BREEDING BIRDS OF BRITAIN AND IRELAND:

A HISTORICAL SURVEY

JOHN PARSLOW

BREEDING BIRDS
OF BRITAIN AND IRELAND
a historical survey

Illustrations by ROSEMARY PARSLOW

T. & A. D. POYSER LTD
Berkhamsted

First published in 1973 by T. & A. D. Poyser Limited,
281 High Street, Berkhamsted, Hertfordshire

ISBN 0 85661 001 1

This book is largely based on material which first appeared in the journal *British Birds* under the title 'Changes in status among breeding birds in Britain and Ireland'. Reference for the original material is as follows:

J. L. F. Parslow 1967–68: Changes in status among breeding birds in Britain and Ireland. *British Birds*, 60: 2–47, 97–123, 177–202, 261–285, 396–404, 495–508; 61: 49–64, 241–255.

Text set in Monotype Ehrhardt and printed and bound in
Great Britain at The Pitman Press, Bath

CONTENTS

TEXT FIGURES

TABLES

ILLUSTRATIONS

PREFACE

The major part of this book first appeared as a series of papers, entitled 'Changes in status among breeding birds in Britain and Ireland', in the journal *British Birds* during 1967 and 1968, and I am able to make use of that material by kind permission of the original publishers, H. F. and G. Witherby Ltd. The original eight-part series of papers was based mainly on an extensive review of the ornithological literature, covering the years up to and including 1965 and 1966. In the latter part of the Systematic List and in the chapter entitled 'Summary of Changes' it was also possible to include some of the more important breeding records for 1967.

Basically, the Systematic List in the present book is that of the original publication, so that terms such as 'now' or 'the present' refer to the late 1960s. I have, however, taken the opportunity of correcting the worst of its errors and adding, where appropriate, the names of a few localities of rare breeding birds now that these places have been taken off the 'secret list'. The most important of these is probably the site of nesting Black-tailed Godwits, Ruff, Pintail, Black Terns and other rare marshland birds—the Ouse Washes on the Cambridgeshire-Norfolk border, where three separate conservation bodies have now established nature reserves.

Since this survey was completed, a number of further important status changes have occurred among our breeding birds, and in order that the story may be brought more-or-less up to date, I have added a chapter covering the years since 1967. Although it is not based on as comprehensive a literature survey as the main part of the book, it does mention all significant breeding records and changes affecting the whole of the British Isles during the last few years, mainly as published in the national ornithological journals.

Further data on the most recent status changes, together with information on the relative abundance and habitat preferences of all birds which have bred in Britain and Ireland since 1940, are given in the text which accompanies the distribution maps at the end of the book.

ACKNOWLEDGMENTS

The main part of this book was first published in *British Birds* and I am most grateful to the editors of that journal, particularly Stanley Cramp and James Ferguson-Lees, for their encouragement and generally patient advice during the course of the survey and when editing the original eight-part series of articles. Dr David Lack, F.R.S., generously provided me with a room and other facilities at the Edward Grey Institute, Oxford, during the two years I was working on this survey, which was financed by a research contract from the Nature Conservancy (later embodied in the Natural Environment Research Council). The Records Committee of the British Ornithologists' Union are thanked for incorporating in their distribution survey questionnaire my request for information on recent status changes among breeding species. My wife kindly checked the references to the original paper and re-drew the later text-figures, as well as producing the illustrations for this book. Miss J. M. Coldrey, Librarian at the Edward Grey Institute, also kindly helped with the original bibliography.

A great many other people also helped during the survey. Numerically, the most important were the hundred or so people who helped to complete the questionnaires, mentioned above, sent out in 1964 by the British Ornithologists' Union. They are listed in the Union's recent publication, *The Status of birds in Britain and Ireland* (Oxford, London and Edinburgh, 1971), and although they are not named individually here, I am most grateful to them all. Many other ornithologists wrote in as the result of a request for information in *British Birds* or kindly answered specific questions that I put to them on status changes among certain groups of birds or in certain regions; they are named below.

J. Anderson, Dr J. S. Ash, K. Atkin, G. Atkinson-Willes, T. S. Baillie, E. Balfour, D. G. Bell, T. H. Bell, J. D. Brown, W. M. Bunce, the late Dr J. W. Campbell, H. A. R. Cawkell, P. J. Conder, Dr P. J. Dare, P. G. Davis, M. J. Everett, T. F. Fargher, R. A. Frost, D. Griffin, the late D. D. Harber, Miss K. M. Hollick, P. Hope Jones, the Reverend G. W. H. Moule, J. R. Mullins, Dr I. C. T. Nisbet, R. E. F. Peal, R. D. Penhallurick, I. Prestt, R. E. Podmore, Dr G. R. Potts, M. J. Rayner, G. A. Richards, R. W. Robson, Major R. F. Ruttledge, F. R. Smith, K. G. Spencer, J. Stafford (Brighstone), Ralph Stokoe, R. C. Stone, A. D. Townsend, R. J. Tulloch, Mrs M. Tugendhat, George Waterston, A. D. Watson and the Honourable Douglas Weir.

INTRODUCTION

Following a similar survey by Nicholson (1926), Alexander and Lack (1944) reviewed the many changes in status which had occurred among the breeding birds of Britain and Ireland during the hundred years up to the time of the 1939–45 war. Since then there has been an enormous growth in the amount of information available on the subject and many further changes are known to have occurred. With the notable exceptions, however, of surveys dealing with a number of individual species (e.g. Moreau 1951, Campbell 1954–55, 1965, Moore 1957, Davis 1958, Peakall 1962, Monk 1963, Ratcliffe 1963, Hudson 1965, Dare 1966, Fisher 1966), this information is scattered through the ornithological literature, particularly in a series of recent county avifaunas and in the now numerous county and regional bird reports which cover virtually every part of Britain and Ireland, mainly on an annual basis. The primary object of the present survey is to review this extensive literature and to summarise for each breeding species the changes in status and distribution which have occurred since about 1940, as well as to relate these recent changes to what is known about the previous fluctuations of the species.

Additional unpublished sources of information have also been used. Most important among these were the summaries of local changes sent in by observers in response to an announcement in the journal *British Birds* in 1965 (*Brit. Birds*, 58: 214–216), and the information on status changes included by many contributors to the distribution survey organised in 1964 by the Records Committee of the British Ornithologists' Union.

Every wild bird which has bred in Britain and Ireland since 1800 is covered in the SPECIFIC LIST beginning on page 6. For completeness, this also includes those species for which there appears to be no evidence of a marked increase or decrease, as well as those which no longer breed or which have bred only sporadically. Three feral species of wildfowl are included which have only recently been admitted to the British and Irish List, the Mandarin *Aix galericulata*, Ruddy Duck *Oxyura jamaicensis* and Egyptian Goose *Alopochen aegyptiacus*, as well as other introduced species such as the Canada Goose *Branta canadensis* and Red-legged Partridge *Alectoris rufa* which have been established here for very much longer.

The amount of information available on each species varies considerably. Those best documented tend to be ones which are scarce or distributed locally, particularly if they are confined to England, and especially to the southern half of the country, where observers are most numerous. The least well documented species are often those which are common and widespread, or those whose range is restricted to the more isolated parts of Britain and Ireland, notably in the north and west, where observers are fewest. Although there are exceptions (and the size and usefulness of the literature on any species is also influenced by other factors), these general rules hold good for the majority. The summaries given in the SPECIFIC LIST therefore include a brief assessment of the present status and distribution of every species breeding in Britain and Ireland, as well as the evidence for any changes which have occurred.

As pointed out by Alexander and Lack, the best evidence for fluctuations is found in those species which have colonised new areas or deserted former ones. Even quite marked fluctuations among populations of common or widespread species may be overlooked unless a special study is being made. When they are recorded, it is usually in such general terms that it is often impossible to judge how extensive a change has occurred, whether it is part of a temporary or longer-term fluctuation, or whether the species has fluctuated similarly in the past. Particularly in recent years, however, most marked changes have probably been recorded. With the encouraging development of the census schemes of the British Trust for Ornithology, future fluctuations of the commoner birds will be quantified and documented in much more detail than has hitherto been possible.

The summaries for each species attempt to cover the main fluctuations, and purely local changes are generally omitted unless these appear to point to a more widespread but otherwise undocumented change. Following Alexander and Lack, I have omitted changes which can be inferred to have taken place owing to known changes in agriculture, forestry and land-use generally, unless there is direct evidence to show that the species has increased or decreased. The survey is primarily concerned with trends over a long period, and temporary fluctuations are noted only if they appear to be an important feature of a species' breeding status in Britain and Ireland. For example, Quail *Coturnix coturnix* and Crossbills *Loxia curvirostra* are more numerous and widespread as breeding birds following one of their periodic invasions, while such species as the Dartford Warbler *Sylvia undata* become less numerous and have contracted breeding ranges after severe winters. An important recent event which caused a marked depletion in the numbers of many British residents and partial migrants was the long and exceptionally severe winter of 1963* (Dobinson and Richards 1964). The numbers of many of these species were still depressed during 1964–66—the most recent years for which information is available through county reports—though they were mostly showing signs of recovery. The effects of this winter were so marked that they tended to obscure the current longer-term trends for a number of species, particularly those which may already have been nearing the end of a phase of

* Throughout, each winter is dated by its January; 1963 is thus used here to signify the winter of 1962/63.

expansion by about 1962. Especially in cases where the information on a species since 1963 is too sparse for any conclusions to be drawn, I have concentrated on its status and trends before the 1963 winter.

To keep the species summaries to a reasonable length and to avoid so far as possible a catalogue style of presentation, a certain amount of generalisation has been necessary. This has also been unavoidable in the accounts of certain rare breeding birds owing to the continuing need for secrecy over some of their nesting sites and numbers. A few recent unpublished breeding records of rare birds are omitted completely. To simplify the summaries of breeding distribution and similar data, the Outer Hebrides and Inner Hebrides are treated as counties in themselves, Rutland is combined with Leicester, London is included in Middlesex, and Monmouth is covered by England rather than Wales. Authorities have not been cited for every statement made, especially when the sources were (a) local or county bird reports, (b) the B.O.U. distribution survey or (c) a widespread change recorded in a great many different county avifaunas.

In the species accounts which follow, and make up the main part of the book, the information is presented in the following manner.

The first paragraph states briefly whether there is any evidence that its status has appreciably altered and, if it has, whether it has increased or decreased generally or in one or more parts of the country (a) before about 1940 and (b) since about 1940. The statement for the earlier period is based entirely on the summary given by Alexander and Lack (1944) (abbreviated to 'A & L') and, in fact, is usually a direct quotation or only slightly abbreviated; in a few instances where subsequent information has come to light which alters or adds to their summary, this is mentioned later in the species account.

At the beginning of the second paragraph a brief statement summarises the present status and breeding distribution of the species in Britain and Ireland. For the reasons mentioned earlier, it seemed desirable that some indication of abundance should be given. In the few cases where an actual figure for the breeding population in the whole or a substantial part of Britain and Ireland is known from a recent special survey, or can be calculated with reasonable accuracy from the literature, this figure has been given. For the great majority of species, however, no such numerical estimate is available. I have therefore attempted to qualify the descriptive terms used for the abundance of each species, basing these terms on the possible number of breeding pairs in Britain and Ireland, as follows:

very scarce: 1–100	fairly numerous: 10,000–100,000
scarce: 100–1,000	numerous: 100,000–1 million
not scarce: 1,000–10,000	abundant: over 1 million

In the cases of many species, particularly those which are either very common or very rare, it was possible to ascribe them to an appropriate category with reasonable certainty. For others, however, there was often considerable doubt as to which of two categories they belonged, either because they appeared to be genuinely borderline or because there was so little evidence to go on. Intuition played a large part in many final decisions, but with almost all doubtful species (and especially those which fluctuate considerably from year to year) I placed them in the lower of the two possible categories. The value of the exercise is in some doubt because mistakes have certainly been made. On balance, however, some such system seems preferable to the use of unqualified terms such as 'common', 'rare', and so on. The system is not new. Fisher (1952) used an almost identical classification for the breeding populations of inland birds in England and Wales, and more recently the 'check-lists' of the Netherlands (1962) and Germany (1964) have also adopted similar systems for classifying the status of breeding birds in those countries.

The remainder of the account for each species attempts to trace in both space and time the fluctuations which have occurred. Causes are given when these are known or can be surmised; a fuller discussion of the possible factors involved will be given in a later section. Where marked changes have occurred elsewhere within a species' breeding range in western Europe, this fact is mentioned. It should be noted, however, that for some parts of the Continent no up-to-date reviews of status changes are available, and these sections should not be regarded as complete.

Finally, the map number given in brackets at the end of each species summary refers to the map which shows its current breeding distribution in Britain and Ireland, in the Appendix, pages 213–266.

Order: GAVIIFORMES *Divers*

Black-throated Diver *Gavia arctica*
Somewhat decreased (A & L). Probably no marked change in recent years, but has extended its range in south-west Scotland.

Scarce, restricted to extensive freshwater lochs in the Scottish Highlands and in some of the Western Isles. Human persecution was held by Alexander and Lack to be the main cause of its earlier decline, and locally reduced numbers through this cause or through increased disturbance have been reported more recently, notably in north Perth (Baxter and Rintoul 1953, H. Boase in MS.). In 1945 the species was said to be becoming scarce in the extreme north owing to increased predation by Foxes *Vulpes vulpes*, but Pennie (1962) did not include it among the birds showing marked changes in breeding status in Sutherland. In south-west Scotland it has shown signs of spreading recently: since 1951 it has become established on Arran (Gibson 1956), while in south Ayrshire, where breeding was first recorded in 1956, it also appears to be becoming established (G. A. Richards 1965 and *in litt.*).

In Sweden it has recently increased and extended its range (Curry-Lindahl 1959–63). Its future status in Scotland is less assured, for it is intolerant of disturbance, which is becoming an increasing problem as more quiet and remote Highland lochs are developed for recreational purposes, particularly boating and fishing. (Map 1)

Red-throated Diver *Gavia stellata*
Decreased in 19th century, somewhat increasing in recent years (A & L). This increase has continued, though there has been no permanent extension of breeding range.

Scarce breeder Scotland, including the Western and Northern Isles, with two or three pairs in Donegal, Ireland. Just as its decline in the 19th century was due to human persecution, so its subsequent increase can be attributed largely to a cessation of this persecution and, especially latterly, to direct protection. It is said to have decreased on the north Scottish mainland during the 1939–45 war (Baxter and Rintoul 1953), but this decrease may have been only temporary or local since the species is not included in Pennie's (1962) survey of status changes in Sutherland. Otherwise, most recent reports on its status—which come mainly from the Scottish isles rather than the mainland—are of continued increase or, at the least, of maintained numbers. In Shetland, for example, there has been a considerable increase and spread since the late 19th century (Venables and Venables 1955), which is continuing (B.O.U. Survey). Similar increases have occurred in Orkney and the Inner Hebrides. At the southern end of its Scottish range, the species first bred on Arran in 1873 and subsequently increased to a few pairs (Gibson 1956).

With the exception of a pair which bred in Ayrshire in 1957 and 1958 (Richards 1958) and a pair which summered and probably nested in Kirkcudbright in 1955 (A. D. Watson *in litt.*), there appears to have been no recent marked extension of breeding range. Two or three pairs still nest in Ireland, in Donegal, where similar small numbers have bred regularly since they were first discovered in 1884. Had the species been affected by changing climatic factors over this period, one might have expected any change to be reflected first (and most obviously) at this outpost. Few changes appear to have occurred elsewhere in its range, but Haftorn (1958) recorded a long-term decline in Norway. (Map 3)

Order: PODICIPEDIFORMES *Grebes*

Great Crested Grebe *Podiceps cristatus*
Marked decrease in 19th century; marked increase in latter part of 19th century, until present time (A & L). Has continued to increase though without any further marked extension in breeding range.

Not scarce; widely distributed on lakes throughout most of Britain and Ireland, but not northern Scotland. Harrisson and Hollom (1932) traced the species' history in detail and showed that, after an earlier decline, it increased steadily from only 42 pairs in England in 1860 to about 1,150 breeding pairs in England and Wales in 1931. A less complete census in Scotland in 1931 produced a total of about 80 pairs. Subsequent sample censuses up to 1955 suggested a further general increase, particularly during 1949–55, though perhaps with temporary setbacks during hard winters (Hollom 1951, 1959). The pattern of increase was, however, confused by the incomplete nature of the sample and by considerable variations in trends from one part of the country to another. Another full census of England, Scotland and Wales was undertaken in 1965. The results showed a considerable increase since 1931 from about 2,800 adults present in the breeding season to over 4,000 (Prestt 1966). No census has been made in Ireland, but there too the species has clearly increased in both numbers and range during this century, particularly since about 1920 (Deane 1954, Ruttledge 1966).

An expansion in range may still be continuing in Ireland and several counties in the south-eastern half of the country have been colonised—some only temporarily—in the last 20 years. Elsewhere in the British Isles there has been little major alteration in range since the 1930's. In north Scotland and south-west England, however, some earlier colonisations have since proved only temporary and there has, for example, been no certain breeding in Devon since 1940, in Glamorgan since 1953, in Ross since 1943, or in Moray since 1953.

Prestt (1966) has shown that the greatest proportional increases since 1931 have taken place in those counties with many newly dug reservoirs and flooded gravel pits, and there can be little doubt that the general increase in population has been due to the enormous growth since the war in these man-made habitats. The initiating cause of the increase in the second half of the 19th century is more obscure. The species was certainly greatly assisted by the cessation of the widescale persecution which hastened its decline earlier in the century, but the recovery in its numbers actually began before protection could have had any marked effect (Harrisson and Hollom 1932). A general increase and northward spread elsewhere in western Europe—especially Scandinavia—since the end of the last century has been linked with the progressive climatic amelioration over the whole continent during this period (Kalela 1949, Merikallio 1958, Haftorn 1958, Curry-Lindahl 1959–63, 1961). High residues of organochlorine insecticides have recently been found in British Great Crested Grebes (Moore and Walker 1964), but, although local population decreases, for example in Northampton (Webster 1966), have been attributed to the effects of toxic chemicals, there is no evidence to suggest that these have had any marked or widespread effect. (Map 4)

Slavonian Grebe *Podiceps auritus*

Recently colonised and somewhat increasing in Scotland (A & L). Still increasing slowly.

Very scarce, probably fewer than 50 pairs, in northern Scotland. Although its numbers are still very small, the species has continued slowly to increase and gradually extend its range, despite the activities of egg-collectors. Its main breeding station remains a group of lochs in Inverness, centred on the one where breeding was first discovered in 1908. In this area Dr I. D. Pennie (in Bannerman 1953–63) put its population at about 15 pairs in 1958, since when it has increased and colonised some neighbouring lochs. Smaller numbers continue to breed more or less regularly in Sutherland and Caithness, and also, more lately, in Moray and Aberdeen. A corresponding increase has taken place in Sweden, while in Norway the species has recently extended its breeding range southwards (Curry-Lindahl 1959, Haftorn 1958). (Map 5)

Black-necked Grebe *Podiceps nigricollis*

Small but steady increase in England and Scotland, and probably much increased in Ireland (A & L). Marked recent decline and now perhaps extinct in Ireland.

Very scarce, regular nesting now confined to about three sites in central Scotland, where the population probably totals fewer than 20 pairs. The recent marked decline has been almost as sudden as was the species' appearance as a breeding bird earlier this century. Outside its few Scottish breeding sites, the chief of which has been occupied regularly since at least the early 1950's, it has probably never become firmly established anywhere in Scotland, or in England and Wales. In the last decade, for example, odd pairs have nested in five widely separated counties from Scotland south to Kent and west to north Wales, but it has nowhere persisted for more than a year or two, presumably because few entirely suitable breeding waters exist.

Until the 1950's its stronghold was in Ireland. Here breeding first took place in 1915 at a shallow water near Briarfield, Roscommon, which remained the summer haunt of up to 15 pairs until it was drained in 1957. In the interim, a remarkable colony was established at Lough Funshinagh in the same county, where up to 250 pairs bred from 1929 to 1932, with fluctuating but much smaller numbers thereafter. Small numbers also bred elsewhere in Roscommon and in three or four other counties. But drainage of these sites led to its apparent extinction (Ruttledge 1966).

Kalela (1949) cited the Black-necked Grebe as providing one of the most striking examples of range extension in Europe as a direct result of changing climatic conditions. As with several other aquatic birds dependent on shallow freshwater lakes for breeding, the dessication of the steppe lakes of the Caspian region earlier this century led to a series of invasions west and north-west across Europe in the years of greatest aridity (see also Frieling 1933). The invasions of Black-necked Grebes were particularly marked around 1918–20, in approximately which period breeding first occurred in England, Ireland, the Netherlands, Denmark and Sweden, and again around 1929–32, which period saw the colonisation of Scotland and Switzerland, and the discovery of the large colony in Ireland. (Map 6)

Little Grebe *Tachybaptus ruficollis*

No evidence of marked change (A & L). Some evidence of increase since end of 19th century, but probably little change in recent years.

A not scarce and widely distributed breeding bird, nesting in every county except Pembroke and Shetland. Although little alteration in range occurred during the period covered by Alexander and Lack, the literature contains several consistent reports of increased numbers from about 1880 onwards, particularly in parts of central and southern Scotland and in northern England (e.g. Baxter and Rintoul 1953, Oakes 1953, Temperley 1951). A general increase may also have occurred farther south. For example, Noble (1906) recorded a 'remarkable increase' in Berkshire in the last two decades of the 19th century, at which time several of the central London parks were also colonised (Homes *et al.* 1957). The species also increased in Warwick (Norris 1947) and perhaps elsewhere. Though the evidence is far from conclusive, that which is available is consistent with the idea that it increased during the main period of climatic amelioration.

Its present trend may now be downward, though the evidence on this point is even more meagre. It disappeared from central London soon after 1950 (Cramp 1966), while within the last 30 years it has gone from some of its former breeding lochs at higher altitudes in Ayrshire, possibly because of the effect of severe winters such as those of 1941, 1947 and 1963 (Richards 1964).

Following the 1963 winter numbers were certainly diminished in the country as a whole, particularly in northern areas (Dobinson and Richards 1964). On the other hand, recent increases have been noted in west Cornwall, as well as in parts of central and eastern England where flooded gravel pits have created additional habitat. (Map 7)

Order: PROCELLARIIFORMES
Petrels

Leach's Petrel *Oceanodroma leucorhoa*
No marked change (A & L). Little positive information, but possibly increased on North Rona and the Flannans.

Not scarce, but largely restricted to only four breeding stations on remote island groups off north-west Scotland, where Atkinson and Ainslie (1940) estimated a total population of about 2,000 pairs, though this figure has doubtful significance. Recent evidence from two of these stations suggests an increased population since the mid-1930's, while at the other two the numbers either appear to be unchanged (Sula Sgeir) or have never been adequately estimated (St. Kilda). On the Flannans, however, the colonies now extend over a wider area than before (Andrew and Sandeman 1953, Robson and Wills 1959), and on North Rona, where 380 pairs were reckoned to be breeding in 1936, a differently based estimate in 1958 put the population at about ten times this number (Bagenal and Baird 1959). Small numbers may also now breed on Foula, Shetland, and perhaps occasionally elsewhere on islands in the Hebrides and off the coast of western Ireland, though there has been no proof of breeding in the latter area for many years. Williamson (1948) recorded an enormous increase in the Faeroes where the species was first discovered breeding as recently as 1934. (Map 8)

Storm Petrel *Hydrobates pelagicus*
No marked change (A & L). Present trends not known.

Numerous but local breeding bird, mainly on rocky west coast islands from Scilly north to Shetland. The inaccessibility of the main colonies and the difficulties involved in censussing a nocturnal species make it likely that even quite major population changes would have gone undetected. Possibly some decline occurred towards the end of the 19th century when the species disappeared from several Scottish islands and decreased markedly at its main colony in the Isles of Scilly (Baxter and Rintoul 1953, Parslow 1965); but conceivably these birds had merely moved elsewhere. In the present century it is said to have decreased in Cornwall (Ryves and Quick 1946) and has disappeared from three Irish islands (Ruttledge 1966). Interspecific competition with the Leach's Petrel *Oceanodroma leucorhoa* has been held to be responsible for its decline on the Flannan Isles (Andrew and Sandeman 1953), while increased predation of adult petrels by Great Black-backed Gulls *Larus marinus* led to a marked decrease on an island in the Minch (Gordon 1965) and may also be having a more widespread effect.

Records of colonies where numbers have increased are few, but new breeding stations are still being discovered, and clearly too little is known about the history of the species to say whether or not any significant changes have occurred in its status in Britain and Ireland. (Map 9)

Manx Shearwater *Puffinus puffinus*

Decrease; many colonies reduced or extinct due to human persecution or introduced rats, but others now protected and flourishing (A & L). Information scanty: decline at some smaller Scottish colonies, but certain large colonies, such as two in south Wales, continue to flourish.

Numerous but local breeding bird, mainly on certain vegetated islands off the western sea-board, from Scilly north to Shetland. Although rather more is known about the history of some of its colonies than of those of the similarly distributed Storm Petrel *Hydrobates pelagicus*, there is little reliable information concerning its numbers at many breeding stations. It is, for example, impossible to be certain whether its present population of perhaps 2,000 breeding pairs on Annet, Isles of Scilly, represents an increase or a decrease since the beginning of the century, when the population was variously 'estimated' from 'hundreds of pairs' up to '100,000–150,000 birds', though from other evidence a decrease seems the more likely possibility. At its other southerly colonies, in Ireland and Wales, there is little or no evidence of any recent widespread decline. Indeed, at Skokholm and Skomer off the Pembroke coast, it is flourishing, and estimates of its population on the former island—about 35,000 breeding pairs in 1964 (Harris 1966)—are now higher than ever before. In recent years, birds have returned to the Calf of Man, where they are now almost certainly breeding again after an absence of more than 150 years.

Little is known about status changes at the main Scottish colonies (including those on Rhum, Canna and St. Kilda), but at some of the smaller ones the species may still be decreasing. In Shetland it is probably extinct on Unst, has declined on Foula, and is believed to have decreased generally throughout the group (Venables and Venables 1955, Jackson 1966). In Orkney the numbers at its only colony on Hoy appear recently to have dwindled (E. Balfour *in litt.*), while on Eigg, in the Inner Hebrides, a marked decrease since 1930 appears to be continuing (Evans and Flower 1967).

On Eigg the Brown Rat *Rattus norvegicus* is believed to be responsible for the decline, and it was through the accidental introduction of this mammal that several island colonies were reduced or made extinct in the last century. On Foula the decline has perhaps been due to inter-specific competition for nest sites with the Puffin *Fratercula arctica*. In several parts of Britain predation by Great Black-backed Gulls *Larus marinus* must have increased markedly this century, and on some 'protected' islands the numbers of gulls are now controlled; however, although the problem has not been studied at the smaller colonies, there is no evidence that this predation has caused a serious depletion in any shearwater population. (Map 10)

Fulmar *Fulmarus glacialis*

Huge increase and spread (A & L). Increase still marked, though it has slowed somewhat since about 1950, particularly in northern areas.

Fairly numerous; probably now slightly over 100,000 occupied nest *sites* (rather fewer breeding pairs) at about 500 colonies, mainly in the north, but also on nearly all suitable cliff-bound coasts of the British Isles (Fisher 1966). There is an extensive literature on the remarkable spread of the Fulmar in Britain and Ireland; the brief summary given here is taken from Fisher's (1966) paper on the sixth and latest (1959) enquiry into its status, which includes a re-assessment of historical data in a series of previous publications (Fisher and Waterston 1941, Fisher 1952a, 1952b, etc.).

Until 1878 the only British breeding station was St. Kilda, but in that year Foula, Shetland, was colonised, probably by birds from the Faeroes. By the end of the century the species had begun breeding at other sites in Shetland and in the Outer Hebrides, and it has since spread progressively southwards to almost every suitable part of the British and Irish coastline, except south-east England. Until the 1950's the rate of increase was so great that colonisation from outside must almost certainly have occurred in all areas. Away from St. Kilda, the breeding population increased by nearly 160% in 1929–39, over 100% in 1939–49, and about 38% in 1949–59, colonisation having slowed earlier in the northern regions than in the newer, more southerly ones. The British and Irish population as a whole is now believed to be increasing at a rate of about 3% a year.

The increase in the Iceland-Faeroes-Britain population of the Fulmar probably began in Iceland more than 200 years ago. The initial increase and the subsequent spread have been connected directly with the Fulmar's adaptation to the role of a scavenger of offal provided first by the northern whaling industry and later by the trawling industry; the significant drop in the rate at which the population increased in the 1950's is consistent with a fall in the amount of offal available to each Fulmar (Fisher 1951, 1966; and others). However, both Wynne-Edwards (1962) and Salomonsen (1965) believed that the spread occurred independently of man's fishing activities, probably through a genotypic change (*cf.* argument and discussion in Fisher 1966).

(Map 11)

Order: PELECANIFORMES
Gannet and Cormorants

Gannet *Sula bassana*

Somewhat increasing (A & L). Steady increase, still continuing.

Fairly numerous, breeding at one mainland and twelve island colonies in Britain and Ireland, where its total population is probably now close on 100,000 breeding pairs. A series of papers, particularly by Fisher (with Vevers, 1943, 1944, 1951; and in Bannerman 1953–63), have dealt at length with the numbers and population trends of the Gannet in the British Isles and the North Atlantic as a whole. The numbers have increased steadily since the end of the 19th century. The last complete survey of the gannetries of the eastern North Atlantic was in 1949, when the 13 British and Irish colonies held about 63,500 out of the total of about 82,400 occupied nests at the 23 gannetries in the area. Although no new British or Irish colonies have been established since 1949, recent evidence from ten of the 13 existing ones indicates that the marked upward trend in population has continued (table 1).

The steady growth of the entire North Atlantic population is attributed to the almost complete cessation of its exploitation by man as a source of food: over a period of about 60 years, during the last century, man's persecution reduced the world Gannet population by about two-thirds (Fisher and Lockley 1954). The only British colony which is still harvested is Sula Sgeir, and here there is now a control on the numbers of young taken. The recent work of Nelson (1964) at the Bass Rock colony indicates that, in summer at least, the species is still well below its food level, and there is no indication when the present phase of expansion will come to an end. (Map 12)

Cormorant *Phalacrocorax carbo*

No marked change (A & L). Probably decreased through human persecution in 19th century. Present trends not clear: decrease in some areas, but marked increase in north-east England and south-east Scotland.

Table 1. Recent estimates of the size of certain British and Irish colonies of Gannets *Sula bassana* compared with 1939 and 1949

The data for 1939 and 1949 are from Fisher and Vevers (1951) and refer to numbers of occupied nest-sites. The recent counts were not standardised, but also relate to the number of apparently occupied nest-sites, except at Ailsa where the figure refers to the number of 'pairs'. The actual number of breeding pairs will normally be smaller than these totals: Nelson's (1965) counts on the Bass Rock in June 1962 showed 5,300–5,700 breeding pairs and an additional 1,300–1,500 pairs with nests or sites but not breeding. The St. Kilda estimate for 1959 is not directly comparable with the earlier ones, though there is additional evidence of an increase (Boyd 1961). Of the six British and Irish colonies not given in the table, a continuing increase is reported at both Noss and Hermaness in Shetland (R. Tulloch *in litt.*); that on Sula Sgeir is probably increasing (Bannerman 1953–63); and there is no change (or no recent information) at Bull Rock and Little Skellig in Ireland and Sule Stack in Orkney.

Colony	Approximate number of nests 1939	1949	Recent count or estimate of occupied nest-sites	
Bass Rock, East Lothian	4,374	4,820	6,600–7,200	1962 (Nelson 1965)
Bempton, Yorkshire	4	2	18	1964 (*Y.N.U. Orn. Rep.*)
Grassholm, Pembrokeshire	5,875	9,200	15,500	1964 (Barrett and Harris 1965)
Great Saltee, Wexford	0	2	100–150	1964 (*Irish Bird Report*, R. F. Ruttledge)
Scaur Rocks, Wigtownshire	1	100	300	1964 (B.O.U. Survey)
Ailsa Craig, Ayrshire	5,419	4,947	11,699	1963 (Richards 1965)
St. Kilda, Outer Hebrides	16,900	17,035	44,526	1959 (Boyd 1961)

Not scarce colonial breeder, widely distributed on rocky western and northern coasts, but very local on east coasts and absent from south-east England; there are single colonies just inland in Scotland and Wales, and a few well inland in trees in Ireland. Its main Scottish breeding sites have been mapped by Mills (1965).

Persecution during the 19th century led to the extinction of a number of colonies, notably those in trees in Norfolk, but also on several parts of the

British coast from Ayrshire south to Dorset. Since the end of the 19th century it has apparently continued to decrease in some areas, though, because of its habit of shifting its breeding site from time to time, it is not always certain whether reduced numbers at one colony reflect a genuine decrease or merely mean that the birds have gone elsewhere. In some places, however, where relatively isolated populations exist, recorded decreases may be genuine. For example, general decreases took place in Shetland after about 1890 (Venables and Venables 1955), in the Isles of Scilly during approximately the same period (Ryves and Quick 1946), at the isolated colony on Lambay Island, Dublin, after about 1930, and probably also at the inland colonies in Ireland which have grown steadily fewer (Ruttledge 1966).

On the other hand, in common with other sea-birds, the species has certainly increased in north-east England. On the Farne Islands Cormorants increased steadily from 40–50 pairs in 1865 to a peak of over 400 pairs in the early 1950's, while on the north Yorkshire coast several sites once abandoned through persecution have now been recolonised (Watt 1951, Chislett 1952, and Local Reports). More recently, the population on the Farnes has been reduced by a half (perhaps through more frequent disturbance by trippers), but at the same time a new colony has been established 50 miles away on The Lamb, East Lothian, which had grown from five pairs in 1957 to 177 pairs by 1965 (Smith 1961, Anon 1965).

While the general long-term trend of the British population has probably been one of decrease, it is not clear whether there has been any recent significant change. Cormorants are still persecuted in several areas, particularly by freshwater fishing interests, a reward being paid for their beaks by several River or District Fishery Boards in England and Scotland (Mills 1965). Haftorn (1958) recorded a probable long-term decrease in Norway, but at its tree-nesting colonies in the Netherlands and in Poland it has generally increased, assisted at least in part by protection. (Map 13)

Shag *Phalacrocorax aristotelis*

No evidence of marked change (A & L) but see below. Marked recent increase.

Fairly numerous colonial breeder, widespread on rocky western coasts, but local on east coasts and absent from south-east England. Alexander and Lack's assessment perhaps held true until about 1930, although during the 19th century the Shag decreased at least locally in north-east England—where colonies at Flamborough Head, Yorkshire, and the Farne Islands, Northumberland, both died out (Chislett 1952, Watt 1951)—as well as in Dorset (Blathwayt 1934) and perhaps elsewhere.

More recently, numbers breeding in south Devon fell during the 1950's, but otherwise virtually all reports of changed status since about 1930 refer to an increase. During the last 20 years especially, this increase has been very marked in some areas, and nowhere more so than in north-east England and south-east Scotland. Two of the main colonies in this area, the Farne

Islands (recolonised 1931, perhaps a little earlier) and the Isle of May, Fife, have been counted fairly regularly over the last 50 years (table 2). The steady increase on the Farnes has averaged about 15% per annum since 1945 and has been supported by immigration from south-east Scotland (Potts 1965). Farther south on the east coast, the Flamborough Head region was recolonised probably around 1949 and numbers there have since increased to more than 50 pairs; farther north, there has been a recent colonisation of north-east

Table 2. Breeding populations (in pairs) of Shags *Phalacrocorax aristotelis* on the Farne Islands (Northumberland) and the Isle of May (Fife)

Data are from Watt (1951), Eggeling (1960), G. R. Potts *in litt.* and Local Reports. The years selected are mainly those for which counts or estimates are available from both stations. The Isle of May figure for 1957 is a minimum and the number may have been as high as 315.

	1918	1924	1931	1936	1939	1946	1950	1953	1957	1961	1965
Farne Islands	(0)	(0)	1	7	15	41	59	108	164	205	362
Isle of May	1	2	?	10	?	12	30	140	301	550	787

Scotland, breeding having occurred in Banff since about 1947 and Aberdeen since about 1950; and a general increase has taken place on the islands in the Firth of Forth.

On the western side of the country, marked increases have occurred on some islands in the Inner Hebrides, in the Clyde area (where strong colonies have been formed on certain islands off Kintyre since about 1930), and on the Solway (the species having spread during the last decade into Kirkcudbright, where it now breeds at several sites). Deane (1954) noted it as increasing in Northern Ireland, and a marked increase has occurred during the past ten years at the colony at Howth Head, Dublin. Breeding was first recorded on Bardsey Island, Caernarvon, in 1930, and numbers subsequently increased (Norris 1953); a marked increase probably occurred on Lundy, Devon, between about 1923 and 1939, after which the population remained stable at a high level (Davis 1954, Snow 1960).

The Shag and several other sea-birds have increased markedly during the present century and, particularly in the period since the 1939–45 war, these increases have been especially noticeable on the North Sea coasts of north England and south Scotland. The precise causes are obscure. In the case of the Shag, protection (and a gradual lessening of persecution) has been suggested, but, although this may have contributed, it scarcely explains either the timing or the rapidity of the increase. Changes in abundance or distribution in the species of fish on which this and the other increasing sea-birds feed, perhaps connected with the environmental or climatic changes which caused the disappearance of the Firth of Forth Herrings *Clupea harengus* in the early 1940's

(Beverton and Lee 1965, Saville 1963), seem a more plausible explanation, though there is no direct evidence to support this view.

In contrast with the recent increase in the British Isles, Haftorn (1958) recorded a general decline of the Shag in southern Norway since the second half of the 19th century. (Map 14)

Order: CICONIIFORMES
Herons

Heron *Ardea cinerea*
No evidence of marked widespread change (A & L). Fluctuates; numbers fall after each hard winter, but then rapidly regain their former level. There was an especially marked and widespread decrease after the 1963 hard winter. A general decrease has occurred in the southern half of Scotland (and probably also in north-east England), which in some counties began in the 1920's.

Not scarce. Herons nest annually at the present time in all British and Irish counties except five in south-east Scotland, Shetland, Denbigh and Flint. National heronry censuses in 1928 (Nicholson 1929, 1930), 1954 (Burton 1956, 1957; Garden 1958) and 1964 (J. Stafford in preparation), and partial annual censuses since 1929, have provided a longer series of data on the size and fluctuations of the breeding population of the Heron in Britain than is available for any other species. The pattern of the main fluctuations is now well known: a marked decrease occurs after each hard winter, but numbers then regain their former level within a few years, providing no further cold winters intervene (*cf.* Lack 1954). A severe decrease occurred over the whole of the country following the exceptionally hard winter of 1963. But, even including the unprecedented low numbers of nest in 1963, the limits within which the population has fluctuated since 1928 have been relatively narrow, probably between rather over 3,000 and under 8,000 nests in the whole of Britain and Ireland. By 1965, at least in England and Wales, numbers were gradually regaining their former strength (J. Stafford in preparation).

Ignoring the short-term effects of hard winters, the population as a whole has probably remained nearly constant since 1928, and probably also for some considerable time before that (Nicholson 1929). Regional fluctuations have occurred, but, in general, decreases in one area have been balanced by increases elsewhere. Disturbance and tree-felling has led to the abandonment of many long-standing heronries, but new ones have also been founded. However, Garden (1958) showed that a marked decrease occurred between the 1928 and 1954 censuses in the numbers of Herons nesting in a wide area of south and south-west Scotland. This decrease appears to have continued steadily in many parts of the country from Perth south to the Borders. Persecution, particularly the killing of the young by fishing interests, has been held as the main cause of the decline (Baxter and Rintoul 1953). In Ayrshire, where there has been a steady marked decrease since the 1920's, many young have been killed in recent years and there are now no large heronries left in the county (Richards 1965).

A fairly general decrease may also have affected parts of north-east England. Several heronries in Northumberland appear to have died out, and the two in Durham are in a precarious state. Numbers are also greatly reduced in parts of Yorkshire, and have been decreasing for some time in Nottingham and Lincoln.

A recent survey of residues of organochlorine pesticides in British birds showed the Heron to contain the largest amounts (Moore and Walker 1964), but there is no evidence to suggest that these chemicals are having a marked adverse effect on the species, particularly since it appears to be recovering its losses caused by the 1963 winter. Unfortunately, the detailed results of the annual heronry censuses since 1962 have not yet been published, but at least up till 1961 (Stafford 1963) they did not suggest that any general decline was taking place. (Map 15)

Little Bittern *Ixobrychus minutus*

Probably bred sporadically in 19th century, and also in 1947.

Although there are no confirmed British breeding records, Little Bitterns are believed to have nested occasionally in East Anglia in the 19th century, in Kent in 1947 and, doubtfully, in Surrey in 1956, when a pair summered. The species breeds right across central and southern Europe as far west as the Netherlands, and occasional breeding in southern England seems conceivable in the future, though the number of suitable localities is very small. (Map 16)

Bittern *Botaurus stellaris*

Huge, widespread decrease, and extinct in most areas by middle of 19th century; re-established itself in Norfolk Broads in early 20th century and has spread in recent years (A & L). This increase and spread has continued, but with set-backs after hard winters.

Very scarce and local breeding species. Its main centre of population is still in East Anglia where it was generally slowly spreading and increasing (particularly in the Suffolk coastal strip) until its numbers were diminished by the 1963 hard winter. Up to that time there were probably about 100 'booming males' in the region. Some recovery is taking place, but the species has not yet returned to all of its previous breeding sites. Outside East Anglia its main phase of expansion appears to have occurred during and shortly after the 1939–45 war when small numbers became established in at least four other counties, north to Leighton Moss, Lancashire, where it has persisted, as many as five pairs breeding in 1965. It has also bred in at least three other counties (making nine in all) since 1940, though in only one of these was breeding regular over a period of years.

Its decrease during the 19th century was attributed to drainage and human persecution. Its increase and spread this century have been assisted by the creation (through various causes) of a limited number of new reed-bed habitats, such as those at Minsmere, Suffolk, and Leighton Moss, and by increased protection. Because it is vulnerable to cold winters it is perhaps significant that its main period of re-establishment in East Anglia occurred when these were fewest, *i.e.* between about 1900 and 1939. The Bittern has recently become re-established in Sweden following its extinction there earlier this century (Curry-Lindahl 1959). (Map 17)

Order: ANSERIIFORMES
Ducks, Geese and Swans

Mallard *Anas platyrhynchos*
No evidence of marked change.

A fairly numerous and widespread resident, breeding in all parts of the British Isles. The best evidence on present population trends is provided by the National Wildfowl Count indices, which, though referring to the wintering population, including immigrants, do also provide by February and March usable indices of the size of the native population which then predominates. The results of these counts indicate that the resident population remained virtually unchanged from 1949 to 1964 (Atkinson-Willes 1963, Atkinson-Willes and Frith 1965). Changes in breeding numbers have been recorded in various parts of the country, but these have been local in nature, without any marked trend being apparent in any one broad region. Decreases have occurred as a result of changes in land-use, such as building development and drainage, while local increases have also taken place through the creation of new waters or in some cases through birds being reared or preserved by shooting interests. (Map 18)

Teal *Anas crecca*
No evidence of marked change (A & L). Little definite evidence, but perhaps slightly decreased.

Not scarce; widely distributed in breeding season except in southern England and Wales where much more local. Atkinson-Willes (1963) has suggested that no great changes have occurred in the breeding population, except possibly in parts of eastern and central Scotland where some former strongholds have been almost abandoned in the last 30 years. In the same period the species has probably also decreased in parts of Galloway (J. D. Brown *in litt.*). This evidence apart, there is little indication of changed status within its main British breeding range. In southern England and south-east Wales (south of a line from the Humber to Carmarthen) it has a scattered distribution and in many counties, particularly inland, breeds only sporadically. Breeding in such counties as Cornwall and Dorset seems to occur even more sporadically now than it did 30 and more years ago, while in such counties as Essex and Suffolk, where breeding is still regular, there appears to have been some decline over the same period. The changes are not marked, however, and, although the present trend of the British population may be towards a decrease rather than an increase, this cannot be asserted with any confidence. (Map 19)

Garganey *Anas querquedula*

Small but definite increase in southern England (A & L). Gradual increase and spread continued till about 1952, but has since been halted.

Very scarce summer resident. The breeding population probably totals not more than 100 pairs (in some years considerably fewer) and is concentrated mainly in six south-eastern counties from Norfolk to Sussex. At the present time the species also breeds regularly in Yorkshire and Somerset and sporadically elsewhere. The British Isles are on the extreme western edge of the Garganey's range and the numbers breeding here each year are largely determined by the very variable size of the arrival in early spring. The gradual increase and spread noted by Alexander and Lack continued for a time after the 1939–45 war, probably until about 1952. Expansion during 1945–48 appears to have been considerable and in this period the species nested in eight more English counties for the first time, though in several of these breeding has not since been repeated. After 1953 there seems to have been a slight contraction of range. Despite a great increase in the amount of field observation and recording, and a marked influx of Garganey in 1959 which led to temporary nesting in several new areas, notably in south-west England, breeding was actually proved in fewer English counties during 1953–65 than in the previous 13 years (table 3).

Table 3. Number of English counties in which Garganey *Anas querquedula* were proved to breed in each of five periods from the 19th century to 1965
Elsewhere the species has bred at least once each in Scotland (1928) and Wales (1936) and twice in Ireland (Armagh 1956, Kerry 1959).

	pre-1900	1900–19	1920–39	1940–52	1953–65
Annually or almost annually	2–3	5	9	10	8
Occasionally	5	4	4	13	12
TOTALS	7–8	9	13	23	20

In the breeding season the species favours marshy areas with shallow pools. Drainage of such areas in parts of Kent, Sussex and the Fens is said to have led to a recent decrease in the numbers of breeding Garganey. Temporarily, at least, the Fenland breeding population was as high as 40–52 pairs in 1952, but has since declined markedly through the drainage of the Nene Washes.

The species' earlier increase in Britain has been attributed to the cessation of spring shooting, but it may also have been connected with a general north-westwards extension of breeding range in Europe. The Swedish population also increased markedly during the 1940's, while in the previous decade the Garganey recolonised parts of Finland from which it had been absent since the 19th century (Merikallio 1958, Voous 1960). (Map 20)

Gadwall *Anas strepera*

Colonised and increasing Scotland; increasing East Anglia; has also nested in northern Ireland since 1933 (A & L). Continued increase in England, partly assisted by introductions.

Scarce resident with patchy, very local distribution (due in part to introductions) and a total population of perhaps 200 breeding pairs. These are concentrated mainly in East Anglia where the species has increased steadily from stock originally introduced into west Norfolk in about 1850. In recent years it has spread into north Norfolk and the Broads, while it has also become much more abundant on the Suffolk coast which it colonised as recently as the 1930's: now 40 or more pairs breed at Minsmere alone. Smaller groups have also been founded elsewhere in England, often by deliberate introductions or by escapes from waterfowl collections. In the last ten to fifteen years small numbers have begun to breed regularly in Essex, Kent, Somerset and Yorkshire, and more sporadically elsewhere. The isolated breeding group established before the war in the Isles of Scilly has recently increased.

Although the Gadwall has increased in Scotland since first nesting there in 1906, it is not certain that it is continuing to do so. Upwards of 20 pairs breed regularly at Loch Leven, Kinross, and a few more at waters near-by in Fife and Perth, but elsewhere in Scotland, despite occasional breeding in several areas during the last 50 years, it has nowhere become permanently established. In Ireland it has bred in four northern counties since 1933, but here, too, it does not yet appear to be firmly established.

Although the spread in Britain has been due partly to artificial dispersion, it is worth noting that the species has also extended its range northwards in Scandinavia and has increased greatly in Iceland this century, presumably in connection with climatic changes (Gudmundsson 1951, Haftorn 1958, Voous 1960). (Map 21)

Wigeon *Anas penelope*

Very marked increase in Scotland and northern England, and has nested in recent years sporadically in north Wales and northern Ireland, and in Kent and Essex (A & L). Little further change, and possibly some recent contraction of range in Scotland; appears never to have become permanently established elsewhere.

Scarce breeding bird in Scotland, also north-west Yorkshire and occasionally elsewhere. The marked expansion of breeding range which occurred in the second half of the 19th century, and which probably continued in southern Scotland until about 1950, seems recently to have been halted. Although the species has been found breeding in Stirling only since 1954, it now nests in only one or two Scottish counties farther south (Selkirk and, possibly, Kirkcudbright), compared with the seven southern counties in 1950 named by Baxter and Rintoul (1953). Little recent information is available from within its main breeding range in northern Scotland, though in Sutherland no significant change in distribution has occurred since 1901 (Pennie 1962). A decrease appears to have taken place in Orkney since the 1940's and the species no longer breeds there regularly.

Outside Scotland it remains very largely a sporadic nester apart from a small population in north-west Yorkshire (also occasionally in Westmorland) which was established in 1957 or earlier. Breeding records elsewhere in England and Wales are probably less frequent now than 20–30 years ago, while some of the few more recent ones from south-east England are believed to have involved escaped or injured birds. It has been recorded breeding only twice in Ireland, in 1933 and 1953. (Map 22)

Pintail *Anas acuta*

Colonisation and marked increase in Scotland, also in Ireland, and has bred sporadically in England in 20th century (A & L). Now breeds regularly in the southern half of England, but is sporadic in Ireland; probably little general change in Scotland.

Very scarce breeder, with curiously scattered British distribution, few sites being occupied persistently over a long period of years. This last factor increases the difficulty of assessing changes in status. In Scotland, for example, Baxter and Rintoul (1953) named three 'settled colonies', at Loch Leven (Kinross) and in Orkney and Shetland. Yet at the first, formerly its Scottish stronghold, there was no confirmed breeding from 1946 till 1962 (since when one or two pairs have again bred annually); at the second it now nests only irregularly; and in Shetland (where breeding has, in fact, probably never been regular) it appears not to have nested for several years. Instead, regular breeding in Scotland now occurs in three quite separate areas—Caithness, Inverness and Aberdeen—and very occasionally elsewhere, such as in Kirkcudbright. Whether these changes in distribution represent any changes in abundance is uncertain, but it seems unlikely that the species has become markedly more or less numerous in Scotland in recent years.

In England sporadic breeding has occurred in several areas since about 1910. In 1951 it was much more widespread than usual and the species nested in five or six counties in the southern half of England. Breeding groups have since become established in two separate areas—north Kent and the Ouse Washes (Cambridge/Norfolk). In Ireland it bred sporadically in five northern counties between 1917 and 1938, and for a time became established in the

Lough Neagh area (Deane 1954). But this group presumably died out and the only recent known breeding was in Derry in 1959. (Map 23)

Shoveler *Anas clypeata*

Huge increase and spread throughout England, Scotland and Ireland: perhaps an earlier decrease (A & L). Gradual increase probably continued until the early 1950's, perhaps later, but present general trend not clear.

Scarce breeding bird, widely but somewhat locally distributed throughout Britain and Ireland. A shortage of suitable lowland marshes accounts for its absence or scarcity in central and western Scotland, while it is also very sparsely distributed in Wales and over central southern England: south-west of a line from the Cheshire Dee to Dungeness, probably the only places regularly supporting more than the occasional breeding pair are the Shropshire meres (where it has increased markedly in recent years) and Chew Valley Lake in Somerset (recently colonised by up to 30 pairs).

The Shoveler's main phase of expansion in Britain and Ireland occurred early this century and was matched by a similar spread in continental western Europe, possibly in connection with increased summer temperatures (Voous 1960). In Scotland the expansion was probably at its height between 1900 and 1920 (Berry 1939) with a subsequently slower rate of spread continuing probably at least until the early 1950's; it is uncertain, however, whether its absolute numbers also went on increasing until that time. Nor is the present trend of the Scottish population known, though it seems unlikely that any major change has occurred in recent years. In Ireland, while the Shoveler is clearly more widespread and numerous than at the beginning of the century, there is also little indication of any recent marked change in status.

In England and Wales, although more evidence is available on changes in local populations, it is not clear whether there has been any general change in abundance in the last 20 or 30 years. Local increases in some parts of the country may have been balanced by decreases elsewhere, neither trend being particularly apparent in any one region. Apart from the increases in Shropshire and Somerset, mentioned above, the species has also increased generally in East Anglia since the 1939–45 war, though the large-scale fluctuations which occur at its strongholds in the Fens, Breckland and the Broads make it difficult to assess how extensive this increase has been, or whether it is continuing. On the other hand, losses of habitat, particularly through drainage, have led to widely scattered records of locally decreased populations. Since the 1930's, for example, it has decreased markedly in Durham and Glamorgan, has declined on Romney Marsh (Kent) and some Essex coastal marshes, and, more recently, has somewhat decreased in parts of Cumberland and Westmorland. In Nottingham, where about 40 pairs were nesting in 1947, drainage of marshland in the Trent Valley and the modernisation of Nottingham sewage-farm have so reduced the amount of suitable habitat that now only a few scattered pairs still nest. (Map 24)

Mandarin Duck *Aix galericulata*

Introduced. Increased since becoming established earlier this century in southern England, but little recent change.

Scarce. Feral populations of this introduced species—only recently admitted to the official British and Irish List—have been established very locally in southern England during this century. Savage (1952) estimated its population at rather more than 500 birds, mostly in Surrey and east Berkshire. Small numbers have also been present for a number of years in the Tay Valley, Perth. Its distribution is limited by a shortage of suitable habitat, and there is no evidence to suggest any marked recent increase or spread (Atkinson-Willes 1963). (Map 25)

Red-crested Pochard *Netta rufina*

Although this species has spread westwards across Europe during this century, reaching the Netherlands in about 1942, the only British breeding records—in Lincoln in 1937 and Essex in 1958—probably involved birds that had escaped from waterfowl collections.

Scaup *Aythya marila*

Has bred sporadically in northern Scotland since the end of the 19th century. One or two pairs nested in Orkney during the 1950's, and since the 1939–45 war occasional breeding has occurred in Wester Ross, probably in the Outer Hebrides and perhaps elsewhere in northern Scotland. Breeding may occur slightly more frequently now than in the past. But this is uncertain and there has evidently been no major change in status. On the Continent, the southern edge of the breeding range has been receding northwards, presumably in association with climatic changes (Voous 1960). (Map 27)

Tufted Duck *Aythya fuligula*

Huge increase and spread throughout British Isles (A & L). Continued marked increase, particularly in England.

Not scarce; widely distributed over much of Britain and Ireland, but absent from parts of north-west Scotland and much of Wales and south-west England. Evidence from Local Reports suggests that more than 500 pairs now breed in England south of a line from the Mersey to the Humber; elsewhere there is much less quantitative information, but what there is suggests a total population in Britain and Ireland of well over 1,000 breeding pairs.

The earlier increase referred to by Alexander and Lack was most marked in Britain in the late 19th and early 20th centuries, and was presumably connected with the species' expansion in western Europe as a whole; Kalela (1949) attributed this increase to climatic changes. In England the population continued to increase, and by the late 1930's Tufted Ducks probably occupied most of the suitable breeding waters then available, and they had also begun to nest sporadically in several areas—notably in parts of south-west England

and Wales—where breeding has not since been repeated. Like the Great Crested Grebe *Podiceps cristatus*, the Tufted Duck has been quick to exploit the many new reservoirs and gravel pits which have been flooded in the last 20 years, and this has led to further marked increases in many parts of central, eastern and southern England, while farther west, in Somerset, a notable concentration of up to 100 pairs now breeds at Chew Valley Lake.

In Scotland, too, there appears to have been some further spread since Berry (1939) wrote that 'only Shetland, the N.W. Highlands and parts of Argyll remain to be occupied'. Breeding now occurs occasionally in Shetland (since 1952) and probably in Skye (since 1954), and the species has increased in north Sutherland and probably also in Argyll. Further increases have been noted in several counties around the Firth of Forth, and there is still a concentration of several hundred breeding pairs at Loch Leven, Kinross. In Ayrshire and Galloway (and also in north Cumberland), however, the increase and spread seems to have slowed up, and in some areas here there may even have been some recent decline.

Since the 1939–45 war the Tufted Duck has continued to extend its range in Ireland, though it is less certain whether it has become more numerous. Deane (1954) suggested that a decrease occurred in Northern Ireland after 1945. The only recent information, however, comes from Lough Beg, where the species has increased during the last ten years. (Map 28)

Pochard *Aythya ferina*

Marked increase and spread throughout England, Scotland and Ireland, still continuing (A & L). Continued increase England, particularly Kent, but probably some decrease Scotland, and still not established anywhere in Ireland.

Scarce breeding bird with fairly wide though very local distribution, nesting only sporadically in many areas, particularly in western Britain. The breeding population in England and Wales is probably of the order of 200 pairs. The only county with a sizeable population is Kent, where it has increased markedly: numbers fluctuate, but up to 70 pairs have bred in some recent years, concentrated mainly in the shallow, reed-fringed, coastal fleets in the north of the county, where it was only an irregular nester until after the end of the 1939–45 war (Gillham and Homes 1950, Harrison 1953). This increase is difficult to understand for in neighbouring Essex little change has occurred in its numbers at the coastal marsh near Tollesbury which has remained its headquarters in that county since breeding was first discovered there in 1886: here, where the habitat has probably remained little changed over the years, 17 pairs bred in 1888, about 15 pairs around 1927, and between five and fifteen pairs today (Glegg 1929, Local Reports).

Taking East Anglia and the Thames Basin as a whole, the Pochard has generally increased over the past 20 years, particularly on certain park lakes in the London area and elsewhere, which, however, were probably originally colonised by 'escapes'. Although gravel pits are sometimes occupied for breeding, this habitat appears to be generally unsuitable, and the species has consequently benefited much less from the growth in the gravel industry than has the Tufted Duck *A. fuligula*.

The total number of counties in England and Wales in which the species now breeds regularly has increased since the late 1930's (table 4), though it

Table 4. Number of counties with breeding Pochard *Aythya ferina* in about 1938 and in 1964

Data for 1938 are adapted from those given in *The Handbook*, which may have exaggerated the regular breeding range in Scotland. Note that the two sets of data for irregular breeding cover unequal periods. The total number of counties in each region is given in brackets.

	Regular breeding counties		Irregular breeding counties	
	1938	1964	1900–38	1955–64
S and SW England (7)	0	1	3	3
Thames Basin (9)	5	5	3	3
E Midlands and Anglia (10)	3	6	5	3
W Midlands (7)	0	1	2	2
N England (8)	2	3	3	1
All England (41)	10	16	16	12
Wales (12)	1	1	2	1
S Scotland (19)	8	4	3	2
N Scotland (14)	9	2	2	5
Ireland (32)	1	1	2	2

should be remembered that in several of these it is extremely local and restricted to one or two sites. The data for Scotland are less strictly comparable, but from table 4 it certainly appears to be much less widely distributed now than it was in the 1930's. Baxter and Rintoul (1953) also considered that it had become less numerous following its increase earlier in the century. Even though it first bred in Ireland as long ago as 1907 it remains no more than a sporadic nester in that country, except at one locality in Roscommon, where it has bred regularly since 1930 (R. F. Ruttledge *in litt.*).

Like the Tufted Duck, but less markedly, the Pochard also extended its range westwards across Europe during the first half of this century (Kalela 1949). (Map 29)

Goldeneye *Bucephala clangula*

Reputed to have bred in Cheshire in 1931 and 1932, otherwise there are no other records of breeding in Britain and Ireland. (Map 30)

Long-tailed Duck *Clangula hyemalis*
Sporadic (A & L). Is believed to have bred once or twice in Shetland in the 19th century and bred in Orkney in 1911, but no recent records. (Map 31)

Velvet Scoter *Melanitta fusca*
Probably bred in Shetland in 1945, but there is no confirmed British breeding record. (Map 32)

Common Scoter *Melanitta nigra*
Colonised and increasing in northern Scotland and north-west Ireland (A & L). Continued gradual increase in Ireland; probably little change in Scotland.

Scarce; small numbers continue to nest in Sutherland, Ross and elsewhere in Scotland, probably south to north Perth, irregularly in Shetland, Orkney and the Inner Hebrides. There is little information concerning the species' recent trends in Scotland, but probably no major changes have occurred. In Ireland, however, numbers have gradually increased to over 50 breeding pairs in Fermanagh (where it first bred in 1905) and to 20–30 pairs in Mayo (where breeding was first proved in 1948) (Ruttledge 1966). (Map 33)

Eider *Somateria mollisima*
Very marked increase and spread; colonised northern Ireland in 20th century (A & L). Has continued to increase (after temporarily decreasing in many districts during the 1939–45 war), spreading south to Walney Island, Lancashire, and further south-west in Ireland.

Not scarce resident, nesting on coasts and off-shore islands in Scotland and northern Ireland, and also in England in Northumberland and, since 1949, at Walney Island, Lancashire. Recent surveys by Taverner (1959, 1963) have traced the species' increase in Britain and have shown that this has been paralleled elsewhere in western Europe and also in eastern North America. A marked rise in the Dutch population has led to increased numbers of non-breeders around English coasts. Almost everywhere the increases have been attributed to protection at the breeding colonies.

The spread of the Eider in Britain began with the colonisation of the Scottish mainland about 1850 (it having been known previously on only a relatively few islands), but its main phase of expansion appears not to have started until towards the end of the 19th century when protection measures were introduced at colonies in many districts. In Shetland, for example, after a marked decrease in the early 19th century, it began gradually to regain its numbers from 1890 onwards, becoming common again by 1922 (Venables and Venables 1955). It continued to increase gradually both in numbers and range up till the 1930's. Ireland was colonised in 1912.

During and immediately after the 1939–45 war several colonies in Scotland and at the Farne Islands, Northumberland, were drastically reduced when large numbers were taken for food. Subsequently, however, with renewed protection, these colonies regained their former strength, and many increased still further. Yet, apart from the now substantial new colony at Walney Island, and a marked south-westward spread in Ireland as far as Sligo, where it is continuing to increase (Cabot 1962, Ruttledge 1966), there has been little southwards extension of breeding range over the past 20 years. In some areas, not only in Britain but also in Sweden, the Eider has generally managed to continue to increase despite increased predation of its young by the larger gulls *Larus spp.*; but some local decreases during this century, for example on the Flannans and on North Rona, may possibly have been due to this cause. (Map 34)

Ruddy Duck *Oxyura jamaicensis*
Introduced; perhaps not yet established.

Very scarce. Within the last few years small numbers have begun to breed regularly at Frampton (Gloucester) and Chew Valley Lake (Somerset), the original colonists having almost certainly come from the waterfowl collection at Slimbridge. Atkinson-Willes (1963) has suggested that further small colonies might be established elsewhere in future years, and it is therefore of interest that it has bred in Stafford since 1961 and at Tring reservoirs (Hertford) in 1965. (Map 35)

Red-breasted Merganser *Mergus serrator*
Very marked increase in Scotland and Ireland (A & L). Increase has probably continued in some areas, though on a much reduced scale; since 1950 the species has colonised parts of north-west England and north Wales.

Not scarce, breeding over much of Scotland and Ireland, and now also in northern England and north Wales (fig. 1). Between about 1885 and 1920 the Scottish population expanded rapidly, and several regions were occupied for the first time, notably the Moray Basin and south-west Scotland. After 1920 the numbers increased more gradually. In parts of Galloway and Dumfries this increase has continued to the present day. Although large numbers are shot throughout Scotland by freshwater fishing interests, the species has suffered no obvious decline and its status over much of the country has remained largely unchanged in recent years (Mills 1962). In Ireland it has also become more numerous and widespread since the beginning of the century and it now nests in all but a few, mainly southern counties; however, no marked change in status appears to have occurred in recent years.

The first proved breeding in England took place as recently as 1950 when a pair nested in Cumberland. The species has since increased considerably and has spread to Westmorland, north Lancashire and north-west Yorkshire. A pair bred as far south as the Lincoln fens in 1962, but it is thought that these birds may have escaped from captivity. North Wales was colonised in 1953 when a pair bred in Anglesey. Here, too, it has subsequently increased (to seven pairs by 1965), and has spread to the mainland of north Wales, breeding in Merioneth by 1957 and in Caernarvon by 1958, while birds are now also present during the breeding season in Montgomery. (Map 36)

Goosander *Mergus merganser*

Colonised and increasing Scotland (A & L). Has since colonised south-west Scotland and northern England, but has somewhat decreased recently in north-west Scotland.

Scarce, breeding on inland waters over much of Scotland and also in northern England (fig. 2). Breeding was first recorded in Scotland in 1871. Many nested after a large winter influx in 1876 and by the end of the century

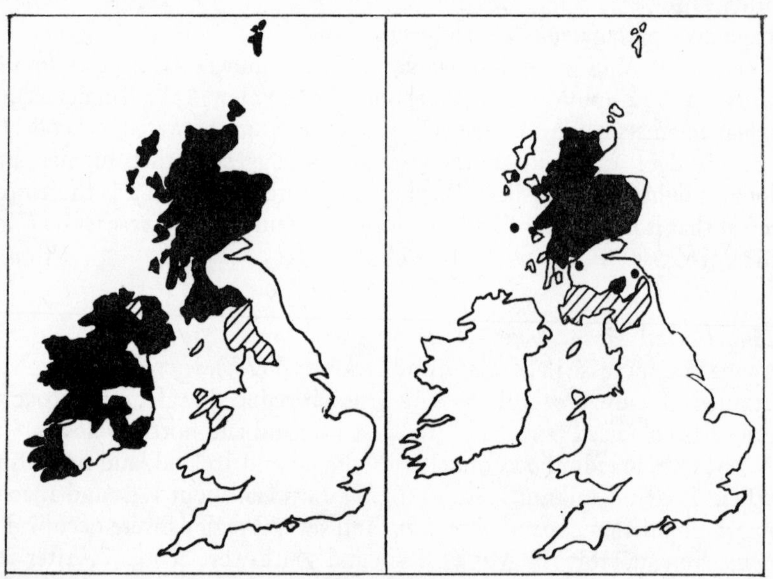

FIGS. 1 and 2. Spread of breeding ranges of the Red-breasted Merganser *Mergus serrator* since 1950 (left) and Goosander *M. merganser* since 1940, shown by hatched areas in each case. Regular nesting was previously confined to the black areas. Isolated breeding records are marked by dots.

the species was widely distributed as a breeding bird over the whole of northern Scotland (Berry 1939). There followed a more gradual expansion and it was not until the 1940's that it began to breed regularly in south-west Scotland and (until the population was shot out by fishing interests) also on the River Tweed in Berwick (Mills 1962). By 1941 it had spread over the border into Northumberland; and Cumberland was colonised in 1950. It has since increased in both these counties, but has not spread farther south.

Despite the systematic shooting of large numbers on most rivers where Salmon *Salmo salar* are fished for in Scotland, it appears to be maintaining its status in many districts. This persecution has, however, led to a recent decrease in the numbers breeding in the extreme north-west and also in Selkirk, while the species would doubtless increase more rapidly in the Border counties were it not for the bounty placed on its head by local fishery boards (Mills 1962). (Map 37)

Shelduck *Tadorna tadorna*

Increasing throughout Britain (A & L). Despite local decreases in some areas, it has continued to increase in Britain as a whole; inland nesting is becoming more frequent.

Fairly numerous, breeding in coastal areas in virtually every maritime county in Britain and Ireland, and regularly in two inland counties of England. The total British population (including non-breeders, but excluding birds of the year) is possibly in the region of 50,000 birds, a figure which is based on the numbers in late summer on the main moulting grounds on the north coast of Germany (Atkinson-Willes 1963).

The Shelduck decreased locally in the 19th century, reaching a low point in Suffolk, for example, in about 1886 (Ticehurst 1932). But it is not clear whether it declined significantly over Britain and Ireland as a whole. Plainly, however, the increase this century has been considerable, and so widespread that it has been commented upon by almost every regional avifauna of the last 30 or 40 years. It appears to have been most marked in eastern and southern England. In Sussex, for example, the species first bred in 1904, had increased to about 500 pairs in the west of the county by 1938, and has spread further since, including to one locality 20 miles inland in 1963 (Walpole-Bond 1938, des Forges and Harber 1963).

Since the last war it has colonised several parts of the coast of eastern, southern and south-western England, spreading in recent years to the extreme west of Cornwall and the Isles of Scilly. A marked feature of its recent spread —reflected also on the Continent, in southern Sweden and Denmark—has been the tendency to colonise inland areas. These nesting sites are usually within a few miles of the sea (such as the New Forest, Hampshire, several sites in Lincoln, the East Anglian fens, the new large reservoirs in Somerset and Essex, freshwater lochs in south-west Scotland, and so on), but are occasionally much farther inland, as in the Trent Valley, Nottingham. However, this last county and Cambridge apart, Shelduck do not yet breed regularly in any other inland county in England.

Against this background of general expansion, increased coastal disturbance has led to recently reduced populations in some areas, notably in south Wales (Glamorgan, Carmarthen) and in parts of Lancashire, Northumberland and Ayrshire; it has also decreased at the inland colony on Loch Lomond. The primary initiating cause of the current expansion is not known, but presumably protection, both here and at the species' moulting grounds in the Heligoland Bight, has been of considerable importance. (Map 38)

Egyptian Goose *Alopochen aegyptiacus*

Scarce. Introduced in England in the 18th century and has long been found in a feral state in several parts of the country, in numbers only in East Anglia, and there mainly in the Holkham Park and Broads areas of Norfolk. Its numbers appear to be fairly stable. (Map 39)

Greylag Goose *Anser anser*

Extinct in England and Ireland in 18th century and decreasing in Scotland in 19th century (A & L). Further decrease this century in Scottish wild population, but under recent protection this decrease has now probably been halted; feral populations have increased.

Wild population scarce, restricted to the Hebrides and the extreme north of Scotland. Prolonged persecution caused the native population to decrease at an 'alarmingly rapid' rate in the 50 years to 1939, by which time its range was very restricted and it was believed to be in danger of extinction (Berry 1939). According to J. W. Campbell (in Bannerman 1953–63), there were by 1956 probably not more than 175 breeding pairs of wild stock in the whole of Scotland; of these, between 125 and 145 pairs were in the Outer Hebrides. At its headquarters on South Uist it had declined from about 200 pairs in 1920 to 45–50 pairs by the early 1950's. Special protection measures were by then beginning to take effect, however, and the population in the Outer Hebrides is now regarded as being in a 'fairly healthy' state (Atkinson-Willes 1963). Small populations of wild birds also survive in Wester Ross (numbers now partly maintained by introductions), Sutherland (numbers augmented by surplus stock originating from a large feral flock) and Caithness.

Flocks of feral origin also exist in some other parts of Scotland and in northern and eastern England. Birds originating from such a flock in Wigtown have recently dispersed over a wide area of south-west Scotland, where they now breed in four counties. Other small colonies have recently been established in the Lake District, Anglesey, Kent and elsewhere by the Wildfowlers' Association. As in Britain, special protection and artificial dispersion has led to the Greylag Goose's revival in some other European countries, following a general earlier decline through persecution. (Map 40)

Canada Goose *Branta canadensis*

Introduced. Increase and spread in recent years due to artificial dispersion.

Not scarce; artificially distributed in many parts of England, and in a few localities in Wales, Scotland and northern Ireland. Jones (1956) organised a national census in 1953 which indicated a July population of 2,600–3,600 adults and young, distributed locally in East Anglia and central England from Berkshire north to Dumfries, with some smaller isolated populations elsewhere. It was then still largely restricted to the lakes in private parks where it had been introduced in the 18th and 19th centuries, its sedentary behaviour appearing to limit the discovery of new waters. On some estates its numbers were controlled and the whole population had probably remained unchanged for some years. At its main British colony, however, at Holkham, Norfolk, it increased from about 200 birds in 1941 to 700–1,000 in 1955, and as many as 1,500–2,000 have been recorded there more recently (Atkinson–Willes 1963).

Since the early 1950's its numbers have almost certainly increased, due to much artificial redistribution of stock by the Wildfowl Trust and others. Several new colonies have been established on flooded gravel pits, lakes and other waters, mainly in England but also in Anglesey and south-west Wales. Some spectacular increases have been noted. In Devon, for example, the species was almost unknown until 1949 when ten artificially reared goslings were released at Shobrooke Park; by 1963 this flock had grown to about 160 and the geese have since spread to several other waters in the county. The species' recent British distribution, including many of the new colonisations, has been mapped by Atkinson-Willes (1963). (Map 41)

Mute Swan *Cygnus olor*

Spreading and increasing Scotland and Ireland (A & L). Continued general increase until 1959, since when slightly reduced in some areas.

Not scarce, breeding over the whole of Britain and Ireland, except Shetland and parts of north-west Scotland. It breeds most numerously in the southern half of England and has increased almost everywhere since the end of the 19th century, including Ireland where it now nests in every county. One notable exception to this pattern of increase has been at the unique colony at Abbotsbury, Dorset, where a marked decrease to a present population of about 800 birds has been due mainly to artificial control of the numbers.

A census in the springs of 1955 and 1956 showed that the total number of breeding pairs in England, Wales and Scotland was probably about 4,000, out of a total population, including non-breeders, of 17,850–19,250 birds (Campbell 1960, Rawcliffe 1958). Numbers were believed to have recently increased and were continuing to rise. A repeat sample census in spring 1961 indicated that no significant change had occurred, though an analysis of winter counts for the intervening years showed that the population had continued to increase markedly to a peak in 1959, but had then fallen almost to the 1955 level (Eltringham 1963). The reasons for the fluctuation are not known. More predictably, numbers fell again in 1963 following the hard winter (Boyd and Ogilvie 1964).

Huge and spectacular population increases have occurred during the last 20–30 years over the whole of the species' range in north-west Europe. (Map 42)

Whooper Swan *Cygnus cygnus*

Became extinct in Orkney in 18th century; colonised and slightly increasing north Scotland in 20th century (A & L). Only one recent published record and, at best, not more than a sporadic breeder this century.

Alexander and Lack's summary and *The Handbook's* 'a few pairs breed

Scotland' seem to have overstated the case; in fact, there are only a very few published records of breeding in Scotland this century, none of them more recent than 1947 (Benbecula, outer Hebrides). Small numbers remain in Scotland every summer and breeding has occasionally been attempted, perhaps slightly more often than the published records suggest. Birds, including apparent pairs, also now over-summer in some years in Ireland. (Map 43)

Order: FALCONIFORMES
Birds of prey

Golden Eagle *Aquila chrysaetos*

In 19th century marked and widespread decrease, becoming extinct in Ireland and some Scottish counties, due to human persecution; local increases in 20th century due to protection (A & L). Possible slight increase, and extension of range into south-west Scotland, following 1939–45 war. Recent sharp decline in breeding success in many parts of Scotland due probably to dieldrin pesticides, but so far only no marked decrease in adult population.

Scarce resident, confined to Scottish Highlands and Western Isles with a few pairs in south-west Scotland. Non-breeders are again resident in the English Lake District, and a pair bred in Northern Ireland from 1953 to 1960. Independent surveys of the Scottish population, summarised by Nicholson (1957), each suggested that in the early 1950's it was in the region of 190 breeding pairs. The recovery of the Golden Eagle, following the intense persecution to which all birds of prey were subjected in the 19th century, probably dates from about the time of the 1914–18 war. There is, however, little quantitative evidence to indicate quite how much more numerous it became during the first half of this century, and in terms of total breeding numbers the increase was probably relatively small. Despite legal protection, it was (and still is) persecuted by game-keepers, shepherds, egg-collectors and others in some parts of the country, while elsewhere it has thrived on the protection afforded to it by sympathetic land-owners.

Assisted by the absence of active keepering during the 1939–45 war, and in western areas by an increase in the amount of sheep and deer carrion available which has tended to offset a long-term reduction in live natural prey (Lockie and Stephen 1959, Lockie 1964), the breeding population probably increased in some districts in the immediate post-war years. In Sutherland there were more eagles by 1947 than there had been for a hundred years, though they have since decreased again, perhaps owing to the lack of Rabbits *Oryctolagus cuniculus* since 1954 (Pennie 1962). There was a notable increase in the Hebrides around 1946, and several former, long-deserted sites were reoccupied. Since 1948 a few pairs have recolonised two counties in south-west Scotland—Ayrshire and Kirkcudbright—after a long absence. One pair even bred on the Antrim coast of Northern Ireland from 1953 to 1960 (Deane 1962); they were the first to do so in Ireland since the population in the west of the country became extinct about 1914. In England the species has returned to the Lake District, but although nests have been built in recent years there has been no actual breeding (Stokoe 1962).

On the other hand, the war-time increase was not a universal one, and in some areas, notably the Cairngorms, there was a decided decrease between the 1930's and 1946 (Gordon 1955, Brown 1955).

Annual surveys in four widely separate mainland regions during 1944–62 indicated that the breeding population maintained a relatively constant, high density throughout, the average area per pair varying from about 11,000 acres in the east Highlands to about 18,000 acres in parts of the west (Brown and Watson 1964). In one study area on Upper Deeside, the population remained stable at eleven pairs from 1944 to 1965 except that there was one extra pair in the late 1940's and early 1950's, and one pair less from 1957 onwards (Watson 1966).

Recent studies have shown that the breeding success of eagles has fallen sharply in the last few years in many parts of Scotland. In a sample population over a wide area of west Scotland the number of pairs rearing young declined from 72% during 1937–60 to 29% during 1961–63 (Lockie and Ratcliffe 1964). Chlorinated hydrocarbon residues, acquired by the eagles from sheep carrion, and by the sheep from sheep-dips, are believed responsible, and relatively large amounts have been found in eagles and their eggs. Unlike the eagles studied in the rest of Scotland, those on Deeside have continued to breed as successfully as before, probably because the birds there hardly ever eat dead sheep (Watson 1966). So far, except perhaps locally in Inverness and Easter Ross, there has been no obvious decline in the numbers of adults. (Map 44)

Buzzard *Buteo buteo*

Huge decrease in 19th century and extinct over much of Britain, due to human persecution; since 1914 beginning to recover markedly, especially in west of England and Wales (A & L). Increase continued till about 1954, but then suddenly marked decline following myxomatosis of Rabbits; in most regions, numbers have somewhat recovered and the population as a whole is perhaps now fairly constant, though smaller than in 1954.

Resident, not scarce. Widely distributed in Scottish Highlands (including Hebrides) and Wales, and in western districts of Scottish Lowlands and England. Absent Ireland and from much of eastern half of England. Moore

(1957) suggested that the Buzzard's period of greatest abundance since the early 19th century was during 1949–54, at the end of which he estimated the total population as approximately 12,000 pairs. Following the myxomatosis of Rabbits *Oryctolagus cuniculus* in 1954 there was a sharp decline in the Buzzard population and also in breeding activity the following year. In some of its strongholds, such as in south-west England, population decreases of up to 50% or more were recorded, while in Shropshire, and in some counties on the eastern edge of its English range, decreases were proportionately even greater. The small number of pairs which in the late 1940's and early 1950's had begun to colonise several Midland counties, east to Oxford and Derby, and perhaps to Huntingdon and Nottingham, disappeared about 1955 or soon after.

In northern Ireland, recolonised about 1951 or a little earlier, ten pairs were breeding by 1954 in Antrim; but these had dwindled to one pair by the early 1960's (Ruttledge 1966, Local Reports).

Except in the New Forest, Hampshire, where after a temporary check about 1955 the numbers continued to increase markedly until 1961 (Cohen 1962) and only then fell, the general population trend in most regions of England and Wales followed a similar basic pattern: a sharp fall in 1955, followed by a gradual recovery in the next few years, and then relative stability at a density below that of the early 1950's. The rate and degree of recovery varied from region to region, while in some areas numbers in recent years appear to have fluctuated rather more than they did when Rabbits were abundant. Local reductions in some areas of England about 1960 were reported by Prestt (1965), but these were perhaps only temporary.

As pointed out by Moore (1957), the history of the species in Britain during the last two centuries is closely correlated in both time and space with the activities of game-preservers. Persecution remains considerable in many parts of Britain, particularly Scotland. In that country, although the Buzzard population was reduced by myxomatosis, the effect appears to have been less marked than farther south, and in some parts, notably in Galloway, Arran, Bute and the Outer Hebrides, the species has continued to increase, perhaps through greater protection.

Prestt (1965) discussed some other possible reasons for recent local changes, but the general influence of myxomatosis overrides all others. (Map 45)

Sparrowhawk *Accipiter nisus*

Though undoubtedly decreased through persecution, it is still not uncommon (A & L). Increased in many areas during 1939–45 war; sudden, sharp and widespread decline, particularly in eastern England, since about 1955.

Resident, not scarce, breeding throughout Britain and Ireland except Outer Hebrides and Northern Isles. In recent years it has virtually disappeard from a wide area of eastern England. Although it remained a widespread resident and its distribution was little changed, the fortunes of this species were, until recently, controlled very closely by the degree of persecution it received from game-preservers. When game-keeping lapsed in both the 1914–18 and 1939–45 wars, Sparrowhawks increased and during the second of these periods there were widespread reports of larger numbers from almost all parts of Britain. It was apparently only in parts of south Wales that they decreased at this time (Ingram and Salmon 1954). There is some evidence to suggest that in many regions the greatest numbers were reached in 1946 and 1947.

In the late 1950's reports suggesting a widespread decrease led to an enquiry being held into the status of the species in 1960. Organised by R. S. R. Fitter, this survey showed that its numbers had fallen over virtually the whole of England and Wales. Only two counties—Flint and Pembroke—reported that no change had occurred (Cramp 1963), though in the latter it was in fact believed to be decreasing (Lockley 1961). The number of nest records submitted to the British Trust for Ornithology fell sharply in 1955 and remained low in succeeding years (Cramp 1963). The number of nestlings ringed annually also showed a similar marked decline from 1955 onwards and, although it is impossible to make precise and completely unbiassed comparisons, this evidence suggests that the numbers of young Sparrowhawks reared during the decade 1955–64 were probably only one-fifth to one-tenth the numbers reared in each of the previous two decades, presumably owing to a decline in the adult population. Regular observations by Ash (1960) on an estate in Hampshire showed a steady decline in the numbers of Sparrowhawks seen after 1953.

A further survey in 1963, this time also including Scotland and northern Ireland, confirmed the extent and severity of the Sparrowhawk's decline (Prestt 1965). In many areas the decrease had become most evident about 1959–60, and by about 1960–63 the combined evidence from Prestt's survey and from Local Reports suggested that the species was then virtually extinct in several eastern counties (Lincoln, Leicester and Rutland, Huntingdon, Bedford, Cambridge, Essex, Middlesex, Oxford and Northampton) and had been reduced to a handful of pairs in several others. Numbers had also been reduced over much of Scotland and Northern Ireland, and even among the few counties mentioned by Prestt as showing little or no change—for example, Dumfries and Kirkcudbright—other evidence suggested that there, too, the species had decreased. Only in Cornwall (where it may actually have increased recently), Devon and parts of south Wales (notably Cardigan) have its numbers remained largely unchanged, although it should be added that, despite a decrease in Hampshire generally, the population in the New Forest has also been unaffected. In Ireland it has evidently decreased considerably in some eastern counties (Ruttledge 1966).

A cause other than persecution is clearly responsible for the Sparrowhawk's recent decline, which has also been noted in Continental countries. Since the mid-1950's the only widespread ecological changes which might conceivably have affected this species would seem to be the introduction of myxomatosis and the advent of chlorinated hydrocarbon pesticides. The reduction in the numbers of Rabbits *Oryctolagus cuniculus* as a result of myxomatosis may have had indirect effects on the Sparrowhawk, but it seems unlikely that these would have been so marked. It is not surprising, therefore, that most contributors to Prestt's (1965) survey attributed the decrease to organochlorine pesticides, residues of which have been found at relatively high levels in both the adult birds and their eggs. The fact that the Sparrowhawk's sharpest decline has occurred in eastern England, especially in lowland agricultural areas, lends support to this view. There is some evidence to suggest that a partial recovery may now be taking place in some southern and Midland counties, but, as with most birds of prey, the breeding success of this species fluctuates and the apparent small improvement may be the result of a single relatively successful breeding season. (Map 46)

Goshawk *Accipiter gentilis*

Bred sporadically in 19th century and apparently regularly in earlier times (A & L). Has nested occasionally since 1938, perhaps earlier.

Up to three pairs bred in Sussex from 1938 (perhaps as early as 1921) until 1951, but they were persecuted by game-keepers and there was no subsequent proof of breeding (Meinertzhagen 1950, des Forges and Harber 1963). Occasional nesting is believed to have occurred in several other widely separated parts of Britain within the last ten years, some apparently the result of the deliberate release of adult birds. Whether the birds that bred in Sussex had escaped or been released is not known, but the female of a pair that nested in Shropshire in 1951 was certainly one that had escaped from a local falconer. Slijper (1963) has recorded a sharp, sudden decrease in recent years in the population in the Netherlands. (Map 47)

Kite *Milvus milvus*

Huge and widespread decrease; now extinct in most of Britain, due to human persecution and decrease of carrion (A & L). The small population in Wales has increased very slightly in the last decade.

Very scarce, confined to a few counties in central Wales, where now about 20 breeding pairs. This represents a higher population than at any previous time this century. Up to the 1939–45 war the number of known pairs fluctuated between about four and ten. An apparent increase from about six known pairs at the end of the war to 15 known pairs during 1951–53 was probably due mainly to the discovery of birds that had previously been overlooked. Since then, however, apart from a slight set-back in 1955 following myxomatosis, the numbers have increased slightly and some Welsh localities have been reoccupied after a long absence. Breeding success varies considerably from one year to another. Nest failures during 1960–63 were generally the result of human interference, but there was also some circumstantial evidence of dieldrin poisoning (Salmon 1964). Even so, seven young fledged from 17 known nests in 1964, and eleven young flew the next year, which was the most successful since 1954 when 15 young were reared. Despite protection, some nests are still robbed of eggs or young. The future of the Kite in Wales remains in some doubt, for it may be threatened by the widespread felling of deciduous woodlands and their replacement with conifer plantations, as well as by the afforestation of sheepwalks. (Map 48)

White-tailed Eagle *Haliaeetus albicilla*
Widespread decrease and now extinct, due to human persecution (A & L). No confirmed breeding since the last nest was found on Skye in 1916.

Honey Buzzard *Pernis apivorus*
Decrease due to human persecution; formerly rare but regular, now only occasional breeder, though in very small numbers.

Very scarce summer visitor. There is now sufficient evidence to show that this unobtrusive species, which is easily confused with the Buzzard *Buteo buteo*, never completely disappeared as a regular breeding bird in Britain. For at least the last 30–40 years it has maintained a population of several pairs in the New Forest, Hampshire, and has sometimes bred elsewhere in southern England north to the Welsh border, as well as almost certainly Fife in 1949. (Map 49)

Marsh Harrier *Circus aeruginosus*
Huge and widespread decrease, in nearly all counties extinct (A & L). Increase after 1939–45 war, but sharp decline after 1958 almost to level of pre-war population.

Very scarce, currently confined to three breeding pairs on a Suffolk reserve and an equal or smaller number elsewhere in England. Persecution and destruction of habitat led to the species' extinction in Ireland by 1917 and to its temporary extinction in England by the end of the 19th century. The occasional pair attempted to breed in Norfolk from 1908 onwards, but it was not until the 1920's that it again became established there; assisted by protection, up to four pairs nested in the county from 1927 onwards. The species began to settle in the Suffolk coastal marshes in the 1930's and, although not actually proved until 1945, probably started nesting there before the 1939–45 war; by 1958 eight pairs were nesting at four localities (Payn 1962). By 1951, perhaps earlier, a few pairs had begun breeding in Dorset (Moule 1965). More sporadic breeding has occurred in four or five other counties in England and one in north Wales since 1945.

By about 1957–58 the British breeding population was probably higher than at any time since the middle of the 19th century, with 12–14 pairs in East Anglia and about five pairs elsewhere (Axell 1964). After this, however, numbers slumped dramatically: the species is not known to have bred in

Norfolk since 1959, nor has it nested in Suffolk away from Minsmere since 1961. From 1963 to 1966, including the three to four pairs at Minsmere, the total population in the whole country was probably only about six breeding pairs each year.

Rooth and Bruijns (1964) noted a similar sharp decline in the Netherlands, which they attributed to a lack of prey, especially Rabbits *Oryctolagus cuniculus*. Increased human disturbance may be one reason for the decrease in East Anglia: Marsh Harriers still prospect apparently suitable reed-beds each summer, without nesting. Axell (1964) suggested that the destruction by Coypus *Myocastor coypus* of extensive areas of reed-bed habitat since the late 1950's may have contributed to the decline, while there also exists the possibility that the species may be affected by agricultural chemicals. (Map 50)

Hen Harrier *Circus cyaneus*

Huge and widespread decrease, becoming extinct almost everywhere, due to human persecution; remnant in Orkney, etc., somewhat increasing, thanks to protection (A & L). Marked increase since about 1940; the species has re-colonised many Scottish counties and several in Ireland, and more recently has begun breeding again locally in England and Wales.

Scarce; now breeding quite widely in Scotland (including its established strongholds in Orkney and the Outer Hebrides); also in at least six counties in Ireland and four in England and Wales. Its total population certainly exceeds 100 breeding pairs and is perhaps much higher; but detailed information is sparse. This species is the only bird of prey breeding in Britain and Ireland which has increased considerably in the last 20 years and which appears to have succeeded in maintaining this increase. By the beginning of this century it had become extinct over much of the British Isles and until the 1939–45 war it was confined as a regular breeder to Orkney and the Outer Hebrides, with the addition of a pair or two in Ireland. Starting about 1939 it began to re-colonise one part of central Scotland, and between then and the mid-1950's it reoccupied a further fives areas of the Scottish mainland. The initial colonisation may have taken place from Orkney, where the species had increased markedly during the war and a peak population was reached in 1949 and 1950 (Campbell 1957, Balfour 1963). It continued to increase and spread and by about 1960 was breeding in Ayr, Galloway and occasionally elsewhere in southern Scotland, as well as in most Highland counties. A parallel increase occurred in Ireland, where by 1964 a total of 34 pairs were nesting in six counties (Ruttledge 1966). Recently a few pairs have also returned to breed in Wales and two counties in northern England.

Campbell (1957) attributed the Hen Harrier's re-establishment on the Scottish mainland to the relaxation of persecution during the war. One factor which has affected its recent increase has been its tendency in many districts to occupy young conifer plantations, which, being unkeepered and relatively undisturbed, have afforded it a safe refuge. (Map 51)

Montagu's Harrier *Circus pygargus*

Although sometimes stated to have greatly decreased, there is no real evidence that this species was ever much commoner than it is at the present time (A & L). Increase in decade following 1939–45 war, but marked decrease since late 1950's.

Very scarce; probably now about 20 pairs breeding in widely separate parts of England and Wales, with perhaps one or two pairs occasionally in Ireland. The British population of this summer visitor has certainly fallen in recent years from Nicholson's (1957) estimate of 40–50 pairs and, though the data are incomplete, the present total of 15–25 pairs is probably roughly similar to that in the 1930's. Following the 1939–45 war the species increased markedly in south-west England (where for a time around 1950 up to 20 pairs bred in Devon and Cornwall), probably also in north-east England and perhaps elsewhere, while it also returned to north Wales after a long absence. In all areas where an increase was recorded the favoured breeding habitat was young forestry plantations. In the early 1950's there were also several records of nesting outside its usual haunts, and these included the first for Scotland (1952, 1953, 1955 in Perth and 1953 in Kirkcudbright) and Ireland (1955 and subsequently, one or two pairs in two counties).

Already by the mid-1950's, however, a decline had begun to take place in several of the six main breeding areas, and by about 1960 the species had decreased to some extent in almost all of them. It decreased most sharply in East Anglia, where since 1958 it has ceased to breed regularly; this population, nesting mainly in reed-beds, was probably the only one in Britain which had bred more or less continuously since the beginning of the century.

Since about 1960 this harrier has bred annually in probably only three counties of England and Wales, though almost annually in about three others. During 1956–65 it bred at least once in a further 12–14 counties, plus two more in Ireland. As the young forestry plantations in which it nests mature there is inevitably some movement from one area to another, and this may account for the sporadic nature of breeding in some counties. In one of its strongholds in south-west England there is evidence of an increase in 1965 and 1966. Rooth and Bruijns (1964) noted a recent decrease in the numbers of pairs breeding in the Netherlands. (Map 52)

Osprey *Pandion haliaetus*

Widespread decrease due to human persecution, and now extinct (A & L). One and later two pairs have bred in Inverness since about 1954.

The history of the recolonisation of Scotland after an absence of almost 50 years has been detailed by Sandeman (1957) and Brown and Waterston (1962). Increased numbers of Ospreys were seen in summer in Scotland from 1951 to 1954, and there is strong circumstantial evidence that a pair nested in the last of these years. Since 1955 one pair (more recently, two pairs) has bred with varying success on Speyside under the watchful eye of the Royal Society for the Protection of Birds and there are now signs of a spread to other parts of Scotland. This recolonisation came at a time when the species had shown a recovery in its numbers in Scandinavia. (Map 53)

Hobby *Falco subbuteo*

Decrease in 19th century due to collectors and gamekeepers, but doubtful if ever abundant; perhaps now holding its own (A & L). Probably little recent change.

Very scarce; 85–100 breeding pairs, virtually restricted to southern England, where concentrated mainly in Hampshire and the five counties adjoining (see table 5). Numbers of this summer visitor fluctuate from year to

Table 5. Breeding population of the Hobby *Falco subbuteo* in England and Wales during 1962–64

Sporadic breeding may also have occurred in as many as five other counties, though proof of this was not obtained in these three years (e.g. bred Worcestershire in 1965)

Regular breeding	Probable number of pairs	Frequent breeding	Minimum number of pairs	Irregular breeding	Number of *years* 1962–64
Hampshire	25+	Devon	2	Radnor	2
Sussex	13	Gloucester	2	Cornwall	1
Surrey	12	Hereford	1	Somerset	1
Wiltshire	10	Oxford	1	Warwick	1
Dorset	9	Buckingham	1	Northampton	1
Berkshire	5	Kent	1	Huntingdon	1
TOTAL	74 + pairs	TOTAL	8 + pairs	AVERAGE	2–3 pairs

year, but there appears to have been little substantial change in status during the past 25 years, or indeed during the present century. Sporadic breeding to the north and north-east of its normal range has perhaps become rather less frequent since about 1950, but this is not certain. On the other hand, the species has bred more frequently in Devon and recently, for the first time, has nested twice in Cornwall. In many parts of its main breeding range, its numbers appear similar to those in the 1930's. However, Ash (1960) recorded a drop in numbers seen in one part of Hampshire from 1952 to 1959, which he suggested might have been due to the activities of egg-collectors or, alternatively, to reduced breeding success following a series of bad summers.

Brown (1957) estimated the total British breeding population at 60–90 pairs, but Richmond (1959) thought this figure was too low and pointed out that there were 'well over 30' pairs in one county (presumably Hampshire) in 1958. Simson (1966) reckoned that in 1963 there were probably 57 pairs in the six main counties, but his estimates for three of these (Hampshire, Sussex and Berkshire) were certainly too low. A revised estimate based mainly on the regional literature, but partly also on Simson (1966) and correspondence, is given in table 5. It has not been possible to provide figures for a single year in the period 1962–64 as the data contained in most Local Reports are too incomplete. For the main areas the maximum number of probable breeding pairs for any of these three years has therefore been given. When breeding, however, the Hobby is extremely elusive and, although in some years its total population may be smaller in some counties than that given here (notably in Sussex, where it declined from 1962 to 1964), nesting pairs are almost certainly overlooked, particularly in the more northerly counties. In most recent years the breeding population has probably totalled 85–100 pairs. (Map 54)

Peregrine *Falco peregrinus*

Marked and widespread decrease due to human persecution; less marked decline in 20th century and probably holding its own by 1939 (A & L). Wartime reduction locally, due to persecution, followed by a rapid recovery; since about 1955 a sudden, marked and widespread decrease, leading to extinction in several southern counties by the early 1960's.

Scarce; apart from a few pairs in south-west England, Wales, the Lake District and south-west Scotland, most are now confined to the Scottish Highlands and parts of Ireland. Ferguson-Lees (1951) showed that in the late 1940's there was little reliable evidence of a widespread desertion of ancient breeding sites, so that any decline due to persecution in the 19th century was probably much less severe than had been claimed. Between about 1900 and 1955 the population in most parts of Britain remained relatively stable, except that locally during the 1939–45 war large numbers were killed by the Air Ministry in the interests of carrier pigeons. When this persecution ceased, the population recovered rapidly. In Cornwall, for example, where the Peregrine had been completely exterminated in the war, 17 eyries were again occupied by 1955 (Treleaven 1961).

Beginning about 1955 in southern England, however, and spreading north to all parts of the British Isles in the next few years, an alarming and drastic decrease then took place (Ratcliffe 1963). A national census (excluding Ireland) in 1961 and 1962 showed that by 1961 two-fifths of the pre-war population of about 650 pairs had disappeared. In the whole country only 82 pairs were known to rear young in 1961, and only 68 pairs in 1962. The regions most severely affected were southern England and Wales, where the species completely disappeared from more than half the counties in which it had been breeding a few years earlier. Only in the Scottish Highlands were Peregrines still present in 1962 in more than half the territories known before the war. A sample census in 1963 and 1964 (Ratcliffe 1965) showed that numbers had fallen further by 1963, but that in 1964 there were some signs that the decline had been halted. A survey in Ireland in 1950, when the species was believed to be increasing, indicated a population of about 190 breeding pairs. But there, too, a decline began and in recent years the population is thought to have fallen to less than 70 pairs, while the species has become extinct in some southern and eastern counties (Ruttledge 1966).

Ratcliffe (1963) has given convincing circumstantial evidence that agricultural toxic chemicals are the cause of the decline, which has affected not only the British population but also those in several Continental countries and eastern North America. (Map 55)

Merlin *Falco columbarius*

Widespread decrease due to human persecution, but in some areas now probably holding its own or increasing where land no longer preserved for game (A & L). In many places there has been a general decrease extending over the past 30–60 years, and recently a more marked and widespread decline.

Scarce; widely but thinly distributed in upland areas of western and northern Britain, and Ireland. Although there is little quantitative information, much indirect evidence suggests that a gradual long-term decrease occurred in several regions during the first half of this century, though locally, for example on some of the Scottish islands, the species probably maintained its numbers quite well, while in south-west England it actually increased on Exmoor and perhaps also Dartmoor.

Areas affected by the general decrease included probably much of Ireland (Kennedy *et al.* 1954, Deane 1954) and Wales (Ingram and Salmon 1954, 1955, 1957, Condry 1955; etc.) and parts of northern England (Chislett 1952, Oakes 1953) and the Scottish mainland (Baxter and Rintoul 1953, Pennie 1962; etc.). It is not clear why this general decrease occurred, nor why, if the 19th century reduction was simply due to persecution, the species did not increase after about 1900 when persecution became less intensive. Changes in habitat, such as the encroachment of forestry on to its open moorland breeding grounds in Northumberland, Durham and Fife, have been held responsible for local decreases, while greater disturbance was probably the cause of the disappearance in about the 1930's of Merlins which bred in some low-lying western areas, for example among the coastal dunes of south Wales and north-west Devon, and on the mosses of south Lancashire.

Since about 1950 a more marked and widespread decrease has occurred, affecting the species throughout almost the whole of its British range. Excluding Ireland, for which little recent information is available, there is evidence of a decrease in the last 10–15 years in at least 31 different counties. In many of these, including six of the seven southernmost in Wales, almost all those in northern England and south-east Scotland, and Sutherland, Caithness and Shetland in the extreme north, the decrease has been recorded as very marked. By 1964 numbers were particularly low in some areas. In that year no Merlins could be found at five former breeding sites in one area of north Yorkshire, no nests were located in Durham where ten years earlier there had been several, many eggs failed to hatch in the six nests found in Northumberland, and on one island in Shetland there was only one successful breeding pair compared with ten to twelve in the mid-1950's.

Despite the widespread nature of the decrease, there appear to be few counties where breeding has ceased altogether since 1950 and during this period nesting has actually been proved for the first time in Cornwall (in 1954).

These results agree with those of Prestt (1965) in that they show that the species is generally diminishing, but they also suggest that the recent decline has been much more widespread than he indicated. Prestt suggested that the decrease had been due mainly to the loss of satisfactory breeding areas, but clearly other factors are also involved. (Map 56)

Kestrel *Falco tinnunculas*

No evidence for marked change (A & L). Fluctuates, but a general marked decrease in eastern England from about 1959 to 1963, though locally with some recovery since.

Fairly numerous, breeding in all parts of Britain and Ireland except Shetland (where it ceased about 1905). Apart from local changes in abundance, usually attributed to increases or decreases in persecution, the Kestrel's status over the country as a whole appears to have remained largely unchanged during much of this century. Especially after 1930, nesting in urban areas, notably in Lancashire (Oakes 1953) and central London (Homes *et al.* 1957), became increasingly more common. There is some evidence for a general increase in southern districts in the decade following the 1939–45 war. Reports of local increases up to the early 1950's were widespread from Surrey west to the Isles of Scilly (recolonised in 1956 after an absence of many years) and far outnumbered reports of decrease.

Recent surveys by R. S. R. Fitter (in Cramp 1963) and Prestt (1965) have shown that between about 1959 and 1963 Kestrels declined very markedly in eastern England, particularly in agricultural areas from Nottingham and Lincoln south to Hampshire, Sussex and Kent. Within this region the decline was less severe in such localities as the New Forest in Hampshire, and the Brecks in East Anglia, than in areas of pure farmland. The only outstanding cause suggested for the decline was toxic chemicals, and this was associated with decreased breeding success (Prestt 1965).

Less marked declines in the same period were also reported from parts of central England, south-east Scotland and eastern Ireland, but at least in some counties these decreases proved only temporary. In most eastern counties the population has remained depressed. Numbers appear not to have fallen further since 1963, however, while in some of the hardest hit areas of Kent, Surrey and Lincoln, and perhaps elsewhere, there was a decided recovery in 1964 and 1965.

In most parts of the country the population and breeding success of the Kestrel (and also the Barn Owl *Tyto alba*) fluctuates cyclically according to the abundance of its main prey, the Short-tailed Field Vole *Microtus agrestis*. Some indication of the fluctuations since the war is provided by the annual totals of young Kestrels ringed by the British Trust for Ornithology (fig. 3). These data generally parallel those for 1950–61 based on the numbers of nest records submitted to another B.T.O. scheme (Cramp 1963), with the notable exception of 1961 for which Cramp's data indicated a sharp fall. Though they need interpreting with caution, these ringing data do suggest that at least some of the fluctuations in numbers and breeding success, which in recent years

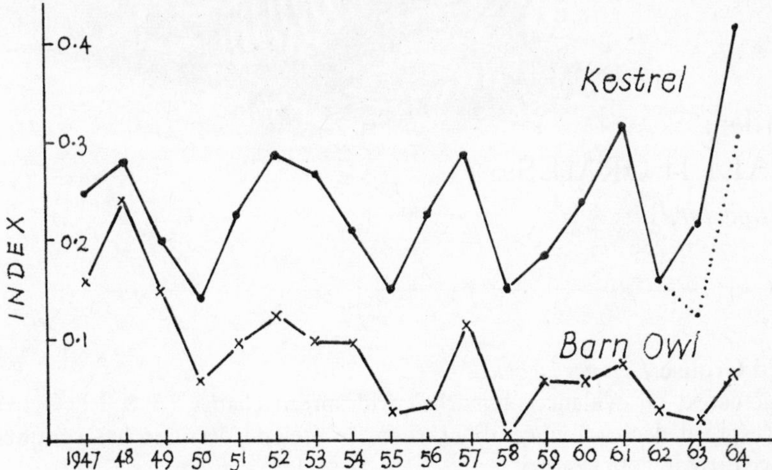

FIG. 3. Numbers of nestling Kestrels *Falco tinnunculus* and Barn Owls *Tyto alba* ringed annually in Britain and Ireland, 1947–64, expressed as a percentage of the annual totals of ringed nestlings of all species. Because of a national survey into its status, special attention was paid to the Kestrel in 1963 and 1964, and the dotted line may better indicate the extent of the fluctuation in these two years compared with previous ones.

have been attributed to other factors, may have been part of this normal short-term cyclical effect. The data are too incomplete to indicate any general trend in the Kestrel population as a whole over the last 20 years. All that can be said is that, unlike those for the Barn Owl, they provide no indication of a decline. Rooth and Bruijns (1964) showed that the Kestrel decreased markedly in the Netherlands from 1961 to 1963, in one area from 28 breeding pairs to only one; the most important single cause was considered to be the decline of voles owing to land improvement. (Map 57)

Order: GALLIFORMES
Game birds

Red Grouse *Lagopus lagopus*

Fluctuates; no evidence of marked widespread change (A & L). General widespread decrease since about 1940; in Ireland decrease has continued since early in 20th century.

Numerous; widespread resident in moorland areas of Scotland, Ireland, Wales and borders, and England from central Stafford northwards; small numbers on Dartmoor and Exmoor where introduced in the 19th century. Shooting bag records and other evidence make it clear that this species has decreased in many parts of Scotland, particularly in the north and west, since the early 1940's, after a period of abundance between the 1914–18 and 1939–45 wars. Reduced numbers since the 1930's have also been noted in most parts of Wales (though there has been some recovery in recent years in Cardigan, Glamorgan and probably elsewhere) and over much of northern England. Disturbance and destruction of habitat led to the species' disappearance from many lowland mosses in Lancashire before the 1939–45 war. It has also declined generally in Ireland during the present century, despite the frequent introduction of birds and eggs from Britain. By about 1950 it seemed to be nearly if not quite extinct in parts of southern Ireland, as well as having become much scarcer in the north (Mackenzie 1952). Except in some parts of Ulster, the decrease has been very marked all over Ireland in the last few years (Ruttledge 1966), though there seem to be few counties from which the species has gone altogether.

Studies into the cause of the decline in Scotland were started in 1956, and this and other research on the species is being continued by the Nature Conservancy's Unit of Grouse and Moorland Ecology in north-east Scotland. The long-term decline appears to have been due mainly to a gradual deterioration in habitat, and particularly a reduction in the productivity and quality of heather *Calluna vulgaris*, on which the species depends for food and cover.

Less efficient management, notably the burning of too much or too little heather, is believed to be primarily responsible for the general impoverishment of moorland studied in the east of the country (Jenkins, Watson and Miller 1963, 1964). Heather growth also depends greatly on spring and summer weather, being better in sunny summers than in wet ones, and this has a crucial effect on the numbers of Red Grouse breeding in the following year. But there is no evidence of any appreciable change in summer weather over the period during which this species has declined in east and central Scotland (Jenkins 1962, 1966). (Map 58)

Ptarmigan *Lagopus mutus*

Widespread decrease and extinct in many areas (A & L). Fluctuates greatly once every decade, but no long-term change this century.

Not scarce; restricted to hill ranges in Scottish Highlands, including Skye and Mull. The distribution has been mapped and fully described by Watson (1965b), on whose papers (Watson 1965, 1965a, 1965b) this summary is based. In the main Scottish Highlands there is no evidence of any change in numbers or range during this century. The population in the Cairngorms fluctuates greatly once every ten years, possibly through changes in behaviour or food; high numbers have occurred in the early years of each decade since the 1910's. Ptarmigan have been extinct as breeding birds in the English Lake District, south-west Scotland, Arran and Rhum since the 19th century, and in the Outer Hebrides since 1938. In recent years, however, the species is said to have been seen again on both Rhum and Harris, and Watson believes that the contraction of range in the Hebrides is only temporary. He explains the decrease in this area as being due to the fact that the areas of suitable habitat are very small and isolated, so that there is a distinct risk of total extinction in years of low numbers. Such local temporary extinctions also occur on isolated small hills in east Scotland. A recent sharp increase in human disturbance by tourists in some parts of the Highlands has had no apparent adverse effects on Ptarmigan numbers, even in the vicinity of ski-lifts. (Map 59)

Black Grouse *Lyrurus tetrix*

Very marked and widespread decrease, due to human destruction and to disappearance of breeding haunts; extinct in most of southern portion of former range (A & L). Evidence of recent increase in new conifer forests in Wales and Scotland.

Fairly numerous; resident Scotland, northern England and Wales, with more isolated populations on the south Pennines, and on Exmoor and the Quantocks in Somerset. Apparent changes in status during this century are summarised on a regional basis below.

Southern England. Extinct in most counties before 1905, and in several more (Cornwall, Wiltshire, Dorset and Hampshire) by 1920. Last seen in the

Braunton area of north Devon in 1933 and on Dartmoor in 1959. Now confined to a few pairs on Exmoor and the Quantocks, where decreasing.

Wales and borders. Indigenous in some eastern districts, but elsewhere probably mainly the descendants of birds introduced in the 19th century. In all parts a general decrease this century, especially in the 1930's, when the species became extinct in Hereford and Glamorgan (perhaps also at this time in Monmouth and Flint). Since about the late 1940's it has increased again and has extended its range in many Welsh counties as a result of the planting and growth of much new conifer forest. With the exception of the counties named above, and also Pembroke and Anglesey, it now breeds in every Welsh county. Small numbers may still breed in south-west Shropshire.

Central and northern England. Disappeared from several Midland counties in last century, from Nottingham and Norfolk early this century, and from Lincoln after 1935. Now breeds in an area of the south Pennines (north Stafford, north-west Derby and east Cheshire) and more widely in northern England. Numbers fluctuate, but appear to have decreased generally in the decade following the 1939–45 war, and locally at least both before and after this period. In some parts, however, numbers have been maintained or have recently increased.

Scotland. Between the end of the 1914–18 war and about 1950 the species decreased generally over most of Scotland and in some districts, particularly in the west, it disappeared altogether. Since about the middle or late 1950's it has become more common again, especially in the new conifer forests, from the border counties north to Sutherland. Locally, however, numbers are still depressed and have shown no signs of increasing. Mackenzie (1952) published game bag figures showing long-term trends in south and central Scotland, and these indicated short-term fluctuations superimposed on longer waves of general abundance with a period of about 30–50 years. Since the mid-19th century the two highest peaks were 1860–70 and 1910–15. Between 1915 and 1949 numbers declined markedly except for a smaller peak in 1933–34. Mackenzie suggested that, if the long-term trend was natural (perhaps due to climatic factors), then numbers should be rising again in the 1950's.

(Map 60)

Capercaillie *Tetrao urogallus*

Extinct Scotland and Ireland before 1800; re-introduced Scotland 1837 onwards. Decrease during both 1914–18 and 1939–45 wars; some increase about 1950.

Not scarce; restricted mainly to east Highlands, from Stirling north to south-east Sutherland. Pennie (1950–51, and in Bannerman 1953–63) has described the species' history and distribution. Following several introductions into Scotland in the 19th century, it increased and achieved a maximum spread by about 1914. Between then and 1949 there was little further colonisation, and in many areas a decrease in numbers or actual extermination, due mainly to the felling of large areas of conifers during the 1914–18 and 1939–45 wars. Recently there has been a tendency for it to spread into younger conifer plantations. By 1959 it had begun to increase again in many areas, though locally its numbers were still depressed. (Map 61)

Red-legged Partridge *Alectoris rufa*

Introduced. Slight contraction of range in western districts since the 1930's, and numbers perhaps reduced in some other areas, but no certain indication of any marked change; local increase in East Anglia since 1959.

Numerous; distributed mainly in east and south England, west to Somerset, north-west to Shropshire and north to north Yorkshire. Howells (1963) suggested that the most important factor limiting the distribution of this species is probably high rainfall. In western districts a maximum distribution appears to have been reached before about 1930, since when it has decreased in Devon (now breeding only doubtfully in the extreme south-east) and probably also in west Dorset; since 1935 it has ceased to breed in Glamorgan. On the other hand, its range limits elsewhere appear to be little changed and may even have extended slightly farther north in Yorkshire, almost to the Westmorland border, in recent years.

There is little definite evidence of a general decline in numbers in southern England, although the species is said to have decreased in several parts of Sussex, Kent and Essex in the last 15–20 years, and in some central counties over a longer period. It is most abundant in East Anglia, where Payn (1962) noted a marked decline in Suffolk beginning about 1945, with a partial recovery in 1959 and 1960 following two dry summers and successful breeding. Middleton and Huband (1966) have shown that the breeding densities on three estates in Norfolk increased markedly after 1959, the average per 1,000 acres rising from 17 pairs in 1953–55 to 63 pairs in 1960–65. An increase of similar proportions was recorded on an estate in Lincoln, while there was also a gradual increase in East Anglia generally from 1961 to 1965, the cause of which is not known. In other parts of the country there was no evidence of an increase. (Map 62)

Partridge *Perdix perdix*

Great decrease in Ireland, but recovering as a result of special legislation for protection, 1932 (A & L). Fluctuates, but steady long-term decrease over most of Britain this century, particularly since about 1940 and accelerating in recent years.

Numerous; widely distributed throughout Britain and Ireland, but local in north-west Scotland and south-west Ireland, and absent from most Scottish islands. The regional literature indicates that this species has decreased widely and markedly over virtually the whole of England, Wales and southern Scotland since the 1930's. Except for temporary and only partial recoveries in some areas, such as in Suffolk in 1959 and 1960 following two good breeding seasons (Payn 1962), the downward trend has become even more marked in recent years. Regional surveys of game-book records, especially for Wales (Matheson 1953, 1956, 1956a, 1957), have indicated that in some areas this trend began towards the end of the last century. G. Howells (in preparation) has shown that this decline has affected all parts of Britain, with the possible exception of northern England and Scotland, and also that it became sharper after the late 1930's; Ireland was not included in his survey. The results of the National Game Census indicate that by 1965 the Partridge population in Britain as a whole was lower than ever before (Middleton and Huband 1966). Howells suggests that the decline is most likely to be the result of human activity (notably changes in agricultural methods brought about by increased mechanisation, such as the grubbing up of hedgerows, rapid ploughing in of stubbles and mechanised hay-cutting) rather than part of a long-term fluctuation due to climatic or other natural factors. More recently, chick survival in many years has been shown to have suffered through an increase in the frequency of cold, wet summers. Further, the availability of insect food for chicks has diminished markedly owing to the widespread use of herbicides which have destroyed those agricultural weeds on which the insects live.

The evidence on present trends in Ireland is conflicting, but it seems possible that the recovery which followed protective legislation in 1930 and the introduction of fresh stocks was only temporary. D. D. Walker (in Bannerman 1953–63) has suggested that the decline there has continued, due mainly to changing farming methods, but perhaps also to climatic changes.

(Map 63)

Quail *Coturnix coturnix*

Very marked and widespread decrease, and now extinct in many former haunts except sporadically in good years; attributed to changed methods of agriculture (A & L). Fluctuates, but since about 1942 at a higher level than earlier this century; it was exceptionally numerous and widespread in 1964.

Scarce; summer visitor breeding regularly in about eight counties in southern England and two in south-east Ireland, fairly regularly in several others, and sporadically north to Shetland. Moreau (1951) traced this species' early history in detail, showing that its numbers reached a low ebb about 1865 and remained low except for occasional 'good years' well into the present century. A slight upwards tendency, noted here and in western Europe generally, began about 1942. In 1947 probably twice as many visited Britain as any earlier year this century. A special enquiry in 1953 (Moreau 1956) showed that in that year probably twice as many occurred in Britain as in 1947, numbers having declined in the interim, reaching a low point in 1951. No obvious correlation was found between the numbers visiting Britain and the weather in the respective springs in France.

No survey has been made since 1953, but the regional literature indicates that numbers have continued to fluctuate considerably, though at a much higher level than in the first three decades of this century. Breeding has probably occurred at one time or another since 1954 in every English county except Middlesex (and perhaps Durham and Devon, where birds were present in summer in 1964 only), though the species is believed to have nested near-annually in Cornwall, Wiltshire, Hampshire, Sussex, Berkshire, Oxford, Hereford and Cambridge (including the Breck). In addition, it has probably bred at least once in six Welsh counties, in seven in the southern half of Scotland, in Caithness in the north, and in the Western and Northern Isles. In Ireland it breeds regularly in Kildare, Carlow and probably Offaly, and perhaps occasionally elsewhere.

Since 1953, notably poor years for Quail were 1956 and 1962; good numbers occurred in 1960 and 1961 and from 1963 to 1965. In 1964 exceptional numbers were recorded over a wide area of Britain and Ireland, and breeding took place in many counties north to Shetland: altogether, well over 600 individuals were heard calling—probably almost twice as many as were present during the 'invasion' of 1953. (Map 64)

Pheasant *Phasianus colchicus*

Introduced. General widespread increase due to artificial rearing and dispersion.

Numerous; resident in all parts of Britain and Ireland, including several islands where numbers are often maintained by fresh introductions and artificial rearing. Except for some regional variation, this species has increased in almost all areas in the last 20 years. G. Howells (in preparation) has shown that numbers have probably increased generally in all parts of England and Scotland (but not Wales) since the end of the last century, though there have been short-term fluctuations, and also temporary decreases during the 1914–18 and 1939–45 wars. The National Game Census figures show that in recent years a peak was reached in about 1960–61, and that there has been a steady increase in numbers reared and released for shooting. In Ireland, re-stocking is taking place extensively and the population is also increasing (Ruttledge 1966). (Map 66)

Order:
GRUIFORMES
Rails, Crakes, Bustard

Water Rail *Rallus aquaticus*
No evidence of marked change (A & L). Decreased locally through drainage, but little evidence of any general change.

Not scarce; distributed generally but very locally in Britain and Ireland, though absent as a regular breeder from many counties, especially in the English Midlands. The regional literature contains little information on status changes of this elusive species, apart from several records of local decrease or extinction as a result of alterations to its breeding haunts, particularly through drainage. Where habitats have remained largely unchanged, so, too, has the status of the Water Rail, though there is very little quantitative information on this point. In Sussex, Walpole-Bond (1938) estimated that up to about 50 pairs nested annually before the 1939–45 war, and a special survey by the Sussex Ornithological Society during 1962–64 showed that the species was still present in summer in at least six or seven widely separated areas, though its numbers appeared to be considerably fewer and only two cases of breeding were proved.

The species is still common in Ireland, where it apparently continues to breed in every county (Ruttledge 1966), and in parts of East Anglia. In England, Scotland and Wales it is known to nest regularly in fewer than half the counties in each country and, although doubtless much overlooked, it is absent from some areas which appear to be suitable for breeding. (Map 70)

Spotted Crake *Porzana porzana*
Decreased with drainage of breeding haunts (A & L). Only occasional breeding during the past 50 years.

Occasional breeder, perhaps just annual at the present time. The main decrease took place before the middle of the 19th century, but the species appears to have lingered on in some eastern counties until the early 1900's. Since then it has remained for the most part a sporadic nester, though for a short time between about 1926 and 1937 it occurred slightly more numerously and probably bred at least once in about ten counties in England and Wales. In one of these years, 1930, four or five pairs bred in Somerset alone (Lewis 1952). There is some evidence to suggest that it has become slightly more frequent again in recent years, with certain or probable breeding in Somerset (1963), Suffolk (1963, 1964) and Sutherland (1966), possible breeding in three other southern counties and one northern one, and a few records of birds seen in summer, for example in Kirkcudbright in 1963 and at two places in Somerset in 1964. Curry-Lindahl (1959–63) mentioned a recent increase and spread in Sweden. (Map 71)

Baillon's Crake *Porzana pusilla*

Bred, apparently only sporadically, in East Anglia in 19th century. The last nest recorded was in Norfolk in 1889.

Corncrake *Crex crex*

Very marked and widespread decrease, probably due to changed methods of agriculture; western Ireland and Scottish islands apparently not affected much as yet; numbers also vary much with the season (A & L). Long-term decline has continued and the species has withdrawn steadily westwards.

Not scarce; for present breeding distribution and contraction of range see fig. 4. A special enquiry into the status of the Corncrake in 1938 and 1939 (Norris 1945, 1947) confirmed that the species had decreased greatly over almost the whole of Britain and Ireland. The decrease began in south-east England and parts of east and central Scotland during the second half of the 19th century, began in eastern Ireland and became especially marked in southern England in the early 1900's, and spread progressively westward to affect most areas by 1939. The species also decreased generally in Europe after about 1920. The decline is generally attributed to changed methods of agriculture, especially the introduction of mechanical hay-cutters. Other factors may have contributed, however. For example, as pointed out by Nicholson (1951), it coincided with the erection of a network of overhead wires in western Europe. He suggested the possibility that the many migrant Corncrakes killed flying into wires might have been sufficient to cause a decrease in breeding numbers.

In Britain the decline has continued at a steady rate over the past 25 years, and may even have become more rapid since the early 1950's, particularly in Scotland. Places affected have included Orkney, Shetland and many in Ireland. The species still remains relatively numerous in western districts of Ireland and in parts of the Hebrides, although locally at least it has also decreased in both these areas. The pattern of a steady long-term decline has sometimes been interrupted locally by a partial recovery in numbers, such as in the Severn valley and elsewhere in the 1930's. Occasional breeding still occurs in central and southern England, and in 'good' years (such as 1959) the

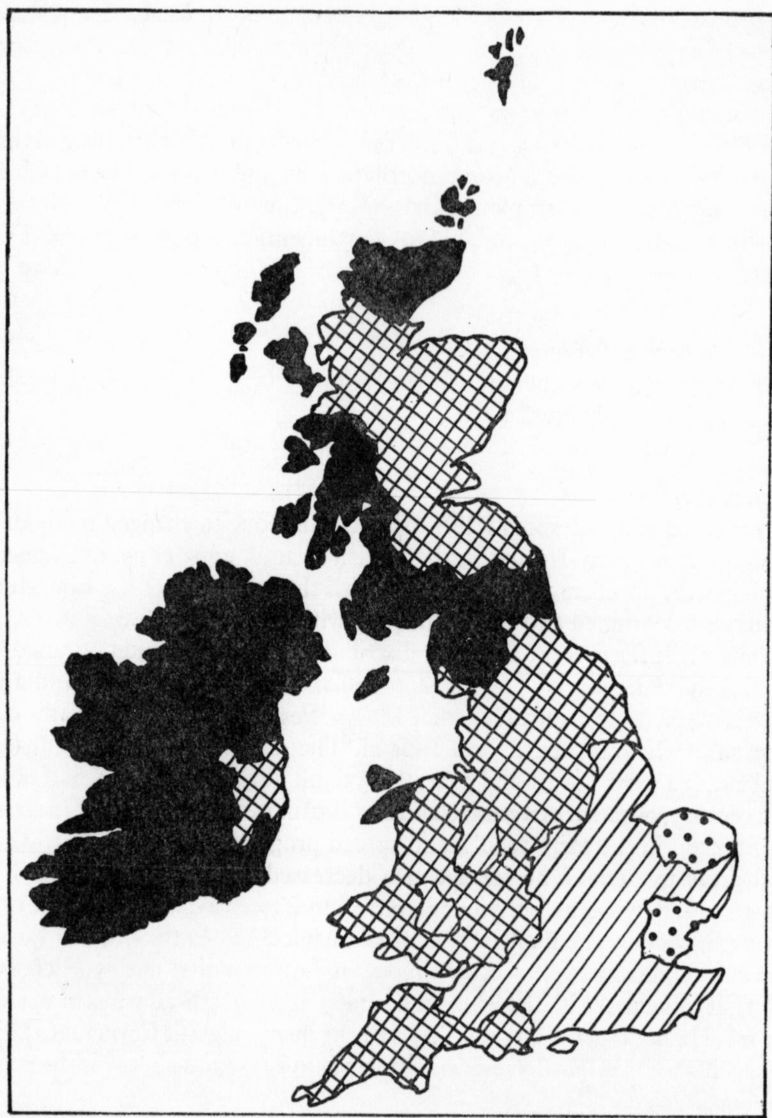

FIG. 4. Contraction of the range of the Corncrake *Crex crex*. The various shadings show the counties in which the species ceased to breed annually before 1900 (dots), after about 1914 (hatched) and after about 1939 (cross-hatched). Breeding still occurred annually in 1964 in the blacked-in counties, although in most of these the numbers have much decreased and in some are now reduced to a few pairs. A very few pairs still breed fairly regularly (but are not known to do so annually) in west Yorkshire, Durham, and perhaps some counties in central Scotland. Irregular breeding occurs in some Welsh counties, and sporadic nesting still takes place in certain counties in central and southern England. The species was never common in Essex and Norfolk, and may in fact never have bred annually in these counties.

odd pair may breed as far south as Cornwall or Hampshire, or as far east as Suffolk. (Map 72)

Moorhen *Gallinula chloropus*

Marked increase Scotland and probably increasing generally, but always common (A & L). Perhaps decreased again Scotland, but no real evidence of any marked change.

Numerous and widespread resident, breeding in all parts of Britain and Ireland, except some islands in the Inner Hebrides. Apart from the mainly temporary effects of hard winters—the frequency of which since about 1940 appears to have caused a general decrease in Scotland (Baxter and Rintoul 1953)—there is no evidence of decreased or increased numbers in recent years other than on a purely local scale. No one trend is apparent in any region, except perhaps for the slight decrease in Scotland. But the evidence for this, and indeed for the species' earlier increase, is very meagre. (Map 73)

Coot *Fulica atra*

Marked increase Scotland (A & L). Little evidence of marked change, but probably decreased Scottish islands and increased England.

Fairly numerous, breeding in all mainland counties (but very scarce north-west Highlands), also Outer Hebrides and Orkney; now absent or only occasional in Shetland and Inner Hebrides. This species is relatively easy to census, yet practically no counts of its breeding numbers have been made anywhere in the country. In Scotland, such information as there is comes mainly from the islands (e.g. Baxter and Rintoul 1953) and this suggests that in at least the last 50 years the numbers have if anything decreased (*cf.* Alexander and Lack's statement above). Since the mid-1950's the species has ceased to breed regularly in Shetland (where it was fairly common early this century) and has decreased in Orkney. An earlier decrease was noted on several of the Western Isles. No clear trend is apparent on the Scottish mainland.

Published information from England is almost as sparse, although there is some indication that in certain counties in the south-east the species has become more numerous this century (e.g. Glegg 1929, Harrison 1953, Payn 1962). In central London, where pinioned birds were introduced in 1926, it has increased markedly and has spread to lakes in most of the Royal Parks (Homes *et al.* 1957, Cramp and Tomlins 1966). In the wider London region it has increased generally, aided by the great growth since the 1939–45 war in the number of flooded gravel pits. It is a highly successful and abundant species on these new waters and, although there is little objective information on this point, it must certainly have increased in eastern England as a whole.

Elsewhere in Britain and Ireland, apart from purely local changes—for example, increases in Monmouth, where the species first bred after 1939 (Humphreys 1963), and in Cornwall, where it has increased and spread since about 1950—there is little indication of any alteration in status. On the Continent there has been a tendency for it to spread northwards this century (Voous 1962) and it may also have recently increased generally over western Europe as a whole. (Map 74)

Great Bustard *Otis tarda*

Extinct before the middle of the 19th century through the enclosing of waste land, and human destruction. Formerly bred many parts of England. Although some birds lingered on in East Anglia until 1838 (and perhaps till 1845) the last recorded nests were in 1830 (Norfolk) and 1832 (Suffolk). Unsuccessful attempts were made to re-introduce the species into Norfolk in 1900. In historic times the species has become extinct in several other parts of Europe including southern Sweden, Denmark and France (Voous 1960).

Order: CHARADRIIFORMES
Waders, Gulls, Auks

Oystercatcher *Haematopus ostralegus*
Marked decrease in eastern and southern England in 19th century; partial recovery in 20th century; possibly increasing in northern Scotland and north-west England (A & L). Very marked increase and expansion of range, particularly in northern areas, but also elsewhere. Some local decreases (e.g. on Welsh mainland) owing to human disturbance and destruction of habitat.

Fairly numerous; breeds round almost whole coastline; widespread inland in Scotland and parts of northern England. The species' present distribution has been mapped by Dare (1966) who recently carried out a detailed survey of its status. The following summary is based almost entirely on his work.

At least 19,000 pairs—and possibly 30,000 to 40,000 pairsb—reed in Britain and Ireland, the great majority in Scotland. The population as a whole is currently expanding, particularly in northern England and southern Scotland, where a remarkable spread in range during this century has led to the colonisation of completely new inland nesting habitats—initially river shingle beds and latterly also surrounding farmland up to a mile or more from the nearest river (see also Buxton 1962). This spread inland is continuing and the species now nests over a wide area north and south of the border counties. Marked increases have also occurred in coastal and inland populations in northern Scotland, where the species has likewise colonised inland areas this century. Recent increases have been especially marked in Orkney and Shetland.

During the last 30 to 40 years several former breeding sites in eastern and southern England have been recolonised. This increase has been most marked in Norfolk, where the establishment of bird sanctuaries at Scolt Head and Blakeney Point was probably largely responsible for an increase in the local population from a mere handful of pairs in 1924 to 200–250 pairs at the present time. In parts of East Anglia Oystercatchers have developed a new tendency to nest in coastal fields rather than on the shore itself, thus following a similar pattern of spread in Belgium and the Netherlands.

Although some populations in the southern half of England and in Wales appear still to be increasing—for example, in Essex and north Kent, and on certain islands off the Welsh coast—others have recently decreased owing to human disturbance, particularly through the growth of tourism. On the mainland coast of Wales, for instance, the species is steadily decreasing almost everywhere. Away from sanctuaries, human disturbance will probably have an increasingly adverse effect.

Oystercatcher populations elsewhere in western Europe have also recently increased and extended their ranges (Dare 1966). In Iceland a sudden colonisation of the north and east coasts since 1920 has been correlated with climatic amelioration (Gudmunsson 1951). Elsewhere, the increase may be due largely to greater protection. (Map 75)

Lapwing *Vanellus vanellus*

Widespread decrease due to decrease in waste land and extensive taking of eggs; marked recovery since the passing of the Lapwing Bill in 1926 (A & L). General increase in north Scotland and Northern Isles this century; widespread decrease elsewhere in 1940's, and in most places more recently as well, probably as a result of changes in agriculture.

Numerous; widely distributed in all parts of Britain and Ireland. Apart from the extreme north of Scotland, where it increased during the first half of this century, the Lapwing appears to have been generally decreasing here since the middle or end of the 19th century. In many areas this trend has been more or less continuous, though locally in parts of England its numbers recovered temporarily between the 1914–18 and 1939–45 wars. In the 1940's, however, it decreased again almost everywhere and, with the possible exceptions of Hampshire and Monmouth where it is said to have increased (Cohen 1963, Humphreys 1963), its numbers have recently declined even further or remained at a low level. Even before the 1963 hard winter, it had disappeared almost completely as a nesting bird from a wide area of south-west Suffolk and central Essex.

In most, if not all, counties of Wales there has been a marked decrease since the late 1920's (e.g. Ingram and Salmon 1955, 1957, Lockley 1961). The species was formerly common on hills in central and north Wales at 1,400 feet, but by the 1950's it had become very scarce at this altitude and most of the small numbers still breeding were below 1,000 feet (Condry 1955). According to Ruttledge (1966), it has also decreased in Ireland and now nests only rarely on arable land. In Scotland numbers decreased markedly following the hard winters of the early 1940's, 1947 and 1963, with a recovery in most areas during the milder periods in between, particularly in the 1950's. In Shetland the species was continuing to increase and spread in the 1950's, several islands having been colonised since 1930 (Venables and Venables 1955). The subsequent fluctuations there are not known, but on Fair Isle there was a steady increase in the numbers breeding, from two pairs during 1950–55 to 16 by 1961, then a sharp fall to three pairs in 1963 and two the next year (Davis 1965).

At least in England and Wales, changes in agriculture—particularly the war-time conversion to ploughland of much permanent pasture and marginal land, increased mechanical farming methods, more intensive grassland cultivation and the drainage of rough lowland pastures—seem to have been largely responsible for the decrease since 1940 (see also Nicholson 1951, Spencer 1953). The increase in northern Scotland is presumably connected with the species' general tendency to spread northwards in Europe since the beginning of this century, which Salomonsen (1948) and Kalela (1949) have attributed to the gradual amelioration of the climate. (Map 76)

Ringed Plover *Charadrius hiaticula*

No evidence of marked widespread change (A & L). Much decreased in many coastal areas of England, Wales and parts of south Scotland, due mainly to human disturbance.

Not scarce. Breeds round almost entire coastline of Britain and Ireland, as well as inland in the Brecks (East Anglia), on river shingle beds in parts of northern England and Scotland, and by several Irish lakes. Coastal development—particularly bungalows, caravan sites and sea-defence works—and greatly increased human disturbance have caused the abandonment of many former breeding sites. As a result, on the coasts of practically every maritime county in England and Wales the numbers of Ringed Plovers are now fewer than at any other time this century. In many areas the species started to decrease well before the 1939–45 war. In east Dorset a decline between about 1930 and 1949 was blamed partly on increased disturbance and partly on the spread of *Spartina* which destroyed its breeding sites in Poole Harbour. On the Yorkshire coast the numbers of nests at Spurn decreased from 70 in 1914 to 36 in 1936 and, after a temporary respite during the war when access to civilians was prohibited, to about 20 in 1949 (Chislett 1952); numbers have since declined to about half this figure. In Devon the species is now restricted to a handful of pairs at two sites on the north coast and one in the south, while on the Cornish mainland it appears to have disappeared altogether in the last year or two. Several other examples of decreases due to disturbance could be given.

On the few parts of the English coast where it is still relatively undisturbed its numbers have been maintained, while in such sanctuaries as those at Blakeney Point and Scolt Head in Norfolk it has increased markedly. At Blakeney Point, where fewer than 20 pairs bred 50 years ago (Rowan 1917), the total of nests in recent years has varied between 45 and 114, with the lowest numbers in 1963 and 1964, perhaps because of high mortality during the 1963 hard winter; at Scolt Head, where up to 150 pairs or more have nested in recent years, there were 67 nests in 1924 (Rivière 1930). In some counties, for example Kent, there has been a recent tendency for more pairs to nest in fields a short way inland from their former nesting beaches; but the habit does not appear to be well developed. There have also been rather more instances in recent years of nesting well inland in some counties from Yorkshire and Lancashire southwards. The unique population which breeds inland in the Brecks has declined markedly this century from an estimated 400 pairs about 50 years ago (Clarke 1925) to fewer than ten pairs at the present time (Easy 1965), owing mainly to the growth of agriculture and forestry.

In northern England the species was increasing and spreading farther inland up rivers in the 1950's in both the Lake District and in north Northumberland (Tyer 1954, Robson 1957). This tendency has been likened to the inland spread of the Oystercatcher *Haematopus ostralegus* in the same areas, though it appears not to have developed to the same extent.

Except in parts of southern Scotland, where the Ringed Plover has decreased in some coastal districts as a result of human disturbance, there is little evidence of any marked widespread change in Scotland or Ireland. Venables and Venables (1955) suggested that it had decreased generally in Shetland, particularly in the previous 20 years; in the last few years, however, it appears locally to have increased there (R. J. Tulloch *in litt.*). (Map 77)

Little Ringed Plover *Charadrius dubius*

Very marked increase and spread since first bred in Britain in 1938; is continuing to increase, especially in the northern half of its range.

Scarce; probably 170–200 breeding pairs, distributed in eastern England from Kent north to Durham and west to Cheshire (fig. 5), almost wholly at gravel pits and other 'artificial' sites, with only one or two pairs on river shingle beds (in Yorkshire). Parrinder (1964 and earlier) has traced in detail the increase and spread of the Little Ringed Plover as a British breeding bird. It first nested in 1938 in Hertford, and next in 1944 in both that county and Middlesex. By 1947 three other counties in the Thames basin and one site in central Yorkshire had been colonised. After that numbers continued to increase steadily: by 1950 about 30 pairs summered in eleven counties, by 1956 about 74 pairs in 20 counties, and by 1962 about 157 pairs in 23 counties. Latterly the greatest increase has occurred in the northern half of the range. In Yorkshire numbers increased from 18 pairs in 1962 to 29 pairs in 1964. From 1962 to 1964 the species also extended its range northward to include the two northernmost vice-counties of Yorkshire, and also Durham. There has been little westward extension of breeding range in the last few years, although between 1962 and 1964 or 1965 its numbers increased greatly in several counties on the western periphery of its range, from Derby south to Berkshire.

Parrinder (1964) showed that the spread had been aided by a parallel increase in the number of 'artificial' habitats, especially gravel pits, which are usually occupied by this species while they are still being worked and before the banks have become overgrown. He suggested that the rate of increase had been held up by the high degree of disturbance at such sites, rather than by a lack of them. In certain counties, however, numbers of Little Ringed Plovers have tended to fluctuate as more or fewer suitable sites become available to them. Parrinder (1964) knew of only one record in Britain—in Derbyshire in 1950—of nesting on a river shingle bank, but in 1964 two such sites were

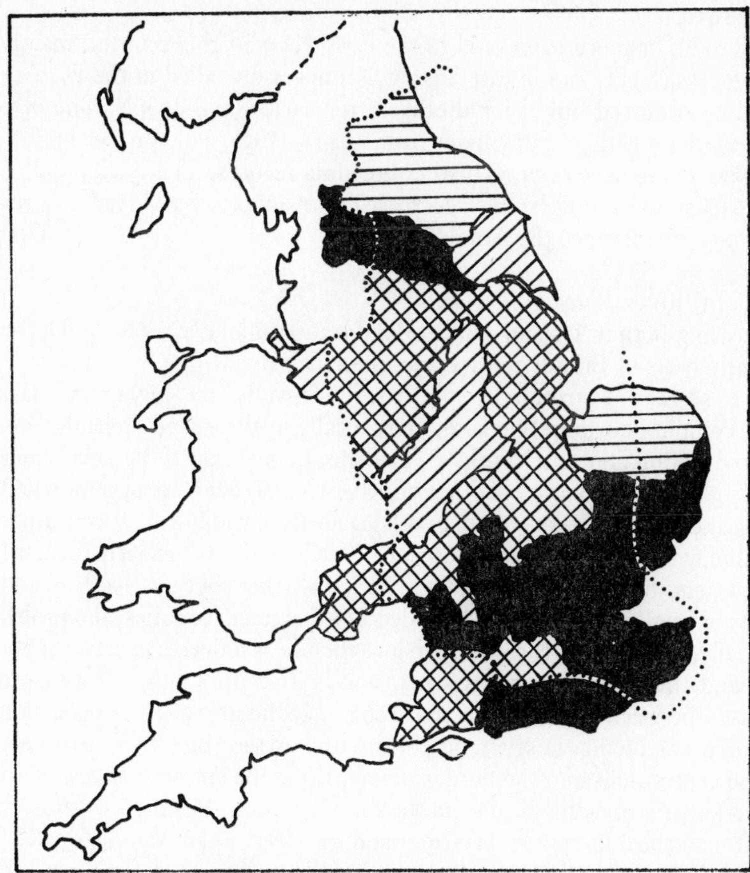

FIG. 5. The spread of the Little Ringed Plover *Charadrius dubius*. Information based on Parrinder (1964) and Local Reports for 1963 and 1964 (also earlier years for Yorkshire). The various shadings show the counties (vice-counties in Yorkshire) in which breeding first occurred during 1944–49 (black), 1950–54 (cross-hatched), 1955–59 (diagonal hatch) and 1960–64 (horizontal hatch). Nesting also occurred in Hertford in 1938. In recent years (1960–64) the species has bred only irregularly in Hampshire and Sussex (in neither in 1964) and Suffolk. The continuous line delimits the approximate breeding range in 1964.

occupied in west and north-west Yorkshire. It will be interesting to see if this habitat—a common one on the Continent and in various other parts of the species' range—is exploited more fully in the northern counties of England in future years. (Map 78)

Kentish Plover *Charadrius alexandrinus*

Always local, decreased steadily and now almost extinct; important causes have been the commercial development of seaside resorts, and egg-collectors (A & L). Now extinct as a British breeding species with no record of nesting since 1956.

Up to 40 or more pairs bred in the early years of this century, mainly at Dungeness (Kent) and in east Sussex. Numbers dwindled in the 1920's and breeding occurred only sporadically in the 1930's and 1940's. One or two pairs bred annually in east Sussex from 1949 to 1956, and one pair in Suffolk in 1952. There have been no further breeding records. The small population in the Channel Islands has also decreased markedly in recent years as a result of human disturbance (R. Arnold verbally). (Map 79)

Golden Plover *Pluvialis apricaria*

Decreasing both in Ireland and Scotland, cause unknown (A & L). Decrease in many parts of Britain and Ireland, perhaps general.

Not scarce; distributed quite widely, mainly on higher moorlands from Pennines north to Shetland, more locally in Wales and Ireland, with an isolated population on Dartmoor. The species was said to be decreasing in 1957 and 1964 in Orkney, but otherwise there is little evidence to show whether it is still decreasing generally in Scotland north of the Forth. It continues to breed in every Scottish county, except Fife where it was formerly regular but ceased to nest after 1947 (H. Boase in MS.). Farther south in Scotland and in northern England its numbers have decreased in many counties, and probably generally, since about 1950. In Ayrshire there was a decrease between about 1945 and 1964 (G. A. Richards *in litt.*) and in Roxburgh numbers were much reduced between about 1953 and 1962 (Medlicott 1963). Stokoe (1962) recorded a reduction in several parts of Cumberland since 1950, particularly on the central fells and the border moors, while the species has disappeared altogether as a breeding bird from the coastal mosses. Numbers decreased by about one-third in north Westmorland between 1950 and 1965 (R. W. Robson *in litt.*). Relatively small numbers still breed on the Pennines south to Derby and north Stafford, but these, too, are currently thought to be decreasing.

During this century the species has probably declined over much of Wales and the Welsh borders. It formerly bred in Monmouth and Glamorgan, and at least occasionally in Hereford, Shropshire and Carmarthen, but in most of these counties it has not nested since the 1939–45 war or earlier. It also ceased to breed in Somerset (Exmoor and, occasionally, the Mendips) more than 50 years ago. On Dartmoor, however, two or three pairs have bred regularly since 1950 after an absence, apart from occasional suspected breeding, of more than 100 years. In Ireland the species has ceased to breed in many counties during this century and is now confined to about six counties in the north and north-west where numbers are small and greatly reduced (Ruttledge 1966).

Although the evidence is meagre, it appears that the Golden Plover is continuing to decrease in many areas, if not generally over the whole of Britain and Ireland. Loss of habitat has been given as the reason for a recent decline in Sweden (Curry-Lindahl 1959–63), but this factor seems unlikely to be responsible for the decrease in Britain and Ireland. (Map 80)

Dotterel *Eudromias morinellus*

Widespread decrease, attributable to former extensive shooting of birds on migration and to collectors (A & L). No evidence of further change except for recent decrease on Cairngorms, due probably to increased human disturbance.

Very scarce; virtually confined as a regular breeder to central Scottish Highlands and perhaps a few sites in Ross. Numbers vary from year to year. D. Nethersole-Thomson has estimated the British population at 60 to 80 pairs (Bannerman 1953–63, Darling and Boyd 1964). The main decline probably occurred during the second half of the 19th century, by the end of which the species had ceased to breed in Sutherland, and had virtually gone from northern England and probably also south-west Scotland. D. A. Ratcliffe records that it probably bred annually somewhere in the Lake District until about 1927 (Bannerman 1953–63), since when it has nested only irregularly (Robson 1957, Stokoe 1962). It may also have bred in Kirkcudbright more than once since the 1939–45 war, and odd pairs may occasionally still breed in Sutherland. The only evidence of a recent decrease within its main range comes from the Cairngorms, where numbers have diminished owing to increased human disturbance (D. Weir *in litt.*).

The recent colonisation of the new polders in the Netherlands by nesting Dotterels (Marra 1964, 1965) represents a remarkable extension of breeding range for a species which is otherwise restricted to mountainous regions and arctic tundras. (Map 81)

Snipe *Gallinago gallinago*

Decrease at beginning of 19th century, but marked increase in southern England about end of that century and beginning of 20th, when it colonised a large area in the south Midlands as well as many districts in southern counties where breeding was previously unknown (A & L). Marked decrease, especially in last 15–20 years, in Midlands and south-east England, though still breeds in most counties; probably little change elsewhere.

Fairly numerous; widely distributed, breeding in every county in Britain and Ireland except Middlesex and the Isle of Wight, though now scarce in several other southern counties. The increase and extension of range which affected many southern counties earlier this century appears to have petered out in the 1930's, although locally—for example, in parts of Hampshire (Cohen 1963) and Warwick (Norris 1947)—it may have continued until the 1940's. In the last 15–20 years this trend has been reversed in practically all counties south of a line from Cheshire to Norfolk, except possibly those in south-west England. In many (e.g. Kent, Essex, Hertford, Wiltshire and Nottingham) it is now restricted to a very few pairs and in Bedford it may no longer nest annually. But only in Middlesex, where the last nest was recorded in 1956, does it appear to have ceased to breed altogether. Drainage of marshland and other losses of habitat are responsible for the decrease in many areas.

As a breeding bird it has also decreased locally in parts of northern England and south-west Scotland, but elsewhere in Scotland and in Ireland and Wales there is no evidence for any recent or long-term change in numbers. Numbers fluctuate according to the severity of the winter and there was, for example, probably a heavy reduction all over the country after the hard winter of 1963 (Dobinson and Richards 1964). (Map 82)

Woodcock *Scolopax rusticola*

In 19th century rapidly increased in England and colonised many parts of Scotland, Ireland and Wales; in 20th century colonised the Isle of Man and continued to increase in Scotland and northern England, but decreased in southern England, Ireland and extreme north of Scotland; main cause of increase probably the cessation of shooting in the breeding season and the protection of coverts in the interests of Pheasants *Phasianus colchicus* (A & L). Little general change, but has probably increased and spread in the new conifer forests in Wales, southern Scotland and East Anglia.

Fairly numerous; widely distributed in woodlands (and in a few treeless areas) over much of Britain and Ireland, but not in south-west England, Pembroke, Anglesey, the Outer Hebrides and Northern Isles, and doubtfully in Donegal. This distribution corresponds closely with that shown by Alexander's detailed survey in 1934 and 1935 (Alexander 1945–46), except that there has probably been some westwards extension of breeding range in Wales. Nor is there much indication that the breeding numbers have altered appreciably in the last 30 years. In some counties in southern England the species has decreased locally where woodlands have been felled. A recent decrease has also been noted in Wester Ross. In East Anglia, however, particularly Breckland (Payn 1962, Easy 1964), and in parts of north Wales (Harrop 1961) and south-west Scotland (A. D. Watson *in litt.*), it has increased over the past 20 to 30 years owing to the spread of new conifer plantations. It is also believed to have increased recently in the Chilterns and central Cotswolds in central southern England. There is no evidence from Ireland that the decrease noted in the 1930's, and attributed to the break-up of estates, has continued. (Map 83)

Curlew *Numenius arquata*

Marked increase in Northern Isles, Inner Hebrides and many parts of England in 20th century; in parts of north and west England, where breeding was formerly almost confined to high ground, now breeds regularly in river valleys and on low moors; cause unknown (A & L). Increase and spread has continued in almost all parts; several more counties in eastern England have been colonised and breeding now occurs widely in lowland areas, including cultivated farmland.

Fairly numerous, now breeding in every county in Britain and Ireland except Kent, Essex, Middlesex, Hertford, Bedford, Huntingdon and Cambridge); has recently colonised the Outer Hebrides (Lewis). A notable feature of the expansion this century has been the occupation of many lowland areas in England and Wales. Already by 1939 the species was nesting on lowland pastures and rough meadows in many places where it was previously unknown. There was no decrease when these were ploughed in the 1939–45 war, and in Northumberland and Durham, for example, pairs took to breeding in cultivated clover and cereal crops. Elsewhere, too, the species has since spread to arable farmland. As well as a continued increase and spread to low ground in almost all those counties in which it was already established before 1939, it has since colonised several in the east Midlands and East Anglia, including Oxford, Berkshire, Buckingham, east Norfolk, Suffolk, Northampton, Warwick, Leicester and Nottingham. In most of these it now breeds regularly, though still only locally. Cambridge was also occupied for a time, but breeding ceased there in the early 1950's owing to drainage and disturbance in the areas concerned.

In addition to the increases on low ground, Curlews have colonised completely new chalk upland areas in the Yorkshire Wolds since 1955, while their numbers in more typical habitats on upland moors in northern England have at least been maintained during this century or have even increased too. In parts of south Wales, however, Ingram and Salmon (1954, 1955, 1957), suggested that the remarkable spread on lower ground since the 1920's had occurred at the expense of the populations on the higher hills.

The species has also spread considerably in Scotland and Ireland during this century. With the colonisation of Armagh in 1948 (Nesbitt 1955) it now nests in every county in Ireland, though it is uncertain whether the increase continues. In Scotland it is believed to be increasing still in Ayrshire, the Lothians and Orkney.

In England, particularly, there was already some indication by the late 1950's that the phase of expansion was slowing down, though there was no sign that it had ceased altogether. It is uncertain whether it is continuing now, for in many areas the populations were reduced by the 1963 winter (Dobinson and Richards 1964) and they have not yet recovered their former level.

A general expansion of range has also occurred in northern Europe, especially Scandinavia, during this century, although in some countries farther south, notably the Netherlands, the species has decreased owing to habitat destruction (Braaksma 1960). (Map 84)

Whimbrel *Numenius phaeopus*

Decreasing markedly; cause unknown (A & L). Now steadily increasing Shetland.

Very scarce; confined to Shetland and the Outer Hebrides (Lewis); very sporadic breeding has been recorded elsewhere in northern Scotland. Small numbers bred regularly in Orkney in the 19th century, but ceased to do so soon after the 1880's. Venables and Venables (1955) stated that the Whimbrel decreased or ceased to breed in most localities in Shetland between 1889 and 1930, but increased again after that. By the early 1950's a total of 50–55 pairs was breeding in four areas. Since then, although no revised population estimate has been published, it has continued to increase gradually and recolonised Whalsay and Yell in the early 1960's. From 1957 one or two pairs have also bred regularly on Lewis in the Outer Hebrides. Elsewhere, however, nesting remains sporadic, and the only recent records are from Sutherland (1960) and St. Kilda (1964). Merikallio (1958) showed that the species disappeared from several districts in southern Finland at the end of the 19th century. (Map 85)

Black-tailed Godwit *Limosa limosa*

Huge decrease and eventual extinction before middle of 19th century, due mainly to drainage of fens and increasing accessibility of breeding haunts; has bred four times 1937–42, so possibly about to become re-established (A & L). Since 1952 it has bred annually in increasing numbers in one area of East Anglia; occasional or sporadic breeding has occurred in six other areas since the 1939–45 war.

Very scarce. One regular breeding site in East Anglia, the Ouse Washes (Cambridge/Norfolk), colonised by one pair in 1952, increasing to about twelve pairs by 1959–61 and to perhaps three times this number at the present day, assisted by protection (P. J. Conder in Brown and Waterston 1962, and *in litt.*). Since the end of the 1939–45 war the species has bred occasionally elsewhere in England and Scotland, most often in Shetland (one or two pairs in several years since 1948 or 1949), but also in Caithness (1946), Orkney (1956) and south-east Scotland (1964, 1965), and almost certainly in west Suffolk (1947, 1949) and Somerset (1963). The races concerned are not known, but it is possible that, as suggested by Williamson (1958), the breeding records in north Scotland refer to the Iceland form *L. l. islandica.*

One factor which may limit any major spread away from the present breeding site in East Anglia is a shortage of suitable habitat—wet, rough, lowland meadows. The species has decreased in many parts of central Europe owing to changes in agriculture, but it has slightly extended its range northwards during this century (Voous 1960). It increased in the Netherlands from about 1920 until at least the early 1950's, probably bred in Finland for the first time in 1955 and 1956, and has increased and spread in Iceland since 1920 (Morley and Price 1956, Merikallio 1958, Gudmundsson 1951). (Map 86)

Green Sandpiper *Tringa ochropus*
The only confirmed breeding records come from Westmorland (1917) and Inverness (1959), and there is no evidence to suggest that this species has ever bred regularly in the British Isles.

Wood Sandpiper *Tringa glareola*
May now be becoming established in north Scotland where a very few pairs have bred since 1959.

Very scarce. A pair bred in Northumberland in 1853 and until recently this stood as the only British breeding record. In 1959, however, and then in most years until 1965, a pair nested at one locality in Sutherland. In a different part of the same county a pair probably nested in 1961 and certainly did so in 1962, while single pairs bred in west Inverness in 1960 and probably in north Perth in 1966. Although these are the only published records of confirmed breeding (to 1966), the species has almost certainly bred in at least one other part of northern Scotland in recent years. (Map 88)

Common Sandpiper *Tringa hypoleucos*
No evidence of marked change (A & L). Apparently decreased in some parts of England, Scotland and Wales since 1950 or earlier, perhaps only locally.

Not scarce; widely distributed in Scotland, Ireland (not extreme south-east), Wales (not extreme south) and west and north England. Over most of the species' British and Irish range there is little evidence or information concerning changes in breeding populations, but there appears to have been no marked extension or contraction of range during this century. It may be significant, however, that about a dozen recent county records which refer to a change in status all concern decreased or probably decreased numbers. In several areas a decrease seems to have begun in the 1920's or 1930's, as in Orkney (Lack 1942–43), in Angus and locally in north Perth (H. Boase in MS.), and in Radnor (Ingram and Salmon 1955). In Orkney the decrease has continued, while in Radnor, as in the near-by counties of Brecon and Carmarthen (Ingram and Salmon 1954, 1957), it was most marked in about the late 1940's, continuing into the early 1950's. Stokoe (1962) recorded a decline in north Cumberland, and R. W. Robson (*in litt.*) has noted slightly reduced numbers both in the valleys and on the uplands of north Westmorland during the period 1950 to 1965. The species is currently believed to be decreasing in Cheshire (T. H. Bell *in litt.*) and there appears also to have been a recent slight decrease in the Peak District, Derbyshire (R. A. Frost *in litt.*). There are no recent breeding records from Glamorgan or Somerset, though it bred at least occasionally in each county earlier this century. In Devon there was a definite decrease in the Dartmoor area in the late 1950's (Dare 1958, and *in litt.*) and breeding was not reported in the county between 1963 and 1965. Apart from the few pairs on Dartmoor, the species appears always to have been only a sporadic nester in England in the area to the south and east of a line from the Severn estuary to Scarborough, Yorkshire. In most southern counties it has never been known to breed, and in the ten years from 1955 to 1964 the only breeding records in this area were in Berkshire (1955), Hertford (1955–57) and Norfolk (1962 and 1963). Ruttledge (1966) made no mention of any change in status in Ireland, though the species is said to have decreased locally on the Antrim-Derry boundary. (Map 89)

Redshank *Tringa totanus*

Great decrease in England at beginning of 19th century followed by steady increase beginning about 1865; in southern Scotland, England and Wales the species spread west and south during the 60 years 1865–1925 till every county but Pembroke and Cornwall had been colonised; cause of increase unknown (A & L). Increase and expansion ended in most districts about 1940, since when there has been some decline in south-east England and locally elsewhere, due to losses of habitat.

Fairly numerous; widely distributed, breeding most commonly in flat coastal regions, but also in every inland county; scarce or absent in south-west England, south-west Wales, and south and west Ireland. Thomas (1942) traced the history of the increase and spread of the Redshank up to 1940. The main period of spread was between 1893 and 1915 when 26 counties in southern England and Wales were occupied for the first time; breeding numbers also increased in northern England and over much of southern Scotland (see above). Since 1940, although Pembroke, Wexford and Kerry (once) have been added to the list of counties in which breeding has been recorded (leaving only Cornwall and three in southern Ireland where it has not), the available evidence suggests that the earlier marked expansion ended soon after 1940, and in south and south-east England numbers then tended to decrease. The decrease appears to have affected inland populations most severely (for example, in Wiltshire, Middlesex, Hertford, Essex and Suffolk), but it has also been noticed in some coastal populations from Hampshire round to Suffolk. At least locally, increased drainage and cultivation of breeding haunts have been partly responsible for the decline. Farther north in England and in southern Scotland there is less evidence of a decrease after 1940, though locally in some western counties one did occur. On the other hand, in some counties, such as Stafford (Lord and Blake 1962), the species may even have continued to increase. In northern Scotland there is little evidence of any change, except in Shetland where it was increasing in the early 1950's and is continuing to increase and colonise new islands at the present time (R. J. Tulloch *in litt.*). Except that a few pairs have bred in Wexford since 1941, there appears to have been little alteration in the species' Irish range in recent years or, indeed, during this century (Ruttledge 1961, 1966).

In 1963 the numbers breeding in many parts of Britain decreased very markedly as a result of mortality during the severe winter (Dobinson and Richards 1964). In south Devon, for example, the small breeding populations which had colonised the Exe and Axe estuaries only a few years earlier disappeared altogether, and no Redshanks bred in the county from 1963 to 1966. In Nottingham only ten pairs bred in 1963 compared with a total of about 110 pairs just four years earlier. Any recovery appears to be taking place only slowly, and it seems possible that the general decrease in southern England since 1940 may be partly connected with the greater frequency with which severe winters have occurred. Contrariwise, the earlier increase and spread corresponded with the period when severe winters in England were fewest (*cf.* Lamb 1965). Yet, despite a decline in south-east England since 1940 and the marked reduction which occurred in many parts of the country after the 1963 hard winter, the Redshank remains very much more widespread and numerous in Britain and Ireland than it was at the end of the 19th century.

According to Voous (1960), the species is decreasing at an alarming rate in Europe as a whole and has virtually disappeared from the cultivated regions of France and Germany. It last bred in Switzerland about 1930 (Glutz von Blotzheim 1962). Haftorn (1958) stated that it had decreased locally in Norway owing to reclamation of breeding haunts. (Map 90)

Greenshank *Tringa nebularia*

Increased in central Scotland in latter half of 19th century (A & L). Recent decrease in this area, but apparently little change farther north.

Scarce; restricted to central and north Scottish Highlands, Skye and the Outer Hebrides; sporadic breeding in Inner Hebrides, Orkney (1951), Shetland (1871) and Berwick/East Lothian (1925). D. Nethersole-Thompson (1951) estimated the Scottish population at roughly 300–500 pairs, which may be an underestimate in some years. Recently numbers have decreased in parts of Inverness, near the southernmost edge of the breeding range. The population on two Speyside deer-forests varied between five and 13 pairs during 1935–39, and then fell to five to eight pairs during 1945–49 and to three to five pairs during 1959–63. Numbers also fell in two adjacent forests. The precise causes of this decrease are not known, but several special local factors may have contributed, while there may also have been a general contraction of range. In the species' strongholds farther north there is no evidence of any decrease (Darling and Boyd 1964). Small numbers now breed on most moors in Lewis (Elkins 1965) and perhaps elsewhere in the Outer Hebrides. This probably represents an increase, since in the late 1930's it was doubtful if any were breeding regularly in the Outer Hebrides (Baxter and Rintoul 1953). (Map 91)

Temminck's Stint *Calidris temminckii*

Sporadic. Bred central Scotland (Cairngorms) in 1934, 1936 and 1956, and central Yorkshire in 1951, each time unsuccessfully. (Map 92)

Dunlin *Calidris alpina*

Possibly decreasing, but evidence hard to assess (A & L). Decrease in certain coastal populations since late 19th century and in parts of Ireland. Little evidence of changes elsewhere and no marked trend apparent at the present time.

Not scarce; distributed quite widely, mainly on moorlands, from Shetland south to north Derby, and locally in central and north Wales and north-west Ireland; one or two pairs breed on Dartmoor (Devon) and occasionally on Bodmin Moor (Cornwall). The evidence is still hard to assess, but in many areas it appears that there has been little change in status. The few records which do refer to a marked change all concern a decrease, however, and this appears to have been most marked among the few mainland coastal or lowland populations. The species ceased to breed in Lincoln after the end of the 19th century (Smith and Cornwallis 1955); several pairs bred at Marton Mere, Lancashire, up to 1916 but not subsequently (Oakes 1953); numbers are much reduced on the Solway salt marshes in Cumberland (Stokoe 1962); and the former large colonies on Tentsmuir, Fife, already decreasing by 1880, dwindled steadily until the last pair nested in 1937 (Grierson 1962). Loss of habitat through afforestation has caused a recent decrease in Kircudbright, and there is some evidence to suggest that in Cardigan and perhaps elsewhere in Wales the species is now becoming scarcer. Small numbers still nest in about eight counties in north-west Ireland, but there appears to be no recent confirmation of breeding in seven other counties where it once nested.

(Map 93)

Ruff *Philomachus pugnax*

Became extinct before middle of 19th century due to drainage of fens and extensive taking for food (A & L). Has bred sporadically since at long intervals and since 1963 has recolonised one area.

Very scarce; restricted to the Ouse Washes (Cambridge/Norfolk) where one or two nests have been found each year since 1963 (to 1966 and later). Ruffs continued to breed in Norfolk until 1871 and there were a number of sporadic breeding records in Norfolk and probably Suffolk until the end of the century. In the 20th century occasional breeding was recorded in Norfolk in 1907 and 1922, in Durham in 1902 and perhaps in Lancashire in 1910. The finding of a nest on the Ouse Washes in 1963 was thus the first authentic record of breeding for 41 years. Although only one or two nests have been found each year during 1963–66, the number of males present at a lek have been very much greater and the species seems likely to establish itself as a regular breeding bird.

(Map 94)

Avocet *Recurvirostra avosetia*

Extinct before middle of 19th century due to taking of eggs for food, drainage of fens, etc.; bred Ireland 1938 (A & L). Bred once Essex and probably Norfolk 1941–46; re-established in Suffolk in 1947 and has increased under protection.

Very scarce; confined as a regular breeding bird to Suffolk. The two main sites are Havergate Island, which was colonised by four or five pairs in 1947, held a breeding population of 97 pairs by 1957, and has had fluctuating but lower numbers since; and Minsmere, where up to four pairs bred in 1947 and again from 1963 to 1966. Protection and careful management of the breeding habitat is responsible for the increases at both these sites. Small numbers have occasionally nested elsewhere in Suffolk since 1948, but outside that county the only known breeding records are from Essex (1954) and north Kent (1958). Since 1930 the numbers breeding in the Netherlands and Denmark have increased as a result of protection, and the species has also recolonised Sweden (Jespersen 1945, van Ijzendoorn 1950, Curry-Lindahl 1959–63). (Map 95)

Black-winged Stilt *Himantopus himantopus*
Sporadic. Three pairs bred in Nottingham in 1945.

Red-necked Phalarope *Phalaropus lobatus*
Big decrease in 19th century almost entirely due to collectors; partial revival in 20th century due to protection; and colonisation of north-west Ireland (A & L). Partial revival appears to have been local and temporary; the species has decreased markedly in Ireland and Orkney since about 1930, and decreased in Shetland until the 1940's, since when there has been some recovery.

Very scarce, restricted to a few Scottish islands and one part of the mainland, and one locality in Ireland. The species is still threatened by egg-collectors, so information on its past and present status in certain areas (e.g. the Outer Hebrides) has often been kept deliberately vague. It is certain, however, that the British and Irish population as a whole has decreased since the early years of this century and, except in Shetland, it may still be decreasing or merely maintaining its numbers at a very low ebb.

Shetland. According to Venables and Venables (1955), the species ceased to breed on Yell, Hascosay and Unst after 1922, but the decrease on Fetlar and Mainland appeared to have ended by 1949 and 1950, when 27–34 pairs were breeding. No revised figure has been published, but numbers are said to have increased slightly in recent years and two islands were recolonised in 1965 after a long absence.

Orkney. Some recovery from about 1910 to 1930, though numbers erratic; believed still breeding on three islands in 1941 (Lack 1942–43), but now confined to one island where about three pairs nest.

Inner Hebrides. Only regular site is Tiree, where first discovered breeding in 1902; a few pairs were breeding in about 1913 and in the early 1950's (Boyd 1958), and probably still do so.

Outer Hebrides. Decrease at end of 19th century and beginning of 20th. A few pairs still nest on the Uists and Benbecula, though at several sites often irregularly; yet, remarkably, the species manages to survive (Darling and Boyd 1964).

Scottish mainland. Since 1963 a few pairs have bred regularly in one area of north Scotland.

Ireland. A colony in Mayo, first discovered in 1902 (*cf.* Inner Hebrides, above), held about 50 pairs in 1905 and about 40 pairs in 1929, but then declined until there are now only one to three pairs. Two smaller colonies in the same county were abandoned by 1944. Odd pairs also bred in Donegal in the 1920's (Ruttledge 1966). (Map 97)

Stone Curlew *Burhinus oedicnemus*

In second half of 19th century became extinct in Cotswolds and east Midlands; has decreased elsewhere due to disappearance of breeding haunts through cultivation and afforestation (A & L). Recovery in some areas in the 1920's and 1930's as a result of less cultivation, but further decrease during and after 1939–45 war owing to loss of downland and heathland habitats.

Scarce; a few pairs breeding near east Suffolk coast and (till 1965) on shingle in Kent; otherwise confined to calcareous soils, especially downland, from east Norfolk to Dorset, Hampshire and Sussex. The British population is probably in the region of 200–400 breeding pairs. Although the species has continued to nest on ploughland and even in woodland 'rides' where agriculture and forestry respectively have supplanted its former haunts, its numbers have fluctuated mainly according to changes in agriculture. When much marginal land in Suffolk and Berkshire, and probably elsewhere, went out of cultivation between 1918 and 1939, Stone Curlews increased (Payn 1962, Jones 1966). When this land, and more besides, was ploughed during the 1939–45 war and kept under cultivation afterwards, Stone Curlews decreased. Now the majority nest on arable farmland, for even in those areas where the original heathland or downland remains it has become overgrown and unsuitable since the myxomatosis of Rabbits *Oryctolagus cuniculus* in 1954. In some areas, however, the species still nests on grassland grazed by sheep.

The most drastic population decreases have occurred in Suffolk, both in the east of the county, where there are now only a few pairs left, and in Breckland, where there were over 300 pairs in 1949, only 60–80 pairs in 1958 and fewer than 50 pairs by 1963 (Easy 1965; Local Reports); in Sussex, where there are now 20–25 pairs compared with 60 before the 1939–45 war and where several sites have been abandoned within the last few years (D. D. Harber *in litt.*; Local Reports); and in Dorset and parts of Berkshire and Oxford, where the species has decreased greatly since the 1940's (Moule 1965, Radford 1966). On the pebble wastes of Dungeness (Kent) up to 17 pairs bred in the early 1900's, later dropping to a fairly constant six to eight pairs for many years up to 1964 (Scott 1965); but only one pair bred in 1965 and none in 1966.

Except that the species finally ceased to breed in Yorkshire after 1938, there has been little change in its British range since Alexander and Lack. The present trend is probably still towards a decrease. Breeding success of many farmland populations seems to be low due to the destruction of nests by agricultural machinery. Locally, however—for example, in parts of Berkshire (Jones 1966) and west Hampshire (Cohen 1963)—numbers may now have become stabilised at a low level or be decreasing only slowly. The future of the species as a British breeding bird is uncertain, and will remain so until a more detailed study of its ecology has been made. Due probably to increased disturbance of its duneland habitat, it has decreased steadily in the Netherlands since 1923 or earlier, and has probably been extinct there since about 1958; in other central European countries it has also decreased markedly in recent years (Voous 1960). (Map 98)

Arctic Skua *Stercorarius parasiticus*

Somewhat decreased 19th century, due to human disturbance, somewhat increased in 20th century where protected (A & L). Increasing Orkney and Fair Isle; little information from elsewhere.

Not scarce; restricted to Scottish islands and Caithness. Venables and Venables (1955) stated that it had certainly decreased in recent years in Shetland in the vicinity of large colonies of Great Skuas *Stercorarius skua*. Foula was cited as an example, but Jackson (1966) considered that the breeding population there of about 130 pairs had not altered appreciably between 1948 and 1963, although towards the end of this period it was being replaced by Great Skuas in some parts of the island. On Fair Isle, recolonised in the early 1920's, there was a steady increase from 15 to 70 pairs between 1948 and 1962 (Davis 1965). There has also been a considerable increase and expansion in Orkney, which was still continuing in 1963: in 1941 the species was believed to be increasing on Hoy and was nesting on two other islands; by 1961 it had increased further on Hoy (to about 200 pairs) and in all was nesting on eleven islands (Bannerman 1953–63).

For a species with such a restricted British breeding distribution, it is curious how little published information exists on the sizes and trends of many of its colonies. The present position of most of the colonies in Shetland and the smaller ones in the Outer Hebrides is not known (except that at the main colony on Lewis 40–50 pairs—'about usual numbers'—were present in 1964). Relatively small and fluctuating numbers still nest on Coll and Jura (Inner Hebrides) and in Caithness. (Map 99)

Great Skua *Stercorarius skua*

Marked decrease in 19th century due to human destruction; marked increase in 20th century due to protection, and extending range southwards (A & L). Continued marked increase; in the past 20 years has spread to the Outer Hebrides (including St Kilda) and the north Scottish mainland.

Not scarce; restricted to Scottish islands and Caithness; has recently begun to breed in Sutherland. In the early 1880's the species was confined as a British breeding bird to two islands in Shetland—Foula (probably about 60 hairs) and Unst (about five pairs). Since then, and especially since about 1920, it has increased steadily and become widespread and numerous in Shetland (see Venables and Venables 1955). On Foula there were about 900 breeding pairs in 1963 (Jackson 1966). Orkney was colonised in 1915, the numbers on Hoy increasing to over 20 pairs by 1941, to 60–80 pairs by 1961, and yet further by 1965; small numbers have also bred on several other islands during the past 20 years. The chief period of increase on Fair Isle occurred between 1950 and 1963 (Davis 1965). Since about 1945 small numbers have bred on Lewis (Outer Hebrides) and in 1962 the species spread to St Kilda. Attempted breeding has occurred regularly at two places in north Caithness since about 1949, and since 1964 a pair or two have begun to nest on the island of Handa in west Sutherland.

Dickens (1964) has suggested that the marked increase which has occurred in Scotland and Faeroe (see also Bayes *et al.* 1964), especially since about 1930, is balanced by a conspicuous decrease in the Iceland population over the same period, and that as a whole the North Atlantic population of the Great Skua has probably not increased during this century. (Map 100)

Great Black-backed Gull *Larus marinus*

Very marked and widespread increase since about 1880; before that was decreasing (A & L). Has continued to increase markedly in all areas.

Fairly numerous, breeding widely on coasts (especially islands off-shore) except in the east from Hampshire to Kincardine. Special enquiries into the breeding status in England and Wales were held in 1930 (Harrisson and Hurrell 1933) and 1956 (Davis 1958). The first of these showed that a remarkable increase had taken place from near-extinction towards the end of the 19th century to an estimated total population in 1930 of between 1,000 and 1,200 breeding pairs. The second indicated that by 1956 there had been an almost threefold increase in many areas compared with 1930, but that this was confined mainly to island populations (notably in the Isle of Man, Anglesey, Pembroke and the Bristol Channel) while mainland ones had remained largely unchanged. (An estimate of 1,600 pairs was given for the total breeding population in 1956, but this figure was probably much too low because it allowed for only 370 pairs in the Isles of Scilly, compared with 600–800 pairs in 1930 and over 1,200 pairs at the present day.) Since 1956 the breeding populations on several islands, especially in the Bristol Channel and Pembroke, have continued to increase. On Skokholm and Skomer, however, recent control measures have reduced the adult populations so that they now number about the same as they did in 1956. The substantial colonies in the Isles of Scilly have also increased, certainly since 1960 and probably since 1956.

Although there are less numerical data from Scotland and Ireland, it is clear that in both these countries the Great Black-backed Gull has also increased considerably during this century. In Scotland there was not the same drastic reduction in the 19th century as there was farther south and in many areas the species appears to have remained numerous, though many colonies fluctuated (and have continued to do so) owing to the activities of man. Its main increase in Scotland seems to have occurred since about 1920, in which time it has colonised or recolonised several parts of south-west Scotland. The increase is continuing, at least in the west and north, and some idea of present abundance can be gained from the fact that just one of several very large colonies in Orkney is estimated to number close on 2,000 pairs (E. Balfour *in litt.*). The largest colonies in Ireland are considerably smaller—Ruttledge (1966) cited Little Saltee, Wexford, as the biggest with 200 pairs—and the fluctuations there closely parallel those recorded in England and Wales. Considerable increases have occurred at several of the larger Irish colonies, such as on the Saltee islands and Inishkea, Mayo, over the past 10–20 years, and numbers around much of the Irish coastline are probably still increasing (Cabot 1963, Ruttledge 1966).

The species is still absent as a breeding bird from large areas of the east and south coasts of Britain. It has bred for the first time in Aberdeen and on the Isle of May, Fife, since 1962 and, more atypically, the odd pair or two have nested occasionally at sites in Poole Harbour, Dorset, since 1957 and at Havergate Island, Suffolk, since 1959. Increasing numbers are now being recorded in summer at seabird stations in north-east England, and it seems only a matter of time before they begin to breed there.

The increase in Britain and Ireland this century is part of a general expansion in the populations of Great Black-backed Gulls on both sides of the Atlantic. The probable main cause has been their exploitation of the abundance of edible refuse now provided by man at such places as fish-docks, rubbish dumps and coastal sewage outfalls, particularly during the winter months. A secondary factor has perhaps been the relaxation of the persecution that the species received in the 19th century, and in part the present increase may represent a return to a former population level. (Map 101)

Lesser Black-backed Gull *Larus fuscus*

'Increasing in Wales, Scotland and Ireland' (A & L). Trends have varied from one region to another; the population as a whole is probably increasing at the present time, though because of a marked decrease in Scotland at and after the end of the 19th century it is doubtful whether the species is currently more numerous than it was 60–70 years ago.

Fairly numerous; widely but locally distributed on western and northern coasts of Britain and Ireland (very local on British east and south coasts), with a few scattered—though sometimes large—colonies inland. Although two surveys have been held into the status of the species as an increasing winter resident (Barnes 1952, 1961), and the histories of a few colonies are known quite well, it is difficult to assess changes in total breeding numbers. In many areas there has been much shifting of colonies, and of populations between adjacent colonies, but the following trends appear to be the main ones. They are summarised by countries since they partly disagree with Alexander and Lack's conclusions. Space does not permit the inclusion of details of many local variations.

England and Wales. A general increase has occurred in most coastal colonies in west England and Wales during this century; several of the more southerly ones, however, were plundered for eggs during the 1939–45 war and the populations at some (but not all) of these have remained depressed ever since. The total numbers breeding in England and Wales have increased since the war, if only through the spectacular growth of the colony at Walney Island, Lancashire, which was founded in about 1930, has now reached a strength of over 10,000 pairs, and is still increasing. The two largest (and long-established) inland colonies in north-west England were abandoned between the 1920's and 1940's in favour of Walney Island, Rockcliffe Marsh in Cumberland, and a new inland colony on the Lancashire Pennines. A substantial inland colony in Cardigan was also abandoned in the mid-1920's. The only permanent east coast colony is on the Farne Islands, Northumberland, where a decrease is said to have taken place in the 1930's.

Scotland. Very substantial decreases occurred both inland and in western and northern Scotland during the late 19th and early 20th centuries (e.g. Mackenzie 1918, Gibson 1952, 1956, Baxter and Rintoul 1953, Venables and Venables 1955, Pennie 1962). Locally, numbers have been increasing again in parts of this area, but there is no indication that they are doing so generally, while in the Northern Isles they may still be decreasing. In east Scotland, however, a steady increase has been recorded on the Isle of May, Fife, since the island was first colonised in 1930, while nesting was first recorded in Aberdeen in 1949 and in Kincardine in 1965.

Ireland. According to Deane (1954) the species has increased as a coastal nester in Northern Ireland while decreasing inland. Kennedy, Ruttledge and Scroope (1954) referred to an 'undoubted increase' in Ireland as a whole. In the last 10–15 years it has increased greatly at the few colonies where checks have been made, and one new colony has been established well inland (Ruttledge 1966). More than 500 pairs now nest on the Saltee islands, Wexford, but other Irish colonies are much smaller and only two or three are known to hold more than 100 pairs.

Although the British and Irish population as a whole may be currently expanding, the species has evidently not increased to the same extent as the Herring Gull *L. argentatus* and Great Black-backed Gull *L. marinus* have done. Indeed, it is uncertain whether it is more numerous now than in the second half of the 19th century. Human interference and disturbance, changing methods of fishing, interspecific competition with Herring and Great Black-backed Gulls, and other factors, have been suggested as reasons for local declines, but it is uncertain whether any one single factor is responsible for the more widespread changes which have occurred. Unlike the Herring and Great Black-backed Gulls, this species is mainly migratory and is also much less of a scavenger. During this century it has colonised Iceland (simultaneously with the Herring Gull), presumably in connection with climatic changes. (Map 102)

Herring Gull *Larus argentatus*

Has increased in Scotland and probably elsewhere, but always abundant (A & L). Greatly increased in virtually all parts of its breeding range, especially during the last 20 years.

Numerous; breeds on all coasts of Britain and Ireland, mainly in west and north, and only locally in east and south-east England; has colonised some areas inland, mainly in Ireland. Although this species has always been numerous, it has undoubtedly increased generally during the 20th century and particularly over the last 20–25 years. There are very few records of decreases, but even where numbers have diminished, this has always been due to exceptional local circumstances: for example, increased human disturbance and predation by Foxes *Vulpes vulpes* at Dungeness, Kent, and changes in the fishing industry in Shetland.

Records of increase are so numerous that they cannot be given in detail. The most spectacular has been the growth of the colony at Walney Island, Lancashire, where Herring Gulls first nested in 1904, had become established by 1928, and subsequently increased to 35 pairs by 1934, 120 pairs by 1947 and between 10,000 and 20,000 pairs by about 1964 (Oakes 1953, Local Report). This colony must now rank among the largest in Britain and Ireland, though the record appears to be held by the one on 59-acre Puffin Island, Anglesey, where Harris (1963) estimated that 20,000 pairs were breeding in 1960. Other notable increases have occurred this century on islands in the Bristol Channel (main colony at Steepholm, where numbers grew from about 700 pairs in the 1930's to 1,250 in 1949 and to about 3,600 in 1956), the Firth of Forth (several islands colonised, including the Isle of May where the first pair bred in 1907, 455 pairs by 1936, 3,000 by 1954, and still increasing), and elsewhere. Any assessment of the scale of the increase in the total population in England and Wales can only be guessed, but it seems probable that numbers have at least doubled over the last 20 years.

Nesting on buildings was almost unknown before the 1939–45 war, but in the 1940's and 1950's this became an established habit on the roofs of houses and factories in many seaside towns in south-west England, Sussex, Kent, Yorkshire, south Wales and elsewhere. The tendency is probably continuing, and in 1965 a pair nested in the town of Inverness for the first time. Another increasing tendency, noticed also in Scandinavia, is for birds to nest inland. This has been particularly noticeable in Ireland where there are now colonies on several lakes and bogs often far inland (Ruttledge 1966), but it has also been apparent elsewhere. Since the 1939–45 war small inland colonies have been established in Scotland, and in England and Wales at places as diverse as china clay pits in Cornwall, an inland cliff in north Gloucester, mountain lakes in Merioneth, a factory roof at Merthyr Tydfil, Glamorgan, and even, since 1961, at the London Zoo.

The increase in the population here has run in parallel with a general and spectacular increase in the North Atlantic population as a whole. This expansion has probably been due primarily to the species' exploitation of the abundance of edible refuse now provided by man at rubbish dumps, fishing ports, harbours and so on, particularly in winter (see Voous 1960). (Map 103)

Common Gull *Larus canus*

Very marked increase in Scotland and Ireland in 19th century still continuing; in 20th century extended its range to north-east Ireland and established small colony near Dungeness (Kent and Sussex) (A & L). Perhaps still increasing, but little real evidence in recent years.

Not scarce; breeds widely in Scottish Highlands and Isles, more locally in south-west Scotland and in north and west Ireland, and at single localities in England (Dungeness) and Wales (Anglesey). Numbers appear to have continued to increase within the main breeding range in Scotland and Ireland until perhaps 1950 (Baxter and Rintoul 1953, Kennedy, Ruttledge and Scroope 1954). Since then little information has been published, though what there is points a further small increase in some areas (for example Kirkcudbright and Mayo) and perhaps generally. Some expansion of range has taken place and small numbers have been found nesting for the first time in Stirling (since 1954), Berwick (since 1960), Dumfries (since 1962), and Longford and Anglesey (since 1963). In England, sporadic breeding by one or two pairs took place in Cumberland and Northumberland between 1910 and 1940, in Yorkshire in 1955, 1957, 1966 and 1967, in Norfolk in 1965–66, in Durham, probably since 1965, and in Nottingham in 1967. However, the only permanent English breeding station is in the Dungeness area, where numbers have decreased from about 30–40 pairs in 1939 to about twelve pairs now, owing mainly to increased predation. (Map 104)

Black-headed Gull *Larus ridibundus*

Great decrease during 19th century, but widespread increase began about the end of the century and has continued (A & L). Much regional and local variation, but as a whole the population has continued to increase, especially on coasts of south-east England.

Numerous; breeding colonies scattered widely in Wales, northern and eastern England, Scotland and Ireland (except extreme south and south-west), and locally in central and southern England; mainly absent from south-west England. National surveys of breeding colonies (excluding Ireland) were held in 1938 (Hollom 1940) and 1958 (Gribble 1962, Hamilton 1962). Both surveys indicated that despite many local and regional fluctuations the total breeding population in England and Wales had increased this century, although there is some evidence to show that it is still less than in the early part of the 19th century. By 1958 approximately 50,000 pairs were breeding in England and Wales, representing an increase of roughly 25% on the 1938 (revised) estimate. However, the increase was by no means evenly spread. The largest colony in both years was the one at Ravenglass, Cumberland, which increased from about 10,000 pairs (Marchant 1952) to between 13,000 and 16,000 pairs. But of seven other colonies holding more than 1,000 pairs in 1938, five (in Cumberland, Lancashire, Lincoln, Norfolk and Dorset) has been deserted by 1958 and the other two (in Montgomery) had decreased. Instead, most of the eight colonies which held more than 1,000 pairs in 1958 were newly established ones situated in Hampshire (three), Kent (two), Essex (two), Suffolk and Westmorland. At least some of the colonies in south-east England have continued to increase. For example, in north Kent (where breeding did not begin until the 1940's) colonies sited mainly on turf saltings on the estuaries of the Medway and Swale totalled about 2,000 pairs in 1955, about 2,500 pairs in 1958, and 4,000 pairs by 1961 (J. N. Humphreys 1963).

In Scotland numbers probably increased between about 1900 and 1938, but again with much regional variation (Hollom 1940, Baxter and Rintoul 1953). The 1958 survey showed that a further large increase occurred in Sutherland, but most other counties were covered too incompletely to indicate trends over the country as a whole (Hamilton 1962, Pennie 1962). No full survey has been carried out in Ireland, though numbers have almost certainly increased generally during this century. It is uncertain whether they are continuing to do so. In Ulster, Deane (1954) noted that the main increase occurred after about 1920.

Fluctuations at individual colonies have been attributed to many different local factors, such as changes in habitat, increased or decreased human interference, competition with other species, and so on (see Gribble 1958). The general increase this century, however, is probably related to the species' expansion in western Europe as a whole (see Voous 1960, Higler 1962). This, in turn, is probably connected partly with its more varied feeding habits in winter, partly with the greater protection of breeding sites, and partly with the climatic amelioration which has led to a marked north and north-westwards extension of breeding range, including the colonisation of Iceland.

(Map 106)

Kittiwake *Rissa tridactyla*

Has increased in Scotland in 20th century (A & L). Steady increase (which continues) in all areas since about 1900, following a decrease during the 19th century due to persecution.

Numerous; breeding colonies are situated mainly on cliffs on all coasts (though only one exists—in Suffolk—between Hampshire and south Yorkshire) with the majority on the North Sea coasts of Scotland and northern England. This and the following statements are based on the results of a national survey carried out in 1959 (see Coulson 1963). This survey showed that the total British and Irish breeding population numbered at least 173,000 pairs, of which about 37,000 pairs nested in England and Wales. Coulson demonstrated that the number of new breeding stations increased at the same rate (3%) as the breeding population between 1920 and 1959. He suggested that the present increase began about 1900, though initially it was confined to existing breeding sites. There was no indication in 1959 that the rate of increase was changing. Coulson regarded the increase this century as representing a return to the population level which existed before the numbers were heavily reduced by persecution in the 19th century. A relaxation of persecution has led to the recent colonisation of low cliffs in many areas, and even to the use of buildings and harbour walls as nesting places, particularly on the east coast. The only colony on the southern part of the east coast was founded by two pairs which nested on the Pier Pavilion at Lowestoft, Suffolk, in 1958; numbers had increased to 26 pairs by 1965. An even more remarkable event has been the nesting since 1962 of a few pairs on a building overlooking the River Tyne at Gateshead, Durham, more than nine miles inland.

The present increase has not been confined to Britain and Ireland, but is also taking place on west European coasts from southern Norway to France (see Coulson 1963). (Map 107)

Black Tern *Chlidonias niger*

Extinct before middle of 19th century through drainage of breeding haunts and extensive taking of eggs (A & L). Two pairs bred on the Ouse Washes (Cambridge/Norfolk) in 1966.

Black Terns ceased to breed regularly in Britain before 1850, although a few pairs bred in Norfolk after floods in 1853 and 1858 and in the Romney Marsh area of Kent till about 1885. The supposed nesting at Pett Level, Sussex, in 1941 and 1942 now having been discounted (des Forges and Harber 1963), the breeding of two pairs on the Ouse Washes in 1966 is therefore the first known breeding record for over 80 years. Breeding in 1966 occurred after a late spring flood; providing water conditions can be artificially maintained to provide suitable nesting habitat on the various nature reserves in this area, there seems no reason why the species should not eventually become established. (Map 108)

Gull-billed Tern *Gelochelidon nilotica*

The only British breeding record is from Abberton Reservoir, Essex, where a pair bred in 1950, and probably also in 1949. (Map 109)

Common Tern *Sterna hirundo*

Local decreases, particularly through human persecution, in 19th century, and local increases where protected in 20th century (A & L). Very marked fluctuations at many colonies, and present trends of population as a whole are uncertain, though a small decrease may have occurred over the last 20–30 years in England.

Fairly numerous; breeds on all coasts of Britain and Ireland, but only very locally in some regions (especially Wales and south-west England); also breeds inland in many Scottish counties and in a few in Ireland and England. No recent checks have been made at most of the Scottish and Irish colonies, and since numbers fluctuate erractically from colony to colony, it is impossible to ascertain present trends in these two countries.

In England, the sites and sizes of practically all colonies are known, and the present (1964–66) total population can reasonably be estimated at 5,500–6,000 pairs. This is certainly more than were breeding in England at the beginning of the century, before the main colonies began to receive protection, but it is probably somewhat lower than in the 1930's. Since the 1939–45 war, and particularly during the last ten years, there has been an increasing tendency for small numbers to nest inland in eastern England, particularly at gravel pits. Such records have come from twelve or more different counties from Kent to south Yorkshire and as far inland as east Stafford, and although several have referred to isolated pairs, the numbers at some inland sites—such as in Lincoln—are increasing.

The population in Scotland (as well as the number of colonies) is much greater than in England, and the fluctuations seem to be even more erratic. Several major colonies have been abandoned or have markedly decreased during this century and, although others have been established, the total population seems more likely to have decreased than increased, at least over the past 20 years. Some northwards extension of range may have occurred, however. Venables and Venables (1955) suggested that Shetland was possibly not colonised until about 1890; numbers subsequently increased and were probably still increasing in the 1950's, although the species was still less numerous then than the Arctic Tern *S. paradisaea*. In Ireland there has been a very marked reduction in the numbers of Common Terns nesting inland, and several large colonies have disappeared. A number of coastal sites have also been abandoned, though there is little evidence to indicate whether the present trends are towards an increase or a decrease (Ruttledge 1966).

(Map 110)

Arctic Tern *Sterna paradisaea*

No evidence of marked change (A & L). Has decreased markedly in Ireland during this century, but there is no evidence of widespread changes elsewhere despite local fluctuations.

Fairly numerous, breeding somewhat locally around Scotland and Ireland, and more locally still in northern England and Wales (no permanent colonies south of Northumberland and Anglesey); very few breed inland. The standard works on the birds of Ireland make it plain that the numbers of Arctic Terns breeding both on the coasts and inland in that country are now much lower than at the beginning of the century, or even during the 1930's; except for one colony now holding a few pairs in Fermanagh, all inland sites have been abandoned during this century. Confusion in the older records between this species and the Common Tern *S. hirundo*, and the marked short-term fluctuations which have occurred at many colonies, make it difficult to assess whether any major changes have taken place in Scotland or northern England. One of the largest and best known populations is that on the Farne Islands, Northumberland, where no marked changes appear to have occurred and the species still far outnumbers the Common Tern. Numbers may currently be decreasing on Anglesey, though they are probably higher now than ever before in north-west England owing to the growth in the colony at Foulney Island, Lancashire.

Farther south, although the odd pair or two nests sporadically among Common Terns (most often in Norfolk), the only permanent colonies appear to have been those in the Isles of Scilly in the last century. The Arctic Tern was then said to predominate over the Common Tern, but in this century it has been recorded breeding there only infrequently, though between 40 and 60 pairs did so on Annet in 1964. (Map 111)

Roseate Tern *Sterna dougallii*

Always local, but great decrease in first half of 19th century; marked increase in 20th century, when recolonised Ireland (A & L). Further increase during and after 1939–45 war, but uncertain whether this increase continues.

Not scarce, but very local, being confined to about 20 colonies mainly on shores of Irish Sea, and in the Isles of Scilly, Northumberland and the Firth of Forth; also breeds occasionally in western Ireland and western Scotland, though probably not at the present time. Like the other terns, it is erratic in its occupation of breeding sites, and in the absence of complete censuses its present population and trends are more difficult to assess than they should be for so local a species. The most recent year for which colony counts or estimates are most complete is 1962 and, after allowing for colonies not covered in that year (but which were occupied in 1961 or 1963), the total population then may be reckoned as approximately 3,500 pairs. Some estimates were doubtfully based, however, and the total figure is heavily dependent upon the accuracy of an estimate of 2,000 pairs for the main colony in Wexford.

Even so, the present population represents a remarkable increase since the end of the last century, by which time the species had been reduced almost to the point of extinction in Britain. Ireland was recolonised by a few pairs in about 1906 and the numbers of birds and colonies have since increased steadily. The Irish east coast now forms the headquarters of the species in Europe. During and after the 1939–45 war small numbers recolonised several islands in the Clyde area of west Scotland and the Isles of Scilly, while there was a marked increase in the Firth of Forth and on the Farne Islands, Northumberland (see especially Sandeman 1963, Hickling 1963). Some colonies, including the main one in Wexford and several in Down, Anglesey and west Scotland, have decreased in the last few years, though it is uncertain whether the population as a whole is also now declining. (Map 112)

Little Tern *Sterna albifrons*

Decreasing, especially where bungalows occupy former breeding grounds (A & L). Has continued to decrease locally through greater human disturbance and development of the coastline.

Not scarce; rather over 100 known colonies scattered on almost all low-lying coasts of Britain and Ireland (absent south-west England, south Wales, and the mainland of north-west Scotland) north to the Outer Hebrides and east Sutherland. The present (1963–65) breeding population in England and Wales may reasonably be estimated at about 800 pairs, the majority of which are concentrated in south-east England from Dorset to Lincoln. Information from Scotland and Ireland is sparse and incomplete, but it seems unlikely that the total population in these two countries approaches that of England and Wales. Few colonies anywhere have ever exceeded 100 pairs (those at Scolt Head and Blakeney Point in Norfolk are the only ones known to have done so) and the great majority number less than about 30 pairs. The largest at the present time are at Blakeney Point (73 nests in 1964, but 120 as recently as 1961), Foulness in Essex (95 nests in 1965), and one in Wexford (75–100 pairs in 1963).

Following a decline at many colonies in the 19th century, numbers appear to have built up again in the early part of the 20th century, and may have reached a peak in the 1920's or early 1930's. Since then, except for a period of respite during the 1939–45 war when several beaches were closed to the public, they have decreased wherever the holiday industry has become more developed. There are few former breeding counties from which the species has disappeared altogether, though Glamorgan and Cardigan were deserted soon before the 1939–45 war and it has now ceased to breed annually in Yorkshire. In several former strongholds in East Anglia and south-east England, however, it has decreased or disappeared altogether in recent years and, although precise comparisons are impossible over the whole area, its numbers in several counties appear to be down to about a half of those 30–40 years ago.

(Map 113)

Sandwich Tern *Sterna sandvicensis*

Decrease in 19th century, local marked increase in 20th century (A & L). Still local and erratic at many sites, but range now more extensive (colonised Shetland, Hampshire and Kerry in mid-1950's) and total population, though fluctuating, is probably higher than at any other time this century.

Not scarce, but very local, being confined to about 40 rather unstable colonies, situated mainly on the east coast and the shores of the Irish Sea. Although the total numbers have fluctuated, they have certainly generally increased during this century and are probably currently higher than ever before. The regional literature indicates a minimum total population in 1962 of about 5,400 pairs; allowing for colonies not counted in that year, the actual total may be nearer 6,000 breeding pairs.

A number of counties have been colonised since about 1920, while few appear to have been abandoned completely. The bulk of the population is found in the area of the Firth of Forth and Farne Islands and in East Anglia. The main fluctuations in these regions are shown in table 6, which also demonstrates the way in which the main colonies may shift from one region to another. Even within the same region the site of the main colony often changes

Table 6. Estimated numbers of pairs of Sandwich Terns *Sterna sandvicensis* in certain years since 1920 on the east and south coasts of Britain south of Fife
The years selected are those for which the data are most complete and which show most clearly the fluctuations both between the different areas and in the population as a whole. The Farne Islands figure for 1920 is an interpolation (see Sandeman 1953 and Watt 1953 for fuller details of changes in the Forth-Farnes area), and the accuracy of some other figures is uncertain. Norfolk was first colonised in 1920, Suffolk not until 1951, and Hampshire in 1954. At the present time, Sandwich Terns also breed in six Irish counties and in Lancashire, Cumberland, Ayrshire, Shetland, Orkney, Caithness, Nairn, Aberdeen and Angus; several of these counties have been colonised since 1920, but the main population is still found in the area covered by the table.

Year	Firth of Forth area	Farne Islands	East Anglia	Hampshire	Total south and east coast north to Fife
1920	few	1,000	1		1,000
1923	400	0	640		1,000
1932	50	2,000	820		2,900
1939	500	2,000	1,000		3,500
1946	1,500	120	1,900		3,500
1954	400	960	380	10	1,800
1957	400	800	1,520	80	2,800
1959	700	1,250	1,220	0?	3,200
1962	1,120	1,480	1,460	57	4,100
1964	500	1,500	2,010	5	4,000

from year to year. In East Anglia, for example, the most numerous colony was at a completely different place in each of the five years from 1955 to 1959.

The decrease that occurred in the 19th century was probably due mainly to human predation, and the increase this century probably represents a recovery to a former population level. This recovery has been greatly assisted by the protection of many of the breeding sites. There is some evidence to suggest that the British population decreased temporarily in the 1950's. In the Netherlands, where between 30,000 and 40,000 pairs bred up till 1955, there has been a very sharp decline over the past ten years, and only 600 pairs nested in that country in 1965; poisoning by an organochlorine insecticide following leakage from a factory was suspected as the main cause (Anon 1966).

(Map 114)

Razorbill *Alca torda*

No evidence of marked widespread change; ceased to breed Sussex about 1878 (A & L). Marked decrease in south-west England and south Wales, but apparently not elsewhere.

Numerous; colonies are widely distributed round coasts of Britain and Ireland, but there is none between southern Yorkshire and the eastern Isle of Wight, and only very locally in north-west and north-east England and on the Irish east coast. The extent of the species' range has remained almost unchanged during this century although it ceased to breed on Culver Cliff in the eastern Isle of Wight in about 1920. At its southernmost colonies in England and Wales there has been a marked decrease over the past 20–30 years. Recent counts at two colonies—Freshwater Cliffs, Isle of Wight, which held about 1,000 birds in 1937, and Lundy, Devon, where there were about 10,500 pairs in 1939—showed that by 1962 the numbers breeding at each had been reduced by about 90%. At another colony—Skokholm, Pembroke—there were 800 pairs in 1928 and 670 in 1947, but only 343 in 1965. Marked decreases have also been recorded at Portland Bill in Dorset, the few mainland colonies in Devon, the Isles of Scilly, and other islands and the mainland of Pembroke. Although the decline has been marked and widespread throughout this southern area, there is little evidence of reduced numbers elsewhere in Britain and Ireland. Indeed, on several islands in the Inner Hebrides the species has increased (Boyd 1958, Evans and Flower 1967).

The decrease at the southern colonies appears to have become noticeable first during the 1939–45 war and to have continued ever since. Lockley *et al.* (1949), Saunders (1962) and others have attributed the losses to oil pollution. But it seems possible that other factors (perhaps a change in the abundance of food) may also be responsible. (Map 115)

Great Auk *Pinguinus impennis*

Formerly bred on St Kilda; species extinct by early 19th century due to human destruction (A & L).

Guillemot *Uria aalge*

No evidence of marked widespread change; ceased to nest Sussex about 1878 and Kent about 1910 owing to cliff falls (A & L). Marked decrease in southernmost colonies in England and Wales during this century, and especially in the last 20–30 years, when local decreases have also been recorded elsewhere.

Numerous; breeding distribution much as for Razorbill *Alca torda*, but usually in far larger numbers where the two occur together. There is some evidence to suggest that the Guillemot has declined rather more widely and over a longer period than has the Razorbill, though like that species the greatest decreases appear to have occurred at the southernmost colonies, particularly those on the English south coast. In the Isle of Wight it ceased to breed at Culver Cliff, at the eastern end of the island, in about 1920. In Dorset, the

Isles of Scilly and perhaps elsewhere, a decline had already become noticeable during the first two decades of this century, though it appears to have accelerated after the 1930's. Numerical estimates from four areas give some indication of this decline. The figures are mostly very approximate, and all southern colonies did not necessarily decrease to the same extent. Except for the Isle of Wight (Freshwater Cliffs) the figures relate to the numbers of pairs, not birds:

Isle of Wight	1937:	3,000	1946:	1,200	1962:	80
Purbeck, Dorset	1932:	3,000	1948:	500	1962:	(<250)
Lundy, Devon	1939:	19,000	1951:	5,000	1962:	<3,000
Skokholm, Pembroke	1937:	220	1947:	110	1963:	60

Particularly in the period during and since the 1939–45 war, diminished numbers have been recorded at several colonies from Pembroke north to the Hebrides in the west, and in the Flamborough Head region of Yorkshire in the east. At some the decreases are thought to have been only temporary, due possibly to excessive oil pollution at sea during the war, but at others, such as on certain of the Inner Hebrides, the decreases may be part of a longer trend and appear still to be continuing. Numbers are also believed to have declined in Ireland over the past 20 years (Ruttledge 1966), but there is little evidence on this point. On the other hand, at many Scottish colonies the numbers are known, or thought, not to have changed significantly. Among the many huge colonies in Shetland, Venables and Venables (1955) knew of only one obviously decreasing colony, and that was at Noss where Gannets *Sula bassana* were spreading and occupying the Guillemots' nesting ledges. On the Isle of May, Fife, several estimates of breeding numbers between 1921 and 1955 showed that little general change had occurred (Eggeling 1955).

Many thousands of Guillemots are killed by oil pollution every year, and it seems probable that this has been the main cause of the decline in the south. Yet this may have begun in the last century, for apart from the desertion of the chalk-cliff sites in Kent and Sussex the species also decreased and then disappeared from similar sites on the French side of the English Channel. More recently it has decreased in Brittany. At least locally, the decreases in Britain have been attributed partly to increased predation by the larger gulls *Larus spp.* Though there is little evidence on this point, it also seems possible that changes in fish abundance and distribution have occurred, perhaps in association with the warming of the sea during the present century.

(Map 116)

Black Guillemot *Cepphus grylle*

Widespread decrease and extinct in former parts of range on coasts of Yorkshire, east Scotland and north Wales; cause unknown (A & L). No evidence of marked change within main breeding range, but is increasing in the Irish Sea area where several new colonies have been established.

Not scarce; breeds on almost all coasts of Ireland and Scotland (but not on the east coast south of Caithness), also in the Isle of Man and (a few pairs only) in Anglesey and at St Bees Head, Cumberland. A pair bred in Yorkshire in 1938, once 'recently' in Kincardine (Baxter and Rintoul 1953), and one to three pairs have done so in Anglesey since about 1962, but otherwise the few former, small and very isolated colonies mentioned by Alexander and Lack have remained untenanted since about the middle of the 19th century, or in some cases earlier. Apart from the colonisation of Anglesey, Black Guillemots have also increased elsewhere in the Irish Sea area this century, most markedly on the east coast of Ireland where several new breeding colonies have been established, often in holes on piers and in old harbour walls, but also in natural sites. The increase and spread in this region appears to be continuing. On the Caernarvon coast birds have been present in recent summers at three places, but breeding has not been proved, while at St Bees Head up to three pairs have bred since 1940 or earlier. On the Isle of Man, however, numbers may have decreased slightly during this century (Slinn 1965). Within the main breeding range—in west and north Scotland and Ireland—there is little evidence that any changes have occurred, other than purely local fluctuations. (Map 117)

Puffin *Fratercula arctica*

Great decrease in some colonies in southern part of range; ceased nesting on cliffs of Kent early in 19th century (A & L). Continued marked decrease at many colonies, especially in south and west, but little change (and locally even some increase) at some in north and north-east.

Numerous; breeding colonies distributed mainly on western islands and coasts from Scilly north to Shetland, and only locally on east and south coasts (none between Yorkshire and Isle of Wight). A number of once large colonies, ranging from the Isle of Wight and the Isles of Scilly north to Lundy, Pembroke, north Wales, Ayr (Ailsa Craig) and the Outer Hebrides (Haskeir Rocks, North Uist), have been abandoned or reduced to negligible proportions during this century. Including those colonies that were similarly reduced in the 19th century, it is clear that the numbers of Puffins breeding in western Britain (and probably also Ireland, where a general decrease is recorded after 1925) must have decreased enormously over the last 100 years.

The decline appears to have been most marked and widespread in the southern part of this area, where the greatest reductions probably occurred between about 1920 and 1950. Among the several colonies which are now extinct (or virtually so) or which contain only tens or hundreds of birds, instead of thousands or tens of thousands (if not actually the 'hundreds of thousands' that were claimed for some) at the turn of the century, may be mentioned: Annet, Isles of Scilly (100,000 birds 1908; under 100 pairs now), Lundy ('incredible numbers' 1890; 3,500 pairs 1939; 93 pairs 1962), St Tudwal's Islands, Caernarvon ('hundreds of thousands' 1902–07; 'thousands' 1935; none 1951 nor since), Ailsa Craig ('huge numbers' 1871; now probably extinct), and Haskeir Rocks ('innumerable' 1881; under 50 pairs 1953). The accidental introduction of Brown Rats *Rattus norvegicus* was almost certainly the cause of the decline or extinction at some of these island colonies, while at others oil pollution and perhaps increased predation by Great Black-backed Gulls *Larus marinus* may also be to blame (Lockley 1953, Thearle *et al.* 1953). A further possible reason for the decline of these more southerly populations is that there has been a reduction in the abundance of food, perhaps owing to climatic amelioration (see Lockley 1953).

Recent evidence suggests that many colonies, including those on the Pembroke coast and islands, in the Isle of Man, the Inner Hebrides and parts of Ireland, are still decreasing, although a few, such as those in the Isles of Scilly and on Great Saltee, Wexford, may now be maintaining their numbers—but at a very low level. In contrast with the decreasing trend in this area, there is little evidence of any marked changes in the extreme north and north-east of the British range during this century. Indeed, on Fair Isle and at several other colonies in Shetland the species has probably increased, and may still be doing so (Venables and Venables 1955, Davis 1965). It is certainly currently increasing on islands in the Firth of Forth, perhaps also on the Farne Islands, Northumberland, while there is little evidence of any changes in the Flamborough Head region, Yorkshire. Shortage of space prohibits discussion of the histories of several other colonies. But no account of the Puffin in Britain would be complete without mentioning the largest colony of all—that on St Kilda, where the species is so numerous that no satisfactory estimate of its numbers (or fluctuations) has yet been made. The effects—if any—of the former intensive human persecution and the recent heavy gull predation are unknown (Lockley 1953, Williamson and Boyd 1960). (Map 118)

Order:
COLUMBIFORMES
Sandgrouse & Doves

Pallas's Sandgrouse *Syrrhaptes paradoxus*
Bred Yorkshire 1888 and Moray 1888 and 1889, following an irruption in the former of these two years. The species has been almost unknown (even as a vagrant) in Britain and Ireland since 1908.

Stock Dove *Columba oenas*
Confined to south and east England in early 19th century, but then increased and spread rapidly, colonising south-west and north England, Wales, south and east Scotland, north-east Ireland and Isle of Man by the end of the century; has continued to increase and spread to north Scotland and south and west Ireland, though not yet established on west coast of Scotland north of Argyll, nor in Kerry (A & L). General expansion of range in Ireland, occupying western parts of Kerry, Mayo and Donegal since 1951, but some contraction of range in northern Scotland; sudden marked decrease, affecting populations in many counties of England and east Scotland from about 1957 to 1963, has perhaps now halted.

Fairly numerous; breeds widely in probably all counties of Britain and Ireland north to southern Argyll in western Scotland and east Ross in the east. Between about 1940 and the mid-1950's no marked changes in abundance appear to have occurred over the country as a whole. In Ireland the earlier slow expansion of range continued, but it was not until after 1951 that the species extended its breeding range to include the far western parts of Kerry, Mayo and Donegal (Kennedy 1961). In Scotland, Baxter and Rintoul (1953) recorded a decrease over the previous few years, while Pennie (1962) noted the species as far less common in Sutherland than at the end of the 19th century, though it was still breeding in the extreme south-east of the county. (By about 1964 it had ceased to breed even there; and it appears never to have become established in north-west Scotland.) Except for decreases in some western counties of central England—notably in Cheshire where it had become virtually extinct as a breeding bird by 1955 (Bell 1962)—its numbers in most parts of England were probably as high or even higher at this time than ever before this century.

By about 1957, however, the first signs of a sudden, sharp decrease were noticed, in that year in about four or five counties north to Lincoln and Lancashire, and by 1961 in most other counties in the southern half of England, as well as in those lying on each side of the Firth of Forth in Scotland. The decline was most severe in the eastern and south-eastern counties of England, but it was also marked in Lancashire and in several central counties south and west as far as Somerset. In some areas the species disappeared altogether, for example from the central London parks, where it had increased and spread between about 1950 and 1957 (Cramp and Tomlins 1966). In Essex, too, it disappeared from much of the county although it managed to maintain its numbers in the north-west. In 1963 the only proved nesting in Essex was at Writtle, near Chelmsford, where of 32 known former breeding sites only two were occupied and at both of these the eggs were infertile (*Essex Bird Report*). So far as is known, Stock Doves farther west in Britain were unaffected by the decline, while locally even within eastern England some populations appear not to have decreased. It is uncertain whether a decrease continues, though there is some recent (1965–66) evidence to suggest that the decline has come to a halt and even that some recovery has begun.

The earlier increase and spread of the Stock Dove in Britain was undoubtedly due to the growth of arable farming in the 19th and early 20th centuries (Murton 1965), while the recent decrease was probably the result of poisoning from agricultural pesticides, particularly organochlorine seed-dressings (Cramp and Tomlins 1966). (Map 119)

Rock Dove *Columba livia*

Marked decrease generally, especially in southern parts of range where now extinct in many places (A & L). Marked recent decrease in Ireland, but little evidence from the present strongholds in the Scottish islands.

Fairly numerous; populations of apparently pure or predominantly pure wild Rock Doves are confined to the northern and western coasts and islands of Scotland and Ireland, although even there feral strains predominate in some areas (e.g. Galway). Coast-dwelling populations in south-west and north-east England, Wales, the Isle of Man, south-west and east Scotland, and south-east and north-east Ireland are now extinct or are wholly or very largely composed of feral pigeons. The long-term decline of this species appears to have continued except perhaps in its strongholds in north and north-west Scotland. Yet even there fluctuations have occurred. On Fair Isle, for example, it was common in the 19th century, had become extinct by about 1895, but has become re-established in small numbers since 1948 or earlier (Davis 1965), while on Eynhallow, Orkney, a remarkable increase took place between 1934 and about 1952 (Duffey 1955). In Ireland, as well as a probable long-term decrease in the north (Deane 1954), there has been a very recent and sharp decline, especially in the south-east, perhaps (though not certainly) attributable to toxic seed-dressings (Ruttledge 1966). Increased competition for food, particularly with the Stock Dove *C. oenas*, has been suggested by Murton *et al.* (1964) as the probable explanation of the Rock Dove's general decline. (Map 120)

Woodpigeon *Columba palumbus*

Very great increase during the 19th century, especially in Scotland due to increase of woodland and increased growth of green crops providing food in winter (A & L). Continued gradual expansion through increased cultivation.

Abundant; widespread, breeding in every county, though only locally in north-west Scotland and very locally in Outer Hebrides and Shetland. Murton (1965) discussed the general increase and spread of the Woodpigeon in Britain over the last 100 years and linked the changes with the development of agriculture, particularly through the increased availability of such food as clover during the winter. He calculated the July population to be not less than five million birds, rising to ten million by September after breeding. High density populations are found in the areas of most intensive arable farming and have probably remained relatively stable for many years. Locally, however, where marginal land has been brought under cultivation, numbers have increased. Certain urban and suburban populations, for example in the London area (Simms 1962, Cramp and Tomlins 1966), have recently increased markedly.

The main expansion of range, particularly in Scotland, occurred during the 19th century, by the end of which the species was breeding in most parts of Britain and Ireland. Since 1939 a few pairs have colonised Shetland, while even more recently some Hebridean islands have been occupied as well as several treeless areas in the extreme west and south-west of Ireland. Since the middle of the 19th century the species has extended its breeding range northwards in Europe, perhaps in association with climatic amelioration (Kalela 1949). (Map 121)

Turtle Dove *Streptopelia turtur*

Increased and extended its range to Wales, Cheshire and Yorkshire before 1865; has continued to increase and has nested occasionally in the northern counties of England and once or twice in eastern Ireland, but has not greatly extended its range in the last 50 years (A & L). Has since extended its range north into south-east Scotland; little change elsewhere except for probable contraction of range in Wales and possible small decrease in western England.

Fairly numerous; breeds most widely in southern and central England, and locally west to Devon, Carmarthen, the Welsh border counties and south Lancashire as well as, in the east, northwards to East Lothian. Murton *et al.* (1964) have shown that the distribution of the species corresponds closely with that of its most important food plant, *Fumaria officinalis*. It nests only occasionally elsewhere, including eastern Ireland. Since about 1940 a slight expansion of range has occurred in the north-east, where the species was formerly represented only by a small and apparently isolated population in north-east Northumberland. Turtle Doves have now been proved to breed for the first time in Scotland (Berwick since 1946, Roxburgh in 1951, East Lothian since 1958), though the numbers involved are very small. A few pairs have also colonised Durham. There appears to have been little further expansion of range on the western side of the country, and south Lancashire (colonised in 1904, steady increase till about 1930) remains as the northern limit of the regular breeding range. In some years since about 1955, however, small numbers have summered in south-west Scotland (Kirkcudbright, Wigtown) and may possibly have bred. A few pairs still breed occasionally in eastern Ireland (Dublin since 1939, Wicklow in 1962).

Some decrease and contraction of range appears to have occurred in Wales, no certain nesting being known in the last ten years in Cardigan, Merioneth or Caernarvon (though it was breeding in all three and increasing generally in north Wales in the 1930's) or in Radnor (where it was described as 'not uncommon' in the early part of this century). Like those of many summer visitors, the numbers fluctuate from year to year, making it difficult to evaluate the subjective records of increase or decrease mentioned in the county bird reports. Recently rather more of these records have tended to lean towards a decrease rather than an increase and, at least locally, there may have been a small decline, particularly in those English counties bordering on Wales. In several counties, however, there have been no noticeable changes and, whether or not the species has decreased slightly in recent years, it is clearly still more widespread than it was at the beginning of the century.

The reasons for the earlier expansion of range and for any recent local decreases are not known; the loss of tall hedgerows is suggested as a possible cause of locally reduced numbers in Worcester and Suffolk (Harthan 1961, Payn 1962). (Map 122)

Collared Dove *Streptopelia decaocto*

Spectacular increase and spread since first colonised Norfolk in 1955; now widespread throughout most of Britain and Ireland.

Not scarce; Hudson (1965) has described and mapped in admirable detail the remarkable spread of this species in Britain and Ireland since it first arrived and bred in Norfolk in 1955. Supported by immigration, the total population had increased by 1964 to about 19,000 or more birds (representing about 3,000 breeding pairs) and the species was then known to be breeding in almost all counties in England, more than half of those in Scotland and Wales, and slightly under half those in Ireland. In 1965 and 1966, although the local literature is still incomplete at the time of writing, it is clear that the rapid expansion has continued. Areas colonised include Shetland in the far north, the Isles of Scilly in the far south, and several more counties in Ireland, where it now breeds in almost all those with a coastline (though probably not in Clare and Limerick) and quite possibly in most inland ones, where it is doubtless overlooked (R. F. Ruttledge *in litt.*).

The expansion here followed an equally explosive one on the Continent, where the species spread from the Balkans north-west to the North Sea in the space of 20 years between about 1930 and 1950 (Fisher 1953, Stresemann and Nowak 1958). (Map 123)

Order: CUCULIFORMES *Cuckoo*

Cuckoo *Cuculus canorus*

No evidence of marked change (A & L). Widespread reports of decrease, especially since the early 1950's; the severity and significance of the decline are hard to assess.

Not scarce; widespread, breeding in every county, but only irregularly in Shetland. The regional literature contains numerous, widespread and virtually unanimous reports of decreased numbers since the early 1950's; yet, because of an almost complete lack of numerical data, the actual extent of the decrease is difficult to assess. Omitting the several records relating to purely local or annual fluctuations, there are 34 reports of a change in status in various parts of England over the whole or much of the period 1953 to 1964. Of these, 24 (13 relating to whole counties) refer to a decrease or marked decrease and the other ten to a slight or probable decrease. In a few areas the numbers are believed to have remained largely unchanged, but nowhere do they seem to have increased. Reports of decreases are widely scattered, with a concentration in eastern counties from Essex north to Northumberland. In some hilly counties, for example in Shropshire (Rutter *et al.* 1964), there is a suggestion that the Cuckoo may have decreased mainly on low ground while maintaining its numbers in upland areas.

There is some evidence that in eastern England the decrease began in about 1953, although in other parts of the country it did not become noticeable until the late 1950's. In Cornwall and south Wales the recent decline may be part of a longer trend, for in both areas a definite decrease had already begun by the 1940's or even earlier (Ryves and Quick 1946, Ingram and Salmon 1957, Lockley 1961). In Ireland the species is believed to have decreased generally during this century (Deane 1954, Kennedy 1961) as well as more markedly in recent years (Ruttledge 1966). In Scotland, however, apart from a 'very big recent decline' in south Kirkcudbright (J. D. Brown *in litt.*), there is little evidence that its status has appreciably changed. Indeed, in Shetland breeding records have probably become more frequent since about 1947, though it is doubtful whether the species has become firmly established there.

(Map 124)

Order: STRIGIFORMES *Owls*

Barn Owl *Tyto alba*
Marked and widespread decrease due to human persecution; in 20th century perhaps holding its own in most districts and increasing in parts of southern Scotland, but has not recovered to the same extent as other owls (A & L). Probable slow decrease till late 1940's, then decreased generally, particularly after 1955.

Not scarce, breeding widely in Britain and Ireland north to southern Scotland, and much more scarcely and locally in the Highlands north to Sutherland. As well as increasing in Scotland after about 1910, the species also became more numerous in northern England; over the rest of England and Wales, however, with certain local exceptions, it probably decreased during the 30–40 years up to 1932 (Blaker 1934). A slowly decreasing trend probably continued through to the late 1940's, although reports of status changes in this period tend to conflict with one another. Some genuine regional variation probably occurred: for example, there was a 'steady . . . very marked' increase in Lancashire (Oakes 1953), but a continued 'slow decline' in Yorkshire (Chislett 1952) after about the late 1930's. Other fluctuations may have been caused by hard winters or by variations in the density of small rodents (see Honer 1963; also fig. 3 on page 63).

Beginning with widespread reports of a decline after the hard winter of 1947, nearly all records of changed status over the past 20 years refer to diminished numbers. Reports of decreases became particularly prevalent after the middle or late 1950's, since when the species has disappeared completely from several places where it was previously not uncommon. A national survey in 1963 (Prestt 1965) indicated that the recent decline was most widespread and sudden in eastern England, although many other parts of Britain had also been affected. A partial reason for the low numbers in that year, particularly in western England, was the high mortality caused by the severe winter (see Dobinson and Richards 1964), but clearly this was not the only factor involved. Contributors to Prestt's survey attributed the decline to loss of habitat (changes in agriculture, leading to a decrease in food; also a lack of breeding sites), disturbance (including game preservation) and poisoning by agricultural chemicals. Of these, the first seems most likely to have accounted for the long-term decline, and the last may possibly be responsible for the apparent sudden decrease in the late 1950's, though there is little evidence of this one way or the other. In Ireland a decrease was first noticeable about 1950 (particularly in Ulster) and became especially marked after about 1960 (Deane 1954, Ruttledge 1966).

Few estimates are available to show the extent of the fall in the British population. The impression from some recent but incomplete surveys in certain counties, for example Essex, is that the number of pairs now breeding is considerably under half those found in 1932 (see Blaker 1934). (Map 125)

Snowy Owl *Nyctea scandiaca*

The nesting of a pair in Shetland in the summer of 1967 was the culmination of a remarkable recent increase in the British records of this arctic owl, Previously known only as a rare winter vagrant, one to three have appeared in Shetland in every summer since 1963 and have remained throughout the year since 1965. Others have also been recorded at various seasons, including summer, in the central and north-east Highlands since 1965. It should be noted, however, that 'surprisingly large' numbers have been imported for sale in the last few years and that some of the recent records, particularly but not necessarily only those in southern England, may therefore refer to individuals that have escaped from captivity (see Harber 1966). (Map 126)

Little Owl *Athene noctua*

Artificially introduced (A & L). Numbers were released, notably in Kent and Northampton, in the late 19th century; they increased rapidly and spread to almost all parts of England and Wales north to central Yorkshire and central Lancashire by about 1925, reached north-west Wales, Durham and Northumberland by the 1930's, Westmorland by about 1944, and other Lakeland counties and Berwick in the 1950's; a decrease began in some southern (especially western) counties around 1940, was more marked after 1947, and affected practically all counties (except perhaps some in the extreme north) between about 1955 and 1961, when numbers fell sharply in many areas; some evidence for a slight recovery by 1965.

Not scarce; widely distributed, breeding in every county of England and Wales (not certainly in Radnor), though only thinly in northern England; also breeds Berwick (since 1958), perhaps Dumfries and East Lothian, but not elsewhere in Scotland. The rapid colonisation of England and Wales by this introduced species is summarised above. After the initial explosive increase, the rate of spread slowed down considerably after about 1930, by which time peak populations had been reached in several areas. By the early 1940's, perhaps associated with a series of cold winters, decreased numbers were noted in some counties south of mid Wales, central England and East Anglia; particularly in some western areas the species has never again attained the high population level of the 1930's. Following the hard winter of 1947 there were reports of further decreases, particularly in counties along the Welsh border, but also as far north as Westmorland. In Radnor, although individuals have been recorded, there has been no certain breeding since 1946, but there appear to be no other counties from which the species has disappeared altogether.

Then, in the period between about 1955 and 1962, many counties, including several in south-east England where the Little Owl population was probably still at an optimum, reported marked and quite sudden decreases. In one area of Essex where 28 pairs nested successfully in 1950, only seven did so in 1961, five in 1962 and two in 1963 (M. Meadows in *Essex Bird Report*). Few comparative figures are available from elsewhere, but the decrease at this time appears to have been fairly general, and perhaps similarly severe, over practically the whole of England and Wales, the winter of 1963 evidently causing a further reduction. There is some evidence (for 1965) of a gradual recovery in numbers in parts of central and south-east England.

The decline beginning in the early 1940's appears to have been partly connected with a succession of severe winters, though it seems possible that it would have occurred in any case since in many areas the initial expansion was already petering out. The more recent severe decline has an unknown cause. Like that of the Barn Owl *Tyto alba*, the Sparrowhawk *Accipiter nisus* and several other birds of prey, it appears to date from about 1955 or 1956 and has been attributed to the effects of certain persistent organochlorine insecticides introduced in agriculture at about that time. (Map 127)

Tawny Owl *Strix aluco*

Decline in 19th century due to human persecution; increase in 20th century, particularly noted in southern Scotland (A & L). General increase this century, continuing in some areas until 1950 or later; no evidence of marked changes in recent years.

Fairly numerous; widely distributed throughout mainland Britain, but entirely absent from Ireland, the Isle of Man, the Northern Isles and many of the Hebrides; it has occasionally been seen or heard on the Isle of Wight but has never been known to nest. A general increase over much of England, Wales and southern Scotland took place between about 1900 and 1930. It continued until 1950 or later in some counties in south Wales (Ingram and Salmon 1954, 1957), in Lancashire (Oakes 1953) and Suffolk (Payn 1962), and probably in several other counties from Hampshire north to Cumberland and Northumberland, as well as into Scotland. In most parts of Britain numbers appear to have remained largely unchanged in recent years. They may decrease somewhat (and certainly fewer breed) in years of low density of small rodents, and recorded declines in parts of southern England and Wales in 1955, 1958 and 1962 were probably due to this cause. Other recent but small decreases were reported to Prestt (1965) or are contained in the local literature. These involve places scattered fairly widely over Britain north to west Ross; nearly all concern very localised areas and only slight and probably temporarily reduced numbers, and their significance is believed to be unimportant.

On the Continent, for example in Finland which was colonised in the late 19th century and where a considerable expansion occurred in the 1920's and 1930's, the Tawny Owl has tended to increase its range northwards during this century (Kalela 1949, Merikallio 1958). (Map 128)

Long-eared Owl *Asio otus*

Has decreased in parts of England probably through human persecution, and increased in many parts of Scotland with spread of plantations (A & L). Very marked decline throughout practically the whole of England, Wales and probably southern Scotland, though not certainly in northern Scotland and doubtfully in Ireland.

Not scarce; distributed thinly but widely over much of Ireland, Scotland (not Outer Hebrides, only irregularly in Shetland) and northern England, but only very locally farther south in England and Wales. Although obviously much overlooked, this species has clearly suffered a marked decline during the present century over practically the whole of Britain north to south-west Scotland. The decrease appears to have begun around the turn of the century —particularly in Wales and the southern half of England—and to have continued steadily ever since. In many counties the species had already become scarce by the 1930's, and in several of these where it was formerly regarded as not uncommon it has since disappeared altogether or been reduced to the odd pair or two. Practically no county in this area appears to have escaped the decline.

Areas farther north appear to have been affected rather later, though by the 1950's a marked decrease had been recorded in virtually all counties in northern England. In Yorkshire, for example, the population appears to have been more or less maintained up until about 1937, but then decreased rapidly (Chislett 1952). Tyer (1954) noted that the species had become rare and almost completely displaced by the Tawny Owl *Strix aluco* in part of north Northumberland, and Stokoe (1962) reported a similar state of affairs in the Lakeland counties where a search in 1958 of former haunts on peat mosses revealed only Tawny Owls.

Baxter and Rintoul (1953) mentioned several instances of diminished numbers in various parts of Scotland, including Wigtown where the decrease was attributed to competition with Tawny Owls. Since the 1930's Long-eared Owls have become much scarcer in Ayrshire and Kirkcudbright, and they are also currently believed to be decreasing in east Inverness. It is uncertain, however, whether the species has declined generally in Scotland, for its status in many of the now mature new conifer plantations is not known. At least locally, such as on Bute and some of the Inner Hebrides, it is believed to have increased. Some increase with the spread of conifer plantations has also been recorded in Ireland, where there is little evidence of any general decline.

Jespersen (1946) noted an apparent decrease in parts of Denmark, although locally it had spread with the growth of new conifer forests; Haftorn (1958) recorded a general increase and spread in Norway. The cause of the decline in Britain is not known, though it seems possible that interspecific competition with Tawny Owls (which have undoubtedly increased) may have contributed. In this connection, it is of interest that no great changes appear to have occurred in Ireland, where there are no Tawny Owls. One of the few places in southern England where the Long-eared Owl is still locally common is the Lydd area of south Kent; it may not be coincidence that, until the first pair arrived in 1965, Tawny Owls were unknown there too. (Map 129)

Short-eared Owl *Asio flammeus*

No evidence of widespread change; marked fluctuations, correlated with numbers of voles (A & L). Somewhat increased in parts of central and north Wales, Yorkshire and Scotland (mainly in newly afforested areas) and a few pairs have recently colonised certain coastal areas in south-east England; perhaps a slight general increase, but evidence uncertain.

Not scarce; breeds regularly in three or four counties of central and north Wales, and in most from mid Lancashire and mid Yorkshire north to Orkney (not Outer Hebrides); also, very locally, in East Anglia and south-east England, and occasionally or sporadically elsewhere, including at least once (in 1959) in Ireland. The erratic breeding and marked short-term fluctuations of this species make it difficult to assess long-term changes, but the evidence suggests that no decline and perhaps some increase has occurred.

Although Short-eared Owls have bred occasionally in the past in East Anglia and southern England, the regular nesting of a few pairs since the early or mid-1950's in coastal areas of north Kent, Essex and Suffolk is a new feature. A few pairs have also bred regularly in Breckland since about 1947, and fairly regularly in Norfolk over a rather longer period. In Wales the species has undoubtedly increased in the centre and north of the country as the result of recent afforestation (Condry 1960), while in Yorkshire, where it formerly bred only occasionally, it has also become a regular breeder since the 1940's (Chislett 1952, Local Reports).

In Scotland, apart from marked population fluctuations associated with the abundance of Short-tailed Voles *Microtus agrestris* (e.g. Lockie 1955), no widespread changes are recorded. Locally, it has benefited from the planting of new conifer forests, which it occupies in the early stages of growth, for example in Ayrshire where it did not become established until the 1940's (Richards 1965) and in Sutherland where it is believed to be currently increasing (Pennie 1962). An earlier increase in Orkney was believed to be due to protection (Lack 1942–43).

The species colonised Iceland in the 1920's and thereafter increased rapidly (Gudmundsson 1951), but few marked changes appear to have occurred on the continent of western Europe. (Map 130)

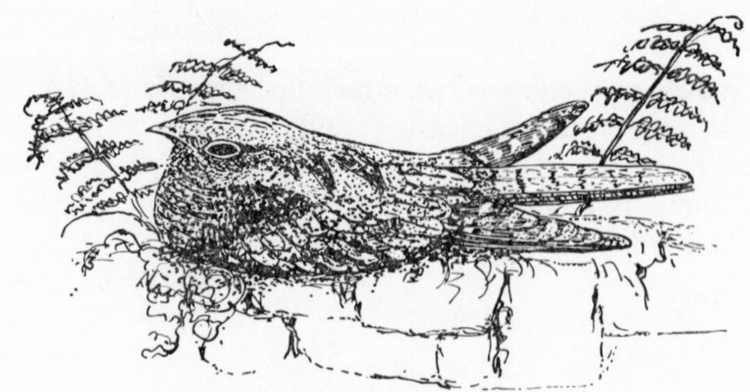

Orders: CAPRIMULGIFORMES, APODIFORMES
Nightjar & Swift

Nightjar *Caprimulgus europaeus*

No evidence of marked change (A & L). Probably decreasing since late 19th century, certainly since about 1930, and markedly in nearly all areas over the last 20 years.

Not scarce; distributed widely but locally throughout most of Britain and Ireland north to south-west Scotland, but only very sparsely over the rest of Scotland north to Sutherland. The species has declined widely in recent years (see also Stafford 1962) and there is much evidence to suggest that it has been decreasing more or less continuously since about 1930, perhaps considerably earlier. Although the decline appears to have been extensive and the species has disappeared from many previous haunts, the extent to which it has colonised new habitats—particularly young conifer plantations—is not known in many parts of the country. A general summary by various regions is given below.

South-west and south England. Stafford (1962) noted the species as common and its recent status as unchanged in each of the seven counties in this region. Since the late 1950's, however, it appears to have decreased in Devon and north Somerset and in several parts of Sussex—where locally a decline had begun by 1930 (H. A. R. Cawkell *in litt.*).

East Midlands and south-east England. A gradual decrease dating from about 1930 (or earlier in several areas) has been noticed in practically every county in this region. It has been particularly marked in the neighbourhood of London and in Suffolk and Essex, while in Oxford and Cambridge the species has probably now ceased to breed. Breeding still takes place regularly in Northampton (*cf.* Stafford 1962). In Essex 18–19 pairs were known in 1952 and 1953, but only about five pairs by 1958 and even fewer more recently. Although the present trend over the region as a whole is probably still a decreasing one, the numbers are apparently now being maintained in some parts where the habitat is remaining undisturbed, for example in parts of east Suffolk.

West Midlands and Wales. A decrease has been recorded in practically every county, dating from the beginning of the century in some areas and since about 1930 in several others. Numbers are still believed to be diminishing in three counties in north Wales and are at a very low ebb in several others in the region. The species is not now known to breed in Carmarthen (where 'not uncommon' about 1905), Brecon ('common' in 1890's, 'fairly common' till 1920's) and Radnor (formerly 'fairly common'), nor regularly in Denbigh and Monmouth.

Northern England. The population breeding to the west of the Pennines has decreased considerably during this century. Numbers fluctuate, but the general decline is continuing, several former breeding sites in Cheshire and the Lake District having been abandoned since 1950. On the eastern side of the region there is less evidence for a marked decline, most of the county avifaunas from Lincoln northwards making no mention of any changes in status. Yet, comparing some mid to late 19th century accounts of the species' status in, for example, Nottingham (Sterland and Whitaker 1879) with those of today it seems evident that it has become less common.

Scotland. Baxter and Rintoul (1953) mentioned few changes except for a steady decrease in the 1930's in Strathspey. In recent years, however, a widespread and general decrease has occurred over practically the whole country from Kirkcudbright and Ayr north to Sutherland. The species has become very scarce in some areas, notably in the west Highlands (Darling and Boyd 1964) and in Ross and Sutherland, where it was locally common in the mid to late 19th century (Pennie 1962). In fact, the decline in Scotland may have been in progress for at least the last 30–40 years, if not longer.

Ireland. Ruttledge (1966) mentioned an earlier westward extension of range, but no recent changes, perhaps because very little information is available on the status of the species. Deane (1954) believed it to be decreasing in Northern Ireland, and there is some evidence to show that it has recently further declined in Down, as well as in Dublin and Wicklow.

Destruction of habitat and increased disturbance are the two causes most commonly given for the decrease or disappearance of this species. While these have certainly contributed, another factor—possibly a climatic one—must also be operating to account for the widespread nature of the decline.

(Map 131)

Swift *Apus apus*

Claimed to be increasing, including in Ireland, but evidence not quite definite enough (A & L). Has perhaps increased in Ireland, but evidence still very meagre.

Numerous, breeding in towns and villages throughout Britain and Ireland north to at least north Argyll in west Scotland and to south-east Sutherland in the east; also at Thurso in north Caithness. In Ireland a 'definite' increase has been noticed since 1932 in western coastal districts, and the species is also believed to have become more numerous in Northern Ireland, Dublin and perhaps over the country as a whole (Kennedy, Ruttledge and Scroope 1954, Deane 1954, Hollohan and O'Connor 1964). Chislett (1952) considered that it had increased in Yorkshire during this century, and the few scattered reports from elsewhere in Britain mostly refer to a possible increase or maintained numbers rather than to a decline. Few significant changes in breeding range seem to have occurred. (Map 132)

Order: CORACIIFORMES
Kingfisher, Bee-eater, Hoopoe

Kingfisher *Alcedo atthis*

Decrease in 19th century due to human destruction; local increases in 20th century; numbers fluctuate owing to heavy mortality in severe winters (A & L). Marked decrease in Scotland, especially since 1947, due possibly to more frequent hard winters or to river pollution; fluctuations but probably no general decline elsewhere.

Not scarce; breeds widely (virtually every county) in England, Wales and Ireland, but in Scotland now occurs only very sparsely (and for the most part irregularly) north to south Argyll and Kincardine (and perhaps south-east Aberdeen). The effects of severe winters on this species outweigh all others and are so marked that most reports of increase or decrease need treating with caution. Mortality during the winter of 1963 was exceptionally severe, not only in Britain but also over the rest of Europe. Although the species' numbers are now gradually recovering, recent assessments of status changes tend to reflect this probably temporary decline rather than any possible long-term changes. Leaving aside the influence of hard winters, there is no evidence to show that the numbers of Kingfishers breeding in most parts of Britain and Ireland have appreciably altered. Indeed, many recent county avifaunas stress this point. Breeding season surveys carried out by the Oxford Ornithological Society showed that numbers in 1961 were similar to those in 1934, when there was an average of one pair to every 1.8 miles on a 68-mile stretch of the River Thames upstream from Maidenhead; after the severe winters of 1940 and 1963, however, numbers fell to approximately one pair to every 30 miles and 20 miles respectively (Local Reports; see also Venables and Wykes 1943). In a few places in central and southern England the species is said to have decreased, notably through river pollution, but there is little definite evidence. Local increases have been recorded too.

In Scotland, however, where it had locally become common in the Lowlands by the 1930's, it has recently decreased very markedly. In several counties the main decline appears to have occurred with the hard winter of 1947 (e.g. Richards 1965), while in those in which the species did not then become extinct it has since gradually decreased almost to vanishing point. With the possible exceptions of Dumfries and Kirkcudbright, there appear to be no Scottish counties in which breeding now takes place annually. River pollution, as well as the effects of severe winters, has been blamed for the decrease in Scotland. (Map 133)

Bee-eater *Merops apiaster*

The only published breeding record involved a group of three pairs that nested, two of them successfully, in Sussex in 1955. A pair also attempted to breed near Edinburgh in 1920. (Map 134)

Hoopoe *Upupa epops*

Sporadic. Although Hoopoes overshoot on spring migration and reach Britain and Ireland in small numbers every year, only a few have ever remained to breed, and then it has usually taken a fine, warm summer to encourage them to do so. Most breeding records come from the south coastal counties of England. The frequency with which proved breeding has been recorded appears not to have changed appreciably over the years, with one record in every decade since the 1830's, but rather more in the 1890's and 1900's (seven between 1895 and about 1904) and four in the 1950's (the latest 1959 and including two in 1955, the year in which the Bee-eaters *Merops apiaster*—another southern species—bred in Sussex). (Map 135)

Order: PICIFORMES
Woodpeckers

Green Woodpecker *Picus viridis*
No evidence of marked widespread change; colonised Isle of Wight in 20th century (A & L). Increase (beginning in about 1920's and becoming marked after 1940's) in northern England; colonised southern Scotland and spread northwards rapidly in 1950's.

Not scarce; widely distributed, breeding in every county in England and Wales, and locally in several counties in southern Scotland, north to Clackmannan and probably Perth. Absent from Ireland and the Isle of Man. Apart from fluctuations caused by severe winters, there is little evidence of markedly changed numbers or distribution over much of England and Wales during this century, apart from the colonisation of the Isle of Wight in 1910. In northern England, however, the species has increased and spread quite considerably in Durham and Northumberland in the east, and in Lancashire, Westmorland and Cumberland in the west. At least in the two eastern counties, the increase (which began about 1913, became noticeable in the 1920's and was most marked in the 1940's) appears to have followed a decline in the mid-19th century. In the west the main increase and spread did not take place until after 1945 (Temperley and Blezard 1951, Stokoe 1962). In 1951 the species bred in Scotland (Selkirk) for the first time. It soon spread to most other Lowland counties from Kirkcudbright north to Midlothian, and then, more gradually, as far as Lanark, Stirling and Clackmannan; it now probably also breeds in Ayr and Perth, and perhaps elsewhere. Mortality during the 1963 hard winter caused marked losses in some counties, but appears not to have checked the spread.

The cause of the increase in northern England and the subsequent colonisation of Scotland is not known. Temperley and Blezard (1951) suggested that the widespread planting of conifers had led to an increase in the Wood Ant

FIG. 6. Breeding range of Green Woodpecker *Picus viridis* before 1950 (black) and the spread since (hatched). The dots show the area of possible breeding.

Formica rufa—a favourite food of the Green Woodpecker in the area—and that this was a possible contributing factor in the bird's increase. Curry-Lindahl (1961) recorded a recent increase and spread in Sweden; Jespersen (1946) mentioned a decline in Denmark in the 19th century, but a partial recent recovery with the spread of plantations in Jutland. (Map 136)

Great Spotted Woodpecker *Dendrocopos major*

Became extinct in Scotland and northern England (north of Cheshire and Yorkshire) in early part of 19th century; during second half of 19th century spread north to central and eastern Scotland and in 20th century colonised Argyll, Inverness, east Ross and east Sutherland; cause of increase unknown (A & L). Further increase and spread in Scotland and northern England until at least mid-1950's; a general increase since about 1890 also affected most parts of England and Wales.

Fairly numerous; widely distributed, breeding in every mainland county of Britain (except possibly Caithness), also in Isle of Wight and Anglesey. Absent from Ireland, Isle of Man, Hebrides and Northern Isles. The marked increase and spread in northern England and Scotland first became noticeable in about 1890 and appears to have continued until at least the mid-1950's, if not actually to the present day. Arran, Mull, west Ross, north Sutherland and (for a time) Caithness have all been colonised since about 1940, and in the same period the species has become more numerous elsewhere in Scotland. Locally in south Scotland (and also in part of Westmorland) numbers may since have fallen from a peak reached in the early 1950's, but there is no evidence to show that the species is declining generally in the region.

As well as the increase in northern districts, there is much evidence to indicate that the period since 1890 has seen a widespread and marked increase in the numbers of Great Spotted Woodpeckers over the rest of England and Wales. Nearly all counties in the southern half of England and in south Wales report a general increase (and none more than very local decreases), especially since the 1920's. The Isle of Wight was colonised after about 1926. The species has become much more tolerant of man and it spread, for example, into London suburban areas and even the central parks in the 1920's. As reported by Upton (1962), it has recently become a regular visitor to garden bird-tables in many parts of the country.

The scale of the increase appears to have been considerable. In several counties in which the species is now widespread and common it was regarded as a rarity in the 19th century. On one estate in Hampshire it increased from two pairs in the 1880's to between eight and eleven pairs during 1940–45 (see Cohen 1963). It is not known whether an increase is continuing, but apart from locally reduced populations (due usually to tree-felling) in, for example, parts of Sussex and Suffolk, the numbers are probably being maintained. Merikallio (1958) recorded an apparent northwards extension of range in Finland 'in recent years', but otherwise few changes in distribution or abundance seem to have been noted on the Continent. (Map 137)

Lesser Spotted Woodpecker *Dendrocopos minor*

No evidence of marked widespread change.

Not scarce; widely distributed throughout England and Wales, but probably absent as regular breeder from Isle of Wight, Pembroke, Anglesey, Durham and Northumberland. Absent from Scotland, Ireland and Isle of Man. Throughout most of its British range this species occurs only at low densities. It is probably much overlooked, but such evidence there is suggests that no marked changes have occurred in either its distribution or abundance. Where status changes are recorded in the regional literature they chiefly appear to be purely local in character and are perhaps often only temporary. Apart from marked decreases in orchard areas of Hereford before about 1938 (Gilbert and Walker 1941) and Somerset during the 1939–45 war (Lewis 1952), in each case due to the removal of old trees planted at the time of the cider boom during the Napoleonic wars, the reports of changed status conform to no regional or chronological pattern. Glutz von Blotzheim (1962) also attributed a decline in Switzerland to the disappearance of old fruit trees. (Map 138)

Wryneck ***Jynx torquilla***

Very marked decrease throughout its British range (A & L). Continued marked decrease and contraction of range, if anything accelerating in 1960's, and species now nearing extinction in Britain.

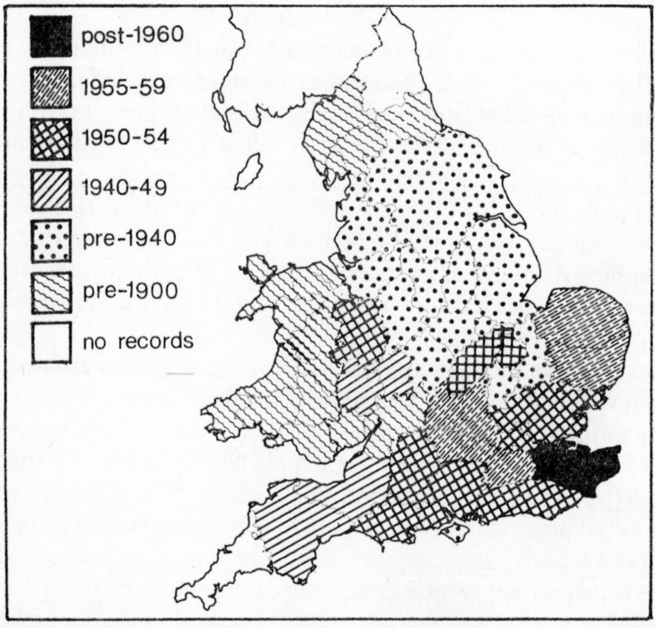

FIG. 7. Decline of the Wryneck *Jynx torquilla*. The various shadings show the years in which the species is last known to have bred in each county. Emphasis has been placed on the recent near-final collapse of the population, which already by 1940 was only a shadow of its former strength (*cf.* Monk 1963).

Very scarce; regular breeding is now confined to a very few pairs in Kent, though a pair or two probably still breed in Surrey and perhaps very occasionally elsewhere in southern England. Monk (1963) documented the history of the steady decline of this species over the last 100 years. In the mid-19th century it was breeding not uncommonly north to Westmorland and west to Hereford and Somerset, and at least occasionally in almost every county in England and Wales (fig. 7). Monk's special enquiry into its status from 1954 to 1958 produced proof of breeding from only ten counties, in only three of which did the actual number of nests found average more than one a year (Kent twelve, Surrey under two, Suffolk about one). Breeding was believed possibly to have occurred in a further eleven counties. In 1958 it was estimated that the total British population was between 100 and 200 pairs, only 15 of which were actually proved to breed (Monk 1963).

Since 1958 there has evidently been a further sharp decline, and outside Kent the only certain nesting records since 1959 were in Suffolk in 1963, Surrey in 1964 and Northampton in 1966. Even within Kent there has been a sharp decline in numbers. In that part of the county covered by the Kent Ornithological Society numbers fell from 16 certain breeding pairs (and a further 69 possible pairs) in 1956 to only two certain breeding pairs (and a further eight to twelve possible pairs) in 1965. Including birds elsewhere, notably in Surrey, it seems doubtful whether the entire British population now numbers more than about 25–30 breeding pairs. Remarkably, two pairs were present, and may possibly have bred, in the Spey Valley, Inverness, in 1965.

To emphasise the recent contraction of range, fig. 7 is based on the year in which breeding was last proved in each county. A series of maps showing the general long-term pattern of decrease may be found in Monk (1963). Although the Wryneck appears to have decreased over most of western Europe, the factors causing the decline are not known. (Map 139)

Order: PASSERIFORMES *Passerine birds*

Woodlark *Lullula arborea*

Marked decrease southern England and Ireland and complete disappearance from northern England (A & L). Gradual increase in southern England and Wales and some expansion of range after 1920; marked increase in England in 1940's, reaching peak in many areas about 1951; decrease from about 1954 onwards, becoming very marked after 1960, with almost total collapse of population in many counties following cold winters of 1962 and 1963.

Scarce; breeds very locally in most counties south-west of a line from Merioneth to Kent, and in Suffolk, Norfolk and Nottingham. Following the marked decline during the last few years, the current distribution is uncertain and the species seems to have disappeared—perhaps only temporarily—from several counties in various parts of England and Wales (see fig. 8). Only about 100 occupied territories were known in the whole country in 1965, but because many must have gone unrecorded it is likely that the actual number of breeding pairs was somewhat higher than this.

Alexander and Lack's assessment tended to over simplify the varied history of this species which has fluctuated over the last 100 years or more as markedly as perhaps any other British breeding bird. The summary which follows attempts merely to outline the main fluctuations.

Around the middle of the 19th century the Woodlark disappeared from several counties of north-west England and Ireland in which it was then said to be breeding; apart from pairs which bred in Wexford about 1905 and in Cork in 1954, none of these counties has been occupied by breeding Woodlarks during this century. Within its main range in the southern half of England and Wales some decrease appears to have taken place towards the end of the 19th century, a low point possibly, though not certainly, having been reached in the 1880's (Harrison 1961).

Soon after 1920 the species began to increase in many counties, particularly in south-east England but also west to Somerset and Brecon, and apart from fluctuations (often caused through a heavy mortality in hard winters) this phase of expansion lasted through to about 1951. Curiously, despite the high incidence of cold winters in the 1940's, this decade, and particularly the latter part of it, seems to have produced the sharpest increase, at least in England if not also in Wales. In the north of its range the species recolonised Yorkshire in 1945 after an absence of 40 years (Chislett 1952), was found to be numerous in Nottingham in the same year (Local Report), and increased and spread in the adjacent county of Lincoln about 1946 (Smith and Cornwallis 1955).

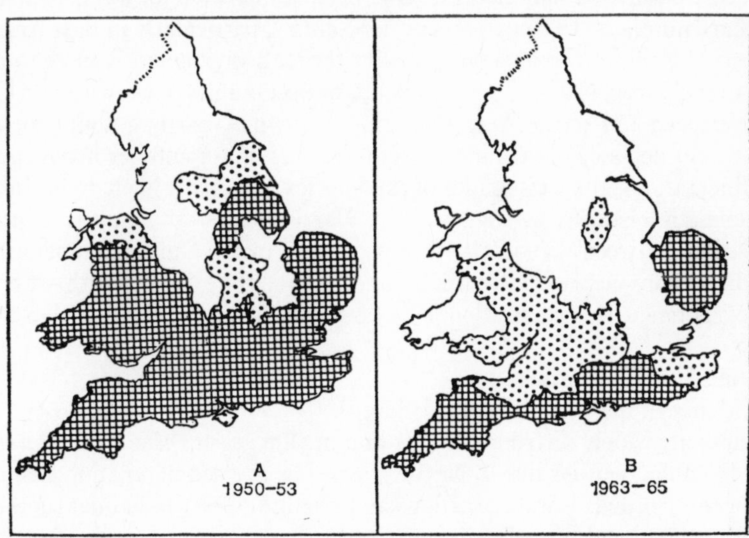

FIG. 8. Breeding range of the Woodlark *Lullula arborea* during (A) 1950–53 and (B) 1963–65. Hatching shows areas (based mainly on counties) in which breeding occurred annually in the period concerned. Dots indicate areas in which breeding is not known to have occurred annually, but a pair or two per county certainly or probably bred in at least one year in the period.

Peak numbers were reached in many areas around 1951 and, although the population remained high for about three years, a decline had already become noticeable in parts of Hampshire, Dorset and other southern counties by about 1954. Breeding results the next year seem to have been poor, and thereafter numbers declined steadily, falling sharply from about 1960, and more sharply still after the cold winters of 1962 and 1963. The species has ceased to breed in a number of counties, including Yorkshire (last nests 1958), Lincoln (last nest 1959), Bedford (last nest 1956) and Essex (last nest 1961), while in several others such as Pembroke and Cardigan, where it was well distributed up till 1962, it disappeared after the 1963 hard winter and was still absent by 1965. In England, despite the obvious effects of the hard winter, it is clear that the decline was already well under way; three examples may be mentioned to show its extent. In the area around London, fewer than nine pairs were known in 1961 compared with 45 pairs in 1950, and none at all could be traced in 1964 (Homes *et al.* 1964, Local Report). In Nottingham, at least 36 pairs were breeding in 1945 and 1950, but there were probably fewer than five pairs by 1961, while in 1963 there was only one report of a single bird (Local Report). On one part of the Suffolk coast, numbers decreased from about 20 pairs in 1956 to two in 1962 (Pearson 1963). Fig. 8 illustrates the recent contraction of breeding range.

At least locally, habitat changes have been responsible for a rise or fall in Woodlark numbers. In some parts of the country, particularly in East Anglia, the loss of Rabbits *Oryctolagus cuniculus* through myxomatosis in the mid-1950's resulted in many Woodlark habitats becoming overgrown with long grass, bracken and scrub. Yet, while this factor may partly account for the more recent decline, and habitat changes of one kind or another may explain local fluctuations, the vicissitudes of this species seem most likely to be linked with climatic changes, as suggested by Harrison (1961). There is a broad correlation between Woodlark numbers and mean annual temperature, though, perhaps because in Britain the species is on the extreme north-western edge of its range, this correlation is by no means precise. (Map 140)

Skylark *Alauda arvensis*

No evidence of marked widespread change.

Abundant; widely distributed, breeding in all parts of Britain and Ireland. Apart from fluctuations due to hard winters, few marked population changes have been recorded. Local reductions as a result of losses in habitat (notably through the ploughing of pastures, and where urban development has occurred) have been reported from some parts of the country. Except in Ireland, where Ruttledge (1966) suggested a possible general decrease in recent years, there is no evidence that Skylarks have declined over a wide area, and most observers report no noticeable change in numbers. (Map 141)

Swallow *Hirundo rustica*

Probably decreasing, particularly in Scotland, but evidence not quite definite enough (A & L). Fluctuates; appears to have decreased, but changes are poorly documented.

Numerous; widely distributed, breeding in all counties in Britain and Ireland, but only very locally in north-west Scotland, and irregularly in Shetland and (probably) the Outer Hebrides. There is some evidence to suggest that the species may have increased slightly in the extreme north-west of Scotland since the end of the last century, when it was regarded there as a rare transient visitor (Baxter and Rintoul 1953). With this possible exception, most records of changed status elsewhere in Britain and Ireland refer to diminished numbers, though because the species fluctuates, and because there are few numerical data, it is uncertain how real or extensive the decline has been, or when it began. Although more than a dozen post-war county avifaunas record a decrease, few go so far as to call it marked—Cornwall (Ryves and Quick 1946), Hampshire (Cohen 1963) and Warwick (Norris 1947) being among the exceptions.

Unfortunately, none of the local censuses of this species made in the 1930's (see Boyd 1936) have since been repeated, except for one in the Sedbergh area of west Yorkshire that indicated a twofold increase in the number of breeding pairs between 1938–42 and 1952–53 (Cuthbertson *et al.* 1954). No wider significance can be attached to these counts, although they do tend to confirm the general impression gained from the local literature of a temporary increase in some parts of the country in the early 1950's. Most Swallows in Britain nest in farm buildings of one kind or another, and it is therefore not surprising that where a local decrease has been recorded it has usually been attributed to agricultural improvements and, more particularly, to the improvement of milking parlours and barns. Voous (1960) recorded an apparent marked general decline in European villages and towns, and suggested that improved farm hygiene (leading to fewer flies) was the most likely cause. (Map 142)

House Martin *Delichon urbica*

Probably decreasing generally (A & L). Widely claimed to be decreasing, but evidence unsatisfactory.

Numerous; widely distributed, breeding in all counties in Britain and Ireland except the Outer Hebrides and Shetland, and only irregularly in Orkney. Numbers breeding at cliff and cave colonies in northern Scotland decreased markedly during the latter half of the 19th century, and throughout this area they have continued to fall until the present time (Pennie 1962). Indeed, in Scotland as a whole, Baxter and Rintoul (1953) suggested that House Martins had become much scarcer, particularly in inland areas. There is, however, some contradictory evidence, while in Ayrshire a decrease noted in the 1920's has since been reversed (Richards 1965).

Elsewhere in Britain the evidence for the long-term decrease that is quite widely held to have taken place is conflicting. Marked local fluctuations have certainly occurred, as indicated by, for example, nest counts at two large colonies on bridges. At one, near Oxford, numbers fell steadily from 513 nests in 1952 to only 65 in 1959, but then rose gradually to 283 nests by 1965 (Radford 1966, Local Report). At the other, in Shropshire, there was a steady increase from 168 nests to 335 nests between 1957 and 1963 (Rutter *et al.* 1964). While local fluctuations of this magnitude are known to occur, it is difficult to know how much credence to give to subjective reports of long-term changes. Although most of these refer to a decrease, they are scattered both in space and time, suggesting (together with the several counties that report no noticeable alteration in the bird's status) that any diminution must on the whole have been slight. There is no evidence that any decrease has occurred in Ireland; in fact, Ruttledge (1966) recorded a recent increase there.

(Map 143)

Sand Martin *Riparia riparia*

Probably decreasing, but evidence not quite definite enough (A & L). No evidence of marked widespread change.

Numerous; widely but locally distributed, breeding in every mainland county in Britain and Ireland and in the Isle of Man; irregular in Isle of Wight, and absent from Outer Hebrides, Orkney and Shetland. In the last century Sand Martins bred regularly on several islands in the Outer Hebrides and Orkney, but in both areas they had ceased to do so by about 1900 (Baxter and Rintoul 1953). This evidence apart, no marked changes in the extent of the range of this species have been recorded.

Although some redistribution of the breeding population has occurred, there is no evidence that Sand Martins have become scarcer in Britain and Ireland as a whole. The great majority nest in man-made habitats—most often at sand, gravel or chalk pits—which are quickly exploited and usually relatively short-lived. In some districts the species has become adapted to nesting in drainage pipes, and in the London area the two oldest existing colonies, occupied permanently for about 50 years, are so situated (Nau 1961). In central and eastern England the considerable growth in the number of gravel pits over the last 20 years has led to an undoubted increase in the Sand Martin population of such counties as Huntingdon. On the other hand, during this period, and perhaps since the beginning of the 20th century, the numbers nesting in such natural sites as river banks (for example, in southern Scotland and the Lake District: Baxter and Rintoul 1953, Stokoe 1962, Medlicott 1963) and coastal cliffs (for example, in Cornwall: Ryves and Quick 1946) have almost certainly become smaller. (Map 144)

Golden Oriole *Oriolus oriolus*

Sporadic. For a time in the mid to late 19th century the occasional pair bred fairly frequently in east Kent (Ticehurst 1909); since then, however, although breeding has been suspected more than once and birds are noted practically every spring, there appear to have been no further cases of confirmed breeding in that county. Elsewhere in Britain the species is said to have bred once or twice in about ten other counties in southern England and East Anglia between about 1840 and 1890; many of these records are probably genuine, but in fact very few are fully authenticated. If anything the species has tended to nest even less often in Britain during the present century, though there appears to have been a slight increase in the number of breeding records during the past 20 years. Breeding has been proved in Somerset (1949), Devon (1951), north Lancashire (1958–59 and possibly 1960–61) and Shropshire (1964), has been strongly suspected in five other English counties, and is believed possibly to have occurred in Pembroke (1954) and Cardigan (1964).

An increase in Denmark and, since 1944, an extension of the regular breeding range into southern Sweden, have been linked with an increase in mean spring temperatures in northern Europe (Salomonsen 1948, Voous 1960). It is presumably the climatic factor that prevents the species from becoming established in this country. (Map 145)

Raven *Corvus corax*

Great decrease in first half of 19th century, when exterminated over a large area of eastern and central England, though a few persisted in Essex till 1890 and in Sussex till a year or so later; increase in 20th century in west and north (A & L). Further increase in 1939–45 war, continuing locally till 1950's, and in some areas until the present time, with tree-nesting becoming more prevalent; but no marked expansion of range.

Not scarce; widely distributed in upland and coastal districts of western and northern Britain, and Ireland. A detailed account of breeding density and a general survey of population trends has been given by Ratcliffe (1962). Since about 1914 the species has gradually recovered much of the ground in Wales and western England that it lost through persecution in the 19th century. Although little extension of breeding range has occurred—the reoccupation of Shropshire (since 1918) and Hereford (since 1924) being among the more notable exceptions—the Raven population in nearly all counties in this area must have increased considerably. The most marked increase appears to have occurred during the 1939–45 war, since when the higher numbers have generally been maintained or, locally, have actually further increased. There have been few signs, however, that the species might recolonise parts of its former range in central and eastern England. The occasional pair or two have nested in Sussex (1938–45), Hampshire (early 1940's), Worcester (1949–50), Stafford (1951–52, attempted only) and north Derby (1967), though there is the possibility that some of these records refer to released tame birds.

In north-west England and south-west Scotland, as well as in the southern part of the range, tree-nesting, which had locally become almost unknown after the late 19th century, began to be more prevalent again after about 1945, and in some areas in Wales and south-west England the habit was re-established as early as the 1920's. In the Lake District and the Scottish border counties the number of cliff-nesting Ravens appears to have been relatively stable since the beginning of the 20th century, so the spread of tree-nesting represents an increase in the breeding population (Ratcliffe 1962, Stokoe 1962). Among cliff-nesting populations studied in four separate parts of Britain from 1945 to 1961, Ratcliffe found no indication of a long-term population trend, and there appeared to be only relatively minor short-term and annual fluctuations.

In north-east England and many parts of Scotland, Ravens are still widely persecuted, and many old nesting sites have remained deserted (e.g. Temperley 1951, Pennie 1962, Ratcliffe 1962). Apart from temporary increases during the 1914–18 and 1939–45 wars, and other minor fluctuations, the breeding population in these areas has remained relatively stable. In Ireland the numbers of Ravens are said to have recovered many of their 19th century losses and here, too, tree-nesting is again on the increase (Kennedy 1961, Ruttledge 1966). (Map 146)

Carrion/Hooded Crow *Corvus corone*

Carrion Crow *C.c.corone* locally decreased (except in vicinity of large towns), especially in south and east England; but increased in south and central Scotland (largely replacing Hooded Crow *C.c.cornix*) and spread to north Scotland and Isle of Man; Hooded Crow decreased in south Scotland and many parts of Ireland (A & L). Carrion Crow very markedly increased in all parts of its British range, with continued northward expansion in Scotland (at expense of Hooded Crow), and recent isolated breeding in Ireland though without yet having become established there; Hooded Crow otherwise maintaining its numbers or, in Ireland, increasing again.

Numerous; widely distributed, breeding in all parts of Britain and Ireland; the Hooded Crow occupies Ireland and the Scottish Isles and predominates in the Isle of Man and throughout most of the Highlands, while the Carrion Crow fills the rest of the range. The zone of hybridisation between the two races has continued to shift farther north in Scotland, and the Carrion Crow is becoming increasingly prominent even in the northernmost mainland counties. In south-east Sutherland, sample counts in 1955 and 1956 showed that Carrion Crows formed less than 15% of the combined Carrion/Hooded Crow population; by 1964 the proportion had risen to 35%, while many of the remainder were hybrids (Macdonald 1965). Except where it is being replaced by the Carrion Crow, the Hooded Crow is not declining, and in west Ross and some of the Western Isles it has recently increased. In Ireland, too, the Hooded Crow has increased considerably over the last 40–50 years in all parts of the country (Deane 1954, Kennedy 1961). The general increase appears to have been maintained in recent years, and since 1950 the species has extended its range into west Donegal (Ruttledge 1966).

There is much evidence to show that the Carrion Crow has increased markedly over almost the whole of its British range during the last 50 years, particularly since the early 1940's. Many county avifaunas note that the increase began with the decline in game-preservation at the time of the 1914–18 war, that it continued during the 1920's and 1930's, and that it became strikingly rapid, particularly in rural areas, with the further reduction in persecution from game-keepers during and after the 1939–45 war. Except possibly in East Anglia, this increase has recently been maintained (*q.v.* Prestt 1965).

The general relaxation of persecution has enabled the Carrion Crow to colonise the outskirts of many large industrial towns, while in rural districts it has spread locally even into sparsely wooded country. On Romney Marsh,

Kent, for example, it is now widespread, and in the absence of trees in the Dungeness area it nests on posts and electricity pylons or in small bushes only a few feet from the ground. Yet breeding was unknown on Romney Marsh till a pair bred in 1919, while at Dungeness—which was not colonised until some time during the 1940's —the breeding density was as high as one pair per 100 acres by 1952 (Axell 1956). (Map 147)

Rook *Corvus frugilegus*

Has spread to areas in north Scotland and Ireland, colonising Orkney, Skye and Outer Hebrides (A & L). Has since colonised Shetland. There is evidence of a fairly general increase in England between about 1930 and 1960, though it is uncertain whether this trend continues; no noticeable change in Ireland.

Abundant; widely distributed, breeding in all counties of Britain and Ireland, but only locally in the extreme north-west mainland and islands of Scotland, while in the Outer Hebrides (colonised 1895) and Shetland (colonised 1952) it is confined to single localities. Although most of the evidence from Scotland suggests a general long-term increase and expansion of range, due largely to 19th century improvements in agriculture and the planting and growth of woodlands (Baxter and Rintoul 1953), there are places, such as north Sutherland, where the species has declined markedly since the end of the last century and where it has continued to do so in recent years (Pennie 1962). On the other hand, censuses in Dumfries in 1908, 1921 and 1963 showed a similar aggregate of nests in each of these years (Skilling *et al.* 1966). Outside Scotland, changes in range have been slight. The species has, however, withdrawn from the centres and suburbs of many towns as these have spread.

A series of sample censuses of rookeries, mainly between about 1930 and 1960, give some indication of the probable population trends over England as a whole during this period. The fullest census, covering nearly one million nests over two-thirds of Britain's land surface, was made during 1944–46, when it was estimated that the total Rook population had increased by about 20% since the early 1930's (Fisher 1948). Subsequent sample censuses in several different parts of England have suggested that this increase was maintained over the next ten to fifteen years—and in some counties, such as Essex, Hertford and Nottingham, considerably improved upon. The only contrary evidence during this period comes from north-west England, where a big decline occurred in south-west Lancashire (Holdsworth 1962) and a less marked one in four other parts of the region. In west Cheshire there was a slight fall after 1944 and a more marked drop—of about 50%—between the early 1950's and the next count in 1964 (Henderson 1965).

Unfortunately, there are few counts after about 1961 to indicate the possible present trend over the country as a whole. In Nottingham, however, where previous censuses had shown a threefold increase in population between 1932 and 1958, numbers fell sharply (by 38%) by 1962 to a level of about that of 1944 (Dobbs 1964). The sudden decrease was believed to be due to mortality caused by toxic seed dressings. The earlier increase in Nottingham, as in several other parts of England, was almost certainly due to the increasing acreage of cereals, despite the fact that grassland (which has decreased) provides for this species the most important single type of feeding ground throughout the year (*q.v.* Sage and Nau 1963). (Map 148)

Jackdaw *Corvus monedula*

General increase, especially in Scotland, where it has spread west and north and colonised the Outer Hebrides and additional islands in Orkney (A & L). Further general increase over practically the whole of the range; has colonised Shetland, but remains local and sparse in the Outer Hebrides and north-west Scotland generally.

Numerous; widely distributed, breeding in all parts of Britain and Ireland, including (since 1943) Shetland. Examples of the great increase and extension of range in Scotland were given by Baxter and Rintoul (1953), and more recent Scottish works suggest that the general increase has probably continued. For example, Richards (1965) recorded a marked increase since about 1950 in Ayrshire; Evans and Flower (1967) noted a steady expansion on Eigg, Inner Hebrides, from the first six breeding pairs in 1933 to around 100 pairs in 1966; and Pennie (1962) showed that the species had increased generally in Sutherland, though it remained rare in the west. The standard ornithological works for Ireland make it plain that it has also increased generally in that country during this century, and Ruttledge (1966) suggested that this trend was continuing.

In England and Wales, although little numerical evidence is available, the local literature is almost unanimous in recording increased numbers during the 20th century. The increase appears to have continued in many parts of the country at least until the 1950's and, even if it cannot be determined whether it is continuing today, it seems improbable that there has been any decline. This expansion appears to have affected populations both in inland areas and on coastal cliffs: among the few numerical estimates is that of Saunders (1962) who showed that on Skomer Island, Pembroke, the breeding population grew from about 20 pairs in 1946 to 200–250 pairs in 1961.

The reasons for the long-term increase are not known, but especially in Scotland they are probably connected with developing cultivation. In Europe, Jackdaws appear to have expanded generally, including in Scandinavia and Finland where they have extended northwards, and in Spain where a marked increase has occurred (Voous 1960). (Map 149)

Magpie *Pica pica*

Marked decrease in 19th century in some parts of England and throughout Scotland; increase in many parts since 1914; increase in Ireland which was colonised towards end of 17th century (A & L). Marked general increase during and after 1939–45 war, continuing or maintained in many districts, but not in East Anglia where a marked decline has occurred since about 1959.

Fairly numerous; widely distributed, breeding in every county in Britain and Ireland north to Forth-Clyde line except in south-east Scotland; more locally in eastern Highlands north to Easter Ross. Like those of other crows, Magpie numbers were at a low ebb at the turn of the century. Despite a marked increase during and after the 1914–18 war, due to the lapse in game-keeping and probably also to an Act of 1911 that prohibited the use of poisoned bait, the species remained scarce in parts of east and south England through to about 1930 or later. Thereafter, and especially during and following the 1939–1945 war, its numbers rapidly increased, and even in some areas where it was previously almost unknown, such as eastern East Anglia, it had become common and widespread by the early 1950's.

Although there are no figures to go on, there can be little doubt that the increase, especially during the 1940's, was considerable and affected all parts of England and Wales, and probably Scotland and Ireland too. As well as many instances of local range extensions, often into places where the only available nest-sites are in low hedgerows or small bushes, there has been a general tendency for the species to spread into suburban areas. This has been observed in districts as far apart as south-west Cornwall, Sussex and Lancashire, while in Scotland the main strongholds of the species are now in the environs of such cities as Edinburgh, Glasgow and Aberdeen. Baxter and Rintoul (1953) attributed the general increase in Scotland largely to the fact that around urban areas the Magpie is safe from persecution from game-preservers. In London the species appears to be on the verge of penetrating the centre itself, as it has done in Dublin and some other large Irish cities and towns (Cramp and Tomlins 1966, Ruttledge 1966).

While over most of Britain numbers have tended to continue to increase, or have at least been maintained, a noticeable decline has occurred in some areas of eastern England since the late 1950's. Particularly in parts of East Anglia, and notably in Essex, west Suffolk, Norfolk, Huntingdon, Lincoln, Bedford and Cambridge, the decrease has clearly been very marked and the species has disappeared almost entirely from some agricultural districts. Elsewhere, for example in parts of Kent and Oxford, the decrease appears to have affected certain rural populations, but not those in suburban areas. The most widely held reasons for the recent decline in East Anglia are the destruction of hedges and the increased use of toxic chemicals (Prestt 1965) but the extensive ploughing of old grassland may also have contributed. (Map 150)

Jay *Garrulus glandarius*

Marked decrease generally, especially in northern England and Scotland, but with local increases, especially in southern England since 1914 (A & L). General increase over the last 50 years and particularly the last 25 years.

Fairly numerous; absent from the Isle of Man, the extreme west and north of Ireland, and parts of southern Scotland, but otherwise generally distributed north to Argyll, Perth and Kincardine. The long-term changes recorded closely parallel those for the Magpie and, as in the case of that species, seem to be closely linked with human persecution or its cessation. In addition, the Jay has clearly benefited from afforestation, particularly in Scotland. Apart from purely local or temporary fluctuations, all the evidence points to a steady and widespread increase since 1914, with a suggestion that this has become even more noticeable since the early 1940's.

In Ireland a marked general expansion has included, since 1936, the re-colonisation of five counties in Ulster and, in the west, the occupation of Mayo (Deane 1954, Ruttledge 1966). In Scotland, although the Jay is still absent from several southern counties, it has recently spread and increased in the new conifer forests of Dumfries, Galloway, Fife and the southern Highlands, without, however, extending its range to the Grampians or farther north. The general increase in England and Wales has included a westward spread in Cornwall and Pembroke, and the colonisation of many suburban areas. In central London, since first breeding there in 1930, the species has steadily increased and now nests in most of the Royal Parks and in several other open spaces (Homes *et al.* 1964).

Apart from a noticeable decrease in the woodland areas of south Cambridge between 1942 and 1963, there is no evidence that the Jay has undergone a recent decline in eastern England similar to that of the Magpie. (Map 151)

Chough *Pyrrhocorax pyrrhocorax*

General decrease extending over two centuries; in Scotland, where in the 18th century the species occurred in numerous inland localities as well as on the east, north and west coasts, it gradually disappeared and by about 1940 was confined to Islay, Jura and some other islands in the extreme south-west; in England, where apparently always coastal, it became extinct in Yorkshire, Kent and Sussex in the first half of the 19th century, and in the Isle of Wight, Cumberland, Dorset and south Devon in the latter half; by about 1940 it had gone from north Devon (last bred about 1910) and survived in only small numbers in Cornwall, but more commonly in Wales, the Isle of Man and Ireland, everywhere confined to the coast except in north Wales (adapted from A & L). Numbers maintained in Isle of Man, Wales and Ireland (perhaps now slowly increasing in latter two), and probably also in Scotland (Argyll) although a sudden sharp decrease occurred there in 1963; has not bred in Cornwall since 1952.

Scarce; a census in 1963 (Cabot 1965, Rolfe 1966) showed a minimum total breeding population of 700 pairs, distributed in Wales (98 pairs, mainly in Pembroke and Caernarvon, but including small numbers in five other counties), the Isle of Man (20 pairs), Scotland (11 pairs, all in Argyll, including the southern Inner Hebrides) and Ireland (567–682 pairs, mainly on western coasts between Donegal and Cork, and also in Antrim and Waterford). The results of the survey indicated that in most areas the populations had recently remained stable or had marginally increased.

In Scotland, however, there was a sharp decline in 1963, perhaps associated with the hard winter. In Cornwall, where four to six pairs bred till the late 1940's, only one bird now remains and no breeding has taken place since 1952; there were actually two Cornish Choughs until spring 1967, but one was then found dead, believed killed by a Peregrine *Falco peregrinus* (R. D. Penhallurick *in litt.*).

Several factors that might possibly have accounted for the general long-term decline of the Chough have been discussed by Rolfe (1966), but no single outstanding cause is apparent. A gradual reduction in breeding range has occurred in central Europe in historic times (Voous 1960). (Map 152)

Great Tit *Parus major*

Increasing in north Scotland, due to increase in woodland (A & L). Now nests over whole of north Scottish mainland; no evidence of marked changes elsewhere.

Abundant; widely distributed, breeding throughout Britain and Ireland excepting the Outer Hebrides (bred 1966) and Northern Isles. Before 1900 it was practically unknown in the three northernmost mainland counties of Scotland, but it now nests widely as far north as the north coast of Sutherland and Caithness. Describing the 'spectacular colonisation' of Sutherland, Pennie (1962) pointed out that, as with a sudden northward spread in Norway since the 1930's, the increase was not obviously due to a spread of plantations; the colonisation of north Norway was, in fact, correlated by Haftorn (1958) with changes in winter climate. Although the outer Scottish isles have not been colonised (apart from a pair that bred at Stornoway, Lewis, in 1966), there is some evidence that breeding has become more frequent on certain of the Inner Hebrides since the 1930's. Except for the colonisation of the Isles of Scilly in the early 1920's and a gradual increase there since, there are no records to suggest that any marked changes in distribution or abundance have occurred over the rest of the British range. (Map 153)

Blue Tit *Parus caeruleus*

Increase in north Scotland and colonised Isle of Man; due to increase of woodland (A & L). No marked long-term change; has colonised the Isles of Scilly and one locality in Outer Hebrides.

Abundant; widely distributed, breeding in all counties of Britain and Ireland except Northern Isles. In the Outer Hebrides it is confined to the Stornoway area where small but increasing numbers have bred since 1962 or 1963. As with the Great Tit, the only noticeable changes in range have occurred in Sutherland and Caithness, where the species has evidently increased and spread during the course of this century (Baxter and Rintoul 1953, Pennie 1962), and the Isles of Scilly, which have been colonised since the late 1940's.

Although marked short-term fluctuations occur, there is no evidence of any long-term population trend over the country as a whole. (Map 154)

Coal Tit *Parus ater*

Spreading in woods of northern Scotland (A & L). Expanding wherever new conifer forests have been planted; otherwise no marked changes.

Numerous; widely distributed, breeding in all of Britain and Ireland except the Outer Hebrides (bred at Stornoway in 1966) and Northern Isles. An increase in Scotland in the 19th century, and in Caithness since 1900, has been attributed to afforestation (Baxter and Rintoul 1953). Similarly, the recent extensive planting of conifer forests in other parts of Britain and Ireland has enabled the Coal Tit to occupy much country that was previously unsuitable (see Chislett 1952, Condry 1955, Ruttledge 1966, etc.). There can be little doubt that this has led to an increase in the total population. Outside the newly afforested areas there is no indication of any marked long-term change in abundance or distribution, apart from a recent spread into certain western coastal areas of Ireland. (Map 155)

Crested Tit *Parus cristatus*

Formerly more widespread in Scotland, but by second half of 19th century appears to have been restricted to Spey Valley; with extensive planting of conifers has now spread to pinewoods throughout the Moray basin (A & L). Slowly increasing and has spread as far as, if not actually into, east Sutherland and Aberdeen.

Scarce; restricted to east Inverness and four other counties of Moray Firth. Nethersole-Thompson (in Darling and Boyd 1964) has estimated that at least 300–400 pairs of Crested Tits nest in Scotland. Though Speyside remains its stronghold, the species has gradually spread to low-lying coastal as well as upland plantations in Nairn, Moray and Banff, almost to the Aberdeen border. It has also spread north in Ross and has recently been seen, but not proved to breed, in east Sutherland (Pennie 1962, Darling and Boyd 1964). Its numbers are reduced after hard winters but they seem quickly to recover. It is generally anticipated that given sufficient suitable habitat—notably old pine forests—the species will gradually regain more of the ground that it lost through the destruction of Scotland's forests more than a century ago. Jespersen (1945) noted a northward spread in Denmark due to afforestation. (Map 156)

Marsh Tit *Parus palustris*

No evidence of any marked widespread change.

Fairly numerous; breeds widely in England and more locally in Wales (probably in all counties except perhaps Anglesey), but in Scotland is confined to Berwick except for a single breeding record from Roxburgh in 1966; absent from Ireland. No significant changes in breeding range have been recorded and there is no good evidence of any widespread change in abundance. Apparent local fluctuations are difficult to interpret in the absence of any objective data, but they appear not to be linked with any wider general trends. (Map 157)

Willow Tit *Parus montanus*

No evidence of marked change (A & L). Apparent decrease and contraction of range in Scotland; no marked changes elsewhere.

Fairly numerous; widely but rather sparsely distributed in England, Wales and the south-west and central Scottish Lowlands; absent from Ireland. Confusion between this species and the Marsh Tit *P. palustris*, the low density of its population, and the fact that it was not recognised in Britain until the end of the 19th century, make it particularly difficult to assess the few status changes that are reputed to have occurred. More competent observation has gradually extended its known breeding range to most parts of England and Wales, and the same factor may be largely responsible for several apparent or claimed local increases in recent years. In Scotland it seems probable that there has been a fairly widespread decrease. The results of the B.O.U. Distribution Survey indicate that since 1955 the Willow Tit is known to have bred only in the south-west and in the Lowland counties of Lanark, Renfrew, Stirling and West Lothian. Since 1930 a sharp decline has occurred in Ayrshire and there are no recent breeding records (Richards 1965). Surprisingly, there appear to be no recent instances of nesting anywhere in the Highlands, which, if true, indicates a considerable contraction in range. Before about 1950 breeding was recorded from several counties north to Ross. On Speyside, Inverness, the species was believed to have become scarcer between 1918 and 1948 (Baxter and Rintoul 1953). (Map 158)

Long-tailed Tit *Aegithalos caudatus*

Fluctuates owing to greatly increased mortality in severe winters, but no evidence of marked long-term changes.

Fairly numerous; widely distributed, breeding in all counties in Britain and Ireland except the Northern Isles, Outer Hebrides (bred 1939) and Caithness (has bred). The species suffers heavily in severe winters, often taking several years to regain its former numbers. These short-term fluctuations apart, however, it shows little evidence of any widespread change in status. It is said to have decreased locally in parts of eastern and southern England since the 1930's; such records are usually attributed to habitat destruction, for example the loss of hedgerows in south-west Suffolk (Payn 1962). Few changes in range are recorded. The species is generally scarce in the north of Scotland, but has probably increased in north Sutherland and was first proved to breed in the west of that county in 1960 (Pennie 1962). Some previous colonisations in north Scotland—in Caithness, on some of the Inner Hebrides and, once, the Outer Hebrides—later proved to be only temporary. (Map 159)

Nuthatch *Sitta europaea*

Increase and extension of range in north-west Wales (Merioneth, Caernarvon, Anglesey) and Cheshire (A & L). Continued gradual increase and spread throughout Wales and over much of the northern half of England.

Not scarce; breeds widely in England and Wales south of a line from the Mersey to the Wash, and much more locally north to Westmorland and Northumberland; absent Scotland and Ireland. Particularly since about 1940 the species has shown signs of increasing over much of the western and northern parts of the range. As well as the increase in north Wales referred to above, it appears to have become much more common and widespread in most counties in mid and south Wales and has spread to several places along the west coast from which it was previously absent (e.g. Lockley 1961, Peach and Miles 1961). The earlier increase in Cheshire has continued, with new ground still being colonised in north-western and north-eastern parts, while since 1945 the species has spread into south-west Lancashire and now breeds regularly there and occasionally elsewhere in that county. Since about 1955 small numbers have become established in several parts of south Westmorland. Local range expansions, especially in the period 1945–55, were also recorded in Stafford and Derby, and more recently in Nottingham, Lincoln and parts of Yorkshire. In the north-east of the range it seems to have disappeared from Durham by the middle of the 19th century, but became re-established there after 1927 and increased and spread north during and after the 1940's (Temperley 1951). The species has now colonised south Northumberland and has recently bred at Alnwick in the northern half of that county (Local Report).

Few changes in status have been recorded from counties in the southern half of England, though what little information there is suggests that some increase may have occurred. Local extensions of range have been noted in southern England. For example, since about 1948 the species has spread into parts of south Dorset, and since 1952 it has probably colonised the Isle of Wight, though breeding has not yet been proved there. Few areas report any decline in numbers. A disappearance from the central London parks (recolonised in 1958) in the late 19th century and from another London park after 1953 were thought to be connected with atmospheric pollution causing the trees to become contaminated with soot (Fitter 1945, Homes *et al.* 1957). The same factor may be responsible for the species' scarcity in the neighbourhood of some other large industrial towns.

The causes of the increase in the north and west are not known. A partial explanation may be that in parts of Derby (Miss K. M. Hollick *in litt.*), Yorkshire (Evans 1964) and other counties, the Nuthatch has become increasingly a bird of gardens, especially in winter when it now makes frequent use of bird tables. (Map 160)

Treecreeper *Certhia familiaris*
No evidence of any marked widespread change.

Fairly numerous; widely distributed, breeding in every county in Britain and Ireland except Orkney and Shetland. A few pairs are now resident at one locality (Stornoway Woods) in the Outer Hebrides, where breeding was first recorded in 1962. The species may now also breed more frequently on some wooded islands of the Inner Hebrides. The local literature provides no evidence of marked changes elsewhere, other than short-term fluctuations due to increased mortality in hard winters. (Map 161)

Wren *Troglodytes troglodytes*
No evidence of any marked widespread change.

Abundant; widely distributed, breeding in all parts of Britain and Ireland. Numerically, this species probably suffers higher losses than any during hard winters, after which the population often takes some years to recover. These fluctuations apart, there is no evidence of any long-term change in abundance, and the species remains the most widely distributed of all British breeding birds. (Map 163)

Dipper *Cinclus cinclus*
No evidence of any marked widespread change.

Not scarce; widely distributed along fast-running streams in western and northern Britain and Ireland, but absent from the Northern Isles and, probably, the Isle of Man. Before 1950 small numbers bred in the Isle of Man and in Orkney (which was colonised in the 1920's), but lately the species appears to have gone from both these areas. Elsewhere there is little evidence of any widespread changes in numbers or distribution, and it seems probable that none has occurred. Locally, river pollution has caused the species to disappear, but on more than one stretch of river later freed from pollution the birds have returned.

In the southern half of England the easternmost limit of breeding range is reached in Dorset, Wiltshire, Gloucester, Worcester and Shropshire. In the first two of these counties a slight eastwards expansion occurred between about 1910 and the 1930's, while the few breeding records from counties farther east have tended to come after that period: Hampshire (1938 to 1950), Oxford (several years since 1949; also 1876, 1899), Warwick (1937). The few other examples of local fluctuations tend not to form any general pattern. Among the counties recording a recent local increase are Pembroke and Shropshire, while those recording a decrease include Cheshire, north Lancashire and Roxburgh. (Map 164)

Bearded Tit *Panurus biarmicus*
Marked decrease and contraction of range in 19th century, due mainly to reclamation of marshland, though also affected by collectors and hard winters;

by about 1900 was practically confined to Norfolk. Thereafter the species gradually increased and recolonised Suffolk, but was nearly exterminated in both counties by the hard winters of 1917, 1940 and 1947. Since the last of these, however, it has steadily increased (the 1963 winter causing only a temporary check) with some recent expansion of breeding range.

Scarce; until recently restricted to Norfolk and Suffolk, but since about 1960 small colonies have become established in Essex and Kent, and breeding has also taken place in at least one other eastern and two southern English counties. Axell (1966) has documented the fluctuations of the British population in detail. As well as the earlier history, briefly summarised above, he traced the rapid increase that has occurred in recent years, including the recovery from apparent near-extinction in 1947. Following the hard winter in that year the population had been reduced to two to four known pairs in Suffolk and a single male in Norfolk. Ten years later, however, the number of known breeding pairs in East Anglia had risen to 108, and by 1962 to 285. This was cut by rather more than half the next year, after the severe winter, but another rapid recovery took place and by 1965 the East Anglian population was estimated at 257 pairs. Eruptive activity was a marked feature of the population in every autumn 1959–65 (and also 1966) and this led to the recolonisation of several ancient breeding sites in Norfolk and Suffolk. Since about 1960 small numbers have begun to breed regularly in Essex and Kent, and occasional breeding has occurred in at least three other counties. The remarkable recent increase here has been paralleled in the Netherlands (*q.v.* Axell 1966). (Map 165)

Mistle Thrush *Turdus viscivorus*

Great increase in first half of 19th century in England, Scotland and Ireland; in northern England and Scotland was rare at end of 18th century and Ireland unknown; first nest found in Ireland in Louth in 1807, and had spread to almost every part of the country by 1850; continued increase in Scotland throughout 19th and into 20th century (A & L). Perhaps further increased locally, notably in young conifer plantations and in neighbourhood of towns and in city parks, but otherwise little evidence of marked change.

Numerous; widespread, breeding in every county except Shetland and the Outer Hebrides, but only irregularly in Orkney and sparsely in the extreme north-west and north of Scottish mainland. The spectacular gains made by this species mainly during the 19th century have been maintained. Earlier colonisations of Orkney (where a pair or two still nest occasionally) and the one suitable locality in the Outer Hebrides appear to have died out in recent years, but otherwise the species nests as widely in Britain and Ireland as it ever did. Over the country as a whole, the trend seems to have been of a gradual, general increase during this century, checked temporarily by hard winters. One feature which seems to be common to many parts, and has been noticed widely also in western and central Europe, has been the species' colonisation of gardens and parks, even in city centres. Having been a gradual process, the occupation of these relatively new habitats has been poorly documented. In Inner London, however, Cramp and Tomlins (1966) described a considerable increase that occurred between 1929 and the 1950's.

The main cause of the 19th century increase and spread is not known. In Scotland it was attributed partly to the planting of woodlands, and this has clearly been an important factor in the increases recently reported from some of the Inner Hebrides and, notably, Ayrshire, where the species now occupies young conifer plantations over an extensive area which was previously unsuitable (Richards 1965). (Map 166)

Fieldfare *Turdus pilaris*

A pair reared three young in Orkney in 1967 (E. Balfour *per* George Waterston) and was the first recorded breeding in the British Isles. Although this may be a parallel to the nesting here in recent years of such typical Scandinavian species as the Wood Sandpiper *Tringa glareola* and Redwing *Turdus iliacus*, it is worth noting that the Fieldfare has been extending its range in central Europe (Rommel 1953) and that since 1960 it has nested on several occasions in Denmark (Pedersen 1966, Poulsen 1967). (Map 167)

Song Thrush *Turdus philomelos*

No evidence of marked widespread change (A & L). Appears to have decreased throughout most of its range during the last 20–30 years, though still remains widespread over the country as a whole.

Abundant; widely distributed, breeding in all parts of Britain and Ireland. In Shetland, however, where it bred regularly between about 1900 and the 1950's, nesting is now only occasional; the initial collapse of the small population there, which numbered at least 22–24 pairs in 1946, came with the hard winter of 1947 (Venables and Venables 1955). Elsewhere no noticeable changes in the extent of the range have occurred except that some islands have been colonised along the west coast of Ireland.

There is much circumstantial evidence to indicate that in many parts of Britain the Song Thrush has become scarcer during this century, particularly since about 1940. Most county avifaunas, in commenting upon the decline, draw comparisons between changes in proportions of Song Thrushes and Blackbirds *Turdus merula* in local populations, and these sources and individual observers both particularly mention changes in the relative numbers of nests found. Even allowing for the fact that the Blackbird has increased, there can be little doubt that the numbers of Song Thrushes have declined appreciably. The changes in the relative abundance of the two species since the 1930's are also indicated by the annual totals of nestlings ringed in Britain and Ireland, summarised in table 7.

It is uncertain when the decrease began and, because recent trends have been obscured by the effects of the 1963 cold winter, it is not clear whether it is continuing. It seems probable that it did not become marked until the cold winters of the 1940's, though decreasing numbers are said to have been noticed in some areas 20 or more years before that. The cause of the decline is not known, though that since 1940 is possibly connected with the greater incidence of cold winters. (Map 168)

Table 7. Numbers of Song Thrushes *Turdus philomelos* and Blackbirds *T. merula* ringed as nestlings in Britain and Ireland in each of three nine-year periods during 1931–65

For various reasons (relative ease with which the nests of the two species are found, brood size differences, etc.) the figures do not necessarily indicate the actual frequency with which the two species occur.

Years	Average annual totals of nestlings ringed			Percentage of Blackbirds in combined total
	Song Thrush	Blackbird	Both species	
1931–39	3,180	2,740	5,920	46.3%
1948–56	1,654	2,577	4,231	60.9%
1957–65	2,161	3,263	5,424	60.2%

Redwing *Turdus iliacus*

Sporadic (A & L). Found breeding almost annually in Scotland in recent years, but only a few pairs, and species perhaps not yet firmly established.

Very scarce, not certainly regular. All known British breeding records up to 1966 were summarised recently in *British Birds*, 59: 500-501. The first nest was found in Sutherland in 1925 and between then and 1941 breeding was suspected or proved in at least seven years in either that county or Shetland, Inverness and Moray. No more breeding birds were found until 1953, since when up to three or more pairs are believed to have nested in almost every year, chiefly in Sutherland or Ross, but also once or twice in Shetland and Inverness; in 1967 breeding was proved in all four of these counties. It is not known whether the species has actually increased or whether it was merely under-recorded in the past; but in any event the numbers appear to be very small. A pair attempted to breed in Ireland (in Kerry) in 1951. (Map 169)

Ring Ouzel *Turdus torquatus*

No evidence of marked widespread change (A & L). Decline in many parts of Britain and Ireland during first half of this century, perhaps continuing, but recent information sparse.

Not scarce; widely distributed on upland moors in western and northern Britain from Caithness (occasionally Orkney) south to Devon, but not in the Outer and most Inner Hebrides, nor apparently now in the Isle of Man; also breeds widely but locally on hill ranges in Ireland. Baxter and Rintoul (1953) presented much evidence to show that the species declined greatly in many parts of Scotland during the first half of this century, and feared that 'unless the decline be arrested we are in danger of losing one of the most characteristic birds of the hill country'. While the present position appears to be not nearly so drastic as this, there is no evidence to suggest that numbers are now increasing. The various works on the birds of Ireland indicate that a decline has occurred there over the same period. For example, Deane (1954) stated that the species had gone as a breeding bird from many moors in Northern Ireland, and Kennedy (1961) referred to its disappearance from a mountain range in Tipperary after 1944.

Ingram and Salmon (1954, 1955, 1957), in their works on Carmarthen, Radnor and Brecon, suggested that a marked decline had occurred in these counties, at least over the previous ten to 30 years. But Condry (1955) knew of no changes in the species' status farther north in Wales. It is said to be still decreasing in Radnor and Carmarthen, though in north Glamorgan and probably in Brecon numbers have recently increased. In the absence of more precise data, and with the probability that local and annual fluctuations occur, it is difficult to assess whether there has been any long-term decrease in Wales, though it certainly seems to be unlikely that the species has increased there.

Similarly, in the various parts of northern and western England in which it breeds, few marked changes have been documented. Although changes in altitudinal range appear to have been little studied, the extent of the breeding range seems hardly to have altered over the years. One exception, however, is in Cornwall where Ring Ouzels were locally common in the early years of this century, but have not been found breeding at all in recent years. There is some evidence to indicate that the species was more numerous in some other parts of England at the end of the 19th century, and it is noticeable that the few records of breeding well outside the normal range—for example, in Kent (1875, 1879, 1887) and Warwick (1887)—were all before 1900. At the lower limits of its altitudinal range (usually around 1,000 feet), where it overlaps with the Blackbird *T. merula*, increased competition with that species may be partly responsible for some local declines or disappearances, as suggested by Meiklejohn and Stanford (1954) and by Rutter *et al.* (1964). (Map 170)

Blackbird *Turdus merula*

Increasing, particularly in Scotland and Ireland, helped by increase in woodlands, but main cause unknown (A & L). Increased generally, and expansion evidently continuing in some areas in recent years.

Abundant; very widely distributed, breeding in all parts of Britain and Ireland. Being already a widespread species, the marked expansion that has occurred during the last 100 years is not evident from a comparison of distribution maps compiled on a county basis. Yet, if unspectacular in the geographical sense, the expansion has been impressive in other ways. Until the mid-19th century the Blackbird was still restricted to its original typical woodland habitat and was unknown as a breeding bird in the neighbourhood of houses.

It was only in the second half of that century that it became the familiar garden bird that it is today, while its spread into the centres of cities came even later (Snow 1958). A further spread from large city parks to smaller squares and gardens did not occur in London until the 1930's, and it seems probable that the expansion there is still continuing (Homes *et al.* 1957, Cramp and Tomlins 1966).

Other impressive range expansions since the end of the 19th century have included the colonisation of many outlying islands of western and northern Scotland, including Shetland where the species was widespread and breeding on most inhabited islands by about 1950 (see Venables and Venables 1951). The original colonists in Shetland were believed to have originated from wintering birds bred in northern Europe, where a northward range expansion has been related to an amelioration of climate (Kalela 1949). As well as its colonisation of islands around Scotland, which continued until the 1950's at least, the species has also established itself on several islands and coastal regions of western Ireland from which it was previously absent. In various parts of England and Wales there has been a recent tendency for it to nest at greater altitudes, both in the new high forests and on more open hills. In most habitats the Blackbird outnumbers the Song Thrush *T. philomelos*, and this disparity has been increasing in recent years (see table 7 on page 148). (Map 171)

Wheatear *Oenanthe oenanthe*

Decrease in England, south Scotland and Orkney in 20th century (A & L). Very marked decrease in southern half of England, becoming extinct or rare in several counties where previously locally common.

Fairly numerous; widely distributed, especially in western and northern Britain and through much of Ireland, but now very local and distinctly scarce in the southern half of England. The very marked decline in England—affecting virtually every county from Lancashire and Yorkshire southwards—appears to have begun around the turn of the century. By about 1914 the species had ceased to breed regularly on the Essex coast and on the heaths south of London, though it was never common in these two areas. By the 1930's numbers had been appreciably reduced in many places, though birds still nested locally in several counties—for example, Nottingham, Cambridge, Berkshire, Oxford and the Isles of Scilly—in which they ceased to do so soon afterwards.

The decline was hastened during and after the 1939-45 war by increased cultivation and afforestation of marginal land. In particular, the ploughing of chalk dowland led to the virtual disappearance of the species from this previously important habitat in such counties as Wiltshire, Hampshire and Sussex. Finally, a widespread and rapid deterioration of many commonland and heathland breeding habitats was caused by the loss of the Rabbit *Oryctolagus cuniculus* in the mid-1950's. On one heath in east Suffolk, where about 40 pairs bred before the outbreak of myxomatosis in 1954, none nested after

1957 (Pearson 1963), while on the heaths of west Suffolk (where some habitat was also lost to afforestation) numbers fell from an estimated 800 breeding pairs in 1947 to fewer than 50 in the early 1960's (Easy 1964).

While loss of habitat has certainly been a major contributing factor in the Wheatear's more recent decline in southern England, it is doubtful whether it alone is the cause of the long-term decline. Evidence of decreased numbers elsewhere in Britain and Ireland is harder to find and, except in south-east Wales and locally in Ireland, it seems improbable that any significant long-term decline has occurred anywhere outside England. (Map 172)

Stonechat *Saxicola torquata*

Decreased locally due to decrease of wasteland (A & L). Fluctuates markedly as a result of heavy mortality in cold winters; has declined in the long-term (especially since 1930's) in the eastern half of Britain and locally elsewhere.

Not scarce; breeds in practically all maritime counties of Britain and Ireland from Orkney southwards, though not regularly on the English east coast apart from a few pairs in Northumberland and East Anglia; very much more local and sporadic inland, especially in England and Wales where the only inland counties in which it is now known to nest regularly are Surrey, Shropshire and Montgomery. Although there is little evidence of any major long-term changes in status in many of its strongholds—notably in Ireland, parts of north-east and west Scotland, west Wales, Cornwall and the New Forest in Hampshire—it is clear that elsewhere in Britain the species has decreased considerably. Away from the south and west coasts where it remains, it formerly nested—often rather marginally—in most counties of England, and continued to do so, though usually in diminishing numbers, through to the 1930's. Following the series of hard winters in the early 1940's, however, it ceased to breed over a very wide area to which it has not since returned.

Magee (1965) investigated the causes of the decline and concluded that it was due partly to the mainly temporary effects of hard winters, but more particularly to destruction of habitat through changes in land-use, and human disturbance. Although losses after hard winters are rapidly made good in optimum habitats, small isolated populations may be wiped out completely. The more isolated and smaller these become through further destruction and fragmentation of suitable breeding habitats, the longer it is before recolonisation takes place. (Map 173)

Whinchat *Saxicola rubetra*

No evidence of marked widespread change (A & L). General decline this century in parts of England, especially in the Midlands and south-east; little evidence of any long-term changes elsewhere.

Fairly numerous; widely distributed, especially in western and northern Britain (not Northern Isles), but only sparsely and very locally in Ireland and in England south of a line from the Severn to the Wash. Over a wide area of the

English Midlands the species has clearly undergone a considerable decline over the last 50-60 years. At the turn of the century it was regarded as a common, even abundant, breeding bird of roadside verges, rough cultivation and a variety of other habitats in such counties as Worcester, Warwick, Leicester and Nottingham, in which it is now much more scarce and localised. It seems never to have been common and widespread in south-east England, especially south of the Thames, but there too numbers have certainly diminished during this century, or locally at least over the last ten to 20 years. Small numbers bred regularly in Sussex, for example, until the 1930's, but have not done so since, and the species has almost gone from Surrey. In recent years the decline in counties around London and in parts of East Anglia, as well as in parts of central England, has taken place at a more rapid rate than that at which suitable habitat is disappearing. Hence some other factor is also involved. But the long-term decline over the southern half of Britain as a whole (excluding the south-west) seems likely to be due to loss of habitat, particularly through improved, mechanised farming and the cultivation of much marginal land.

While lowland or coastal breeding populations have disappeared or been reduced in many parts of northern England (though locally in the north-east they have been increasing again recently), there is no evidence that upland populations have been affected either there or in other parts of Britain. Indeed locally, notably in parts of south-west and north England, Wales and south-west Scotland, the species has probably benefited from an increase in one favoured habitat—young, open conifer plantations. In Ireland the species is on the edge of its range and has always been extremely local; the information is incomplete, but apparently after a general long-term decline in many areas the current trend there is towards an increase. (Map 174)

Redstart *Phoenicurus phoenicurus*

Very marked decrease throughout southern, eastern and central England, and to a lesser extent in Scotland; cause unknown (A & L). No evidence of further decrease, and has in fact increased in parts of southern England.

Fairly numerous; widely distributed, breeding regularly in all mainland counties of Britain except Cornwall, Cambridge and Caithness, but most commonly in the west and north; absent Isle of Man and breeds only erratically in Ireland. In the southern and south-eastern parts of its range this species has fluctuated quite markedly over the past 100 years. Yet apart from Cambridge, where it has ceased to breed since the 1930's, and Cornwall, where it now breeds only irregularly, there are no English counties from which it has disappeared altogether. The 'very marked' decrease referred to by Alexander and Lack has certainly halted over the last 20–25 years, and in the south of the range, particularly from Berkshire west to Devon, there is much evidence of an increase in this period (e.g. Lewis 1966, Ellicott and Madge 1959). Although there are many records of local, annual and other short-term fluctuations from the rest of Britain, there is little indication of any significant or widespread long-term changes in abundance or distribution. The very few breeding records from Ireland are mainly for the periods 1885–95 and 1955–60, and there is no evidence that it has ever been more than an erratic nester there. (Map 175)

Black Redstart *Phoenicurus ochruros*

After breeding sporadically for some years, now established as regular breeder in very small numbers in southern and eastern England (A & L). Has bred annually in south-east England and sporadically elsewhere since 1939; numbers reached a peak in 1950–52 and there has apparently been a gradual decrease since that time.

Very scarce; breeds regularly or fairly regularly on coasts of Sussex and Kent and in the London area, also less often near coasts of East Anglia; has bred sporadically west to Cornwall, Shropshire and Lancashire, north to Nottingham and Yorkshire. This is one of the very few species to have colonised Britain in recorded times. Apart from two or three isolated earlier attempts, the Black Redstart first nested in Britain in 1923 and has done so regularly since 1939. Its breeding history has been documented in a series of papers by R. S. R. Fitter, and the following summary is taken from the information in his latest survey (Fitter 1965). Nearly all known breeding has taken place in eastern and south-eastern England, and in many years more than half the breeding pairs and territory-holding males have been located on bombed sites in the City of London and at Dover, Kent. In the country as a whole the numbers of territorial males recorded (including those known to have bred) reached a peak of 53–55 in 1950–52. Except for a temporary increase in 1958 after a big immigration in April, the numbers have since apparently declined to a low of 16 males in 1962. The disappearance of the bombed site has been a major factor in this, but there is evidence that the birds have actually scattered and that the decline is less than supposed. Nowadays one favoured—if limited—habitat seems to be the large industrial power station. (Map 176)

Nightingale *Luscinia megarhynchos*

Perhaps decreasing, but evidence meagre (A & L). Only a slight contraction in breeding range, but numbers have declined over the last ten years.

Not scarce; distributed widely in south-east England to a line from Dorset to the Wash, and rather more locally farther west and north to Devon, Monmouth, Hereford, south-east Shropshire, Warwick, extreme south Yorkshire, and Lincoln. Except that the species once bred much more widely in Yorkshire (see Chislett 1952), this distribution corresponds closely with that recorded at other times this century. Some slight changes have occurred at the periphery, and in recent years these have all referred to contractions in range—sometimes, however, following an earlier expansion into the same areas in the 1930's. There are a few records of sporadic or occasional breeding beyond the normal range, for example in Derby and also in some parts of south-east Wales, but practically none of these has been in recent years.

A study of the population fluctuations of this species near Gloucester has been carried out annually by M. Phillips Price over a remarkable 41-year period, from 1927 to 1967 (Price 1961, and unpublished). The figures show a low population in 1927–33, a sharp increase in 1934–36, a relatively high population from then until 1956 (with an exceptional peak in 1949–50), a sharp fall in 1957–59, and very low numbers since. These fluctuations were not correlated with changes in habitat and their cause is obscure. There is a strong indication that they reflect not only population changes elsewhere in that part of England but also over a much wider area of the country. Certainly the peak around 1950 was noticed in several other counties, while the sharp decline over the last ten years has been commented upon in at least a dozen other southern and eastern counties. Locally—for example, in parts of Hampshire, Kent, Hertford and Suffolk—habitat losses (notably the grubbing up of thick hedgerows and small copses) have been responsible for the disappearance of the species. The over-riding cause of the recent decline is not known, but it is possible that slight climatic changes are also responsible. In some counties, the greatest decrease appears to have occurred among populations present on higher ground. (Map 177)

Robin *Erithacus rubecula.*

No evidence of marked widespread change.

Abundant; very widely distributed in all counties of Britain and Ireland, breeding also on most major islands and archipelagos with the exeption of Shetland. Apart from short-term fluctuations, often caused by increased mortality in cold winters, and local changes, especially among small, isolated island populations, there is no evidence that the numbers or distribution of this widespread species have altered appreciably over the last 100 years. It has never been known to breed in Shetland—the only county from which it is absent—although it has been established in Orkney since at least the late 18th century. (Map 179)

Grasshopper Warbler *Locustella naevia*

No evidence of marked widespread change (A & L). Locally decreased in parts of south-east England, but no general decline over Britain as a whole and has, if anything, increased recently.

Not scarce; widely but rather thinly distributed, breeding throughout practically the whole of Britain and Ireland north to Argyll, Stirling, probably Inverness and, at least occasionally, Aberdeen. Destruction of habitat has caused the species to become gradually scarcer in parts of Sussex, west Kent, Surrey and Middlesex (where it has now ceased to breed), as well as in a few other localised areas in lowland England (Norris 1947, Homes *et al.* 1957, des Forges and Harber 1963, etc.). But in south-east England generally no marked changes in status have occurred in places where the habitat has remained undisturbed.

Even more than most passerine summer-visitors, Grasshopper Warblers are particularly prone to local fluctuations from one year to another, and they are often extremely erratic in their occupation of some breeding sites. For these reasons it is especially difficult to assess reported changes in status on a long-term basis, but such evidence as is available suggests that the species may have become commoner in recent years.

Certainly the post-war boom in forestry should have benefited it. As in the cases of so many other species, young conifer plantations now form one of its most important (if not the most important) breeding habitats, particularly in the western half of Britain, but also in counties such as Berkshire and Buckingham in central southern England. No great changes in the extent of the British range have been recorded, but in Ireland the species has extended westwards to the Atlantic coast and is believed to have increased generally over the country as a whole (Deane 1954, Kennedy 1961, Ruttledge 1966). (Map 181)

Savi's Warbler *Locustella luscinioides*

Extinct in mid-19th century soon after its discovery in Norfolk and the fens of East Anglia (A & L). Very small population established in Kent since 1960, perhaps several years earlier.

Very scarce. Pitt (1967) has described the recent discovery of a small population at a locality in Kent (Stodmarsh) where from one or two to twelve singing males were located annually between 1960 and 1967, and evidence of nesting was obtained in four of those years. Birds may first have arrived there as early as 1951. Throughout its period of absence as a British breeding bird it remained locally common in the Netherlands, although latterly it was believed to be decreasing as a result of habitat destruction (van Ijzendoorn 1950). There is little information on its current trends in westernmost Europe, but in Poland and Germany there are signs of a recent westward expansion (Mrugasiewicz and Witkowski 1962), while since 1943 it has reappeared in Switzerland (Glutz von Blotzheim 1962). (Map 182)

Moustached Warbler *Acrocephalus melanopogon*

The breeding of a pair in Cambridge in 1946 was remarkable for the fact that the species normally nests no nearer to Britain than the Mediterranean countries. (Map 183)

Reed Warbler *Acrocephalus scirpaceus*

No evidence of marked change (A & L). Many local changes due to destruction or establishment of suitable habitat, but no single regional trend emerges from the records, apart from a recent expansion in south-west England.

Fairly numerous; widely distributed in East Anglia and southern and central England, becoming very much more localised in west and north; in fact, breeds in every English county except Durham, but only occasionally in Cumberland and at single localities in Westmorland and Northumberland; in Wales nests only at a few sites in Glamorgan, Brecon, Denbigh and Flint; absent Scotland and Ireland, where it has bred once—in Down in 1935. Throughout most of its range it is highly dependent upon the presence of the reed *Phragmites communis*, and many local changes in status are due to the often temporary destruction of this plant (most commonly through dyke and canal clearance) or to its colonisation of new waters, in recent years notably of flooded gravel pits.

Local records of increase and decrease form no clear regional pattern, except in south-west England. Here there has been a considerable expansion in recent years, beginning apparently with an increase in south Devon (the species benefiting from a cessation of commercial reed cutting) and followed a spread into Cornwall, where it reached various places in the west of the county, including the Isles of Scilly, between 1956 and 1962. In the same period there is some indication that it may also have increased in parts of the extreme north of its range, though the numbers involved are very small. Since the late 1950's a few pairs have bred at single localities in Westmorland and Northumberland. Lakeland breeding records are not unprecedented (Stokoe 1962) and, although the species had not previously been known to nest in Northumberland, there are a few 19th century records from Durham (Temperley 1951). A recent range expansion in northern Europe (see Merikallio 1958, Voous 1960) has included a continuing increase in numbers in southern Norway since that country was first colonised in 1947.

(Map 184)

Marsh Warbler *Acrocephalus palustris*

No evidence of marked change (A & L). Marked decrease during last 15–30 years, and now virtually confined as regular breeder to a few localities in Gloucester and Worcester.

Very scarce; fluctuating but very small numbers restricted to a few localities in the valleys of the Severn and Avon in north Gloucester and south Worcester, with a few pairs perhaps still nesting regularly in south Somerset and Dorset; breeds at least occasionally in Sussex and Kent, but now only very sporadically elsewhere in southern counties of England. Always scarce and very local, this species has clearly declined over the last 30 years, particularly since about 1950, and is now one of our rarest breeding birds. Although nests have been recorded in 20 southern and western English counties in all, regular breeding over a period of years has been known to occur in only seven or eight: Oxford, from 1893 to 1904 (also 1960); Kent, from 1926 to about 1946 (and at intervals since); Sussex, up to 20 pairs from 1920 to 1939, but none after 1947 until four separate pairs were discovered in 1966 (and also one pair in 1967) in an area where the species had probably been overlooked before; Dorset, from about 1893 to about 1954, but apparently only irregularly since; perhaps Wiltshire, where recorded in many years, and certainly nested in some, between about

1900 and 1922; Somerset, regularly in many parts in 1920's and in diminishing numbers through to the 1950's (perhaps still, though no reports in 1964 or 1965 and only one singing bird found during extensive search of old strongholds in south of county in 1966); Hereford, annually from 1938 to 1953 at up to four or five localities, but none since; and Worcester and Gloucester, where small numbers are still to be found.

Habitat destruction has been responsible for the decline or disappearance from some localities. This is, however, clearly a marginal species in Britain and it seems probable that some other factor, perhaps climatic, is the main cause of the general decrease. (Map 185)

Sedge Warbler *Acrocephalus schoenobaenus*

Colonised Orkney in mid-19th century and Outer Hebrides in 20th (A & L). No marked recent changes in range or numbers.

Numerous; widely distributed, breeding throughout Britain and Ireland except Shetland. Evidence of further change is restricted mainly to the Scottish islands, notably on some of the Inner Hebrides where there has been a recent increase (Boyd 1958, Evans and Flower 1967). The southern Outer Hebrides were first colonised during the 1920's, and in about the 1950's the species 'spread' north of the Sound of Harris (Dr J. W. Campbell *in litt.*); in Lewis, although the first positive record of breeding was not established until 1963 (*Scot. Birds*, 2:442), the Sedge Warbler could be described only two years later as 'fairly common, breeding in all suitable localities' (Elkins 1965). Following the original colonisation of Orkney, the species is said to have increased there by the end of the 19th century, but apparently declined again afterwards (Lack 1941–42); during the last 20–30 years, however, it has considerably increased once more—to a greater extent than any other breeding passerine in Orkney (E. Balfour *in litt.*). Over the rest of Britain there is no indication of any marked changes in range or abundance. Loss of habitat through drainage is suggested as having caused some decrease in the long-term, for example in Yorkshire and Hereford. On the other hand, new breeding and, perhaps just as importantly, pre-migratory feeding areas, have been provided since the last war by the increase, particularly in southern England, in the number of new reservoirs and flooded gravel pits with heavily vegetated banks. In recent years there is some evidence that the species has been expanding into drier habitats to breed, for example in Northumberland (Tyneside Bird Club 1967) and in young conifer plantations in Nairn (B.O.U. Survey).

Icterine Warbler *Hippolais icterina*

Eggs belonging to either Melodious Warbler *H. polyglotta* or this species were taken in Sussex and Surrey near the end of the 19th century. In May 1907 a bird was flushed from a nest with three eggs at Mildenhall, Wiltshire, and these were subsequently collected and identified, 'with hardly any doubt', as those of Icterine Warbler.

Blackcap *Sylvia atricapilla*

Increased in Ireland in second half of 19th century and increase perhaps continuing (A & L). Irish increase doubtful (though currently increasing locally in the north-east); no evidence of marked widespread change.

Numerous; widely distributed, breeding in all parts of England and Wales, more locally in southern Scotland (north to Stirling and south Fife), and very sparsely further north as far as Inverness; also very locally, patchily and probably erratically in several parts of Ireland. There is no evidence of a general long-term increase or decrease in Britain. Fluctuations occur from year to year and are noticed particularly near the northern limit of the range in Scotland. Pairs have actually bred as far north as Orkney (in 1949) and Shetland (in 1948), but occasional individuals seen on the north and north-east Scottish mainland in summer are perhaps mainly unmated males.

Observer coverage in Ireland is poor and it is extremely difficult to assess the significance of the changes recorded there. But the impression to be gained from the literature is of an erratically fluctuating population rather than one that shows any long-term tendency to increase or decrease. For example, Kennedy *et al.* (1954) described the species as numerous and widespread in Wicklow and mentioned nine counties from which it had apparently disappeared during this century. Recently, however, Blackcaps have reappeared and suddenly increased in north-east Ireland, have bred as far west as Limerick (two pairs in 1964) and have been found in summer in Galway and Fermanagh as well as elsewhere. Wicklow remains the chief stronghold of the species in Ireland. (Map 187)

Garden Warbler *Sylvia borin*

Possibly increasing in Ireland in second half of 19th century, but more probably overlooked earlier; still very local (A & L). No evidence of widespread change; perhaps some increase in Britain, some decrease in Ireland.

Numerous; range similar to that of Blackcap *S. atricapilla*, but in Scotland extends slightly further north in the west (to south Argyll), also to Inverness, occasionally east Ross, and Aberdeen; curiously local in Ireland, where found mainly in the Shannon valley. The few records of local changes in Britain during this century have tended to refer to increased rather than decreased numbers. But, in the absence of any quantitative information, all that can be concluded is that it seems unlikely that any general decrease has occurred. There is some evidence of a northwards expansion of range in Scotland during the last ten to 15 years, birds having been found in some years in parts of Sutherland and the Outer Hebrides, for example, where the species was previously unknown. Most of these records, however, refer to singing (and probably unmated) males, not nests, though a pair did breed in Orkney for the first time in 1964. Like that of the Blackcap, the distribution in Ireland is a complex one, and the species is absent from wide areas of apparently suitable country. In recent years it has been recorded breeding in only half-a-dozen widely scattered localities, to some of which it has remained faithful for many years, while others have been occupied only erratically. But, in the absence of more detailed information, nothing can be deduced about changes in the Irish population as a whole, though locally the species appears to have become less common. (Map 188)

Whitethroat *Sylvia communis*

Colonised Outer Hebrides in second half of 19th century; increasing in northern Scotland (A & L). No evidence of marked widespread change.

Abundant; widely distributed, breeding in all counties in Britain and Ireland except the Northern Isles, but only locally in north-west Scotland and Hebrides. This is another common and widespread species for which there is no satisfactory evidence of a change in numbers or distribution. Short-term fluctuations occur, and it appears to have increased recently in parts of northern Scotland and on some of the Inner Hebrides. Small numbers still nest in the Outer Hebrides, at Stornoway, but whether the species has bred there annually since the first nest was discovered in 1881 is uncertain. Other minor extensions of breeding range, such as the first recorded breeding in the Isles of Scilly in 1965, may be due to better observation today. Some local decreases in southern England, notably in the eastern half of the country, have been attributed to hedgerow trimming or destruction. In Ireland, Ruttledge (1966) suggested that a general decrease might have occurred recently, but there is no evidence of this in Britain. (Map 189)

Lesser Whitethroat *Sylvia curruca*

'Has probably increased in England and certainly in Wales; spread west to Cornwall, Pembroke and Anglesey in 20th century' (A & L). No evidence of widespread change in numbers or range (breeds only exceptionally in Cornwall and still very sparsely and locally in Wales).

Fairly numerous; widely distributed in southern half of England, west locally to east Devon and into Wales, and north locally to Cumberland and Northumberland; has bred Isle of Man and Scotland, but not recently. Despite Alexander and Lack's statement, there is little indication of any permanent westward expansion of range. The species has been found breeding on only two or three occasions in Cornwall (also two pairs in the Isles of Scilly in 1965), and Lockley *et al.* (1949) were able to cite only on breeding record for Pembroke. Throughout Wales it remains an extremely scarce and local nesting bird and, although very small numbers are usually present and believed breeding as far west as Pembroke and Anglesey, it is apparently absent from wide areas in mid and south Wales. There are no recent breeding records from Scotland, but Baxter and Rintoul (1953) gave several instances of nests being found at intervals between 1896 and 1949, mostly in southern Scotland but also as far north as west Ross and Inverness, without the species ever becoming established. There is no evidence of any long-term changes within the main breeding range in England. Populations fluctuate considerably from one year to another, and numbers of both unmated males and breeding pairs near the western edge of the range appear to depend partly on weather conditions during the species' immigration into Britain in spring. (Map 190)

Dartford Warbler *Sylvia undata*

Widespread decline, extinct in many counties (A & L). Further contraction of breeding range (now confined to three counties) and marked population 'crashes' in 1962 and 1963, with only slow recovery since.

Very scarce; now confined as regular breeder to a few localities in Dorset and Hampshire and the odd site or two in Sussex. Numbers decline markedly after severe winters, then gradually build up again over several years. When the population is high the species may spread very locally into Devon (last bred 1954, unmated males present 1964–66), Wiltshire (probably last bred 1957), Isle of Wight (last bred 1961, pair present 1964) and Surrey (last bred 1961). Outside these counties the most recent records of sporadic breeding have been in Essex (1948) and Cornwall (1940), but formerly such cases were reported from as far north as Shropshire and perhaps Stafford, while at one time the species nested regularly west to Cornwall and east to such counties as Kent and Suffolk.

Tubbs (1963, 1967) showed that the whole area of suitable habitat has been steadily shrinking and becoming increasingly fragmented over a long period of time, but that the process has been particularly rapid in recent years. He discussed the recent population fluctuations in some detail and showed that, after reaching a peak of probably nearly 450 pairs in 1961, the breeding numbers were reduced by two successive hard winters to only ten known pairs by 1963—probably the lowest total ever reached. By 1966 some recovery had taken place and, of 22 known breeding pairs, all but six were in Dorset where winter survival had been highest owing to a locally milder climate. Tubbs (1967) suggested that the Dartford Warbler's ultimate survival as a British breeding bird may depend on the extent to which the remaining Dorset heathlands can be saved from afforestation and agriculture. (Map 191)

Willow Warbler *Phylloscopus trochilus*

Colonised Outer Hebrides and increasing Orkney in 20th century (A & L). Perhaps general recent decrease in parts of southern England, but evidence uncertain; no marked changes noticed elsewhere.

Abundant; very widely distributed, breeding commonly in all counties except Shetland (where bred in 1901 and 1949), but only locally in the Outer Hebrides and Orkney (both actually colonised in latter part of 19th century). In the Inner Hebrides, as well as in many other parts of Scotland and also Wales, the species has tended to spread with the increase in afforestation and now occupies young plantations in areas that were previously desolate moorland. In Cornwall, too, Almond (1960) noted a recent tendency for it to extend its range to some hill areas with only slight cover. Evidence of recent decreases in southern England is, however, provided by breeding censuses made in two areas of predominantly oak woodland. The first, carried out in Gloucester by Price (1961 and unpublished) from 1928 to 1967, showed an initial high average population with a peak of 18 territories in 1939, followed by a general steady decline to 1964, after which there was none at all during 1965–67. The other, in Surrey, showed a similar marked decline from 21 to about two territories between 1950 and 1963 (Beven 1963). In neither case were the decreases obviously related to local environment changes, but whether these results reflect a general trend over a wider area of southern England is uncertain. Some other evidence, for example from parts of Kent and Cambridge, suggests a decline in numbers over part or most of these periods. On the other hand, over the country as a whole it seems unlikely that any drastic decrease has occurred. The yearly national ringing totals, for instance, provide no indication of any marked fall in the numbers of nestlings ringed, such as might be expected if the census results from Gloucester and Surrey had a wider application. (Map 192)

Chiffchaff *Phylloscopus collybita*

Marked increase in Ireland in second half of 19th century (A & L). Recent increase and perhaps some spread in Scotland; no evidence of marked change elsewhere.

Numerous; widely distributed in southern Britain north to Ayrshire and, locally, Argyll in west, but in east becoming rather sparse and local north of south Yorkshire, though breeding regularly to Lothians and, since 1958, south Fife; occasionally breeds still further north, as far as Ross (where perhaps regular); widespread in Ireland. A general increase appears to have occurred in Scotland since the early 1950's. As well as having become far more numerous in south-west Scotland, singing birds have been found almost regularly in summer in parts of Caithness, Sutherland and the Outer Hebrides (Stornoway), in each of which the species was previously unknown. Breeding has been suspected, but not proved, in some of these areas; and in 1959 a pair bred in the Inner Hebrides (on Rhum) for the first time. In many parts of Scotland the distribution appears to depend on the presence of the rhododendron *Rhododendron ponticum*, which in early spring is important in providing shelter in periods of cold weather (Meiklejohn 1952, Richards 1965).

In Ireland, where the species was apparently confined to only seven counties in the mid 19th century, it is now common and widespread, a further expansion of range taking place recently in Kerry (King 1960). In England and Wales there is no evidence of any marked change in status. Price's 41-year census in Gloucester (1961 and unpublished) has shown a relatively stable population of singing males, but a slow and very recent decline in the number of breeding pairs. (Map 193)

Wood Warbler *Phylloscopus sibilatrix*

Not recorded north of Inverness or from Ireland till second half of 19th century; in Ireland still extremely rare, but in Scotland has increased and now breeds Ross and south-east Sutherland (A & L). Probably never became established in Ireland where it has now not bred for nearly 30 years; increase maintained in northern Scotland, but appears to have decreased in many parts of England.

Fairly numerous; widely but locally distributed throughout mainland Britain, generally most numerous in western half of country and most local down eastern side; absent Ireland and perhaps now gone from Isle of Man. The increase and spread in northern Scotland appears to have been maintained and the species has reached north Sutherland only since the 1940's; this northwards spread has been paralleled in Norway (Pennie 1962). In Ireland, however, the species never became established and there has been no record of breeding since pairs nested in Down in 1932 and Cork in 1938.

Although there is no evidence of a decrease in Wales and some of its strongholds in England, reports of status changes from many English counties between about 1940 (sometimes earlier) and about 1963 nearly all refer to decreased numbers. In eastern England, between Kent and south Yorkshire, the species has always been scarce and local, but lately it has become even more so. In East Anglia it has now practically ceased to breed (a few pairs nest still in north Norfolk) and the same is true of Nottingham and possibly Oxford. Some decrease has occurred in Worcester, Stafford and Cheshire, and numbers are said to have been much reduced in the Lakeland counties between about 1950 and 1964 (Stokoe 1962 and *in litt.*). Richards (1965) noted a recent decline in Ayrshire.

The significance of the apparent decline is hard to assess. Short-term fluctuations in numbers evidently also occur, and there is evidence that since about 1964 there has been a small recovery in at least some places where the species was declining. Often local populations comprise a high proportion of unmated males (e.g. Oakes 1953). Wood Warblers favour rather open, mature deciduous woods with sparse secondary growth, and the species' disappearance from some traditional haunts has been correlated with the under-storey becoming too thick (e.g. Harthan 1961). (Map 194)

Goldcrest *Regulus regulus*

Increased in 19th century, partly at least due to planting of conifers and perhaps also milder winters; still increasing and spreading in Scotland and Ireland with increase of conifer plantations (A & L). Further increase due to extensive planting of conifers.

Numerous; widely distributed, breeding throughout Britain and Ireland, but not in Shetland, only irregularly in Orkney, and locally in the Outer Hebrides, north-west Scotland and parts of eastern England. Population 'crashes' correlated with severe winters are a feature of this species' biology, but numbers are usually made good within a very few years. The Goldcrest is the dominant bird in older conifer plantations and there is no doubt that the extensive recent planting of these woods has led to a considerable increase in its total numbers. During this century it has colonised several islands, for example in the Hebrides and the Isles of Scilly, as the conifer plantations have matured. (Map 195)

Firecrest *Regulus ignicapillus*

Since 1961 small numbers (up to nine singing males) have been found in the breeding season in the New Forest, Hampshire, and breeding was proved in 1962 and 1965 (Adams 1966). There were the first authentic breeding records for the British Isles, though the extent to which the species might have been overlooked in the past is not known. (Map 196)

Spotted Flycatcher *Muscicapa striata*

Apparently increasing somewhat in northern Scotland (A & L). No evidence of marked widespread change.

Fairly numerous; widely distributed, breeding in all counties of Britain and Ireland except Shetland, but only locally and in small numbers in Caithness, the Hebrides and Orkney; in the Hebrides it has become established only fairly recently (probably since about 1940's) and in Orkney only in the last few years. There is no evidence of any other changes in the extent of the breeding range. Locally at least, numbers tend to fluctuate, but, although the few records of local changes in breeding status tend to refer to a decrease rather than an increase, it is impossible to assess how real or extensive this trend has been. Except that three reports of decrease come from areas in south-west England and one from west Pembroke (perhaps indicating a general decline in western coastal districts) these local records are scattered and form no geographical or chronological pattern. (Map 197)

Pied Flycatcher *Ficedula hypoleuca*

Definite increase in northern England and southern Scotland (A & L). General increase and expansion of range since about 1940, particularly up to 1952.

Not scarce; distributed widely but locally in Wales (extending east into Gloucester, Worcester, Shropshire and Cheshire) and from north Derby and central Yorkshire through northern England into southern Scotland, with small isolated populations still further north, mainly in Perth and Inverness; also breeds locally in south-west England (Exmoor and south Devon); has nested occasionally in recent years in several other western and northern counties from Cornwall to east Ross. Campbell (1954–55, 1965) described in detail the distribution and history of this species in Britain up to 1962. A slow gradual increase in numbers and range has apparently been in progress since the second half of the 19th century, when the species first spread into southern Scotland. Between about 1940 and 1952 there was a phase of more marked expansion: established breeding groups increased and birds spread into several new areas, for example south Devon and parts of the west Midlands and Scottish Highlands. After 1952 the increase slowed down considerably and locally was even reversed; a nest-box population studied since 1942 in the Forest of Dean (Gloucester) reached a peak in 1951 and declined slightly during the following two or three years, but thereafter remained relatively stable.

The factors responsible for the general increase (and the fluctuations in the shorter term) are not known. Campbell (1954–55) suggested that the most probable reason for the previous absence of the Pied Flycatcher from the Scottish Highlands was the sequence of deforestation and re-afforestation, though climatic factors might also have been involved. (The species has increased generally in northern Europe, while Merikallio 1958 reported an enormous increase in northern Finland after about 1947). Elsewhere the provision of nest-boxes has undoubtedly aided the spread, and some populations, for example that in south Devon, appear to be almost entirely dependent for nest-sites on these artefacts. (Map 198)

Dunnock *Prunella modularis*

No evidence of marked widespread change, but more probably increased than decreased.

Abundant; widely distributed, breeding in all parts of Britain and Ireland except Shetland. In the Outer Hebrides and Orkney breeding was first recorded in the second half of the 19th century and in each area the species subsequently became established and increased. Evidence of changes elsewhere is virtually non-existent, but what little information there is suggests that the Dunnock has almost certainly increased rather than decreased in the period since the 1939–45 war. Most recent reported increases have been from east and south-east England, and they seem to have been particularly noticeable in and around towns. Cramp and Tomlins (1966), for example, recorded a marked increase in the central London parks since the early 1950's. (Map 199)

Meadow Pipit *Anthus pratensis*

No evidence of marked widespread change, but perhaps decreased, at least in southern half of England.

Abundant; widely distributed, breeding in every county, commonly in the west and north, but only locally, often very sparsely, in counties in the south and east English Midlands. Again, as with most widespread and abundant breeding birds, there is very little information on population changes, particularly in the north and west where the species has always been, and remains, most common. There is some evidence of a decrease in parts of southern and eastern England owing to loss of habitat, for example in Suffolk where much marginal land has been cultivated or afforested. Possibly, though not certainly, a more general decline has occurred in the southern half of England, for the species has become scarce or is now absent from many apparently suitable habitats in Hampshire (Cohen 1963) and within recent years has disappeared completely as a breeding bird from the Isles of Scilly, where Ryves and Quick (1946) and previous authors described it as common. Less definite reports of decrease (which contrast, however, with none of increase) come from parts of Sussex, Essex, Cambridge, Worcester, Shropshire and Nottingham, as well as Brecon, Northern Ireland and elsewhere. On the other hand, frequent estimates and censuses since 1928 of a breeding population on Skokholm Island, Pembroke (Barrett 1959, Local Reports), give no indication of any long-term changes, although numbers have fluctuated in the short-term between a minimum of 'perhaps only 16 pairs' in 1955 and a maximum of 60 pairs in 1950. (Map 200)

Tawny Pipit *Anthus campestris*

The breeding record from Sussex in 1905, together with that of probable breeding from the same county in the following year, is now no longer regarded as valid (Nicholson and Ferguson-Lees 1962).

Tree Pipit *Anthus trivialis*

No evidence of marked widespread change (A & L). Northward expansion of range in northern Scotland during the last 80 years; probably somewhat decreased in parts of England, especially in the south, though locally has benefited from the planting of new conifer forests.

Numerous; widely distributed, breeding in all British counties except the Northern Isles, Outer Hebrides, Caithness and Anglesey, but tending to occur less commonly and widely in lowland woods of south-east Britain than in hill woods of west and north; also breeds Isle of Man, but not recorded nesting in Ireland. On the north Scottish mainland, north of Inverness, the species has increased and spread considerably since the latter part of the 19th century, and in Sutherland, where once almost unknown, it is now one of the commonest breeding birds in almost every mature birchwood (Pennie 1962, Yapp 1962). A similar expansion of range took place in Norway during the same period (Haftorn 1958).

Further south in Britain, subjective assessments of local status changes point towards the species having become gradually less numerous, though here and there it has recently benefited from the planting of new conifer forests which it occupies in the early stages of growth. Reports of recent decreases come mainly from south-eastern England. For example, on the fringes of the East Anglian Breck, Payn (1962) stated that numbers were down to only 10% of those in the 1930's, while in north-east Surrey, where Pounds (1952) noted the species as common, it is now restricted to only one or two localities (M. J. Rayner *in litt.*). As well as other reported local decreases in south-east England, Tree Pipits have evidently also declined in places west to Dorset, Gloucester, Worcester and Cheshire; while as far north as the Lake District, a decrease is believed to have occurred in some areas over the past ten to 15 years (Stokoe 1962, R. W. Robson *in litt.*). (Map 201)

Rock Pipit *Anthus spinoletta*

No evidence of marked widespread change.

Fairly numerous; breeds, almost entirely on rocky shores and islands, around whole coastline except Dumfries, Lancashire and between Kent and south Yorkshire, but confined to only single localities in Cumberland, Cheshire and Hampshire (though breeds in the Isle of Wight). Except that the species then nested more commonly in Hampshire, at least occasionally in Lancashire, and at least once in Kent and inland in Radnor, the present distribution corresponds closely with that around the turn of the century. Few other marked changes in range have occurred, although the species seems to have virtually disappeared from along the Sussex coastal cliffs during a 40-year period up to 1932; it then became re-established about 20 pairs being located along the coast in 1935 and about 45 pairs in 1965 (Porter 1966). Recently, there have been a few local reports of a decline—for example, at Portland Bill, Dorset, and in part of Kirkcudbright where J. D. Brown (*in litt.*) thinks it has decreased more than any other passerine—but there is no evidence of any general or widespread change in abundance. Estimates or counts of some island breeding populations over many years—for instance, at Skokholm, Pembroke, and the Isle of May, Fife—indicate relatively stable numbers: at Skokholm, the highest estimate since 1928 was 67 pairs in 1959 and the lowest 24 pairs in 1965. (Map 202)

Pied/White Wagtail *Motacilla alba*

Decrease in Scotland in recent years (A & L). No evidence of marked widespread change; has increased in Ireland, but perhaps decreased slightly in some parts of England.

Numerous; widespread, breeding regularly in all counties of Britain and Ireland except Shetland, and only locally in Orkney and Outer Hebrides; the Pied Wagtail *M. a. yarrellii* is the usual race, but the White Wagtail *M. a. alba* also nests here sporadically, most often in Shetland. In Ireland, the Pied Wagtail is said to have increased greatly during this century, especially in western coastal districts from which it was once absent (Kennedy 1961); in the country as a whole it 'is now one of our most common and widespread passerines' (Ruttledge 1966). No corresponding decrease has been recorded in Britain. Except for a recent decline in Orkney, the earlier Scottish decrease has not been sustained. The few relevant records from England point to some decrease having occurred locally, though with one or two exceptions this decline is nowhere said to have been other than slight or 'probable'. Indeed, the great majority of counties report or infer no change in numbers. In east Sussex, however, H. A. R. Cawkell (*in litt.*) believes that numbers may now be down to about half those of 30 years ago, the bird having disappeared particularly from many farmyards. Populations of small islands are notoriously prone to extinction and fluctuation, and wider emphasis should not be put upon such examples. Nevertheless, it is curious that none has been recorded breeding in the Isles of Scilly since early this century, when Clark and Rodd (1906) noted it as nesting on all the larger islands there.

Most reliable records of the White Wagtail breeding in Britain are from Scotland, especially Shetland, but there is no evidence that such records have become more or less frequent at any time during the present century.

(Map 203)

Grey Wagtail *Motacilla cinerea*

Marked increase in south-east England (A & L). General increase in eastern and southern England during this century, most marked in 1950's, with some decrease since about 1960 and especially after the 1963 hard winter.

Not scarce; widely but rather locally distributed, breeding most commonly in hilly districts in the west and north (but absent from the Northern Isles and very scarce or irregular in Outer Hebrides), and most locally in lowland, south-east Britain, where nests only irregularly in some counties. As well as a general, gradual increase over much of southern England during the first half of this century, a more rapid expansion during the 1950's affected many parts of the same area. Breeding was recorded for the first time in Essex and Leicester in 1951 and in Nottingham and Huntingdon in 1955; in several counties (for example, Suffolk, Northampton and Kent) where the species had previously been erratic or scarce, it now became established in small numbers and in others (Berkshire and Oxford, for instance) it increased. This upsurge in numbers during the 1950's may have been general throughout the British Isles, and Sharrock (1964) suggested that a recent peak in breeding numbers or breeding success was reached in 1959. Unfortunately, there is little regional evidence of changes outside southern England, though the species was recorded nesting in the Outer Hebrides for the first time in 1957.

Since about 1960 a decline has set in in some parts of the country, and the very cold winters of 1962 and, particularly, 1963 resulted in severe losses in breeding strength, especially in south-east England (Dobinson and Richards 1964). Around Banbury, Oxford, numbers were reduced from about 21 breeding pairs in 1961 to only one in 1963. In Essex, where five to seven pairs bred in 1957, numbers had fallen to only one pair in 1962, and none has nested since. In Surrey, at least 35 pairs were located in 1961, only ten or eleven in 1962 and 1963, but 20 in 1965. In Sussex, where Walpole-Bond (1938) estimated the average breeding population at 60–70 pairs, no breeding records were reported to the *Sussex Bird Report* in 1963, only two in 1964, and eight in 1965; P. G. Davis (*in litt.*), however, wrote in 1965 that 'there are certainly more than 60 pairs today'.

Clearly, a gradual recovery from the effects of the severe winter is taking place, though it is uncertain whether the species will regain its abundance of the late 1950's. Apart from the effects of hard winters, the reasons for the fluctuations are not known. In Europe as a whole, the species is spreading and increasing: it is thought not to have become established in central Europe until after about 1850, while during this century it has been expanding its range northwards in the north-west (Voous 1960). (Map 204)

Yellow Wagtail *Motacilla flava*

British race *M. f. flavissima* decreased in Scotland and Ireland with complete disappearance from some localities where it formerly nested; in Northumberland it became very rare during 19th century, but has increased during last 20 years; Blue-headed Wagtail *M. f. flava* perhaps increasing somewhat in south-east England, but very local and perhaps overlooked earlier (A & L). Further decrease Scotland (has gone from Stirling and Dumfries) where now confined to the Clyde area; last regular breeding in Ireland was in 1941, but occasional pairs have bred erratically since 1956; decrease in parts of southern England, perhaps a continuation of general trend during this century, but few changes (and perhaps even some increase) in northern England. Blue-headed Wagtail breeds occasionally, but seems never to have become firmly established, except perhaps in certain parts of Sussex during the course of the 1920's and 1930's.

Fairly numerous; widely but rather locally distributed in England (very local in south-west, but including a pair or two in most years in west Cornwall); in Wales restricted to border counties and Carmarthen, in Scotland to a few pairs in the Clyde area, and in Ireland to the occasional pair or two (in recent years most often in Wicklow). Nominate *flava* breeds occasionally, sometimes with *flavissima*, within (e.g. East Anglia, Cheshire), on edge of (e.g. Northumberland, Devon, Cornwall) or sometimes beyond (e.g. Belfast 1963, Kerry 1965, Isles of Scilly 1966) the normal range of *flavissima*. Two pairs showing the characters of the Ashy-headed Wagtail *M. f. cinereocapilla* bred in Northern Ireland in 1956; and birds (or occasionally, for a few years, small groups) resembling Sykes's Wagtail *M. f. beema* or other forms have been found breeding in southern England, but these may be hybrids. The discussion which follows refers only to the British race *flavissima*.

Smith (1950) made a detailed study of the distribution and status changes of the Yellow Wagtail in the British Isles. He concluded that during the first half of this century it had decreased in many parts of southern England and south Wales, but increased generally in north-west England. In Scotland, however, where it once bred as far north as Aberdeen, it had seriously decreased in all areas with the possible exception of Renfrew, to which county, together with adjacent parts of Lanark and Ayrshire, it had become restricted (see also Baxter and Rintoul 1953). In Ireland two sizeable and long-established breeding groups, one on the borders of Mayo and Galway, the other around Lough Neagh, gradually decreased and finally died out by about 1928 and 1941 respectively.

Since 1950, apart from a few minor changes, the extent of the species, regular breeding range in Britain has remained practically unaltered. There has been a continuing tendency for most records of changes in numbers in southern England to refer to a decrease, and for records from northern England, for example currently in Northumberland, to refer to an increase (or at least to relatively stable numbers). In Ireland there was no record of breeding between 1942 and 1955, but since 1956 occasional pairs have nested in some years, most often in Wicklow, but also in Down, Antrim and perhaps Tipperary.

Smith (1950) could gather little information to account for the fluctuations. Locally, changes in habitat were clearly responsible for an increase or decrease, but the earlier declines in Scotland and Ireland took place in the absence of any obvious environmental changes and the reasons for them are obscure.

(Map 205)

Red-backed Shrike *Lanius collurio*

Marked decrease in northern, western and parts of southern England, also in Wales (A & L). Decrease and contraction of range even more marked over last 20 years, apparently continuing, though more slowly in its last strongholds in East Anglia, Surrey and Hampshire than elsewhere.

Scarce; apart from the occasional pair (for example, in Gloucester in 1966), is now restricted to a few parts of southern England south of a line from the Wash to the Exe estuary, Devon, with a total population of 125–200 pairs. Peakall (1962) traced the history of the species' decline in Britain over the last 100 years and showed that the decrease seemed to have accelerated after about 1940 (see fig 9a). By 1960, the year of his survey, there was a total of only about 172 known breeding pairs, of which 119 (69%) were found in the four counties of Hampshire, Surrey, Suffolk and Norfolk. A survey of the latest county bird reports—mainly for 1966, though in some cases 1965—together with information from Dr J. S. Ash on a population in part of Hampshire in 1966, indicates a current known breeding population of about 127 pairs, of which 108 (85%) are in the four counties mentioned above. The distribution of these pairs, by counties, is shown in fig. 9b. Except that the total for the Norfolk part of Breckland is here included under that county (and not under Suffolk), this map may be compared with fig. 2 in Peakall (1962). Because of different intensities of coverage, however, and some local seasonal variation (for example, in 1960 temporarily high numbers in Essex and part of Hampshire, and low numbers in Breckland), the two sets of figures give a false impression of the extent of the changes in some counties.

Nevertheless, the general picture over this period seems clear: a continuing general decline outside the species' main strongholds, but with numbers holding up reasonably well or declining less rapidly within them. The most marked decrease in the period has been in the three adjacent counties of Essex, Middlesex and Hertford, where the total number of pairs has fallen from 35 to seven. In Hampshire there has been a general decrease, though it has been less conspicuous where the greatest density occurs: the population of one such area fluctuated between 27 and 29 pairs during 1956–61 except that there were 39 pairs in 1960; when next censused in 1966 the area held 23 pairs (Dr J.S. Ash *in litt.*). The evidence from East Anglia is harder to evaluate, for, although the total numbers reported now are actually higher than in 1960, some local populations that have been studied closely have continued to decrease gradually. It seems probable that some pairs present in 1960 were not recorded.

Durango (1950) found that the Red-backed Shrike had decreased considerably throughout north-west Europe since about 1930, and Peakall (1962)

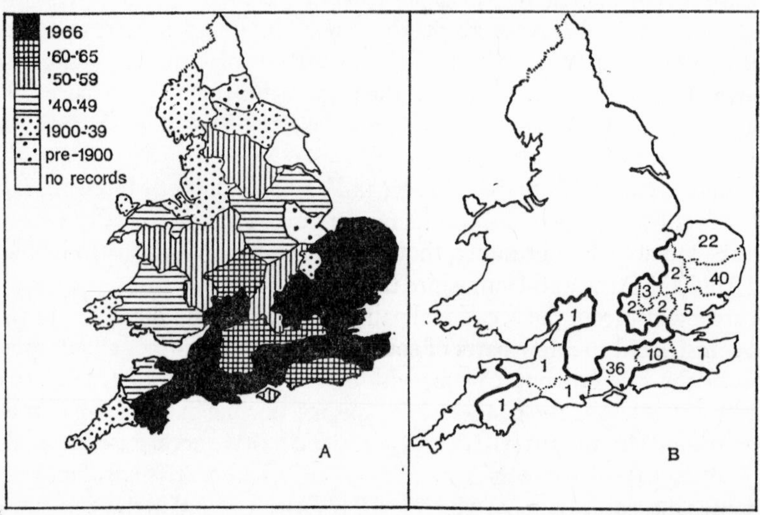

FIG. 9. Decline of the Red-backed Shrike *Lanius collurio*. In A the various shadings (based mainly on counties) show the period in which the species is last known to have bred in each county (occasionally vice-county). The species still breeds in the blacked-in counties and the approximate number of known pairs per county in 1966 is shown in B. Information for 1960 and earlier is based mainly on Peakall (1962), with some minor amendments.

showed that this decrease had continued in several countries. Both these authors concluded that the pattern of the decline was consistent with long-term climatic changes. The apparent rapidity of the decrease in Britain during the 1940's, when some local populations of up to a score or more birds disappeared within the space of a year or two, might repay further investigation. (Map 206)

Starling *Sturnus vulgaris*

Following earlier marked decrease, and extinction in many parts of northern and western Britain (though not in the Scottish isles), increased between about 1830 and 1880 and recolonised most parts of northern England and southern Scotland, also extending west to Cornwall and into western Wales; from that time onwards continued to increase and spread into the Scottish Highlands and many parts of Ireland (A & L). Some expansion of breeding range is still taking place near western coasts of Britain and Ireland, and numbers elsewhere have probably at least been maintained.

Abundant; widely distributed, breeding throughout Britain and Ireland. There is no evidence to show whether the population over the whole of Britain has continued to increase, but it seems unlikely that any decline has occurred. In certain western coastal districts of Britain the breeding distribution is still local and patchy, and the occupation of some localities somewhat irregular. It seems clear, however, that a gradual expansion of range is still going on: for example, in Wales in Carmarthen, Pembroke, Cardigan and Caernarvon, and in Scotland in Kirkcudbright, Ayrshire and Sutherland. Ruttledge (1966) recorded a continued spread of breeding range in parts of western Ireland, including the occupation during or since the 1950's of several new areas in Kerry, Galway, Mayo and Donegal. The causes of the steady expansion of this species and the earlier decrease are not known. (Map 207)

Hawfinch *Coccothraustes coccothraustes*

Possibly only began breeding in England at beginning of 19th century and till about 1850 was apparently confined to south-east England and Midlands; has since spread west to Devon and Wales and north to south and east Scotland (A & L). Only a slight expansion of breeding range has occurred during the past 40 years; numbers fluctuate considerably, perhaps only locally, but long-term trends over country as a whole are not known.

Not scarce, breeding widely but locally in England (absent Cornwall) and very locally in Wales and southern Scotland. Mountfort (1957) discussed the distribution of the Hawfinch and its earlier expansion in Britain in some detail. He believed that the rapid spread in breeding range between approximately 1835 and 1915 had continued, 'though at a much slower pace'. Except that breeding occurred in south-west Devon (at Plymouth) in 1953 and has now been proved in Merioneth (in 1964), no further expansion of breeding range has been recorded; and in southern Scotland, where Baxter and Rintoul (1953) described the species as 'now not uncommon', the few reports of current status suggest that it has since declined.

The Hawfinch is such an elusive and little studied species, and its occupation of many sites apparently so erratic, that few conclusions can be drawn from existing information concerning its longer-term population trends over much of England. Numbers appear to fluctuate more violently than those of most birds. There is some indication that in several parts of the country, notably in the west Midlands, numbers have generally decreased since the early 1950's, or perhaps earlier. Tree-felling in north-east Derby recently eradicated what was, until the early 1960's, a thriving population of about 50 pairs (R. A. Frost *in litt.*). On the other hand, some local populations are known or believed to have increased—at least temporarily—particularly in northern England. The reasons for these local and apparently wider fluctuations, and for the earlier increase, are not known. Only one breeding record is known for Ireland, in

Kildare in 1902; birds were also seen in Leix in 1934, but there has been no suggestion of nesting since. (Map 208)

Greenfinch *Carduelis chloris*

Increasing and spreading in woods of northern Scotland (A & L). Has increased in built up areas and slightly extended its range in parts of western Britain and Ireland.

Numerous; widely distributed, breeding in all parts of Britain and Ireland except Shetland. Little further expansion of breeding range has been noted over the past 25 years apart from a general increase in the Hebrides, including the colonisation of several of the inner islands (Boyd 1958, Evans and Flower 1967), an increase in Cornwall and the colonisation of the Isles of Scilly (Ryves and Quick 1946; Local Reports), and a recent spread to parts of western Mayo and Donegal (Ruttledge 1966). Elsewhere in Britain and Ireland it is widely reported as having become much commoner in urban and suburban areas, both as a breeding bird and in winter. During this century it has colonised the inner suburbs and centre of London, and has considerably increased there in recent years. Similar increases have been noted in several other towns in central and southern England. At least part of the species' recent success in towns is due to the increased amount of food, especially seed and peanuts, now put out for birds in gardens. (Map 209)

Goldfinch *Carduelis carduelis*

Huge decrease everywhere in 19th century, but in 20th century marked increase in England, southern Scotland and Ireland; important factors have been the extensive catching of Goldfinches as cage-birds and then the cessation of this, also the spread or decrease of thistles, and the incidence of hard winters (A & L). Numbers fluctuate, but increase seems to have continued.

Fairly numerous; widely distributed in England (especially in the southern half), Wales and Ireland, and more locally in Scotland north to Perth and Inverness. Since 1940 most reports on the species' local breeding status have referred to increased numbers, and it seems possible that the general expansion noted during the first four decades of the century has continued. It is difficult to be certain of this, or to assess its extent, for year-to-year fluctuations are sometimes marked and there is an absence of numerical data on population size. In recent years, high numbers occurred in 1961—following a big immigration that spring—and relatively low numbers in 1963.

There has evidently been little alteration in the extent of the range. In Scotland, although the species has expanded again since the turn of the century (following an earlier recession), it remains generally scarce north of the border counties. It occasionally nests as far north as Ross, but at one time the range reached Sutherland. In recent years an extension of breeding range has been reported from western Ireland, and the species has colonised the Isles of Scilly. Some expansion into new habitats, such as sheltered upland valleys in western

England and, more widely, surburban gardens and town parks, has also taken place. (Map 210)

Siskin *Carduelis spinus*

Increasing in Irish woods (A & L). Numbers fluctuate erratically, but are apparently gradually increasing, while the species appears to be becoming established in several parts of England and Wales where it was previously absent.

Not scarce; distributed quite widely in north-east Scotland, rather locally elsewhere in that country and in parts of Ireland; has recently bred in several parts of England and north Wales, and may now be established in some areas. Though the scale of its eruptions are less marked than those of the Crossbill *Loxia curvirostra*, the Siskin is another species whose numbers and breeding range fluctuate markedly and erratically. Little is known about long-term changes in Scotland, but it seems probable that it has increased there during this century, both in its strongholds in the north-east (where a noticeable decline is said to have occurred in the late 19th century owing to the activities of bird-catchers) and, especially recently, in the south-west, where it has been helped by afforestation. The introduction of the Scots pine *Pinus sylvestris* into Northern Ireland is said to have led to the Siskin's establishment there in the second half of the 19th century (Deane 1954). In Ireland as a whole the breeding range has expanded during this century, though Ruttledge (1966) noted a serious decline in numbers in recent years.

In England and Wales, however, where the species has always been an extremely erratic breeder, there has been a considerable increase in the number of summering and nesting records over the last 25 years and especially the last ten. Although in part this may be attributable to increased observation, it seems probable that the increase has been an actual one and that it is largely connected with the spread of conifer forests. Since 1942 many counties from Northumberland south to Kent, Hampshire and Devon, and from Caernarvon and Merioneth east to Suffolk, have recorded breeding for the first time. In some parts, such as the New Forest in Hampshire, and in new areas of forest in Devon, East Anglia, Northumberland and north Wales, Siskins are now present annually in summer, and are known or believed to have been breeding for some years. (Map 211)

Linnet *Acanthis cannabina*

Decrease in 19th century, and increase in 20th century in parts of central and southern England and perhaps elsewhere (A & L). Perhaps decreased in northwest Scotland; no satisfactory evidence of marked widespread change elsewhere, though possibly generally decreased as a result of agricultural improvements.

Numerous; widely distributed, breeding in all parts of Britain and Ireland except north-west Scotland (where very local), the Outer Hebrides and Shetland. Except that it seems to have vanished from the Outer Hebrides, has decreased or disappeared from some other west Scottish islands, and has gone again from Shetland which was temporarily colonised for some years from about 1934, no marked changes in the extent of the breeding range are on record. Information is too incomplete to show whether the species is increasing or decreasing over the country as a whole. On balance, however, there have in recent years been more records of locally declining than increasing numbers, most of which have been attributed to loss of habitat, notably of waste land to agriculture and, locally, the eradication of gorse. (Map 212)

Twite *Acanthis flavirostris*

Marked decrease in northern England and southern Scotland with complete disappearance from some areas, for example the Cheviots and Pentland Hills (A & L). Continued contraction of range in Scotland and apparent further decrease in northern England, though with possible resurgence in southern Pennines in last few years; the causes of the fluctuations are not known.

Not scarce; locally distributed in Scotland (chiefly in the Northern Isles, Hebrides and north-west) and Ireland (chiefly near northern and western coasts); also very locally in moorland areas of northern England south to north Stafford. A considerable contraction of range towards the north and west has occurred in Scotland since the beginning of the century. At one time or another the species has been recorded as resident in every Scottish county except Kinross, East and West Lothian and Wigtown (Baxter and Rintoul 1953), but it is now practically unknown as a breeding bird south of the Highlands and seems also to have disappeared from much of north-east Scotland. There is little evidence of any marked changes in status in its strongholds in the north and north-west. In some areas marked short and medium-term fluctuations occur, while on Fair Isle there has been a general decline which became marked after about 1955 (Davis 1965).

In northern England the general picture is of a continued decline and the species has disappeared as a regular breeder from parts of the Lake District, Yorkshire and the Lancashire mosses. In Northumberland there has been no certain breeding on the Cheviots since about 1953. It does, however, still breed as far south as the southern Pennines, and here there has been a recent increase in the number of breeding records, including the rediscovery during 1964–67 of the species in east Cheshire, north Derby and north Stafford. These records almost certainly reflect a genuine increase and do not seem to be merely the result of renewed interest in a little known and much overlooked species. In 1967 a nest was found on an area of salt marsh in north Wales (J. R. Mullins *in litt.*); the only previous Welsh breeding record was in Merioneth in 1905—just a year after the only known breeding in southern England, in Devon in 1904. (Map 213)

Redpoll *Acanthis flamma*

Small but definite increase throughout Britain, especially in northern Scotland where increase is marked (A & L). Marked general increase in England and Wales since about 1950, facilitated by spread of new conifer forests.

Fairly numerous; widely distributed in Britain and Ireland, but scarce or absent in parts of Midlands and southern half of England, and not known to breed at all in Cornwall, Pembroke, Caithness, and the Outer Hebrides and Northern Isles. Most information on status changes comes from central and southern England where Redpoll numbers have evidently fluctuated considerably both in the short and medium term over the last 60–70 years. Though there are some inconsistencies in the records the main fluctuations seem to have been: a marked increase in many lowland counties from about 1900 to 1910, when the chief breeding habitat appears to have been damp woodlands, especially alder and sallow, and also high, thick hawthorn hedges; next a widespread decline, leading to the species' complete disappearance from many lowland areas in the 1920's; and then, from about 1950, another expansion in numbers and range, this time mainly in those districts where extensive areas of conifer forest had been planted.

In Devon, for example, post-war afforestation has allowed the Redpoll to colonise many parts of the county since about 1953; before that only one isolated case of nesting was known. Similar marked increases have been recorded in the new conifer forests of East Anglia and northern England. In Northumberland the recent increase is described as 'spectacular' (Tyneside Bird Club 1967). The Redpoll has probably benefited more than any bird from afforestation in Wales: Condry (1960) noted that it was scarce and local up to the 1920's, but that by the late 1950's it was breeding in young conifer plantations across north and central Wales from sea-level to nearly 2,000 feet.

In many parts of its British range its numbers are irregular and variable. Apart from these short-term fluctuations, there is little information concerning the species' general trends in Scotland and Ireland. Though common in some years, Pennie (1962) did not find that there had been a general increase in the northernmost part of its range, in Sutherland. (Map 214)

Serin *Serinus serinus*

A pair reared at least two young in southern England in May 1967 and it is thought possible that the species may also have nested in one other county (Ferguson-Lees 1968). The Serin has been spreading steadily northwards in Europe over the last 100–150 years and, in addition to having reached the Channel coast of France, now breeds further north than southern England in many places from the Netherlands, Denmark and southern Sweden through northern Germany and Poland to the Baltic States. Further colonisation of Britain seems likely. (Map 215)

Bullfinch *Pyrrhula pyrrhula*

Spreading in woods of northern Scotland and Ireland (A & L). General, widespread and marked increase, especially since about 1955.

Numerous; widely distributed, breeding in every mainland county with the possible exception of Caithness; absent from the Isle of Man, Outer Hebrides and Northern Isles. Even in the absence of much numerical data and any marked alteration in the extent of the breeding range, there can be no doubt that the Bullfinch has increased considerably over a wide area of Britain and Ireland in recent years. Records of an increase are probably more numerous and widespread for this than any other species, and come from practically every county in England as well as several in Wales, Ireland and southernmost Scotland. In the long term at least, the species has also increased and extended its range in Scotland generally, but it is not known whether the whole of that country has been affected by the recent expansion. In Ireland, however, where there has been a gradual spread westwards, the recent general increase has been described as 'tremendous', especially in the southern half of the country (Ruttledge 1966).

Although there are several records of increasing numbers of Bullfinches in many widely scattered parts of England and Wales during the 1940's and early 1950's, the very marked expansion appears not to have begun until about 1955 or a little later. From 1957 onwards there were widespread reports—from eastern Ireland as well as from many urban areas in England—of Bullfinches spreading into new habitats, especially gardens and town parks. In many rural areas, where it had previously been relatively scarce and confined to thick cover, it was increasingly noted in more open habitats, and has since become common in them. Bud-eating increased and in many orchard districts the Bullfinch became a serious pest.

Newton (1967) discussed the recent increase and concluded that an important factor has probably been a change in the habitat tolerance of the species. This behavioural change was perhaps initiated by the decline of the Sparrowhawk *Accipiter nisus*, which, when common, may have deterred the Bullfinch from feeding far from cover. (Map 216)

Crossbill *Loxia curvirostra*

Fluctuating, but on the whole marked increase in numbers of nominate race, mainly due to immigration from the Continent and the recent planting of conifers (A & L). Fluctuations still very marked; basic breeding population currently larger and more widespread in England than in past, but no definite evidence that breeding now occurs more commonly in Britain following invasions, while in Ireland it has become less frequent.

Not scarce; the endemic Scottish race, *L.c. scotica*, is resident in the eastern Highlands; the nominate race breeds regularly in East Anglia and Hampshire, near-annually in several other English counties, mainly in the south-east, but only rarely now in Ireland (see fig. 10). Marked short-term fluctuations, related to food supply, occur in the populations of both races. Little is known about long-term trends in the Scottish Crossbill. Numbers may sometimes be large—for example, hundreds of pairs nested in one part of Speyside in 1936, 1952 and 1958—though they seldom are in any one particular wood in consecutive years (Darling and Boyd 1964).

The numbers and breeding range of the nominate form are, and appear always to have been, highly dependent on the size and frequency of irruptions from the Continent. In years following an invasion, breeding now tends to be

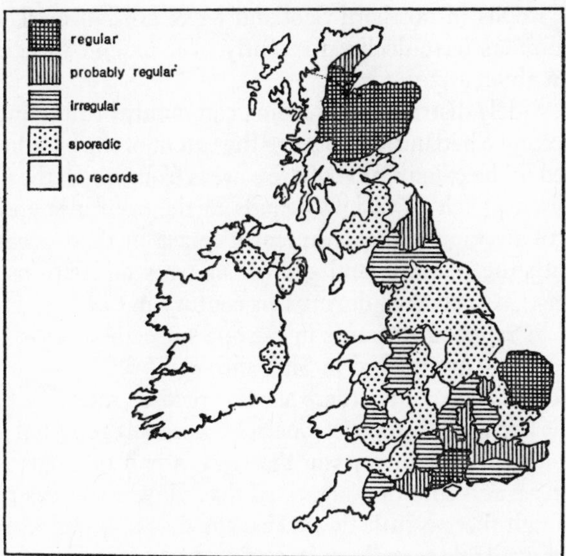

FIG. 10. Apparent breeding status of the Crossbill *Loxia curvirostra* in Britain and Ireland. Shadings indicate the frequency with which breeding occurred in each county during the decade 1957–66: 'sporadic' means that the species bred or probably bred in only one or two of these years; 'irregular' that it bred more often, though probably not annually.

reported from more English counties than in the past, but this may be partly due to increased observation, though possibly also to more habitat being available through the post-war increase in conifer forests. In Ireland, where the species at one time became established in several areas, the frequency of breeding, even in years following sizeable invasions, has become much less since about 1937 (Ruttledge 1966). Sizeable immigrations into Britain occurred in five out of the eleven years between 1956 and 1966, and this increased frequency may partly account for a recent increase in the number of areas in England in which the species is now thought to breed annually. In about 1940 regular breeding was known only in Norfolk and Suffolk, but it now occurs also in Hampshire, probably in Surrey and east Dorset, and possibly in several other southern counties and Northumberland (see fig. 10). Even so, numbers are often very small and it is uncertain whether the species could survive in any of these areas without being periodically reinforced by further immigration. (Map 217)

Parrot Crossbill *Loxia pytyopsittacus*

Following an unprecedented irruption of the species into Britain in autumn 1962, a pair is believed to have nested in Surrey the following April (see Davis 1964).

Chaffinch *Fringilla coelebs*

Spreading in woods in northern Scotland (A & L). No marked changes in range, but numbers have declined recently over much of England, perhaps after a peak in about 1950.

Abundant; widely distributed, breeding commonly in all counties of Britain and Ireland except Shetland. Changes in the extent of the breeding range have been restricted to the colonisation of a few areas from which the Chaffinch was previously absent, such as various islands in the Hebrides and the Isles of Scilly. The colonisation and subsequent increase in these areas is probably connected with the planting and growth of trees and shrubs. Although a general increase has occurred during this century in Orkney, and the species has extended its range northwards in Europe since about 1930, it has shown no sign of becoming established in Shetland.

Over the rest of the country there are few records referring to a change in status until the late 1950's, when the species was widely reported as decreasing, especially in agricultural habitats in the eastern half of England. There the evidence from several counties suggested that a low point was reached about 1960–62. Though there is little doubt that the decrease was real and marked, few figures are available to indicate its timing or extent, or to confirm whether it followed, as is generally believed, an earlier increase. One of the few sets of figures concerns an oakwood population in Surrey which decreased from a peak in 1951 (about twelve territories) to a minimum in 1959 (two territories), then increased again; the pattern over the whole period seemed to indicate a natural fluctuation in the population (Beven 1963). Perhaps one of the best indications of a general decline through the 1950's and early 1960's is provided by the figures for the numbers of nestlings ringed annually under the national ringing scheme. These show that, despite a steady increase in the totals for all species combined, the numbers of nestling Chaffinches ringed fell from a peak of just over 1,000 in 1950 to a little over 300 in each year from 1963 to 1965. Except for a sharp fall (shared, incidentally, by several other species) in 1955, the decline was relatively steady from 1950 to 1963. The reasons for the decline are not known. (Map 218)

Brambling *Fringilla montifringilla*

The species is reported as having bred in northern Scotland on several occasions (see Baxter and Rintoul 1953) and it has summered and possibly bred in at least one recent year. But the only firm published record is of a pair that nested in Sutherland in 1920.

Yellowhammer *Emberiza citrinella*

No evidence of marked widespread change (A & L). Evidence uncertain, but perhaps generally decreased.

Numerous; widely distributed in all British and Irish counties except the Inner Hebrides and Orkney (where local) and the Outer Hebrides and Shetland (where absent). No marked changes in the extent of the range are recorded, though at its northernmost limit in Britain, in Orkney, it has been gradually decreasing in recent years (E. Balfour *in litt.*). In Ireland the species has withdrawn from some west coast islands and from Rathlin Island (Ruttledge 1966). Except for a few reports of local increases—for example, in Pembroke, Brecon and parts of Lancashire—most statements concerning its recent status refer to decreased numbers. In some cases these have been attributed to locally adverse factors, such as the destruction of hedges and increased urbanisation affecting the bird's habitat; and in a few to the introduction of the persistent organochlorine pesticides; but in others the causes are largely unknown. In nearly all the timing and severity of the decrease is in some doubt. There does seem to be general agreement, however, that, in parts of eastern England at least, numbers fell sharply in the late 1950's. In Essex, for example, the decline was clearly very marked around 1959–61 when the species disappeared from some places where it had previously been very common. A partial recovery has since been reported both in Essex and in some other counties where a decline was recorded. The ringing figures (*cf.* Chaffinch *Fringilla coelebs*) do indicate a general decline from 1956 to 1961, though, because the rate of decrease and sample size were smaller than in the Chaffinch (and unknown forms of bias are inherent in the data), its significance is uncertain. (Map 219)

Corn Bunting *Emberiza calandra*

Marked decrease reported in Sussex, Essex, Suffolk, the Clyde and Tay basins, and some Scottish islands, and suspected decreases elsewhere (A & L). Very marked decrease in Ireland, Wales, Scottish islands, west-central and south-west England, with complete disappearance, especially since 1930's, from many areas where it was once common.

Not scarce; widely but irregularly distributed in England and Scotland from Cornwall north to Shetland, generally most common in eastern Britain, but absent from wide areas of south-west England, west Midlands and central Scotland; now almost entirely absent from Wales, and in Ireland confined to a few scattered localities around coasts. This species has undergone a very sharp decline in many western areas of the British Isles, but in eastern Britain it is uncertain whether there has been a general decrease. The information is summarised below by countries.

Ireland. The species was once found in most counties and was common in many coastal areas. But by the early 1950's it had disappeared from nearly all inland and many coastal and island localities. The decline has continued and the Corn Bunting has now gone even from some places in which it was common as recently as 1945. It now seems to be confined to a few isolated coastal areas in Kerry, Mayo, Donegal, Down, Wexford and Waterford.

Scotland. The species has declined steadily during this century in Shetland, Orkney and the Western Isles, and between the 1930's and 1950's it disappeared completely from several islands in each of these areas. The decline appears to be continuing, and in Orkney, for example, the bird has now become very scarce (E. Balfour *in litt.*). A general, but poorly documented, decrease has apparently also affected the Scottish mainland (Baxter and Rintoul 1953, G. Waterston *in litt.*). At least in the east and south, however, the decline does not appear to have been very marked.

Wales. Widely distributed and common in coastal areas at the turn of the century, when described in Anglesey, for example, as one of the most conspicuous breeding birds. Before or during the 1920's it decreased markedly in many places, and by about 1945 it had disappeared completely from almost the whole of Wales. A few pairs persisted in parts of Pembroke until 1949 or a little later, and occasional birds have been seen in that county, Glamorgan and Carmarthen in the last few years. But the only known recent breeding in Wales has been in Flint, where a few pairs nest near to the border with Cheshire.

England. Widespread and general decline in the south-west and in the west Midlands. In the former area the species has disappeared from Devon since about 1945 (though one pair bred in the north in 1957) and from the Isles of Scilly since the 1930's, and decreased markedly in Cornwall (where now mainly restricted to parts of the north coast), especially between about 1934 and 1946. In the west Midlands the distribution has always been irregular, but even where the Corn Bunting was once locally common—for example, in Shropshire and Worcester—numbers declined considerably before about 1940. Since the 1930's the species has ceased to breed in Stafford, and numbers in other counties in the region are now very small. Over the rest of England there is much less evidence of a general decline, though many local fluctuations have been recorded. Some of these have been correlated with changes in agriculture. In the south, for example, the increase in cultivation during the 1939–45 war seems to have triggered off a spread in several counties, including Sussex where it was earlier said to have declined. Other fluctuations, however, are unexplained, and often neighbouring populations seem to fluctuate independently of each other, thus giving rise to conflicting statements about status changes, even within a single county. Over the country as a whole, as well as the clear decrease in south-west England and the west Midlands, recent records tend to refer more often to a decrease than an increase. But, except possibly in the Lake District and some other parts of northern England, it is doubtful whether there has been any marked, general decline.

The reasons for the general and very marked decline of the Corn Bunting in western districts of the British Isles are not known. The species is highly dependent on agriculture, but it seems unlikely that farming changes in these areas have been sufficiently marked to account for the decrease. Instead, as suggested by Evans and Flower (1967), the decline might be correlated with an increase in rainfall, attendant on the climatic amelioration during this century. (Map 220)

Cirl Bunting *Emberiza cirlus*

Possibly colonised southern England only at end of 18th century; some evidence of increase in 20th century in southern England, though range extends less far north than in 19th century (A & L). No longer breeds in Wales or Hereford, and records of occasional nesting in central and northern England have become less frequent; but no evidence of any marked reduction in numbers within main English range.

Scarce; restricted to southernmost counties of England, with main population in south-west and a few pairs north as far as the Malvern Hills (Worcester) and the Chilterns (Oxford, Buckingham, Hertford). Through to the 1930's breeding occurred very locally in many counties in Wales, but this seems to have ceased soon after. In the Isle of Wight it was a relatively common bird until about 1910, but it then declined markedly and has remained very scarce there ever since (J. Stafford *in litt.*). The species has also disappeared from Hereford, but otherwise there have been no other marked changes in the extent of the breeding range. Since about 1950, however, records of sporadic breeding in central and northern England have become less frequent, though pairs did nest in Leicester in 1951 and even as far north as Cumberland in 1955. There is also some indication that on the eastern and northern periphery of the present range, in counties such as Sussex, Kent and Oxford, numbers have declined in recent years. But within the main range, although there have been local decreases due to loss of habitat, and some short-term fluctuations caused probably by severe winters, there is no evidence of any marked change in numbers. (Map 221)

Reed Bunting *Emberiza schoeniclus*

No evidence of marked widespread change (A & L). Some increase in Scottish isles, and probably a general increase in many parts of Britain owing to recent expansion into drier breeding habitats where previously absent.

Numerous; widely distributed, breeding in all counties of Britain and Ireland. Baxter and Rintoul (1953) believed that a general increase had occurred in Scotland, and the recent evidence suggests that the species is at least expanding in the Scottish isles. It has recently colonised two islands and increased on others in the Inner Hebrides, has steadily increased in Orkney, and since about 1949 has spread to Shetland where one or two pairs nest regularly in the extreme south. Although no figures are available, there is general agreement that numbers have increased in many parts of Britain and

Ireland in recent years. This may have been brought about by an expansion of the ecological range of the species, as pointed out by Kent (1964). In many areas Reed Buntings are now found breeding in dry habitats, often long distances from surface water, which once seemed to form an essential part of their habitat requirements. As well as Kent's survey in Nottingham, which showed that a substantial proportion of Reed Buntings were nesting in dry habitats, this apparently recent extension in habitat tolerance has been recorded in many southern counties and in northern England and south-west Scotland. A considerable variety of habitats is now occupied. Less widespread, and probably involving relatively few individuals, has been an increasing tendency to come into urban areas in winter to feed in gardens and on bird-tables. (Map 222)

Snow Bunting *Plectrophenax nivalis*

Numbers always very small, but evidence suggests that breeding occurred more frequently and over a wider area of northern Scotland before 1914 than it has done since.

Very scarce; breeding confined to the Cairngorms, where perhaps not annual, and in any case not more than three known pairs in any recent year. Nethersole–Thompson (1966) discussed the whole history of the Snow Bunting as a Scottish breeding bird, and correlated the long and short-term fluctuations in its numbers with climatic changes. Before about 1914 the species evidently bred more frequently and widely in Scotland than in the milder period since. From about 1886 to 1913 nesting was proved on hills in Sutherland, Ross and Perth, on Ben Nevis and in the Cairngorms, as well as once, in 1901, on St. Kilda. During the last 30 years, however, apart from the small Cairngorms population, the only confirmed breeding record has been on Ben Nevis, where a brood was seen in 1954. In the same period the Cairngorms population has varied from only a few unmated males in some years up to three known pairs and several unmated males in others. (Map 223)

House Sparrow *Passer domesticus*

Huge increase in Scotland and Ireland; in England the bulk of a similar increase probably occurred before 19th century; decrease in towns in 20th century owing to disappearance of the horse (A & L). No evidence of marked widespread change, but total numbers have probably further increased owing to the growth of suburbs.

Abundant; widely distributed, breeding near human habitations in nearly all parts of Britain and Ireland, though scarce and local in some upland and western coastal areas. By 1940 or earlier the species had already reached most of the remoter parts of the British Isles in which it is now found. Some further expansion has recently been recorded in Sutherland and in some coastal and upland areas in west Wales. On the other hand, in the extreme west of Ireland the species is believed to be undergoing a general decline which began before

1950. Decreases have been recorded on a number of islands around the coasts of Britain and Ireland, and these have usually been correlated with decreases in human population; on some islands completely evacuated by man the House Sparrow has quickly disappeared also. Other local changes in House Sparrow populations can usually be linked with changes in farming practice, such as an increase or decrease in poultry farming (Summers-Smith 1963). One steady and continuing decrease which is unexplained, however, is that reported from central London (Cramp and Tomlins 1966). So far as is known, there has been no comparable decline in suburban areas, in which, as shown by Summers-Smith, the greatest House Sparrow densities are found. Indeed, as Summers-Smith pointed out, the continuing steady growth of suburban Britain must benefit the species considerably and lead to a rise in total numbers.

(Map 224)

Tree Sparrow *Passer montanus*

Colonies are local and fluctuate markedly for unknown reasons (A & L). General increase in numbers since about 1958, with explosive range expansion during 1961–66, when breeding colonies established in many parts of Scotland, Ireland and Wales from which the species had been absent for up to 25 years or had never previously been known to breed.

Fairly numerous; distributed widely in England (but absent from Cornwall, Devon, Dorset and much of Hampshire and Sussex), and much more locally in Scotland and Wales, while in Ireland it breeds locally but increasingly, mainly in coastal counties. Since about 1958 there has been a remarkable expansion in the numbers and range of this species in the British Isles. The cause of the increase is not known, but in many areas, and perhaps over Britain and Ireland as a whole, it followed an earlier phase of decrease which lasted through the greater part of the first half of this century; this had led to the complete disappearance of the species from many parts of Scotland, Ireland and Wales, and a few areas in south-west England.

In England, east Wales and southern Scotland, the recent increase is commented upon in many county bird reports and other regional publications. The records of several closely studied nest-box populations confirm that numbers increased enormously from about 1961 to 1964. Beginning in 1961, there was also a remarkable, explosive increase in range—into areas in which Tree Sparrows had never previously been known to nest, as well as into others from which it had been absent for up to 25 years or more. Counties and other areas in Britain colonised or recolonised during 1961–67 included the Isles of Scilly, Glamorgan, Carmarthen, Pembroke, Anglesey, Kinross, Aberdeen, Orkney, Fair Isle, Shetland, and St. Kilda and some other Hebridean islands. In Ireland the increase since 1961 has been impressive. Though never widespread or common, the species had by the 1950's been reduced to the status of a sporadic breeder, and there was no evidence of nesting anywhere in Ireland in 1959 or 1960. In 1961, however, Tree Sparrows bred in three coastal localities (in Mayo, Derry and Donegal); in 1962 small colonies were found in

Dublin and Down; in 1963 five more counties were occupied; and by 1964 breeding was known in 13 counties (Ruttledge 1966). The increase and spread in Ireland has continued since then, and small colonies are now widespread, though they are still confined mainly to coastal counties. (Map 225)

SUMMARY OF CHANGES

Between 1800 and 1967—the period covered by this survey—216 species are known to have bred in Britain or Ireland on at least one occasion. This total includes the four introduced and one re-introduced species admitted to the *Check-list of the Birds of Great Britain and Ireland* (1952). On the other hand, it excludes such introduced species as the Mandarin Duck *Aix galericulata* and Egyptian Goose *Alopochen aegyptiacus* which were omitted from that list, and the Ruddy Duck *Oxyura jamaicensis* which has only recently established feral breeding populations. It also excludes some species which have almost certainly bred during the period, but for which the evidence falls short of published proof.

Occasional and sporadic breeders

Of the 216 species which have nested since 1800, 19 can be regarded as never (or not yet) established as regular breeding birds in Britain or Ireland during the period. These are listed in table 8. The great majority of them have been found nesting here on fewer than five occasions, and most only once or twice. A few, such as the Hoopoe *Upupa epops*, Golden Oriole *Oriolus oriolus* and Scaup *Aythya marila*, have nested rather more frequently, though none of them appears to have succeeded in establishing a regular breeding population. Two species, the Whooper Swan *Cygnus cygnus* and Goshawk *Accipiter gentilis*, bred regularly before 1800; the Goshawk may also have done so in recent years, but the evidence and the origin of the birds are uncertain and it seems best to include this bird here. On the other hand, some recent colonists—the Wood Sandpiper *Tringa glareola*, Redwing *Turdus iliacus* and Firecrest *Regulus ignicapillus*—have been placed, perhaps optimistically, among the regular breeders. Time will tell whether this is justified or not.

Of the 19 exceptional breeders listed in table 8, five are only known to have bred in the period before 1940. They include two species which have mainly southerly breeding ranges in Eurasia, these being the irruptive Pallas's Sandgrouse *Syrrhaptes paradoxus* (bred 1888, 1889) and Baillon's Crake *Porzana pusilla* (occasionally to 1889), while the other three—the Goldeneye *Bucephala clangula* (reputed 1931–2), Long-tailed Duck *Clangula hyemalis* (1911) and Brambling *Fringilla montifringilla* (1920)—have mainly northerly breeding ranges. Seven species in table 8 have been recorded breeding only since 1940, each only in one year. Three of these—the Black-winged Stilt *Himantopus himantopus* (1945), Bee-eater *Merops apiaster* (1955) and

Moustached Warbler *Acrocephalus melanopogon* (1946)—have predominantly southerly ranges, while the Snowy Owl *Nyctea scandiaca* (1967) and Fieldfare *Turdus pilaris* (1967) are chiefly northerly breeders. The last two of these seven post-1940 species—the Gull-billed Tern *Gelochelidon nilotica* (1950) and Serin *Serinus serinus* (1967)—breed regularly at British latitudes on the Continent. Both the Fieldfare and the Serin are known to have been expanding their ranges in Europe in recent years, and both may be about to

Table 8. Species which bred in Britain and Ireland during 1800–1967 without becoming firmly established

Species lacking definite or published proof of breeding are omitted except Goldeneye for which the 1931–2 records are now doubted.

	Breeding recorded	
	Before 1940	After 1940
Scaup *Aythya marila*	×	×
Goldeneye *Bucephala clangula*	× ?	
Long-tailed Duck *Clangula hyemalis*	×	
Whooper Swan *Cygnus cygnus*	×	×
Baillon's Crake *Porzana pusilla*	×	
Green Sandpiper *Tringa ochropus*	×	×
Temminck's Stint *Calidris temminckii*	×	×
Black-winged Stilt *Himantopus himantopus*		×
Goshawk *Accipiter gentilis*	×	×
Gull-billed Tern *Gelochelidon nilotica*		×
Pallas's Sandgrouse *Syrrhaptes paradoxus*	×	
Snowy Owl *Nyctea scandiaca*		×
Bee-eater *Merops apiaster*		×
Hoopoe *Upupa epops*	×	×
Golden Oriole *Oriolus oriolus*	×	×
Fieldfare *Turdus pilaris*		×
Moustached Warbler *Acrocephalus melanopogon*		×
Serin *Serinus serinus*		×
Brambling *Fringilla montifringilla*	×	

become established here. The seven remaining of the 19 species in table 8 have been recorded nesting in Britain both before and after 1940. No clear pattern emerges from a comparison of the frequency of breeding of the four northerly species and the two southerly ones. (The seventh, the Goshawk, is widely distributed in Europe.)

Extinctions and colonisations

Omitting these 19 exceptional breeders, there remains a total of 197 species that can be regarded as having bred regularly in Britain or Ireland at some time since 1800. No less than 27 of these have either become established here during this period or, conversely, have ceased to breed altogether or for a considerable number of years. Species whose status has altered thus drastically are listed in table 9. One striking point which emerges from this tabulation is that in recent

Table 9. Extinctions and colonisations among breeding birds in Britain and Ireland during 1800–1967

In many cases the dates are very approximate. Those in the second column ignore occasional nesting and aim to show when the species became firmly established.

	Extinct as breeding species	Recolonised or first colonised (*introduced)
FORMER BREEDERS NOW ABSENT		
Great Auk *Pinguinus impennis*	1812	
Great Bustard *Otis tarda*	1832	
White-tailed Eagle *Haliaeetus albicilla*	1916	
Kentish Plover *Charadrius alexandrinus*	1956	
FORMER BREEDERS NOW SPORADIC		
Black Tern *Chlidonias niger*	1858	sporadic
Spotted Crake *Porzana porzana*	1900	sporadic
FORMER BREEDERS NOW RECOLONISED		
Avocet *Recurvirostra avosetta*	1844	1946
Black-tailed Godwit *Limosa limosa*	1847	1952
Savi's Warbler *Locustella luscinioides*	1855	1960
Bittern *Botaurus stellaris*	1868	1910
Ruff *Philomachus pugnax*	1871	1963
Osprey *Pandion haliaetus*	1903	1954
FIRST COLONISED ONLY SINCE 1800		
Tufted Duck *Aythya fuligula*		1830
Wigeon *Anas penelope*		1834
Capercaillie *Tetrao urogallus*		1837*
Gadwall *Anas strepera*		1850*
Pintail *Anas acuta*		1869
Goosander *Mergus merganser*		1871
Little Owl *Athene noctua*		1874*
Black-necked Grebe *Podiceps nigricollis*		1904
Slavonian Grebe *Podiceps auritus*		1908
Black Redstart *Phoenicurus ochruros*		1939
Little Ringed Plover *Charadrius dubius*		1944
Redwing *Turdus iliacus*		1953
Collared Dove *Streptopelia decaocto*		1955
Wood Sandpiper *Tringa glareola*		1959
Firecrest *Regulus ignicapillus*		1961

years gains have far outnumbered losses: since 1940 only one species has ceased to breed, while ten have become established or re-established. Indeed, there are currently more species known to be breeding in Britain and Ireland than at any other time since 1800. Regular breeders now total 190, while in most recent years the Spotted Crake *Porzana porzana* has also nested, as have an average of about four of the sporadic breeders named in table 8. In 1967 the total number of breeding species probably topped 200.

Two factors are probably responsible for this apparently satisfactory state of affairs. First, there has been the preservation as bird reserves of the few remaining areas of important coastal and inland marshes and other wetland habitats in East Anglia and south-east England. This has enabled some rare species to survive or to become firmly re-established following what might otherwise have been only temporary recolonisations. Most of the British populations of the six re-established species listed in table 9 nest on bird reserves. Some other very scarce species, such as the Marsh Harrier *Circus aeruginosus*, are also mainly confined to such reserves at the present time.

Second, it seems reasonable to suppose that the total number of species found breeding in any year has also depended on the ability and number of active ornithologists in the field, and on their willingness to impart information on rare species. Undoubtedly there are more observers today than ever before and more local and regional bird reports in which they can publish their observations. Hence the chances of a rare bird breeding unnoticed or unrecorded are now smaller than they were, especially in the cases of inconspicuous species or those which nest in remote and hitherto little watched regions. Thus it seems possible that such breeding birds as the Redwing and Wood Sandpiper in Scotland or the Savi's Warbler *Locustella luscinioides* and Firecrest in southern England may at times have been overlooked in the past.

Yet if the total number of species now known to be breeding in Britain and Ireland is higher than at any other time since 1800, it should be added that the populations of a number of species are extremely low or else restricted to a very few localities. Thus, with the marked exception of the Collared Dove *Streptopelia decaocto* and the lesser one of the Little Ringed Plover *Charadrius dubius*, all the species listed in table 9 as having colonised or recolonised Britain and Ireland in the 20th century have breeding populations of under 100 pairs. Perhaps, however, the fact that only one species—the Kentish Plover *C. alexandrinus*—has become extinct as a British breeder during the last 50 years is sufficient encouragement for us to believe that no more than this are likely to cease breeding in the next 50 years.

Changes in the avifauna as a whole

The chief aim of the species accounts in this book has been to document recent changes in status among breeding birds in Britain and Ireland. For completeness, however, these recent changes (that is, since about 1940) were related to previous fluctuations in each species, usually as recorded by Alexander and Lack (1944). Table 10 is an attempt to summarise for both the earlier and the recent periods (1800–1940 and 1940–1967) the marked changes in status that have been recorded. It takes into account all species that are known to have bred in either of the two periods.

The analysis is necessarily crude and oversimplified, and in comparing the figures several points should be borne in mind. First, of course, is the fact that the two parts of the table span very different lengths of time. Therefore, although short-term fluctuations—for example, ones due to severe winters—have been ignored as far as possible, it is likely that there are more instances of

Table 10. Status changes among different groups of British and Irish breeding birds during 1800–1940 and 1940–1967

'Marked fluctuation' during the 1800–1940 period refers to a decrease followed by a later increase, but during the 1940–1967 period it refers to an increase followed by a later decrease (see also text). 'Seabirds' comprise the petrels, shearwaters, gannets, cormorants, gulls, terns and auks; 'Wildfowl' are confined to the ducks, geese and swans; 'Birds of prey' also include the owls; 'Passerines' also include the near-passerine groups of cuckoos, nightjars, swifts, kingfishers, bee-eaters, hoopoes and woodpeckers; and 'Others' comprise the divers, grebes, herons, game-birds, rails, bustards, sandgrouse and pigeons.

	Increase	Decrease	Marked fluctuation	No marked change	Introduced	Sporadic
1800–1940						
Seabirds	6	6	6	8	0	0
Wildfowl	13	1	0	2	1	4
Waders	3	9	5	2	0	2
Birds of prey	0	11	3	4	1	1
Passerines	12	13	12	48	0	3
Others	7	7	3	6	3	2
TOTALS	41	47	29	70	5	12
1940–1967						
Seabirds	13	5	1	5	0	2
Wildfowl	7	0	4	5	1	2
Waders	7	8	0	5	0	4
Birds of prey	4	4	5	4	1	2
Passerines	22	15	8	42	0	6
Others	7	5	0	10	3	1
TOTALS	60	37	18	71	5	17

these remaining in the 1940–1967 section of the table than in the other. This is particularly so in the case of the 'Marked fluctuation' column, where a change from a marked increase to a decrease (or, in some cases, a probable decrease) has occurred in the space of the 28-year period, usually in the early 1950's. There were sufficient such changes to justify the inclusion of this column, though it must be added that in some cases it is still uncertain whether the very recent reversal of a previous increase represents a genuine switch in a long-term trend or merely indicates a temporary fluctuation.

Second, as noted earlier, the amount of information available on a species is often in inverse proportion to that species' abundance. Evidence of marked change is therefore biased towards the rarer species, and many of the records of increase or decrease in table 10 refer, in fact, to changes among very small populations. As pointed out earlier, changes among common birds which can be inferred to have taken place owing to land-use changes have been omitted, unless there is direct evidence to show that a species has decreased or increased.

Third, though purely local changes have been ignored so far as possible, it has sometimes been difficult to distinguish between a local and a widespread change. Further, records of increase or decrease in either section of table 10 can refer to one or more of several different effects. For example, an increased species can be one that has become established or re-established here, or one that has expanded its range either geographically or ecologically, or one that has increased its numbers within its existing range.

Fourth, the groupings of species are necessarily rather arbitrary and broad. For convenience they follow those adopted by Alexander and Lack.

Despite these several qualifications, the general picture that emerges from table 10 is not without interest. It is perhaps rather surprising to find that, omitting the introduced and sporadic species, no less than 115 out of 186 regular breeding birds in the recent period have shown noticeable changes in status in the course of only 28 years. During this same time several of the remaining 71 species have had local or temporary fluctuations and the status of some of the five introduced breeders, such as the Little Owl *Athene noctua* and Canada Goose *Branta canadensis*, has also changed markedly. The first half of the table indicates that in the earlier period, 1800–1940, significant status changes occurred in a very similar proportion of the avifauna: 117 out of 187 regular breeding species. A direct comparison is probably invalid, however, since status changes are more likely to have gone unrecorded then, especially among the passerines. It should be made clear that 181 regular species are common to both periods, that the 187 in the earlier period omits the five post-1940 colonists listed in table 9 and that the 183 in the recent period omits the six pre-1940 losses listed there. (Increases known to have occurred amongst certain woodland species in Scotland, following reafforestation in the 19th and early 20th centuries, have been omitted here: if included, however, as was done by Alexander and Lack in their analysis, a further 16 species may be added to those with a marked change in status during the 1800–1940 period.)

Table 10 also shows that, while decreases and increases are about balanced in the earlier period, there is a preponderance of increases in the recent one. This is not entirely unexpected since the latter total includes the nine species, already mentioned, which have colonised or recolonised Britain or Ireland since 1940. Also, over the last ten to 15 years the number of species showing a decreasing trend has become larger ('Marked fluctuation' column), so that currently the numbers of species that are decreasing roughly balance those that are increasing.

Nevertheless, even though the total gains and losses in each period are more or less balanced, there is a great deal of variation from one group of birds to another. The main trends shown by each group are briefly discussed below.

Seabirds (Procellariiformes, Pelecaniformes, and Laridae and Alcidae of Charadriiformes). Most species have tended to increase in the 20th century and many are continuing to do so. The few exceptions include the Little Tern *Sterna albifrons*, now the scarcest of all our seabirds, whose nesting beaches have become increasingly disturbed by man, and also the southern populations of the three most common auks. Various reasons have been put forward to account for the decline of the Razorbill *Alca torda*, Guillemot *Uria aalge* and Puffin *Fratercula artica* in south-west Britain and Ireland, but it is by no means certain what has been the chief factor involved. Among the gulls and skuas, the only species which is not certainly known to have increased in recent years is the Common Gull *Larus canus*, though even it may be spreading, judging from recent breeding records in Durham, Yorkshire, Nottinghamshire and Norfolk in 1965–67. Increases among the larger gulls, notably the Great Black-backed Gull *L. marinus* and the Herring Gull *L. argentatus*, have been spectacular, not merely here but also elsewhere in their breeding ranges. Other species to have shown considerable increases include the Shag *Phalacrocorax aristotelis* and Gannet *Sula bassana*, while the increase and spread of the Fulmar *Fulmarus glacialis* has been almost the most dramatic of any species. Many of the changes appear to have been due in one way or another to man's activities: in the cases of the larger gulls, and the Fulmar, probably to the provision of additional sources of food; in the case of the Gannet, and perhaps some other species, to the relaxation of persecution. On the other hand, in the cases of marked changes among some other seabirds human factors do not seem to have played a major role, and the primary causes are often not known.

Wildfowl (Anseriformes). This is another group in which striking increases have occurred. Especially in the earlier of the two periods, when only one species—the Greylag Goose *Anser anser*—markedly decreased, increases among the Anatidae have easily outnumbered decreases. No less than five species of duck are believed to have colonised Britain and Ireland in the 19th century (see table 9), and three of these, together with four others, are probably still increasing at the present time. On the other hand, earlier increases among three shallow-water breeding species—the Garganey *Anas querquedula*, Shoveler *A. clypeata* and Pochard *Aythya ferina*—appear to have slowed up or been reversed since about 1950, at least in some areas. The evidence is hard to evaluate, but, certainly locally, loss of habitat through drainage has had an effect. Despite this, many species of wildfowl must have benefited from the greatly increased acreage of inland fresh water in southern England in the form of flooded gravel pits and new reservoirs. The latter particularly afford safe refuges in winter, and both gravel pits and reservoirs have enabled the Tufted Duck *Aythya fuligula* to increase its breeding numbers. Human protection has been important in the cases of the increase of the coastal Eider *Somateria mollissima* and Shelduck *Tadorna tadorna*.

Waders (Charadriiformes excluding Laridae and Alcidae). In the earlier period there were clearly more losses than gains among the waders. Loss of habitat through drainage was an important adverse factor among marsh and fenland species. Today the effects of drainage are more insidious: the scale is smaller, but the gradual eradication of water meadows and small inland marshes is slowly leading to the disappearance of such species as the Snipe *Gallinago gallinago* from many inland counties in lowland Britain. In the 1940–1967 period, however, status changes among the regularly breeding waders are about equally divided between decreases and increases. Human activities have evidently been important in the cases of some of these changes. The Avocet *Recurvirostra avosetta*, for example, has clearly benefited from protection, while the growth of the gravel industry enabled the Little Ringed Plover to colonise Britain and become established here. In contrast, the disappearance of the Kentish Plover as a British breeding species and the decrease of the Ringed Plover *Charadrius hiaticula* in many areas have been due to the development of the coast, especially for the holiday trade. Some other changes are less easily explained. Thus the cause of the recent colonisation of northern Scotland by a small number of Wood Sandpipers is not known. Nor is that of the marked increase and expansion into new habitats of both the Curlew *Numenius arquata* and the Oystercatcher *Haematopus ostralegus*.

Birds of prey and owls (Falconiformes and Strigiformes). The proportion of species to show a decrease in the 1800–1940 period was much higher in this group than in any other. This was due almost entirely to the extensive destruction of birds of prey, especially in the 19th century. In the 1940–1967 period species showing a noticeable change in status are almost equally divided between an increase (Red Kite *Milvus milvus*, Hen Harrier *Circus cyaneus*, Osprey *Pandion haliaetus* and Tawny Owl *Strix aluco*), a decrease (Merlin *Falco columbarius*, Kestrel *F. tinnunculus*, Barn Owl *Tyto alba* and Long-eared Owl *Asio otus*) and an increase to about the early 1950's followed by a sharp decline (Buzzard *Buteo buteo*, Sparrowhawk *Accipiter nisus*, Marsh Harrier, Montagu's Harrier *Circus pygargus* and Peregrine *Falco peregrinus*). The causes of many of these fluctuations are not known. In the case of the Buzzard a noticeable decrease was correlated with the myxomatosis epidemic among Rabbits *Oryctolagus cuniculus*, while in the Peregrine and Sparrowhawk the much more marked declines coincided with, and were almost certainly caused by, the introduction of certain organochlorine insecticides.

Passerines and near-passerines (Passeriformes, Cuculiformes, Caprimulgiformes, Apodiformes, Coraciiformes and Piciformes). This is by far the largest grouping, in terms of both numbers of species and numbers of individual birds involved. Because it includes nearly all the commonest land-birds, it has, for the reasons stated earlier, a relatively high proportion of species for which there is no evidence of any noticeable long-term change in status. Thus in the 1800–1940 period no marked changes were noted for 48 out of the 85 regular breeding species, and in the recent period for 42 out of the 87. Several instances of increase or decrease are found among scarce species with restricted and comparatively easily studied populations. Severe declines causing a marked contraction of range among widespread species have been rare, though the few that have occurred have sometimes been very marked: the decline of the Red-backed Shrike *Lanius collurio* and Wryneck *Jynx torquilla* affected most of England and that of the Corn Bunting *Emberiza calandra* much of western Britain and Ireland, while the decrease of the Woodlark *Lullula arborea* in southern England was sudden and severe from about 1953 onwards. In most cases the causes of these fluctuations are not known. Recent declines have also been recorded among some more widespread birds, such as the Cuckoo *Cuculus canorus* and Nightjar *Caprimulgus europaeus*, though without there being any major alteration in breeding range. Again, some species have decreased in some parts of the country, but not necessarily in others; in southern England the recent decreases of three closely related species—the Wheatear *Oenanthe oenanthe*, Stonechat *Saxicola torquata* and Whinchat *S. rubetra*—may be connected with the loss of wasteland and heathland, though there are probably other causes as well.

Instances of increase among passerines and near-passerines have rarely been spectacular in terms of range extensions. The most marked examples in recent years have been recolonisation by the Tree Sparrow *Passer montanus* of parts of western Britain and Ireland and, on a much smaller scale, the steady northward push into Scotland of the Green Woodpecker *Picus viridis* and the rather erratic colonisation of parts of England and Wales by the Siskin *Carduelis spinus*. The Siskin is only one of several species of finch which in recent years—in most cases in the last ten to 15—have expanded into new habitats (see Newton 1967).

The causes of many of the fluctuations among passerine and near-passerine species are not known. In the cases of summer visitors to Britain the causes of a decrease may, of course, lie outside this country. In this connection it is of interest to note that apart from the newly established Firecrest and Savi's Warbler none of the 22 species that increased during the 1940–1967 period are summer visitors to Britain; on the other hand, summer visitors form about half the decreases.

Others (Gaviiformes, Podicipediformes, Ciconiiformes, Galliformes, Gruiformes and Columbiformes). Included in this grouping are the divers, grebes, herons, game-birds, rails and pigeons. Human activities have played a large part in the increases of the Great Crested Grebe *Podiceps cristatus* (mainly through the provision of such suitable habitats as gravel pits and reservoirs) and the Woodpigeon *Columba palumbus* (mainly through the development of agriculture). Weather, particularly hard winters, is known to affect the numbers of the two breeding herons—the Heron *Ardea cinerea* and the Bittern *Botaurus stellaris*. The causes of fluctuations among some other species in this group are not known. Though that most spectacular of all invaders—the Collared Dove—clearly found a vacant niche for itself once it arrived here, the cause of its original spread is still a mystery.

BIBLIOGRAPHY

To save space in view of the large number of references cited in this survey, the following bibliography is given in an abbreviated form, with titles of papers and articles omitted.

ADAMS, M. C. (1966): Brit. Birds, 59: 240–246.
ALEXANDER, W. B. (1945–46): Ibis, 87: 512–550; 88: 1–24, 271–286, 427–444.
ALEXANDER, W. B., and LACK, D. (1944): Brit. Birds, 38: 42–45, 62–69, 82–88.
ALMOND, W. E. (1960): Rep. Cornwall Bird-Watching & Pres. Soc., 29: 58–66.
ANDREW, D. G., and SANDEMAN, G. L. (1953): Scot. Nat., 65: 157–166.
ANON. (1965): Bird Notes, 31: 403.
ANON. (1966): Rep. Netherlands State Inst. for Nature Conservation Res., 1965: 61.
ASH, J. S. (1960): Brit. Birds, 53: 285–300.
ATKINSON, R., and AINSLIE, J. A. (1940): Brit. Birds, 34: 50–55.
ATKINSON-WILLES, G. L. (ed.) (1963): Wildfowl in Great Britain (London).
ATKINSON-WILLES, G. L., and FRITH, J. C. (1965): Rep. Wildfowl Trust, 16: 21–29.
AXELL, H. E. (1956): Brit. Birds, 49: 193–212.
AXELL, H. E. (1964): Bird Notes, 31: 95–98.
AXELL, H. E. (1966): Brit. Birds, 59: 513–543.
BAGENAL, T. B., and BAIRD, D. E. (1959): Bird Study, 6: 153–179.
BALFOUR, E. (1963): Bird Notes, 30: 215–216.
BANNERMAN, D. A. (1953–63): The Birds of the British Isles (Edinburgh and London).
BARNES, J. A. G. (1952): Brit. Birds, 45: 3–17.
BARNES, J. A. G. (1961): Bird Study, 8: 127–147.
BARRETT, J. H. (1959): Field Studies, 1: 1–16.
BARRETT, J. H., and HARRIS, M. P. (1965): Brit. Birds, 58: 201–203.
BAXTER, E. V., and RINTOUL, L. J. (1953): The Birds of Scotland (Edinburgh).
BAYES, J. C., DAWSON, M. J., JOENSEN, A. H., and POTTS, G. R. (1964): Dansk. Orn. Foren. Tidsskr., 58: 36–41.
BELL, T. H. (1962): The Birds of Cheshire (Altrincham).
BERRY, J. (1939): The Status and Distribution of Wild Geese and Wild Duck in Scotland (Cambridge).
BEVEN, G. (1963): Brit. Birds, 56: 307–323.
BEVERTON, R. J. H., and LEE, A. J. (1965): In: The Biological Significance of Climatic Changes in Britain, ed. C. G. Johnson and L. P. Smith (London and New York).
BLAKER, G. B. (1934): The Barn Owl in England and Wales (Roy. Soc. Prot. Birds).
BLATHWAYT, F. L. (1934): Proc. Dorset Nat. Hist. Fld. Cl., 55: 165–209.
BOASE, H. (1962): Birds of Angus (private publ.).
BOYD, A. W. (1936): Brit. Birds, 30: 98–116.
BOYD, H. J., and OGILVIE, M. A. (1964): Rep. Wildfowl Trust, 15: 37–40.
BOYD, J. M. (1958): Brit. Birds, 52: 41–56, 103–118.
BOYD, J. M. (1961): J. Anim. Ecol., 30: 117–136.
BRAAKSMA, S. (1960): Ardea, 48: 65–90.
BROWN, L. (1955): Eagles (London).

BROWN, L. H. and WATSON, A. (1964): Ibis, 106: 78–100.
BROWN, P. E. (1957): Brit. Birds, 50: 149.
BROWN, P. E., and WATERSTON, G. (1962): The Return of the Osprey (London).
BURTON, J. F. (1956): Bird Study, 3: 42–73.
BURTON, J. F. (1957): Bird Study, 4: 50–52.
BUXTON, E. J. M. (1961): Bird Study, 8: 194–209.
CABOT, D. B. (1962): Irish Nat. J., 14: 59–61.
CABOT, D. B. (1963): Irish Nat. J., 14: 113–115.
CABOT, D. B. (1965): Irish Nat. J., 15: 95–100.
CAMPBELL, B. (1954–55): Bird Study, 1: 81–101; 2: 24–32, 179–191.
CAMPBELL, B. (1960): Bird Study, 7: 208–223.
CAMPBELL, B. (1965): Bird Study, 12: 305–318.
CAMPBELL, J. W. (1957): Brit. Birds, 50: 143–146.
CHISLETT, R. (1952): Yorkshire Birds (London and Hull).
CLARK, J., and RODD, F. R. (1906): Zool., 10: 242–252, 295–306, 335–346.
CLARKE, W. G. (1925): In Breckland Wilds (London).
COHEN, E. (1962): The Birds of Hampshire and the Isle of Wight (Edinburgh and London).
CONDRY, W. M. (1955): Nature in Wales, 1: 25–27.
CONDRY, W. (1960): Q. Jl. For., 44: 357–362.
COULSON, J. C. (1963): Bird Study, 10: 147–179.
CRAMP, S. (1963): Brit. Birds, 56: 124–138.
CRAMP, S., and TOMLINS, A. D. (1966): Brit. Birds, 59: 209–233.
CURRY-LINDAHL, K. (1959): Sveriges Natur Årsbok, 1959: 87–108.
CURRY-LINDAHL, K. (1959–63): Vår Fåglar i Norden (Stockholm).
CURRY-LINDAHL, K. (1961): Bijdragen tot de Dierkunde, 31: 27–44.
CUTHBERTSON, E. L., FOGGITT, G. T., and TYLER, G. E. (1954): Brit. Birds, 47: 204–205.
DARE, P. J. (1958): Devon Birds, 11: 22–32.
DARE, P. J. (1966): Fishery Investigations, ser. 2, 25, 5: 1–69.
DARLING, F. F., and BOYD, J. M. (1964): The Highlands and Islands (London).
DAVIS, P. E. (1954): A List of the Birds of Lundy (Lundy Field Soc.).
DAVIS, P. E. (1964): Brit. Birds, 57: 477–501.
DAVIS, P. E. (1965): 'A list of the birds of Fair Isle' in Fair Isle and its Birds, by K. Williamson (Edinburgh and London).
DAVIS, T. A. W. (1958): Bird Study, 5: 191–215.
DEANE, C. D. (1954): Bull. Belfast Mus. & Art Gallery, 1: 120–193.
DEANE, C. D. (1962): Brit. Birds, 55: 272–274.
des FORGES, G., and HARBER, D. D. (1963): A Guide to the Birds of Sussex (Edinburgh and London).
DICKENS, R. F. (1964): Brit. Birds, 57: 209–210.
DOBBS, A. (1964): Brit. Birds, 57: 360–364.
DOBINSON, H. M., and RICHARDS, A. J. (1964): Brit. Birds, 57: 373–434.
DUFFEY, E. (1955): Scot. Nat., 67: 40–51.
DURANGO, S. (1950): Fauna och Flora, 46: 49–78.
EASY, G. M. S. (1964): Rep. Cambridge Bird Club, 37: 39–42.
EGGELING, W. J. (1955): Scot. Nat., 67: 70–89.
EGGELING, W. J. (1960): The Isle of May (Edinburgh and London).
ELTRINGHAM, S. K. (1963): Bird Study, 10: 10–28.
ELKINS, N. (1965): The Birds of the Isle of Lewis, 1963–65 (private publ.).
ELLICOTT, P. W. C., and MADGE, S. G. (1957): Devon Birds, 10: 34–38.
EVANS, P. R. (1964): Naturalist, 890: 93–98.
EVANS, P. R., and FLOWER, W. U. (1967): Scot. Birds, 4: 404–445.

FERGUSON-LEES, I. J. (1951): Bird Notes, 24: 200–205, 309–314.
FERGUSON-LEES, I. J. (1968): Brit. Birds, 61: 87–88.
FISHER, J. (1948): Agriculture, 55: 20–23.
FISHER, J. (1952): South-Eastern Naturalist and Antiquary, 47: 1–10.
FISHER, J. (1952a): Ibis, 94: 334–354.
FISHER, J. (1952b): The Fulmar (London).
FISHER, J. (1953): Brit. Birds, 46: 153–181.
FISHER, J. (1966): Bird Study, 13: 5–76.
FISHER, J., and LOCKLEY, R. M. (1954): Sea-Birds (London).
FISHER, J., and WATERSTON, G. (1941): J. Anim. Ecol., 10: 204–272.
FISHER, J., and VEVERS, H. G. (1943): J. Anim. Ecol., 12: 173–213.
FISHER, J., and VEVERS, H. G. (1944): J. Anim. Ecol., 13: 49–62.
FISHER, J., and VEVERS, H. G. (1951): Int. Orn. Congr., 10: 463–467.
FITTER, R. S. R. (1945): London's Birds (London).
FITTER, R. S. R. (1965): Brit. Birds, 58: 481–492.
FRIELING, H. (1933): Zoogeographica, 1: 485–550.
GARDEN, E. A. (1958): Bird Study, 5: 90–109.
GIBSON, J. A. (1952): Scot. Nat., 64: 179–180.
GIBSON, J. A. (1956): The Birds of the Isle of Arran (Rothesay).
GILBERT, H. A., and WALKER, C. W. (1941): Herefordshire Birds (Hereford).
GILLHAM, E. H., and HOMES, R. C. (1950): The Birds of the North Kent Marshes (London).
GLEGG, W. E. (1929): A History of the Birds of Essex (London).
GLUTZ von BLOTZHEIM, U. N. (ed.) (1962): Die Brutvögel der Schweiz (Aarau).
GORDON, S. (1955): The Golden Eagle (London).
GORDON, S. (1965): Brit. Birds, 58: 445.
GRIBBLE, F. C. (1962): Bird Study, 9: 56–80.
GRIERSON, J. (1962): Scot. Birds, 2: 113–164.
GUDMUNDSSON, F. (1951): Int. Orn. Congr., 10: 502–514.
HAFTORN, S. (1958): Sterna, 3: 105–137.
HAMILTON, F. D. (1962): Bird Study, 9: 72–80.
HARBER, D. D. (1966): Brit. Birds, 59: 280–305.
HARRIS, M. P. (1963): The Breeding Biology of the Larus Gulls (Ph. D. thesis, Swansea).
HARRIS, M. P. (1966): Ibis, 108: 17–33.
HARRISON, J. M. (1953): The Birds of Kent (London).
HARRISON, C. J. O. (1961): Lond. Bird Rep., 24: 71–80.
HARRISSON, T. H., and HOLLOM, P. A. D. (1932): Brit. Birds, 26: 69–92, 102–131, 142–155, 174–195.
HARRISSON, T. H., and HURRELL, H. G. (1933): Proc. Zool. Soc. Lond., 1933: 191–209.
HARROP, J. M. (1961): Nature in Wales, 7: 79–82.
HARTHAN, A. J. (1961): A Revised List of Worcestershire Birds (Worcester).
HENDERSON, M. (1965): Rep. Lancashire & Cheshire Fauna Committee, 35: 37.
HICKLING, G. (1963): Scot. Birds, 2: 450–452.
HIGLER, L. W. G. (1962): Limosa, 35: 260–265.
HOLDSWORTH, K. (1962): Merseyside Nat. Assoc. Bird Rep., 1960–62: 61–64.
HOLLOM, P. A. D. (1940): Brit. Birds, 33: 202–221, 230–244.
HOLLOM, P. A. D. (1951): Brit. Birds, 44: 361–369.
HOLLOM, P. A. D. (1959): Bird Study, 6: 1–7.
HOLOHAN, S., and O'CONNOR, R. J. (1964): Irish Nat. J., 14: 287–296.
HOMES, R. C., *et al.* (1957): The Birds of the London Area since 1900 (London).
HONER, M. R. (1963): Ardea, 51: 158–195.
HOWELLS, G. (1963): Rep. Game Res. Assoc., 2: 46–51.

HUDSON, R. (1965): Brit. Birds, 58: 105–139.

HUMPHREYS, J. N. (1963): Kent Bird Rep., 10: 44–51.

HUMPHREYS, P. N. (1963): The Birds of Monmouthshire (Newport).

INGRAM, G. S. C., and SALMON, H. M. (1954): A Handlist of the Birds of Carmarthenshire (Tenby).

INGRAM, G. S. C., and SALMON, H. M. (1955): The Birds of Radnorshire (Hereford).

INGRAM, G. S. C., and SALMON, H. M. (1957): Brycheiniog, 3: 182–259.

JACKSON, E. E. (1966): Scot. Birds, 4: special supplement.

JENKINS, D. (1962): In: Rep. Nature Conservancy 1961–62: 80–81.

JENKINS, D. (1966): Field, 13 Jan. 1966.

JENKINS, D., WATSON, A., and MILLER, G. R. (1963): J. Anim. Ecol., 32: 317–376.

JENKINS, D., WATSON, A., and MILLER, G. R. (1964): Scot. Birds, 3: 3–13.

JESPERSEN, P. (1946): The Breeding Birds of Denmark (Copenhagen).

JONES, E. L. (1966): In: The Birds of Oxfordshire and Berkshire, by M. C. Radford (London).

JONES, N. G. B. (1956): Bird Study, 3: 153–170.

KALELA, O. (1949): Bird Banding, 20: 77–103.

KENNEDY, P. G. (1961): A List of the Birds of Ireland (Dublin).

KENNEDY, P. G., RUTTLEDGE, R. F., and SCROOPE, C. F. (1954): The Birds of Ireland (Edinburgh and London).

KENT, A. K. (1964): Bird Study, 11: 123–127.

KING, F. (1960): Irish Nat. J., 13: 188.

LACK, D. (1942–43): Ibis, 84: 461–484; 85: 1–27.

LACK, D. (1954): Brit. Birds, 47: 111–121.

LAMB, H. H. (1965): In: The Biological Influence of Climatic Changes in Britain, ed. C. G. Johnson and L. P. Smith (London and New York).

LEWIS, L. R. (1966): In: The Birds of Oxfordshire and Berkshire, by M. C. Radford (London).

LEWIS, S. (1952): The Breeding Birds of Somerset and Their Eggs (Ilfracombe).

LOCKIE, J. D. (1955): Bird Study, 2: 53–69.

LOCKIE, J. D. (1964): Scot. Nat., 71: 67–77.

LOCKIE, J. D., and RATCLIFFE, D. A. (1964): Brit. Birds, 57: 89–102.

LOCKIE, J. D., and STEPHEN, D. (1959): J. Anim. Ecol., 28: 43–50.

LOCKLEY, R. M. (1953): Puffins (London).

LOCKLEY, R. M. (1961): Nature in Wales, 7: 124–133.

LOCKLEY, R. M., INGRAM, G. S. C., and SALMON, H. M. (1949): The Birds of Pembrokeshire.

LORD, J., and BLAKE, A. R. M. (1962): The Birds of Staffordshire (West Midland Bird Club).

MAGEE, J. D. (1965): Bird Study, 12: 83–89.

MARCHANT, S. (1952): Brit. Birds, 45: 22–27.

MACDONALD, D. (1965): Scot. Birds, 3: 366.

MACKENZIE, J. M. D. (1952): J. Anim. Ecol., 21: 128–153.

MARRA, N. (1964): Limosa, 37: 1–4.

MARRA, N. (1965): Limosa, 38: 2–5.

MATHESON, C. (1953): Brit. Birds, 46: 57–64.

MATHESON, C. (1956): Brit. Birds, 49: 112–114.

MATHESON, C. (1956a): Nat. Libr. of Wales J., 9: 287–294.

MATHESON, C. (1957): Brit. Birds, 50: 534–536.

MEDLICOTT, W. S. (1963): The Birds of South Roxburghshire (private publ.).

MEIKLEJOHN, M. F. M. (1952): Scot. Nat., 64: 114–116.

MEIKLEJOHN, M. F. M., and STANFORD, J. K. (1954): Scot. Nat., 66: 129–145.

MEINERTZHAGEN, R. (1950): Bull. Brit. Orn. Cl., 70: 46–47.
MERIKALLIO, E. (1958): Fauna Fenn. 5: 1–181.
MIDDLETON, A. D., and HUBAND, P. (1966): Rep. Game Res. Assoc., 5: 14–25.
MILLS, D. H. (1962): Rep. Wildfowl Trust, 13: 79–92.
MILLS, D. H. (1965): The Distribution and Food of the Cormorant in Scottish Inland Waters (H.M.S.O.).
MONK, J. F. (1963): Bird Study, 10: 112–132.
MOORE, N. W. (1957): Brit. Birds, 50: 173–197.
MOORE, N. W., and WALKER, C. H. (1964): Nature, Lond., 201: 1072–1073.
MOREAU, R. E. (1951): Brit. Birds, 44: 257–276.
MOREAU, R. E. (1956): Brit. Birds, 49: 161–166.
MORLEY, A., and PRICE, K. L. H. (1956): Brit. Birds, 49: 258–267.
MOUNTFORT, G. R. (1957): The Hawfinch (London).
MRUGASIEWICZ, A., and WITKOWSKI, J. (1962): Brit. Birds, 55: 245–271.
MOULE, G. W. H. (1965): A Revised List of the Birds of Dorset.
MURTON, R. K. (1965): The Wood-Pigeon (London).
MURTON, R. K., WESTWOOD, N. J., and ISAACSON, A. J. (1964): Ibis, 106: 174–188.
NAU, B. S. (1961): Lond. Bird Rep., 25: 69–81.
NELSON, J. B. (1964): Ibis, 106: 63–77.
NELSON, J. B. (1965): Brit. Birds, 58: 233–288, 313–336.
NETHERSOLE-THOMPSON, D. (1951): The Greenshank (London).
NETHERSOLE-THOMPSON, D. (1966): The Snow Bunting (Edinburgh and London).
NEWTON, I. (1967): Ibis, 109: 33–98.
NICHOLSON, E. M. (1926): Birds in England (London).
NICHOLSON, E. M. (1929): Brit. Birds, 22: 269–323, 333–372.
NICHOLSON, E. M. (1930): Brit. Birds, 25: 159–161.
NICHOLSON, E. M. (1951): Birds and Men (London).
NICHOLSON, E. M. (1957): Brit. Birds, 50: 131–135, 146–147.
NICHOLSON, E. M., and FERGUSON-LEES, I. J. (1962): Brit. Birds, 55: 299–384.
NOBLE, H. (1906): In: The Victoria County History of Berkshire (London).
NORRIS, C. A. (1945): Brit. Birds, 38: 142–148, 162–168.
NORRIS, C. A. (1947): Notes on the Birds of Warwickshire (Birmingham).
NORRIS, C. A. (1947): Brit. Birds, 40: 226–244.
NORRIS, C. A. (1953): Brit. Birds, 46: 131–137.
OAKES, C. (1953): The Birds of Lancashire (Edinburgh and London).
PARRINDER, E. R. (1964): Brit. Birds, 57: 191–198.
PARSLOW, J. L. F. (1965): Brit. Birds, 58: 522–523.
PAYN, W. H. (1962): The Birds of Suffolk (London).
PEACH, W. S., and MILES, P. M. (1961): Nature in Wales, 7: 11–20.
PEAKALL, D. B. (1962): Bird Study, 9: 198–216.
PEARSON, D. J. (1963): Trans. Suffolk Nat. Soc., 12: 293–300.
PEDERSEN, E. T. (1966): Dansk. Orn. Foren. Tidsskr., 60: 95–100.
PENNIE, I. D. (1950–51): Scot. Nat., 62: 65–87, 157–178; 63: 4–17, 135.
PENNIE, I. D. (1962): Scot. Birds, 2: 167–192.
PITT, R. G. (1967): Brit. Birds, 60: 349–355.
PORTER, R. F. (1966): Sussex Bird Rep., 18: 56–57.
POTTS, G. R. (1965): Trans. Nat. Hist. Soc. Northumberland, Durham & Newcastle upon Tyne, 15: 184.
POULSEN, H. R. (1967): Dansk. Orn. Foren. Tidsskr., 61: 111–112.
POUNDS, H. E. (1952): Notes on the Birds of Farleigh and the North Downs of Surrey (London).
PRESTT, I. (1965): Bird Study, 12: 196–221.

PRESTT, I., and MILLS, D. H. (1966): Bird Study, 13: 163–203.
PRICE, M. P. (1961): Brit. Birds, 54: 100–106.
RADFORD, M. C. (1966): The Birds of Oxfordshire and Berkshire (London).
RATCLIFFE, D. A. (1962): Ibis, 104: 13–39.
RATCLIFFE, D. A. (1963): Bird Study, 10: 56–90.
RATCLIFFE, D. A. (1965): Bird Study, 12: 66–82.
RAWCLIFFE, C. P. (1958): Bird Study, 5: 45–55.
RICHARDS, G. A. (1964): A Check-list of the Birds of Ayrshire (private publ.).
RICHMOND, W. K. (1959): British Birds of Prey (London).
RIVIERE, B. B. (1930): A History of the Birds of Norfolk (London).
ROBSON, M., and WILLS, P. (1959): Scot. Birds, 1: 110–117.
ROBSON, R. W. (1957): The Changing Scene, 1: 26–35.
ROLFE, R. L. (1966): Bird Study, 13: 221–236.
ROMMELL, K. (1953): Vogelring, 22: 90–135.
ROOTH, J., and BRUIJNS, M. F. M. (1964): Report on the Working Conference on Birds of Prey and Owls (I.C.B.P.), 107–109.
ROWAN, W. (1917): Annotated List of the Birds of Blakeney Point.
RUTTER, E. M., GRIBBLE, F. C., and PEMBERTON, T. W. (1964): A Handlist of the Birds of Shropshire.
RUTTLEDGE, R. F. (1961): Bird Study, 8: 2–5.
RUTTLEDGE, R. F. (1966): Ireland's Birds (London).
RYVES, B. H., and QUICK, H. M. (1946): Brit. Birds, 39: 3–11, 34–43.
SAGE, B. L., and NAU, B. S. (1963): Trans. Hertfordshire Nat. Hist. Soc., 25: 226–244.
SALMON, H. M. (1964): Bird Notes, 31: 91–94.
SALOMONSEN, F. (1948): Dansk. Orn. Foren. Tidsskr., 42: 85–99.
SANDEMAN, G. L. (1963): Scot. Birds, 2: 286–293.
SANDEMAN, P. W. (1957): Brit. Birds, 50: 147–149.
SAUNDERS, D. R. (1962): Nature in Wales, 8: 59–66.
SAVAGE, C. (1952): The Mandarin Duck (London).
SAVILLE, A. (1963): Rapp. Cons. Explor. Mer., 154: 215–219.
SCOTT, R. E. (1965): Bird Notes, 31: 261–265.
SHARROCK, J. T. R. (1964): Brit. Birds, 57: 10–24.
SIMMS, E. (1962): Brit. Birds, 55: 1–36.
SIMSON, C. (1966): A Bird Overhead (London).
SKILLING, D., SMITH, R. T., and YOUNG, J. G. (1966): Trans. Dumfries and Galloway Nat. Hist. and Antiq. Soc., ser. 3, 43: 49–64.
SLIJPER, H. J. (1963): Het Vogeljaar, 11: 81–88.
SLINN, D. J. (1965): Proc. Isle of Man Nat. Hist. and Antiq. Soc., 6: 597–614.
SMITH, A. E., and CORNWALLIS, R. K. (1955): The Birds of Lincolnshire (Lincoln).
SMITH, R. W. J. (1961): Scot. Birds, 1: 475–479.
SMITH, S. (1950): The Yellow Wagtail (London).
SNOW, B. (1960): Ibis, 102: 554–575.
SNOW, D. (1958): A Study of Blackbirds (London).
SPENCER, K. G. (1953): The Lapwing in Britain (London).
STAFFORD, J. (1962): Bird Study, 9: 104–115.
STAFFORD, J. (1963): Bird Study, 10: 29–33.
STERLAND, W. J., and WHITAKER, J. (1879): A Descriptive List of the Birds of Nottinghamshire (Mansfield).
STOKOE, R. (1962): The Birds of the Lake Counties (Carlisle).
STRESEMANN, E., and NOWAK, E. (1958): J. Orn., 99: 243–296.
SUMMERS-SMITH, J. D. (1963): The House Sparrow (London).
TAVERNER, J. H. (1959): Brit. Birds, 52: 245–258.
TAVERNER, J. H. (1963): Brit. Birds, 56: 273–285.

TEMPERLEY, G. W. (1951): Trans. Nat. Hist. Soc. of Northumberland, Durham & Newcastle upon Tyne, 9: 1–296.

TEMPERLEY, G. W., and BLEZARD, E. (1951): Brit. Birds, 44: 24–26.

THEARLE, R. F., HOBBS, J. T., and FISHER, J. (1953): Brit. Birds, 46: 182–188.

THOMAS, J. F. (1942): Brit. Birds, 36: 5–14, 22–34.

TICEHURST, C. B. (1932): A History of the Birds of Suffolk (London).

TICEHURST, N. F. (1909): A History of the Birds of Kent (London).

TRELEAVEN, R. B. (1961): Brit. Birds, 54: 136–142.

TUBBS, C. R. (1963): Brit. Birds, 56: 41–48.

TUBBS, C. R. (1967): Brit. Birds, 60: 87–89.

TYER, E. G. (1954): Trans. Nat. Hist. Soc. of Northumberland, Durham & Newcastle upon Tyne, 11: 61–76.

TYNESIDE BIRD CLUB (1967): Rep. Tyneside Bird Club, 1966: 11–29.

UPTON, R. (1962): Great Spotted Woodpecker Enquiry 1959–60 (private publ.).

van IJZENDOORN, A. L. J. (1950): The Breeding Birds of the Netherlands (Leiden).

VENABLES, L. S. V., and VENABLES, U. M. (1952): Ibis, 94: 636–653.

VENABLES, L. S. V., and VENABLES, U. M. (1955): The Birds and Mammals of Shetland (Edinburgh).

VENABLES, L. S. V., and WYKES, U. M. (1943): Brit. Birds, 36: 153–155.

VOOUS, K. H. (1960): Atlas of European Birds (London).

WALPOLE-BOND, J. A. (1938): A History of the Birds of Sussex (London).

WATSON, A. (1965): J. Anim. Ecol., 34: 135–172.

WATSON, A. (1965a): Bird Notes, 31: 379–383.

WATSON, A. (1965b): Scot. Birds, 3: 331–349.

WATSON, A. (1966): Rep. Nature Conservancy Unit of Grouse and Moorland Ecology, 12: 59–60.

WATT, G. (1951): The Farne Islands (London).

WEBSTER, B. (1966): Birds of Northamptonshire (Northampton).

WILLIAMSON, K. (1948): The Atlantic Islands (London).

WILLIAMSON, K. (1958): Brit. Birds, 51: 209–232.

WILLIAMSON, K., and BOYD, J. M. (1960): St. Kilda Summer (London).

WYNNE-EDWARDS, V. C. (1962): Animal Dispersion in Relation to Animal Behaviour (Edinburgh and London).

YAPP, W. B. (1962): Birds and Woods (Oxford).

Postscript
THE YEARS SINCE 1967

As we have already seen, a surprisingly high proportion—the majority—of bird species breeding in Britain and Ireland have undergone changes in their status and distribution during the past century and a half, often to a marked degree, and in several cases within the space of a short period of time. Therefore, it is not surprising to find that since the completion of the original survey in 1967, further marked changes have occurred in the status of a number of our breeding birds. The purpose of the present chapter is to highlight the more dramatic of these. Unlike the main part of the book, however, it is not based on a comprehensive review of the regional ornithological literature (although a great many county bird reports have in fact been consulted) but instead has relied chiefly on the more important national events as recorded in *British Birds* and the *Irish Bird Report*, and in the relatively new (and, to the authors of surveys such as this, most welcome) annual bird reports covering the whole of Scotland and Wales respectively.

The changes in bird populations which have occurred in the past few years need to be viewed against those recent natural and man-made factors which may be causing them. Most important of these is probably the succession of mild winters which have occurred since the exceptional freeze-up of early 1963. This has enabled populations of the traditional main hard-weather sufferers such as Herons, kingfishers and Green Woodpeckers, to recover, in most cases, after a slow start, to numbers approaching their pre-1963 strength. Even Dartford Warblers, reduced to only about ten pairs in England after the 1963 winter, are gradually coming back, their rate of increase accelerating in the last few years, until by 1971 their population totalled just over 140 pairs, most of which were in Dorset; a pair or two were back in Surrey again in 1969 after an absence of eight years. On the other hand, some range contractions recorded after the 1963 winter have not yet been made good. By 1971, for example, Redshanks had still not recolonised south Devon, and Woodlarks, already declining before 1963, have decreased still further almost everywhere.

Potentially, one of the most important events affecting many of our diurnal birds of prey and owls, was the introduction in 1962–66 of voluntary bans on the use of dieldrin and certain other persistent organochlorine insecticides as seed-dressings on spring-sown wheat. Following their introduction for this use in the mid-1950's, populations of several birds of prey, notably the Peregrine and Sparrowhawk, and locally the Kestrel and Barn Owl, decreased alarmingly. In Scotland, the breeding success of Golden Eagles dropped markedly in districts where the birds fed largely on sheep carrion following the introduction of dieldrin as a sheep-dip—a use that was banned in 1966. Since the withdrawal of some, but by no means all, uses of dieldrin in agriculture, the populations of these birds of prey have recovered at least locally, and Golden Eagles appear to be breeding normally again. (Sparrowhawks, though, remain very scarce in arable eastern England, and Peregrines are still absent from most of their former southerly breeding sites in England and Wales, as well as from many coastal sites in Scotland.) Had these voluntary bans not been introduced the outlook for many of our birds of prey and owls would indeed have been bleak. Even so, despite the recommendation of the appropriate government committee more than three years ago that dieldrin should be withdrawn as a dressing for winter-sown wheat, it is still being used very widely for this purpose, and quite probably remains a factor in preventing a full recovery among those species of birds of prey which inhabit areas of arable farmland in eastern Britain.

Pollution abatement of another kind—The Clean Air Acts—has also had locally beneficial effects on bird populations. The enormous reduction of smoke in the London area, for example, has led to an increase in the amount of 'aerial plankton' available to species such as House Martins and Swifts, both of which have penetrated, and now breed in, areas close to the centre of the city from which they had been absent almost since the 19th century.

On the other hand, some other forms of pollution, particularly in the marine environment (where the majority of persistent pollutants eventually end up) have continued virtually unchecked. March 1967 saw the wreck of the *Torrey Canyon* off Land's End, Cornwall, and the death through oil pollution of a minimum of 10,000 Guillemots (and other seabirds); the small breeding population in the Isles of Scilly was particularly hard hit. Accidental, or at times wilful, oil pollution continues to kill thousands of seabirds every year. In 1967, too, another industrial pollutant, the polychlorinated biphenyls (PCBs) were first recognised as a contaminant of wildlife in Britain. Their toxicological significance is uncertain. They appear to be of particular ecological importance in aquatic, especially marine, situations, and they may have been a contributory factor in the massive mortality of at least 12,000 Guillemots and other seabirds in the mysterious Irish Sea wreck in autumn 1969. This event led to a marked diminution in the numbers of Guillemots breeding at many Irish Sea colonies in 1970, but, happily, the situation seems to have improved somewhat since then.

Although they have not been restricted to the last five or six years, mention should also be made of the rapid changes which are occurring in our environment as the result of new agricultural practices and other developments. Farmland of one kind or another covers about four-fifths of the land surface of Britain. The most rapid and immediately noticeable alterations in our agricultural landscapes have occurred in eastern Britain and have involved particularly the removal of hedgerows and hedgerow trees. Though the effects on birds have been studied only locally, it can be inferred from these studies that the numbers of typical hedgerow species, such as Whitethroats, Yellowhammers and Chaffinches have been reduced considerably wherever arable farmland predominates. (A well documented, very large—70%—reduction in Whitethroat numbers throughout Britain and Ireland in 1969 was caused by an unknown, but probably natural, factor, possibly in their winter quarters or on migration; as yet their numbers have not recovered.) Another comparatively recent event has been the destruction of old pastures (on farmland through ploughing, and in parkland for housing developments). This has almost certainly had adverse effects on species such as Magpies and Green Woodpeckers, for which the abundant invertebrate fauna of old grassland is so important.

Finally, before coming to an assessment of the main changes in status of various bird groups in recent years, two further developments should be mentioned. The first is afforestation, partly beneficial (certainly in young conifer plantations for species such as Short-eared Owls and Grasshopper Warblers, and in older ones for Coal Tits and Crossbills) and partly detrimental (as when ornithologically rich oak woods are felled to make way for introduced species of conifers). The second is the developing threat to one of our most important, restricted and ecologically sensitive habitats—estuaries. Several of these are threatened by development of one form or another—Foulness by an airport, the Wash and perhaps Morecambe Bay and others by reservoir barrage schemes, yet others by industrial expansion. Of greatest ornithological importance for their wintering and migrant wader and wildfowl populations, estuaries do nevertheless form important nesting and feeding grounds for many of our less common breeding birds.

SPECIES BREEDING FOR THE FIRST TIME IN BRITAIN AND IRELAND

Since 1967 no less than six species have nested in Britain for the first time, three of them (two of southern origin, one of eastern) in southern England and three (of north European origin) in Scotland. In chronological order, the first of these was a pair of Bluethroats *Luscinia svecica* which nested unsuccessfully in Strathspey in north-east Scotland in 1968. Although the nest was found, only the female of the pair was seen and so the subspecies involved could not be determined. It seems most likely that the birds belonged to the northern, nominate race. Also in 1968, a pair of Mediterranean Gulls *Larus melanocephalus* bred successfully among the huge colony of Black-headed Gulls at Needs Oar Point, Hampshire; another male there mated with a female Black-headed Gull, and a female mated with a hybrid between the two species. In subsequent years only the hybrid (mated with a female Black-headed Gull) was proved to breed. Great Northern Divers *Gavia immer* have frequently been recorded in Scotland in summer but it was not until 1970 that a pair bred (in Wester Ross) for the first time, successfully rearing two young. None was found in 1971, although in that year a hybrid Great Northern/Black-throated Diver, paired with a Black-throated Diver, bred in west Scotland. Also in 1970, a pair of Goldeneyes *Bucephala clangula* nested successfully in east Inverness, and breeding again took place there in 1971 and 1972. Apart from the supposed breeding in Cheshire in 1931 and 1932, these are the first definite records for Britain.

At the time of writing, the status of the next new species remains in some doubt. Since 1969 birds closely resembling Short-toed Treecreepers *Certhia brachydactyla* have been identified in several places in southern England, and in 1971 a pair was proved to breed in east Dorset. The species is extremely difficult to distinguish from the Treecreeper *Certhia familiaris*, and it is still uncertain how many of the recent identifications are correct; it is also unknown whether the species has recently spread into England (from France) or has been previously overlooked. There is no doubt, however, that the sixth of these new breeding species, Cetti's Warbler *Cettia cetti*, which nested successfully for the first time in southern England in 1972, has spread here from France. In recent years it has spread northwards in that country and has colonised the Channel Islands, and the English breeding record came after an increasing number of sightings in southern counties. Given a continued run of mild winters, there seems no reason why this largely sedentary warbler should not spread to other localities in southern England.

OTHER RECENT MARKED STATUS CHANGES

Seabirds

During 1969–71 the Seabird Group carried out a survey ('Operation Seafarer'), the aim of which was to census all seabirds breeding around the entire coastline of Britain and Ireland. The results of this survey have not yet been published, but they will undoubtedly form a valuable inventory of present seabird populations against which future changes can be measured. One result of 'Operation Seafarer' was the discovery of a small new Gannet colony on the Flannans, Outer Hebrides, in 1969.

Even in the absence of the full 'Seafarer' records, several trends in the status of our breeding seabirds are clear. Those species which were markedly expanding in the early 1960's have continued to do so. The spread of Fulmars continues apace, particularly in the southern parts of its range—Kent and Carmarthenshire (in 1967 and 1971 respectively) having been added to the counties in which it breeds. Gannet numbers have gone up at virtually all of their colonies; in 1971, for example, 14,347 nests were counted on Ailsa Craig (Ayrshire)—23% more than in 1963, or an average increase of about 3% per year. Kittiwakes and the larger gulls are still expanding their range; among several new colonies of the larger gulls, the discovery of a large mixed colony of Herring and Lesser Black-backed Gulls (totalling about 1,250 pairs in 1971) at Orfordness, Suffolk, represents a remarkable expansion in range. Odd pairs of Lesser Black-backed Gulls have also nested recently in the English Midlands. Coastal colonies of Black-headed Gulls in south-east England have also continued to do well: one at Needs Oar Point, Hampshire, numbered no fewer than 17,000 breeding pairs by 1970.

Little Terns were the subject of a special survey in 1967, which showed that the total population in Britain and Ireland was about 1,600 breeding pairs. Common Terns have continued to spread inland in southern England and small numbers are now breeding, usually on islands in flooded gravel pits, in most inland counties. Among our scarcer seabirds, Roseate Terns have been discovered at a few places in western Ireland, while Great Skuas are still spreading in Orkney and elsewhere in northern Scotland, where they now nest in small numbers on the mainland of Caithness and Sutherland, as well as on islands off the Sutherland coast such as Handa (10 pairs in 1971) and Eilean nan Roan (one pair in 1972).

The continued decline of Guillemots at a number of their colonies has already been mentioned, but the most dramatic decrease among auk populations has occurred among Puffins at two of their major colonies—St Kilda and the Shiants (Outer Hebrides)—and probably also at a third, the Clo Mor in north-west Sutherland. These declines represent the loss of tens of thousands of birds within the space of less than a decade. The cause remains obscure (possible reasons are discussed in *Bird Study*, 19, 1–6 and 7–17) and appears not to have affected Puffins elsewhere, at least not to the same extent. Indeed, on the Isle of May (Fife) their numbers appear to be increasing.

Wildfowl

Apart from the first breeding of Goldeneyes, already mentioned, few dramatic changes in status have occurred. Feral populations of Greylag Geese, Canada Geese, Mandarin Ducks and Ruddy Ducks appear to have increased locally, while a pair of Red-crested Pochards (undoubtedly 'escapes') bred in Gloucester in 1970. Another introduced species, the Wood Duck *Aix sponsa* appears to have established small feral breeding populations in East Anglia and Surrey.

Red-breasted Mergansers have spread further in Wales; in addition to counties in the extreme north-west, it now nests regularly in north Cardigan and in 1970 there were probable breeding records in Montgomery and Glamorgan. On the other hand, breeding records of Garganey in England and

Wales seem to be getting scarcer, continuing the trend noted earlier. Other scarce breeding wildfowl have shown few changes in status, although the nesting of a pair of Whooper Swans in Inverness in 1963 was the first confirmed record in Scotland since a pair bred on Benbecula, Outer Hebrides, in 1947.

Waders

Most recent information concerns the rarer species. The Ouse Washes (Cambridge/Norfolk) specialities, Black-tailed Godwit and Ruff, have continued to do well, up to 65 pairs of godwits and up to 21 reeves having nested there in 1971. A few pairs of Black-tailed Godwits have nested in several other parts of England and Scotland, from Kent to Shetland, in the last few years, one of the most regularly occupied localities being in south-east Scotland. Ruffs have summered at a few places, notably in Norfolk, but apart from the Ouse Washes and the probable nesting of a male plus two females in Anglesey in 1970, no other breeding records have been published.

The increase and spread of Little Ringed Plovers has continued and the total breeding population must now number about 300 pairs. The species reached Northumberland in 1968 (in which year it also bred as far north as the Clyde Valley in western Scotland) and it has since spread to north-east Wales and Worcester. Ringed Plovers, while continuing to decrease in many coastal areas, notably in south-west England and Wales, have, like Common Terns, begun nesting in small numbers in some inland areas in southern England—for example in Cambridge (1969), Essex (1970) and Buckingham (1971). Oystercatchers, too, which underwent an expansion to inland areas in northern Britain some years ago, have recently (1966 onwards) taken to nesting inland in small numbers much farther south, for example in southern Yorkshire, Nottingham, Stafford, Leicester, Cambridge and probably Warwick.

While the number of Avocets breeding at Havergate Island (Suffolk) has hovered around (usually just above) 100 pairs, at the other Suffolk coastal reserve of the Royal Society for the Protection of Birds, Minsmere, their population has gradually increased until, by 1972 thirty-four pairs were breeding on the lagoons specially constructed for them and other birds. Among the scarce, northern waders, probably the most interesting recent event has been the summering of one or two pairs of Temminck's Stints in Easter Ross during 1969–71. A pair bred successfully in the last of these years —only the fifth British breeding record, and the first in which young have been reared. Wood Sandpipers now seem to be firmly established (in very small numbers) in the far north of the Scottish Highlands, while the Whimbrel, formerly confined to Shetland (plus a pair or two on Lewis, Outer Hebrides) has bred in two or three recent years in Orkney and, since 1969, has spread to a locality on the north Scottish mainland, where it had increased to four or five pairs by 1971. Another rare wader which is showing signs of expansion in Scotland is the Dotterel, which has bred in at least one recent year in Sutherland. Red-necked Phalaropes, on the other hand, are decreasing in Orkney and probably elsewhere. A recent survey showed that the Scottish population (plus the few pairs in Mayo, western Ireland) fluctuated between 28 and 65 pairs during 1968–70.

Birds of prey and owls

Reference has already been made, at the beginning of this chapter, to the effects of the introduction of certain organochlorine insecticides (and their subsequent partial withdrawal) on the populations of some of our birds of prey. The following summary considers mainly recent status changes among our least numerous birds of prey, which include, incidentally, some of Britain and Ireland's rarest breeding birds.

Still restricted to a single British breeding pair are the Snowy Owls of Fetlar (Shetland) which nested annually during 1967–72. Next, in terms of rareness, are Marsh Harriers, two or three pairs of which maintain a precarious toehold at Minsmere and Benacre in Suffolk, occasional birds or apparent pairs sometimes summering elsewhere in the country. Fast diminishing, and now facing imminent extinction as a British breeding bird, is the Montagu's Harrier. Although a breeding pair has now returned to Norfolk (during 1970–72) and odd pairs have occasionally bred in recent years in, for example, Suffolk, Hampshire and Dorset, it has decreased considerably in its main breeding haunts in Cornwall, from seven known pairs in 1968 to only one (perhaps two) in 1970. The number of Montagu's Harriers in Britain is now almost certainly smaller than the number of Ospreys, which by 1971 were nesting at seven places in the Scottish Highlands. Of these seven pairs, the eggs of one (at the original site at Loch Garten, Inverness) were robbed and those of another failed to hatch; but the five remaining pairs successfully reared a total of eleven young. Honey Buzzards are probably present in Britain in similar numbers to Ospreys. While no information is available on the current strength of the New Forest (Hampshire) population, it has now been revealed that at least one pair has been nesting in the English Midlands for a number of years.

In Wales, the Kite population continues to show a gradual improvement in numbers and breeding success: 24 pairs bred in 1970 (when 17 young were reared from 11 successful nests) and 22 pairs in 1971 (16 young reared). Hen Harriers have also continued to increase, particularly in Ireland, where they now nest in about a dozen counties. In Scotland, a revised estimate of Golden Eagle numbers has put the breeding population at 250–300 pairs, and since 1969 a single pair has nested in the English Lake District, successfully rearing young in each year during 1970–72.

One further raptor, the Goshawk, should also be mentioned. Pairs have bred recently in at least six widely separated areas of England, Scotland and Wales, in two or three of them regularly. Their origin, however, is suspect since, as with the female of the Shropshire pair mentioned earlier (p. 55), many are believed to be birds liberated by or escaped from falconers.

Passerines and near-passerines

If among the already common and widespread breeding birds it was the Bullfinch and Tree Sparrow which showed the most striking increases in the early 1960's, it was the Redpoll and probably also the Grasshopper Warbler which increased most noticeably in the period 1967–71. The Redpoll expansion had already begun when the main part of this survey was completed (see p. 175) and reports during the last few years suggest that it has made widespread gains throughout much of Britain and Ireland. Grasshopper Warblers, too, as well as having occupied much new territory in northern Scotland have increased markedly in eastern England, particularly in Essex, a county in which it was formerly a very scarce bird.

Although the period involved (mainly 1967–71) is a short one, there are signs of range expansion among several other passerine birds. Pied Flycatchers, for example, have gained much ground in Devon and spread into Wester Ross, Sutherland (1970–71) and Anglesey (1971), as well as having bred sporadically beyond their normal range in the New Forest, Hampshire (1968) and again in Cornwall (1969). Reed Warblers have spread westwards in Wales and have nested in Anglesey since at least 1968 and Carmarthen since 1971; breeding birds also reached the Isles of Scilly in the 1960's. Siskins have continued their rather erratic colonisation of new areas in England and Wales; birds bred in Brecon and Carmarthen for the first time in 1971. Although they have not yet returned to Wales (outside Flint), a pair of Corn Buntings bred in Monmouth in 1970 (for the first time since 1903), and in the west Midlands, Cheshire and Shropshire the species was showing signs of a considerable increase and spread in the middle and late 1960's.

Several of our rarer passerine birds have increased in the last few years. The partial recovery of Dartford Warblers from the 1963 winter has already been remarked upon, but another formerly very local and rare bird, the Bearded Tit, has recently undergone a remarkable expansion in range. Its spread from East Anglia into Essex and Kent after about 1960 was mentioned in the main part of the book. It has since increased and spread in both these counties (nesting in 1970 at three localities in Essex and five in Kent) and beyond them along the south coast at least as far as Hampshire and Dorset (nesting at three localities in the latter county in 1971) and north in eastern England at least as far as Lincoln; it also bred in Anglesey in 1967.

Three rare southern species are also increasing. Firecrests, which have been breeding in the New Forest, Hampshire, for a number of years, have now been discovered elsewhere in southern and eastern England, notably in Buckingham, where at least two pairs bred in 1971 and no fewer than 23 singing males were located in 1972. Firecrests have also bred in Somerset and have been found in the breeding season in Dorset, Kent, Bedford and Suffolk in the last two years. Savi's Warblers, established in Kent for some years, have recently been found in the breeding season in a number of counties (including Somerset, Hampshire, Cambridge and Norfolk) and have bred at two localities in east Suffolk since at least 1970. Serins, which first nested in southern England in 1967, have since bred in other years in at least two southern counties.

In northern Scotland, Redwings now appear to be firmly established, about 50 occupied territories being located in 1971. Fieldfares, which nested for the first time in Britain in Orkney in 1967, bred the following year in Shetland, where they have lately nested on several other occasions; breeding has also been recorded in east Inverness and in one year in England.

On the debit side, the rapid decline of the Red-backed Shrike continues throughout virtually the whole of the final remnant of its range. By 1970–71 its numbers appear to have totalled only about 70 pairs—or nearly half those estimated to be present in 1966 (see p. 169). Wrynecks, too, have almost gone from south-east England: the last breeding record from Surrey was in 1968, while in Kent, by 1970, the species was recorded in summer at only a handful of localities and no reports of breeding were received. By way of compensation, however, following its occurrence in several successive summers on Speyside (east Inverness) no fewer than three Wryneck nests were found there in 1969—the first time the species had ever been proved to breed in Scotland. Birds have been present in each summer since then.

Other Orders

Included in this grouping are the divers, grebes, herons, game-birds, rails and pigeons. Apart from the continued decline of the Corncrake, most recent changes which need to be remarked upon concern increases. The spectacular spread of the Collared Dove has continued, so that it now nests throughout Britain and in virtually every Irish county. The rate of its increase has been geometrical, as illustrated in Fig. 11.

The first breeding of Great Northern Divers in Britain has already been mentioned. Great Crested Grebes have spread in Wales, where by 1971 it was nesting in all counties except Pembroke and Cardigan. The two rarest grebes remain Scottish specialities: the Slavonian Grebe population was estimated at 52–58 pairs in 1971, while the only permanent colonies of Black-necked Grebes in the British Isles remain the two in the central Scottish lowlands. Heron numbers have now recovered from the 1963 hard winter, and it is doubtless the succession of recent mild winters (and perhaps also protection) which has enabled the Bittern population in Anglesey to make rapid progress: at least ten pairs were breeding there by 1971. Remarkable numbers of Quail were present throughout Britain and Ireland in 1970, when their numbers probably equalled the influx of 1964. Spotted Crakes continue to elude ornithologists in search of confirmed breeding records; there have, however, been several recent records of birds summering (and probably breeding in a few cases) in Scotland—in Sutherland, Ross and notably on Speyside, Inverness.

Finally, mention should be made here of those introduced species of pheasants, omitted from the previous systematic list, but now mapped in the chapter which follows. They are the Golden Pheasant *Chrysolophus pictus* and Lady Amherst's Pheasant *Chrysolophus amherstiae*, both of which, because they

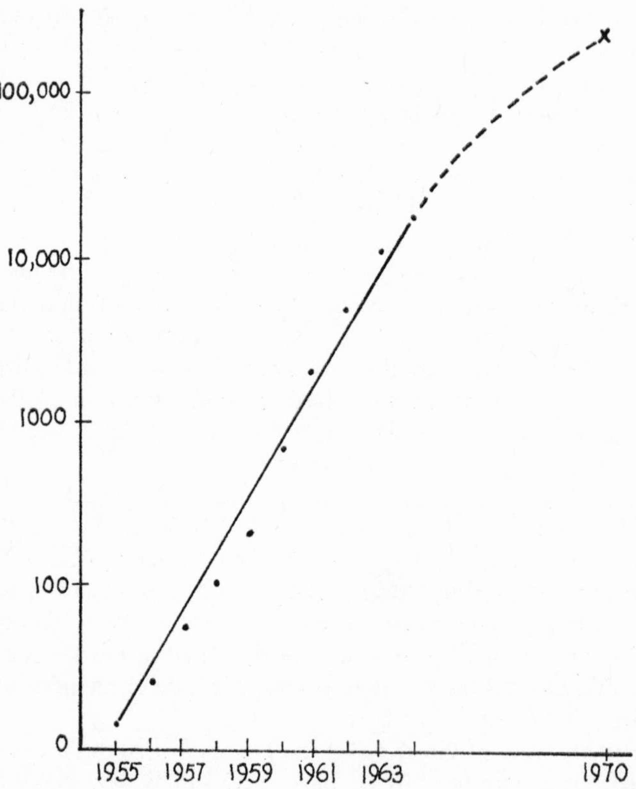

FIG. 11. Geometric increase in the Collared Dove *Streptopelia decaocto* population in Britain and Ireland. Based on R. K. Murton and data on total post-breeding numbers collected by R. Hudson. Since 1964 the species has become too numerous for accurate population estimates to be made; the rate of increase has certainly slowed down and the broken line indicates the probable population trend.

have been established in small numbers in Britain for several decades, have now been admitted to the official British and Irish List; and Reeve's Pheasant *Syrmaticus reevesii* which may now be established in Scotland and central England. Another recently introduced game-bird, the Bobwhite Quail *Colinus virginianus*, has been breeding in a feral state on Tresco, Isles of Scilly, for a number of years and may also be successfully maintaining itself in East Anglia and south-east England.

Appendix

CURRENT STATUS AND DISTRIBUTION OF BREEDING BIRDS IN BRITAIN AND IRELAND

The aim of this Appendix is to provide at-a-glance information on the current distribution, abundance, status changes and nesting habitats of all bird species breeding in Britain and Ireland at the present time. Included also are those species which have nested, or almost certainly nested, on one or more occasions since 1940, as well as the one regular breeding bird which has ceased to nest in Britain in this period, the Kentish Plover.

The Appendix also includes a few introduced game-birds and one duck that do not appear in the main part of the book. These species are those which seem to have established self-sustaining feral populations in Britain, mostly in comparatively recent years. The composition of the avifauna during 1940–72 is made up as follows:

Regular breeders (187) + Introduced (13)	200
Sporadic breeders (21) + Probable (4) + Extinct (1)	26
Total breeding species	226*

Of the total of exactly 200 species which have been classified as regular breeding birds in Britain and Ireland today, more than half (105) are residents, 30% (60) are summer visitors, and the remainder (35) are partial migrants. Fifty-eight species (29%) have breeding populations totalling less than 1000 pairs and 53 (26.5%) have populations of over 100,000 pairs. The actual distributions for each logarithmic abundance class are shown in the Fig. 12 overleaf.

* 225 species are mapped; Parrot Crossbill (a probable breeder) is mentioned under Crossbill. Red-crested Pochard is omitted from the total since the few breeding attempts refer to escaped birds.

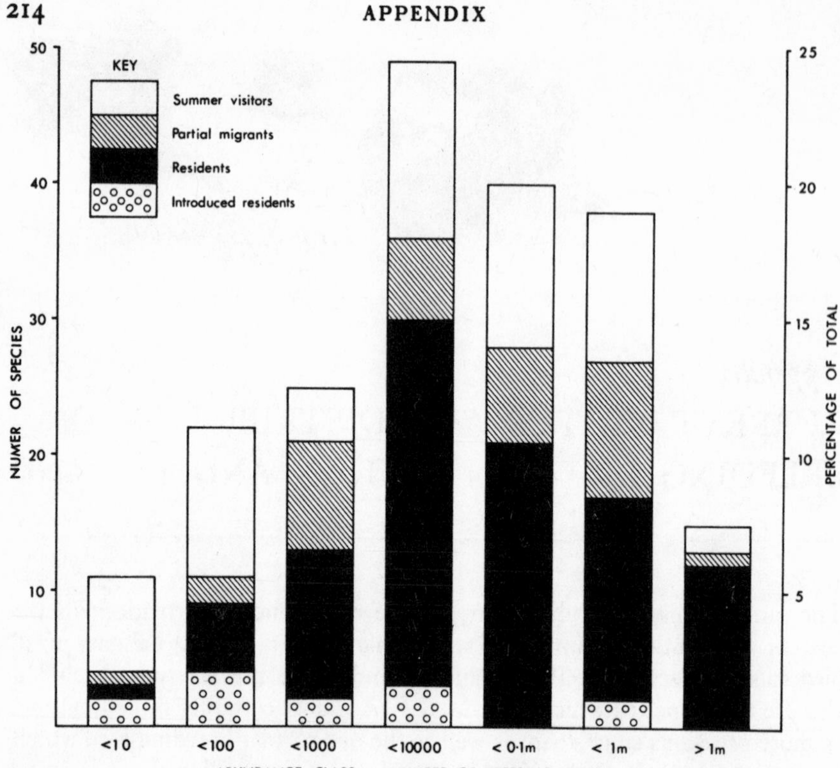

FIG. 12. Abundance class distribution of species breeding regularly in Britian and Ireland

The maps

The bases of most of the distribution maps are the ones I compiled for the *Reader's Digest Book of Birds* (1969) and subsequently revised in two later editions of that work. Modified versions of them were also published in the English language editions of Heinzel, Fitter and Parslow's *Birds of Britain and Europe* (Collins, 1972). The present maps have been further updated and modified to include additional data on sporadic breeding and more precise information on colonial species. An explanation of the various shadings and symbols used is given on the example map.

Text

The brief text for each species gives information on two aspects of its breeding status. First, any current or very recent (1967–72) data on population and distribution trends, or in the case of sporadic nesting birds, dates of recent records. Second, a line or two on its main habitat requirements in the breeding season—often, in view of the limited space, in a very generalised form.

Key to text symbols

The symbols—to the right of each bird's name—show immediately whether a species is a resident, migratory or sporadic breeding bird in the British Isles and, by the number of symbols, its relative abundance.

MIGRATORY STATUS

●—Resident: the whole (or in a few cases, the great majority) of the British and Irish population remains here throughout the year.

⊙—Partial migrant: a substantial part of the population winters outside the British Isles, the remainder remaining here throughout the year.

○—Summer resident: the whole (or virtually the whole) of the breeding population winters beyond the British Isles.

△—Sporadic breeding bird—i.e. one that nests less than annually at present.

ABUNDANCE STATUS

○—1–10 breeding pairs
○○—11–100 ,, ,,
○○○—101–1000 ,, ,,
○○○○—1001–10,000 breeding pairs
○○○○○—10,001–100,000 ,, ,,
○○○○○○—100,001–1 m. ,, ,,
○○○○○○○—over 1 million ,, ,,

Key to map shadings and symbols

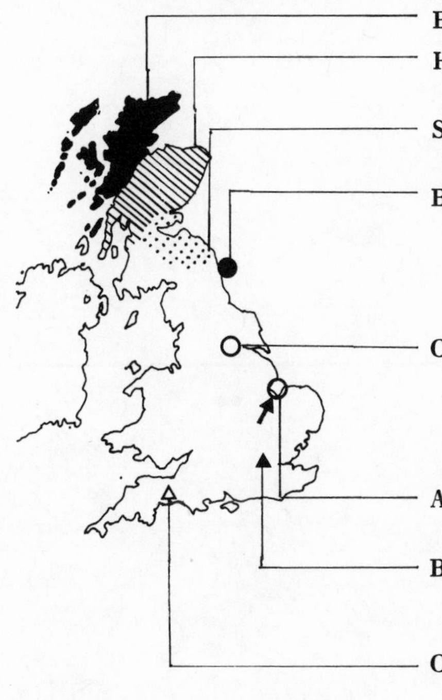

Black—Main breeding range.

Hatch—Breeds regularly but in smaller numbers or more locally than in black areas.

Stipple—Breeds fairly regularly but not annually.

Black dot—Isolated or discrete breeding locality or colony. Used most often for colonial seabirds for which larger-sized dots on some maps denote biggest colonies.

Open dot—Isolated, occasional breeding records beyond normal range. For sporadic species, these usually cover all records since 1940; for commoner species only selected recent records are shown.

Arrow—Used to draw attention to detail which might otherwise be overlooked.

Black triangle—Approximate position of isolated regular breeding site (precise locations suppressed for security reasons).

Open triangle—Approximate position of sporadic breeding sites (precise locations of which have not yet been disclosed).

EXAMPLE MAP

(Fictitious species; Orkney/Shetland inset omitted)

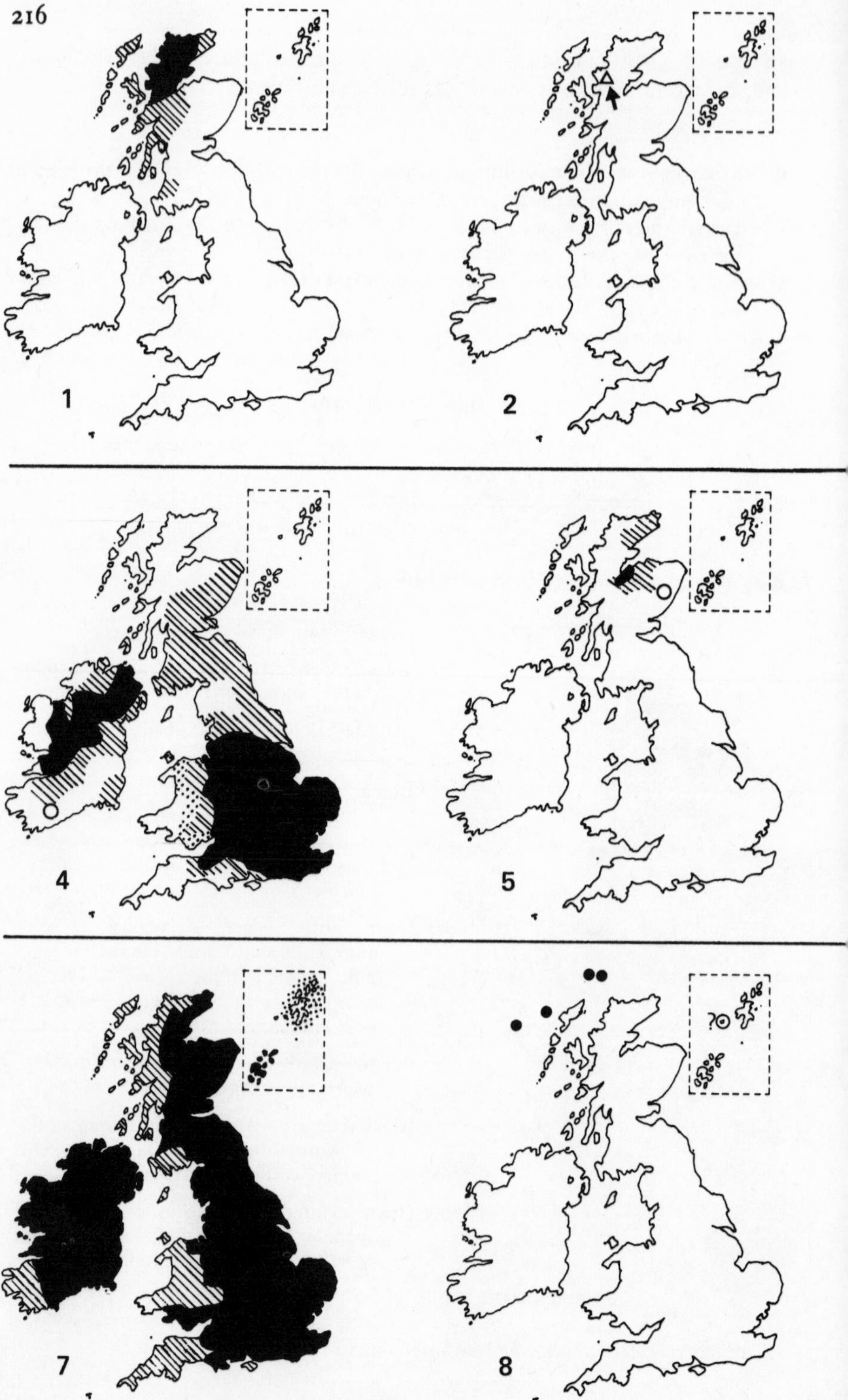

1

2

4

5

7

8

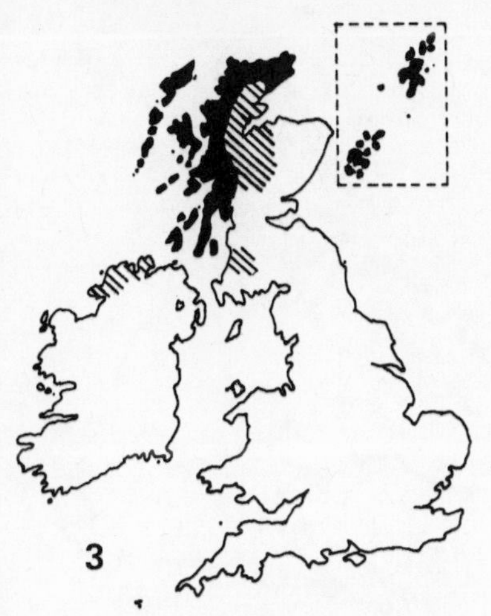

1 **Black-throated Diver** ⊙⊙⊙
Gavia arctica
Perhaps 150 pairs. No marked change.
Large freshwater lochs with tree-less islands.

2 **Great Northern Diver** △
Gavia immer
Sporadic: bred 1970 only (W. Ross).
Large freshwater loch.

3 **Red-throated Diver** ⊙⊙⊙
Gavia stellata
Locally slightly increased.
Small moorland pools, usually near sea.

4 **Great Crested Grebe** ●●●●
Podiceps cristatus
About 3000 pairs. Marked increase.
Large lakes, especially flooded gravel pits.

5 **Slavonian Grebe** ●●
Podiceps auritus
50–55 pairs. Slightly increased.
Freshwater lochs with reedy bays.

6 **Black-necked Grebe** ○○
Podiceps nigricollis
Recent decrease; now only two regular sites.
Shallow, eutrophic lakes.

7 **Little Grebe** ●●●●
Tachybaptus ruficollis
No marked change.
Lakes, ponds, sluggish rivers and backwaters.

8 **Leach's Petrel** ○○○○
Oceanodroma leucorhoa
Perhaps locally increased.
Outlying maritime islands.

9 **Storm Petrel** ○○○○○○
Hydrobates pelagicus
Trends not known.
Rocky maritime islands.

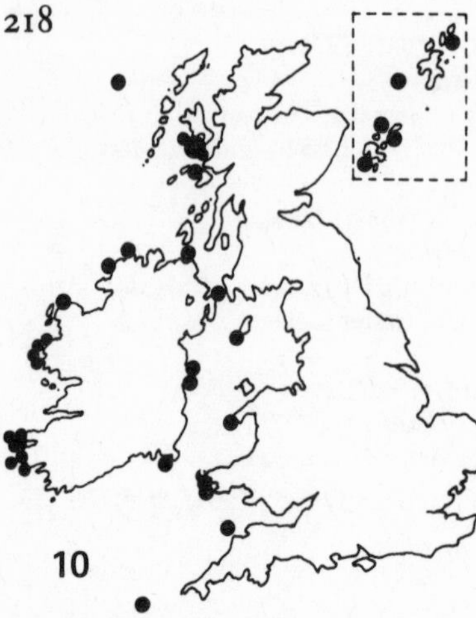

10

11

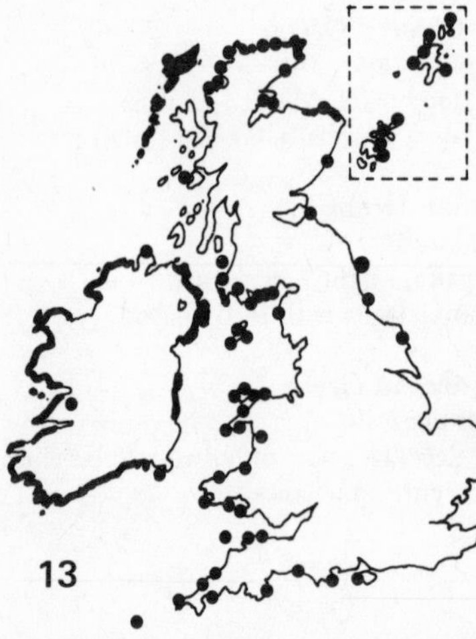

13

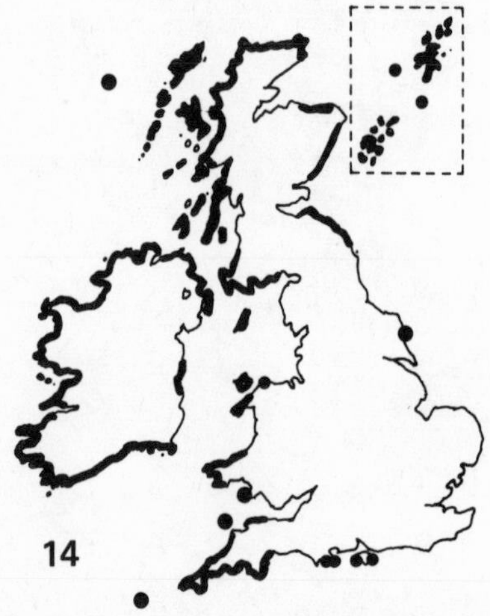

14

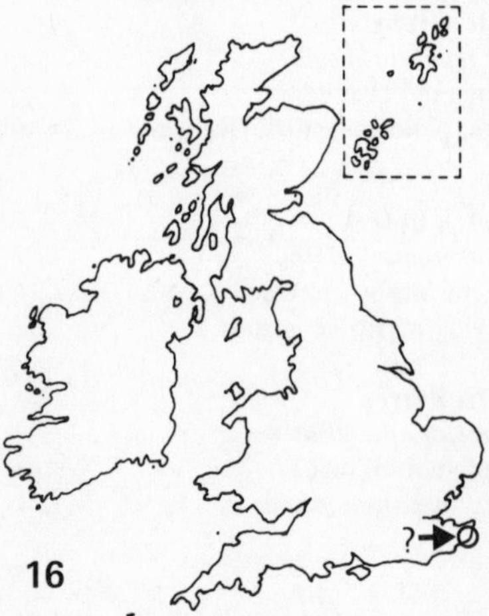

16

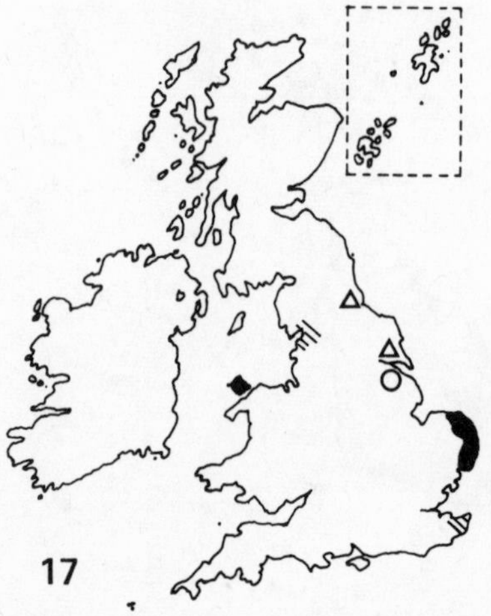

17

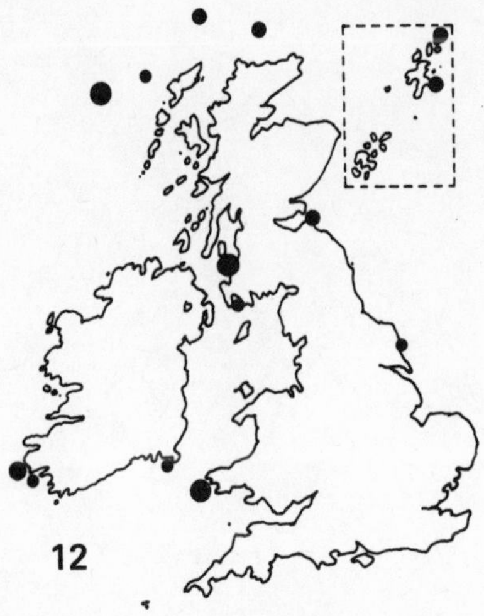

10 **Manx Shearwater** ○○○○○○
Puffinus puffinus
Local changes (up and down) but overall trend unknown. Vegetated maritime islands.

11 **Fulmar** ⊙⊙⊙⊙⊙⊙
Fulmarus glacialis
Marked increase and spread.
Seacliffs, islands.

12 **Gannet** ⊙⊙⊙⊙⊙⊙
Sula bassana
Marked increase.
Maritime islands; one mainland cliff colony.

13 **Cormorant** ⊙⊙⊙⊙
Phalacrocorax carbo
Main trend not clear, but increase on N. Sea coasts. Seacliffs, maritime islands and locally islands in lakes.

14 **Shag** ●●●●●
Phalacrocorax aristotelis
Generally increasing.
Rocky islands and coasts.

15 **Heron** ●●●●
Ardea cinerea
About 5000 pairs; recovery since 1963 hard winter. Colonies usually in trees, also sea-cliffs, reed beds.

16 **Little Bittern** △
Ixobrychus minutus
(Sporadic.) Probably bred Kent 1947 (also in 19th C.). Marshes, usually with *Phragmites* beds.

17 **Bittern** ●●
Botaurus stellaris
Perhaps 80 pairs. Increasing Anglesey and and Lancashire. Shallow wetlands with large *Phragmites* beds.

18 **Mallard** ●●●●●●
Anas platyrhynchos
No evidence of marked change.
Neighbourhood of freshwater of all kinds.

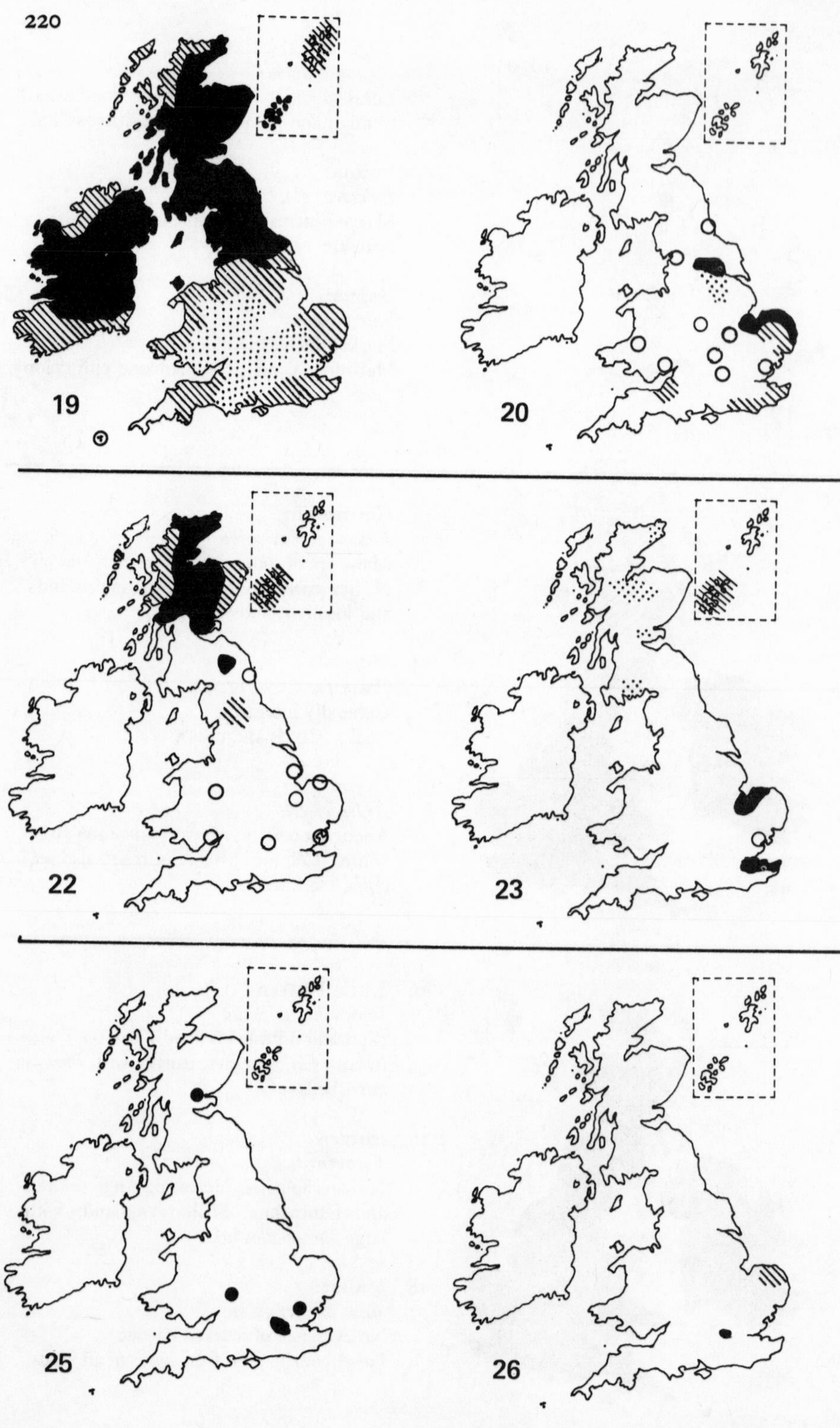
19
20
22
23
25
26

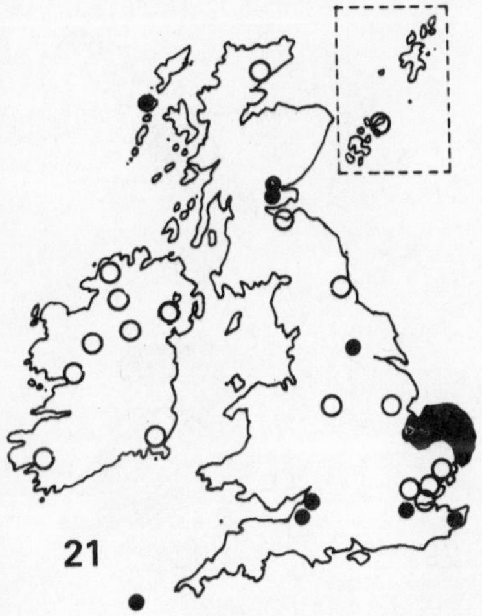

21

19 **Teal**
Anas crecca
No evidence of marked change.
Neighbourhood of freshwater, especially moorland pools.

20 **Garganey**
Anas querquedula
Fluctuates, but has recently tended to decrease Marshes and other lowland shallow wetlands.

21 **Gadwall**
Anas strepera
About 260 pairs. Increasing, aided by artificial dispersion. Shallow lowland lakes, usually with reed cover.

24

22 **Wigeon**
Anas penelope
About 350 pairs; no recent change.
Mainly near waters on upland moors.

23 **Pintail**
Anas acuta
Fluctuates (over 100 pairs in some years).
In England, mainly marshes or wet rough grassland.

24 **Shoveler**
Anas clypeata
Probable recent decrease.
Shallow, muddy wetlands with much aquatic vegetation.

25 **Mandarin Duck**
Aix galericulata
About 200 pairs. Introduced; little recent change. Small ponds in woodland, usually with rhododendron cover.

26 **Wood Duck**
Aix sponsa
Introduced. Very small feral population.
Woodland ponds

27 **Scaup**
Aythya nyroca
Not annual. Usually single pairs but three Perth, 1970. Moorland pools and lochs.

28

29

?
31

?
32

34

35

30

28 **Tufted Duck** ●●●●
Aythya fuligula
Increasing.
Lakes, in south especially large flooded gravel pits.

29 **Pochard** ⊙⊙⊙
Aythya ferina
About 250 pairs. Increasing in England.
Lakes and coastal fleets with areas of shallow water and reeds.

30 **Goldeneye** △
Bucephala clangula
Sporadic. Bred E. Inverness 1970–72.
Nests tree-holes (also nest boxes) near wooded lochs.

33

31 **Long-tailed Duck** △
Clangula hyemalis
Sporadic. Probably bred 1969, otherwise last nest 1911. Moorland lochs.

32 **Velvet Scoter** △
Melanitta fusca
(Sporadic.) Probably bred Shetland 1945.
Moorland lochs or marine islands.

33 **Common Scoter** ●●
Melanitta nigra
About 90 pairs; fluctuates.
Small moorland lochs; in Ireland wooded islands in large lochs.

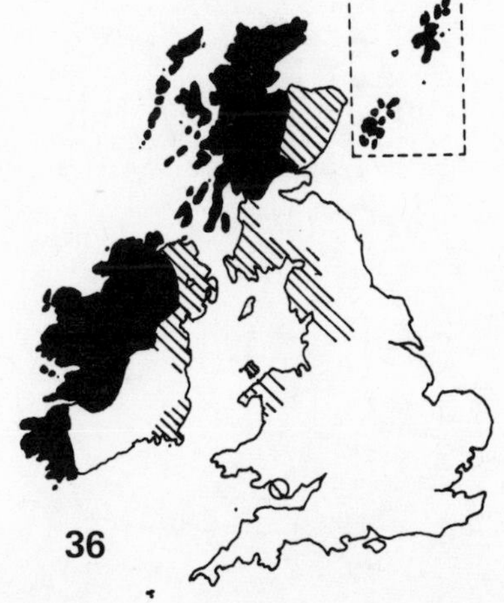

34 **Eider** ●●●●
Somateria mollissima
Increasing.
Coasts and marine islands.

35 **Ruddy Duck** ●
Oxyura jamaicensis
Introduced. Slow increase and spread.
Large lakes.

36 **Red-breasted Merganser** ●●●●
Mergus serrator
Gradual increase and spread, especially in Wales. Lakes, rivers, coastal inlets and estuaries.

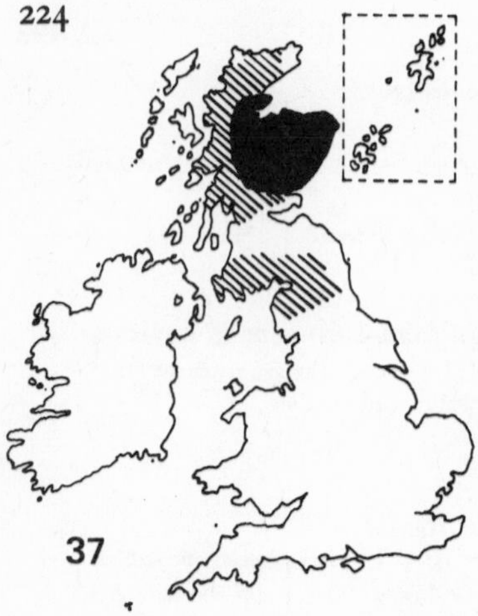

37

38

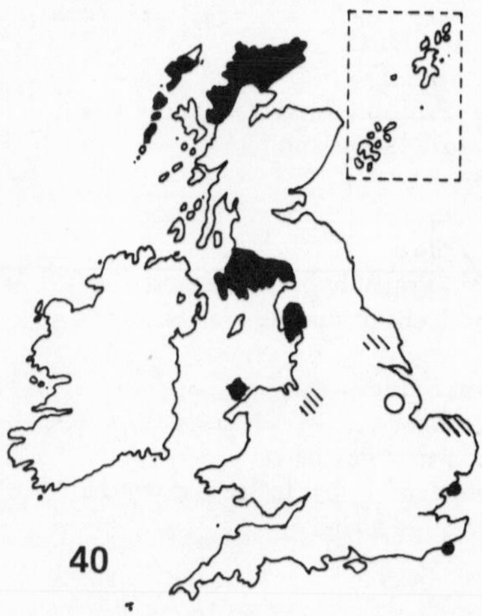

40

41

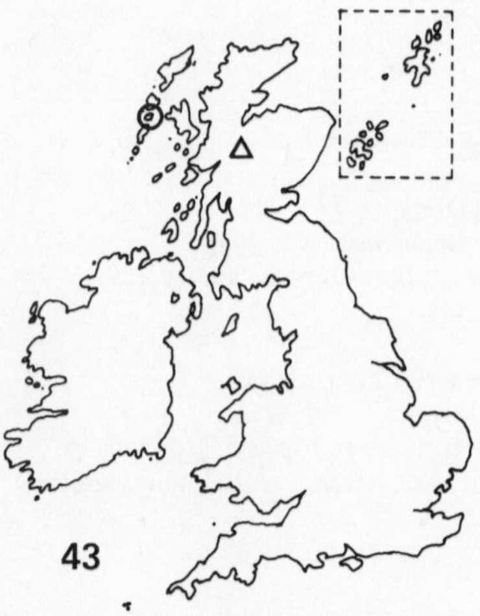

43

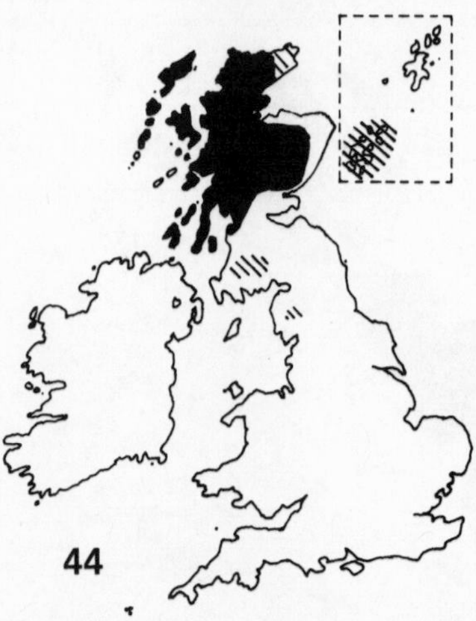

44

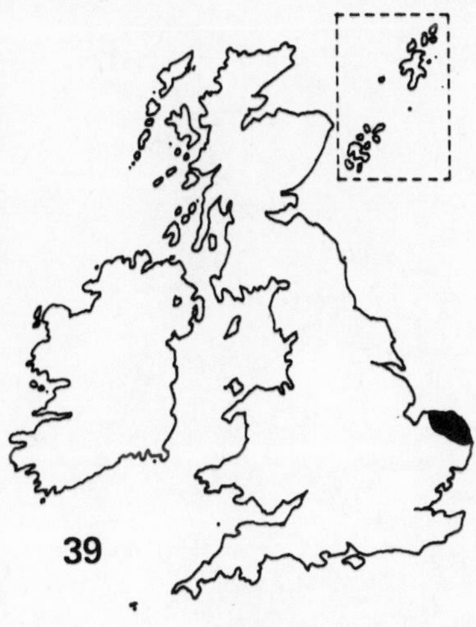

37 **Goosander** ●●●
Mergus merganser
Some increase in south of range.
Larger rivers and lochs, usually wooded.

38 **Shelduck** ⊙⊙⊙⊙⊙
Tadorna tadorna
Increase perhaps sustained in some areas.
Low coasts; increasingly near lakes inland.

39 **Egyptian Goose** ●●
Alopochen aegyptiacus
Introduced; no recent change.
Mainly lakes in parkland.

40 **Greylag Goose** ●●●
Anser anser
Feral population increasing, aided by artificial spread. Native birds, moorland lochs. Feral birds, lowland waters, etc.

41 **Canada Goose** ●●●●
Branta canadensis
Introduced. Increasing, aided by artificial spread. Freshwater lakes, especially in parkland.

42 **Mute Swan** ●●●●
Cygnus olor
Numbers stable or slightly decreased.
Waters of many kinds, usually fresh.

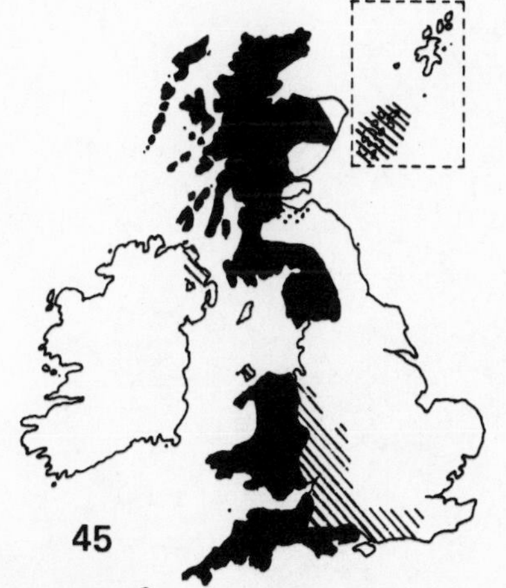

43 **Whooper Swan** △
Cygnus cygnus
Sporadic; most recently 1947 (Hebrides), 1963 (Inverness). Freshwater lochs.

44 **Golden Eagle** ●●●
Aquila chrysaetos
About 300 pairs. Has recently recolonised Lake District and Orkney. Crags in open mountainous country.

45 **Buzzard** ●●●●
Buteo buteo
Decrease since 1954 but numbers now apparently stable. Varied: open moorland, seacliffs to well wooded farmland.

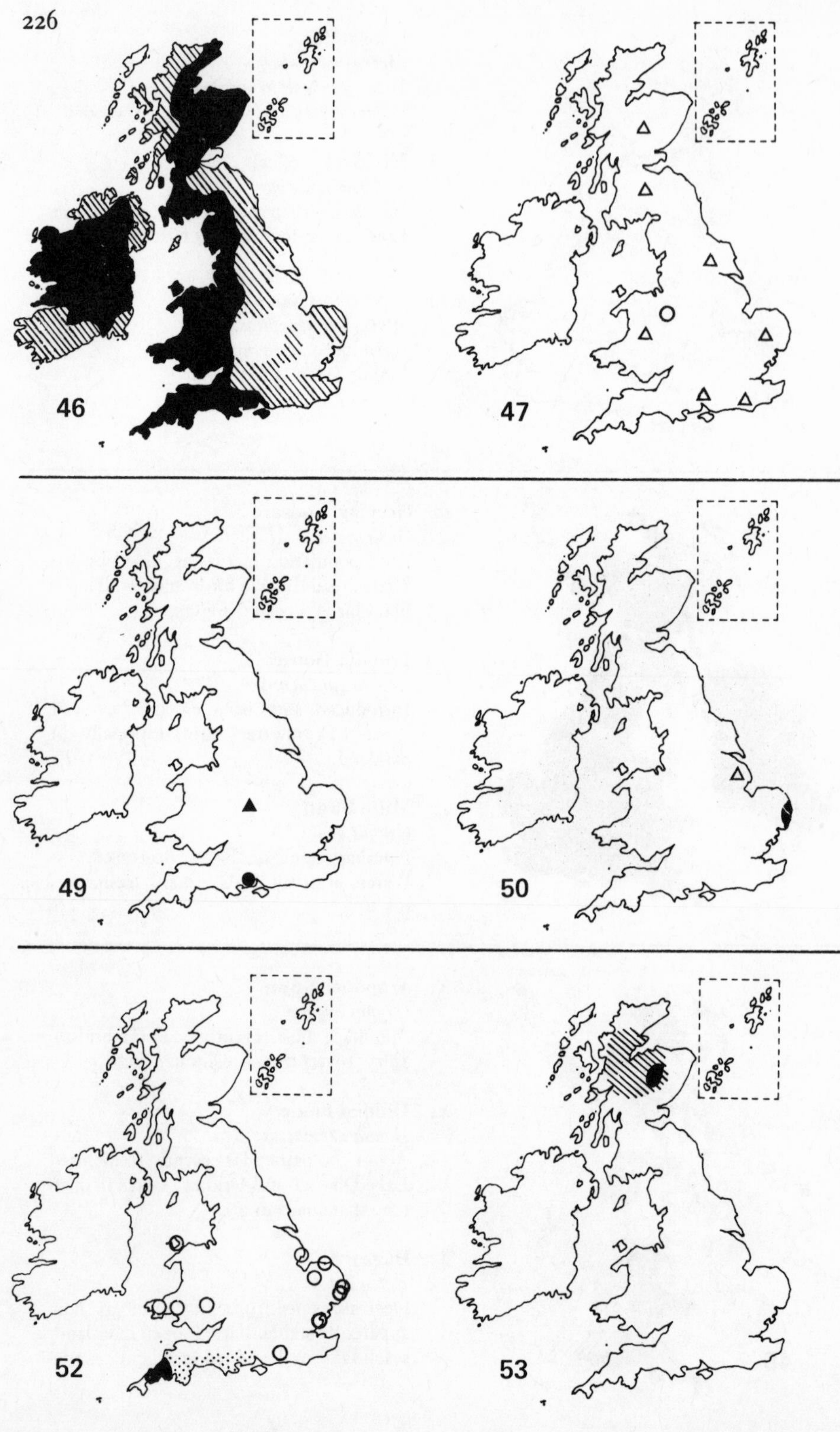
46
47
49
50
52
53

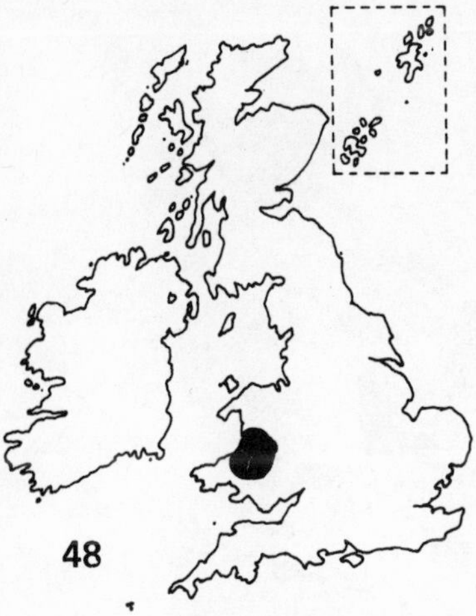

46 **Sparrowhawk** ●●●●
Accipiter nisus
Some recovery in west, remains rare in lowland east. Woodlands, especially conifers; sometimes scrub.

47 **Goshawk** △
Accipiter gentilis
Birds of unknown (probably captive) origin have bred most recent years. Extensive woods with large clearings.

48 **Kite** ●●
Milvus milvus
Increasing very slowly, now 26 pairs. Steep valley woods with open country nearby.

49 **Honey Buzzard** ○
Pernis apivorus
About eight pairs; number presumed stable. Mature deciduous woodland.

50 **Marsh Harrier** ⊙
Circus aeruginosus
Some decrease and now only 3–5 nests annually. Lowland marshes with extensive *Phragmites* beds.

51 **Hen Harrier** ⊙⊙⊙
Circus cyaneus
Perhaps 600 pairs. Increasing, especially in Ireland. Damp moorland; overgrown young conifer plantations.

52 **Montagu's Harrier** ○
Circus pygargus
Continued decrease and now only 5–10 pairs annually. Mainly rough moorland edges with young conifers; also reed beds.

53 **Osprey** ○
Pandion haliaetus
Gradual increase to seven nests 1971, when other birds present. Usually nests in mature Scots Pines near lochs or large rivers.

54 **Hobby** ○○
Falco subbuteo
Just under 100 pairs. Numbers probably stable. Typically heathland or downs with scattered pine clumps.

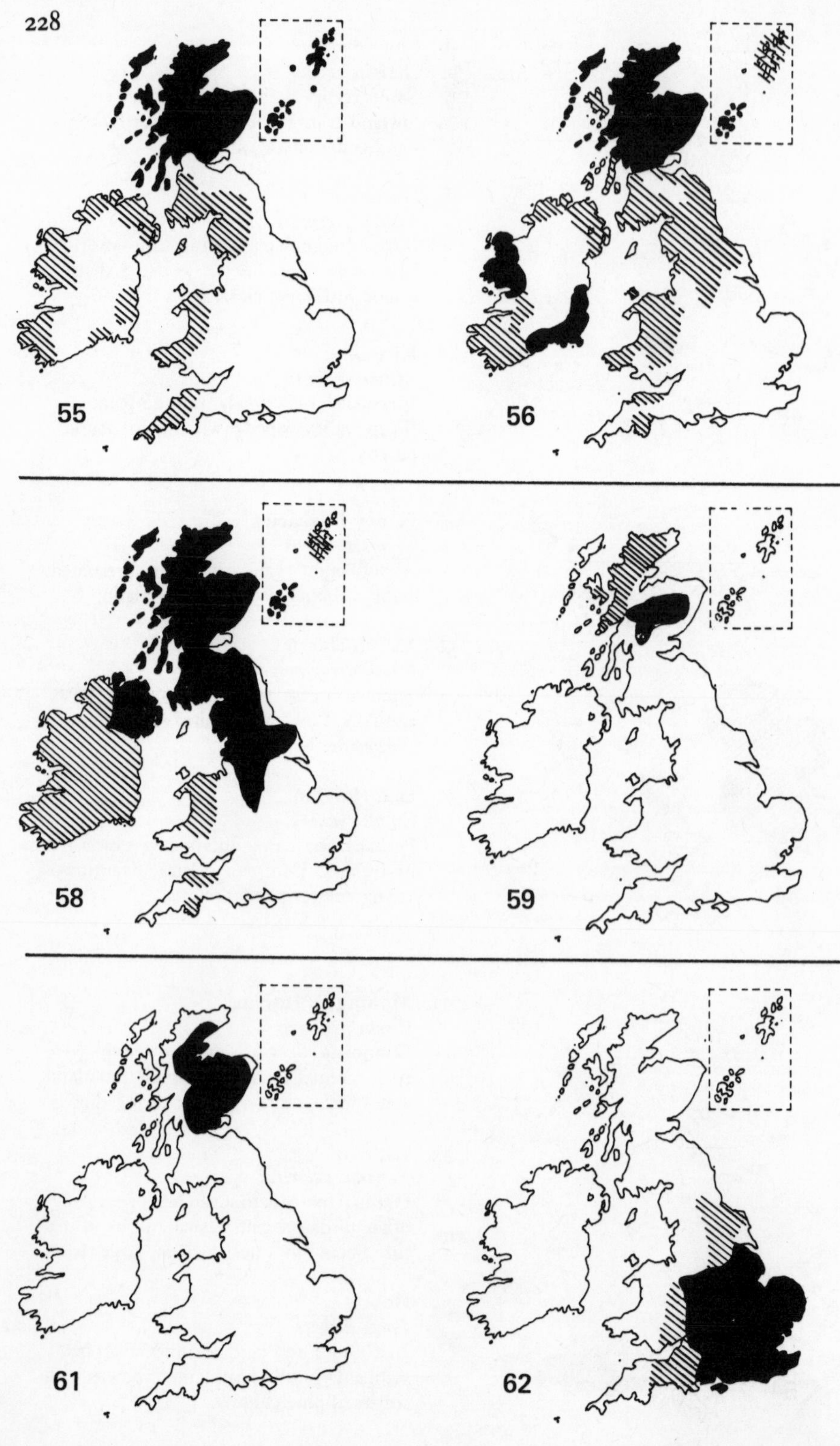
55
56
58
59
61
62

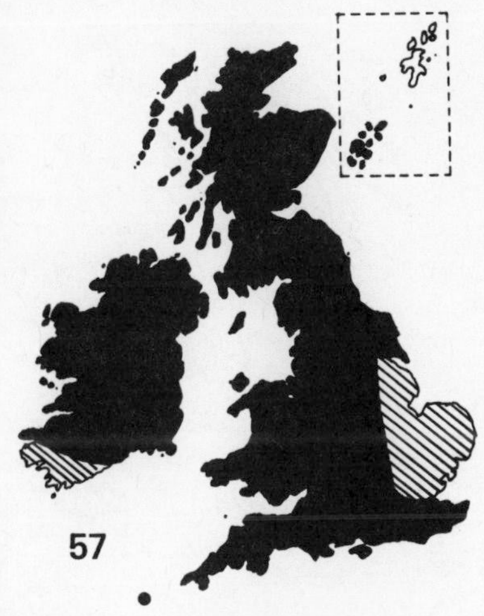

55 **Peregrine** ●●●
Falco peregrinus
Some recovery, mainly inland, but still fewer than 200 successful pairs. Inland and coastal cliffs.

56 **Merlin** ⊙⊙⊙
Falco columbarius
About 500 pairs; perhaps still decreasing. Open moorland, nesting thick heather or occasionally trees.

57 **Kestrel** ⊙⊙⊙⊙⊙
Falco tinnunculus
Fluctuates; still scarce in arable parts of E. England. Open or lightly wooded country of all kinds, including urban areas.

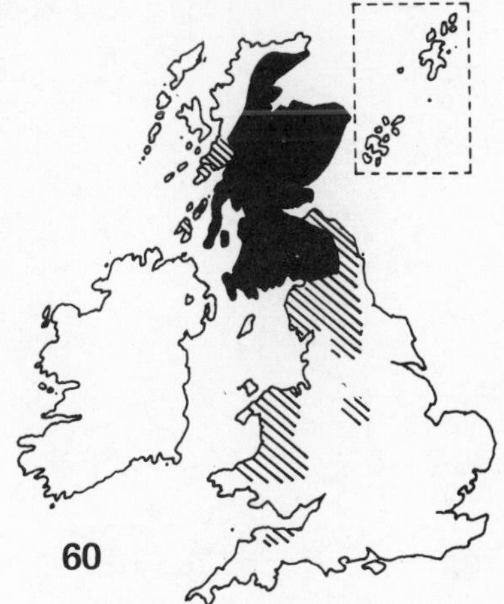

58 **Red Grouse** ●●●●●●
Lagopus lagopus
No further changes known.
Heather moors.

59 **Ptarmigan** ●●●●●
Lagopus mutus
Numbers fluctuate.
Barren ground on higher mountains, generally above 800 m.

60 **Black Grouse** ●●●●●
Lyrurus tetrix
Numbers fluctuate; probably still increasing Wales. Open conifer woods at moorland edge, including young plantations.

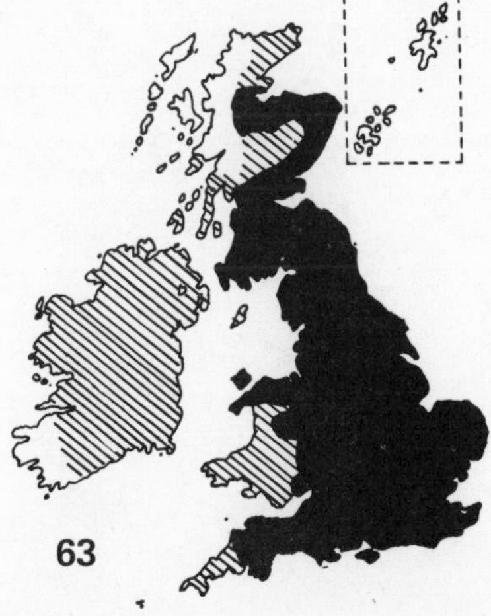

61 **Capercaillie** ●●●●
Tetrao urogallus
No recent marked changes known.
Mature, open pinewoods.

62 **Red-legged Partridge** ●●●●●●
Alectoris rufa
Further introductions (usually temporary) beyond mapped range. Farmland and other open country with well-drained soils.

63 **Partridge** ●●●●●●
Perdix perdix
Continued sharp decline till at least 1970.
Mainly farmland.

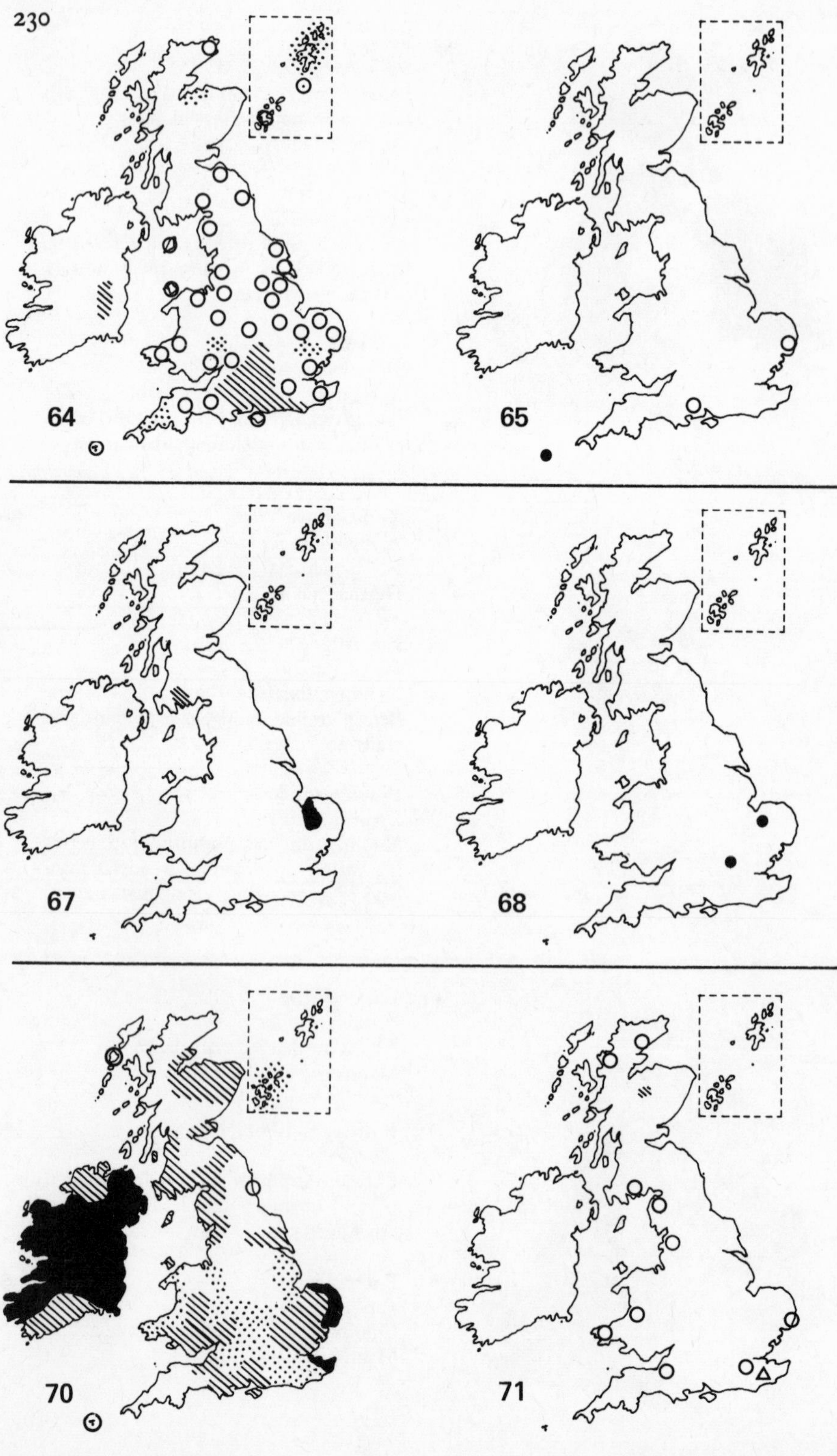
64
65
67
68
70
71

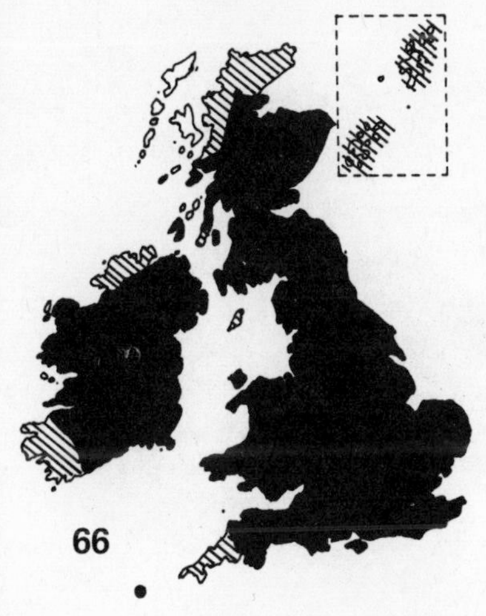

64 **Quail** ○○
Coturnix coturnix
Fluctuates; widespread (over 100 pairs) in 1970. Chiefly in cereal crops; also other long herbaceous vegetation.

65 **Bobwhite Quail** ●●
Colinus virginianus
Introduced; feral population has persisted Scilly since early 1960s. Wooded farmland.

66 **Pheasant** ●●●●●●
Phasianus colchicus
Numbers maintained artificially.
Farmland, woods, upland scrub to 300 m.

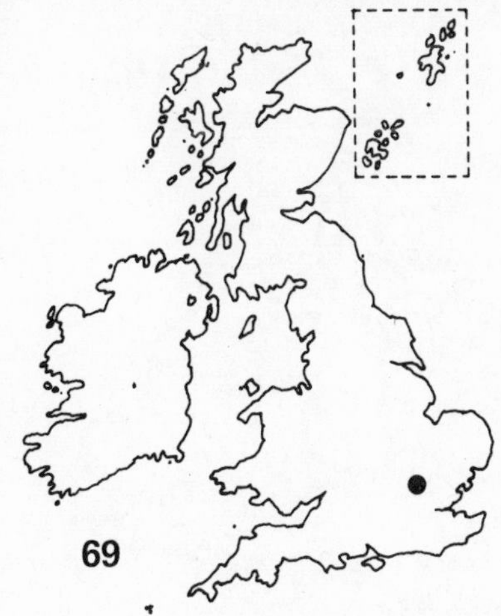

67 **Golden Pheasant** ●●●
Chrysolophus pictus
Introduced; apparent recent increase.
Open parts and surrounds of conifer woods.

68 **Lady Amherst's Pheasant** ●●
Chrysolophus amherstiae
Introduced; largely restricted to one area. Open woods, parklands, especially with rhododendron.

69 **Reeves's Pheasant** ●●
Syrmaticus reevesii
Introduced; largely restricted to one area.
Open woods and parkland.

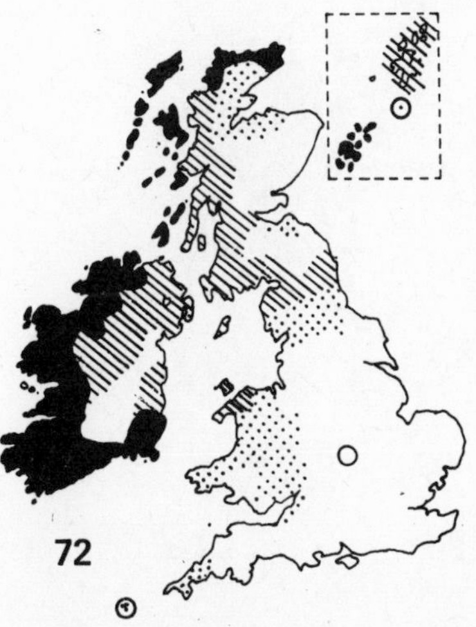

70 **Water Rail** ●●●●
Rallus aquaticus
No recent changes known.
Marshes and other lowland wetlands with dense vegetation.

71 **Spotted Crake** ○
Porzana porzana
Barely annual; sporadic most areas, though overlooked. Marshes and other wetlands with dense aquatic vegetation.

72 **Corncrake** ○○○○
Crex crex
Apparently still declining everywhere.
Rough pastures, hayfields, nettle beds.

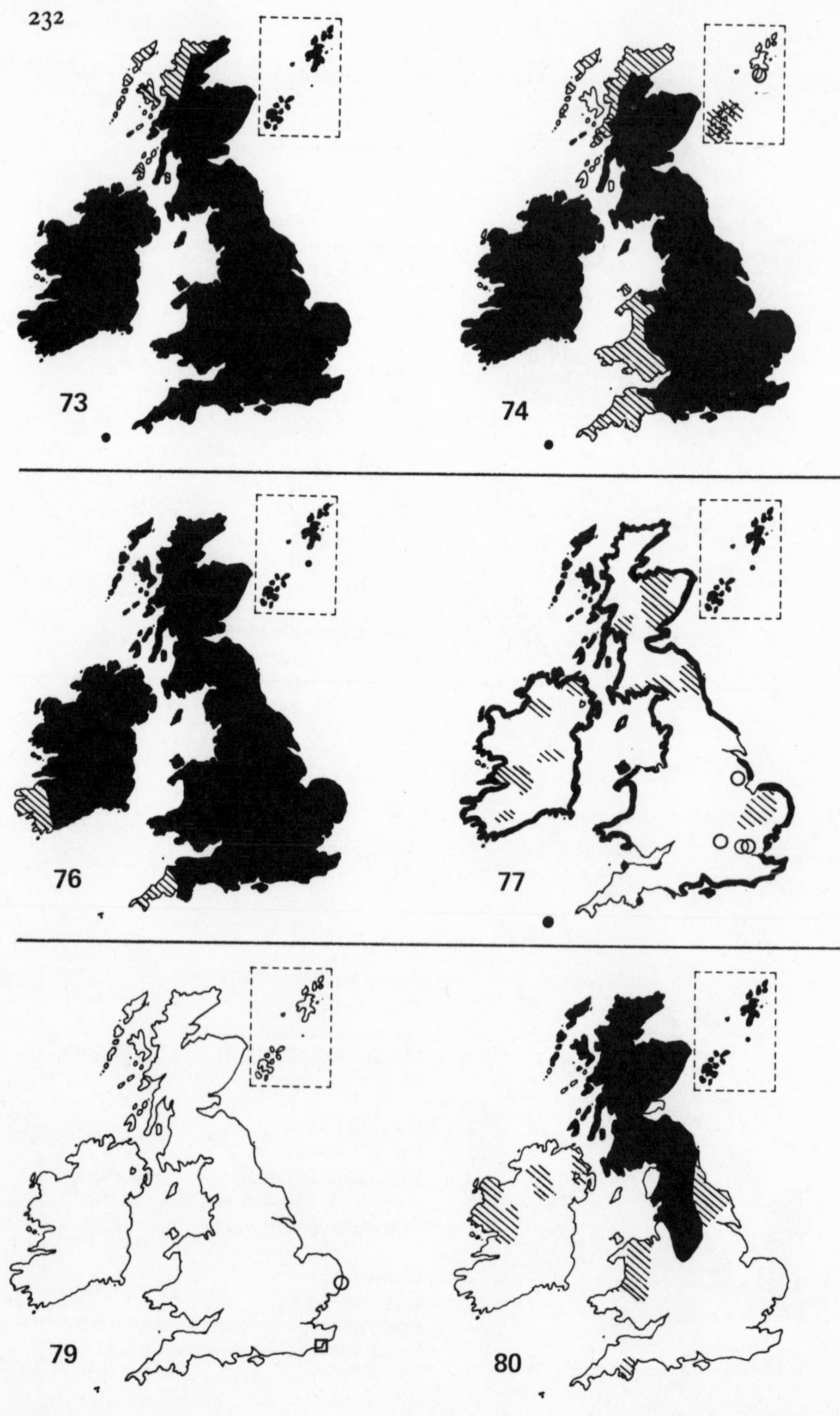
73
74
76
77
79
80

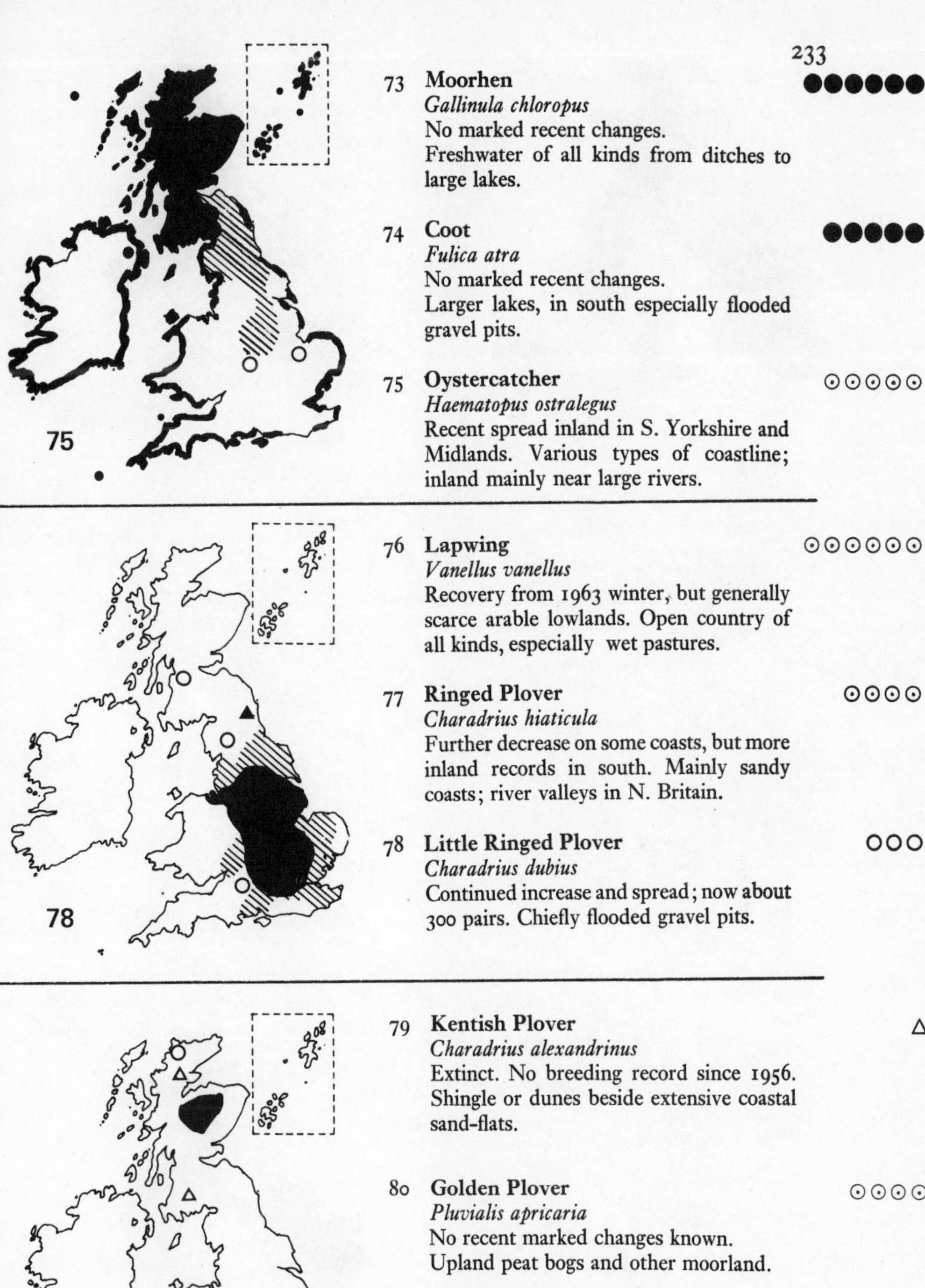

73 **Moorhen** ●●●●●●
Gallinula chloropus
No marked recent changes.
Freshwater of all kinds from ditches to large lakes.

74 **Coot** ●●●●●
Fulica atra
No marked recent changes.
Larger lakes, in south especially flooded gravel pits.

75 **Oystercatcher** ⊙⊙⊙⊙⊙
Haematopus ostralegus
Recent spread inland in S. Yorkshire and Midlands. Various types of coastline; inland mainly near large rivers.

---

76 **Lapwing** ⊙⊙⊙⊙⊙⊙
Vanellus vanellus
Recovery from 1963 winter, but generally scarce arable lowlands. Open country of all kinds, especially wet pastures.

77 **Ringed Plover** ⊙⊙⊙⊙
Charadrius hiaticula
Further decrease on some coasts, but more inland records in south. Mainly sandy coasts; river valleys in N. Britain.

78 **Little Ringed Plover** ○○○
Charadrius dubius
Continued increase and spread; now about 300 pairs. Chiefly flooded gravel pits.

---

79 **Kentish Plover** △
Charadrius alexandrinus
Extinct. No breeding record since 1956. Shingle or dunes beside extensive coastal sand-flats.

80 **Golden Plover** ⊙⊙⊙⊙
Pluvialis apricaria
No recent marked changes known.
Upland peat bogs and other moorland.

81 **Dotterel** ○○
Eudromias morinellus
Perhaps slightly increased—rather more recent records beyond main range. Bred Wales 1969. Barren ground on higher mountains, generally above 800 m.

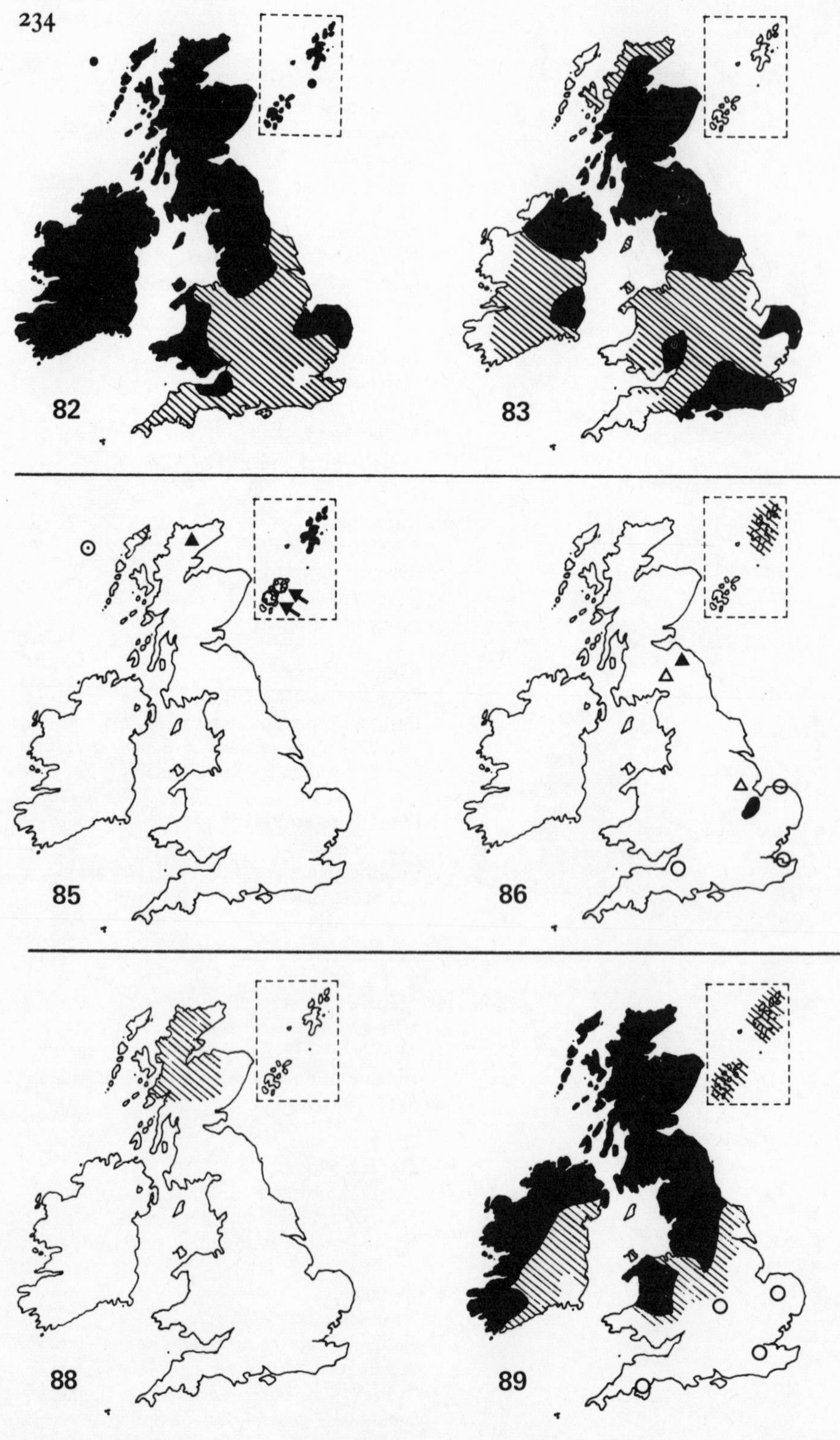

82
83
85
86
88
89

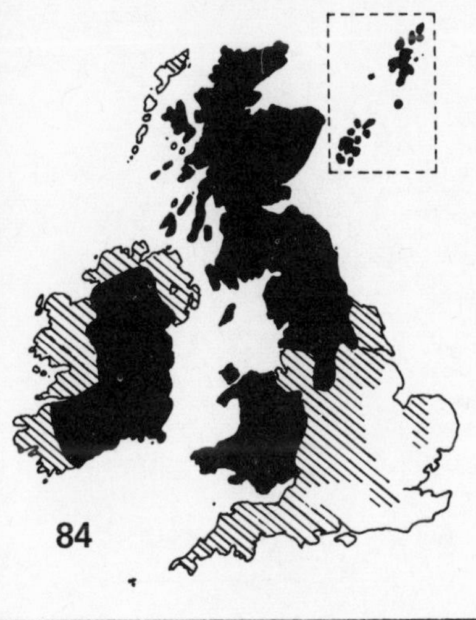

82 **Snipe** ●●●●●
Gallinago gallinago
No recent marked changes known.
Wet moorland and pastures, marshes.

83 **Woodcock** ●●●●●
Scolopax rusticola
No recent marked changes.
Chiefly woodlands with light ground cover: also heathland.

84 **Curlew** ⊙⊙⊙⊙⊙
Numenius arquata
No indication of further spread in south of range. Mainly wet moorland and heaths.

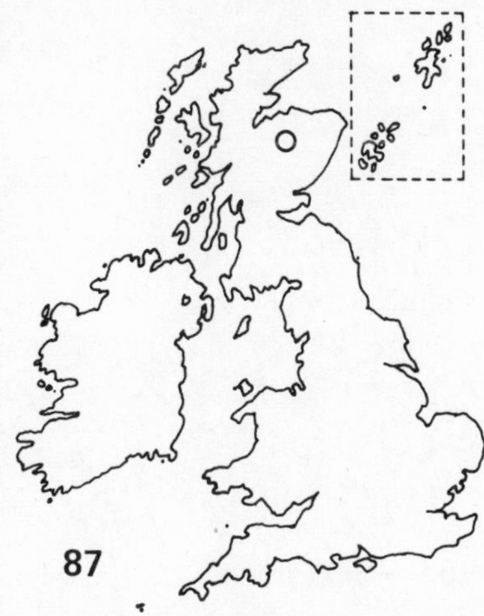

85 **Whimbrel** ○○○
Numenius phaeopus
About 160 pairs (mainly Shetland); recent spread to Scottish mainland. Peat bogs and other moorland.

86 **Black-tailed Godwit** ○○
Limosa limosa
About 70 pairs, chiefly on Ouse Washes. Grazed washlands.

87 **Green Sandpiper** △
Tringa ochropus
Sporadic. Bred Inverness 1959.
Wet moorland with scattered pines.

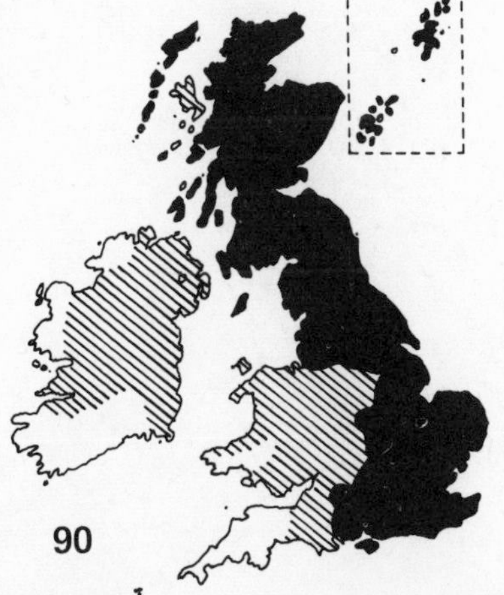

88 **Wood Sandpiper** ○
Tringa glareola
No change; numbers still very small.
Moorland near small, eutrophic lochs.

89 **Common Sandpiper** ○○○○○
Tringa hypoleucos
Perhaps some further local decreases.
Clear streams, rivers, lakes, coastal inlets with stony shores.

90 **Redshank** ⊙⊙⊙⊙⊙
Tringa totanus
Recovery from 1963 winter, but still absent e.g. S. Devon. Marshes, wet pastures and grass moors.

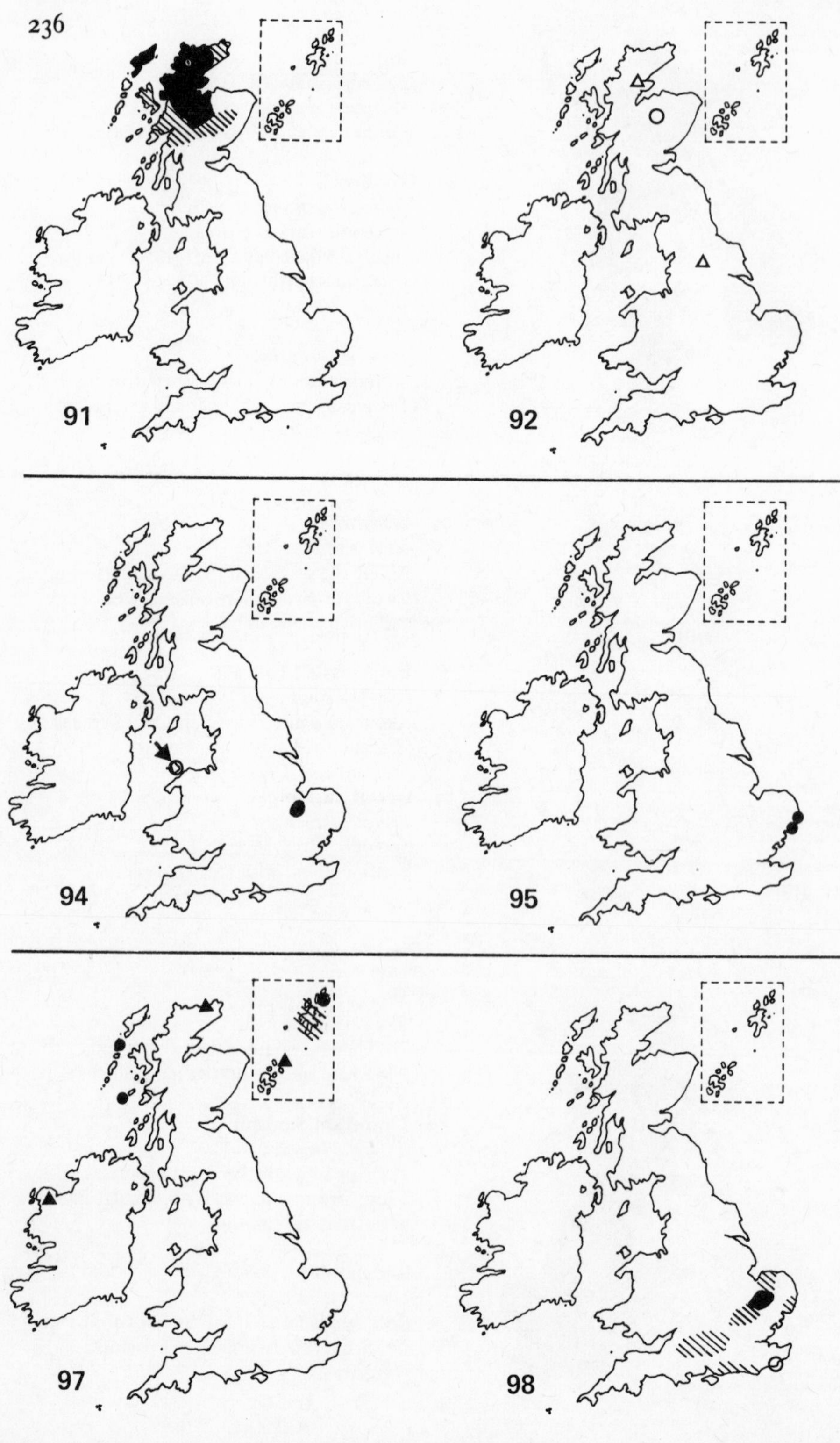
91
92
94
95
97
98

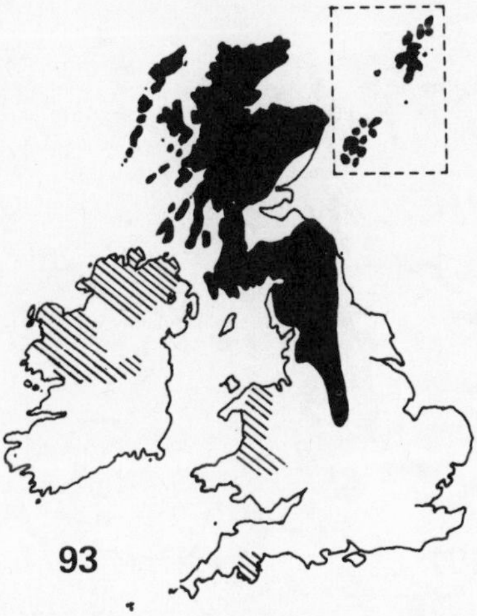

91 **Greenshank** ○○○
Tringa nebularia
Some decrease in southern part of range. Open or lightly wooded moorland with scattered pools.

92 **Temminck's Stint** △
Calidris temminckii
Sporadic; bred E. Ross (1–2 pairs) 1969–71; previously only 4 records. Lightly wooded country near pools.

93 **Dunlin** ⊙⊙⊙⊙
Calidris alpina
No recent changes known.
Peat bogs; also coastal saltings, *machair*.

94 **Ruff** ○○
Philomachus pugnax
Recent Ouse Washes recolonist, up to 20 nests (1971). Grazed washlands.

95 **Avocet** ⊙⊙⊙
Recurvirostra avosetta
About 150 pairs (1972); gradually increasing. Shallow, brackish lagoons with bare mud or shingle islands.

96 **Black-winged Stilt** △
Himantopus himantopus
Sporadic; 3 pairs bred Nottingham, 1945.
Sewage farm settling lagoon.

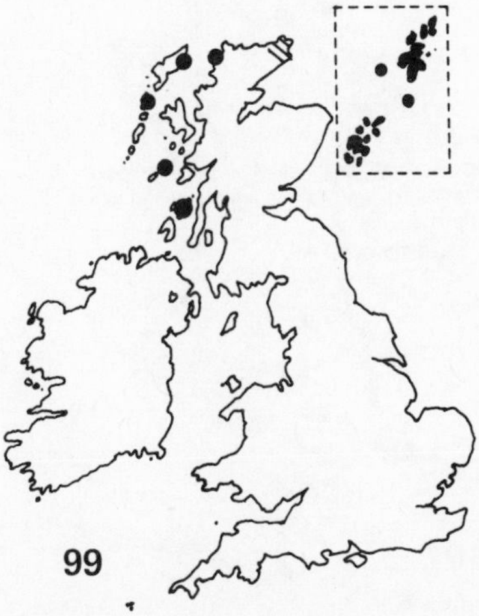

97 **Red-necked Phalarope** ○○
Phalaropus lobatus
Fluctuates; 28–65 pairs during 1968–70.
Flooded peat cuttings, small shallow lochs.

98 **Stone Curlew** ○○○
Burhinus oedicnemus
About 200 pairs. Further decrease; none now Kent. Sandy heaths and chalk downland, even after ploughing.

99 **Arctic Skua** ○○○○
Stercorarius parasiticus
Some continued increase.
Paramaritime moors and peat bogs.

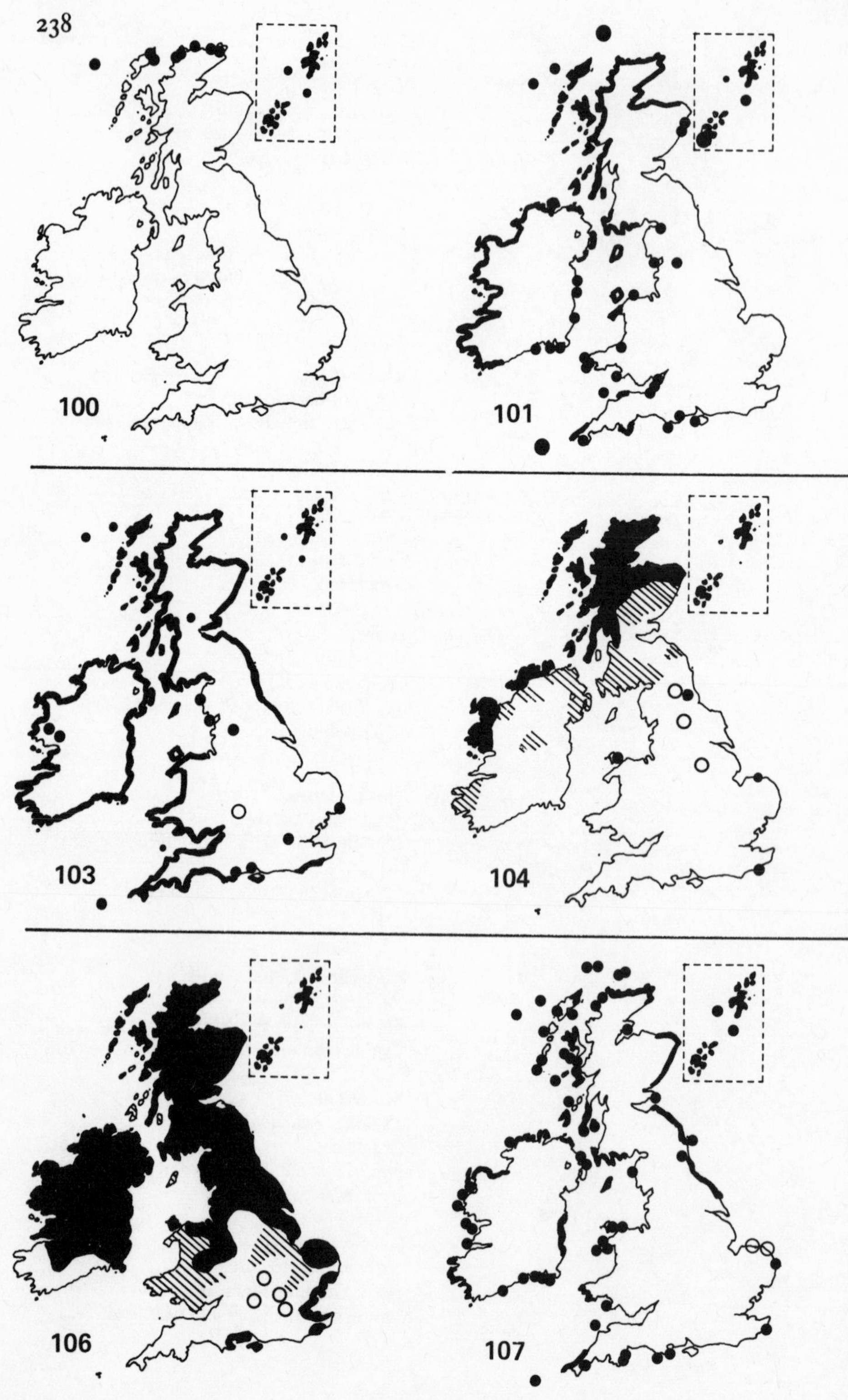
100
101
103
104
106
107

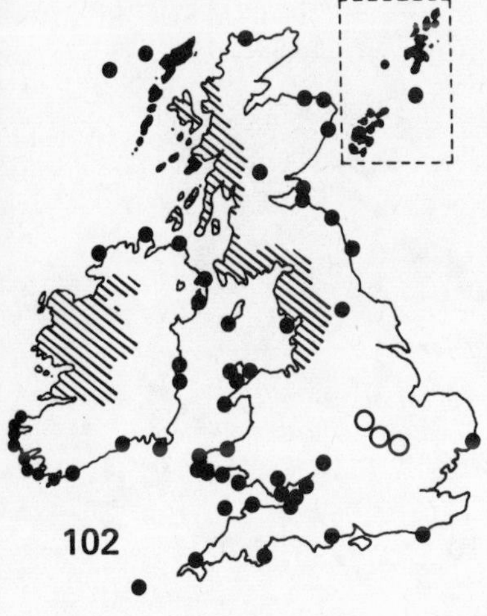

100 **Great Skua** ○○○○
Stercorarius skua
Increase and spread in Sutherland and Caithness. Paramaritime moors and peat bogs.

101 **Great Black-headed Gull** 
Larus marinus
Increase and spread continues.
Chiefly marine islands, stacks, headlands; also inland moors.

102 **Lesser Black-backed Gull** ○○○○○
Larus fuscus
New colony Suffolk coast and odd pairs in English Midlands. Mainly coastal islands, also seacliffs and moors inland.

105

103 **Herring Gull** ●●●●●●
Larus argentatus
Increase. New colony Suffolk coast.
Typically seacliffs and islands, also seaside buildings.

104 **Common Gull** ●●●●
Larus canus
Probably increasing; evidence of southward spread. Chiefly islands in fresh and sea lochs

105 **Mediterranean Gull** △
Larus melanocephalus
Bred Hampshire 1968 and odd hybrids or cross-mated birds since. Salt marsh among Black-headed (with which hybridising).

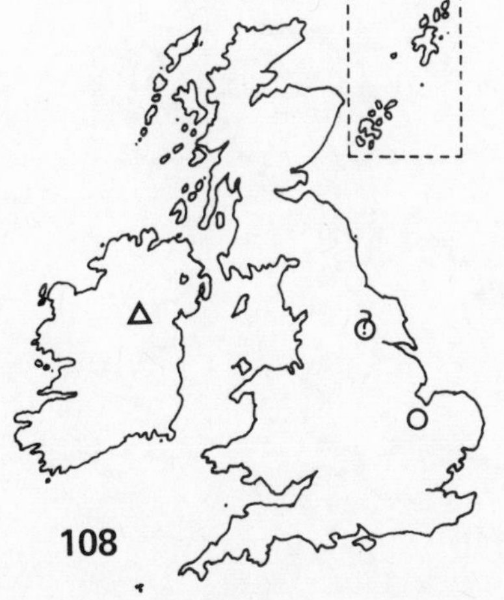

106 **Black-headed Gull** ⊙⊙⊙⊙⊙⊙
Larus ridibundus
Huge local increase in S. Hampshire.
Salt marshes, dunes, freshwater marshes, boggy-edged pools.

107 **Kittiwake** ⊙⊙⊙⊙⊙⊙
Rissa tridactyla
General increase probably continues.
Typically seacliffs; locally piers, buildings next sea.

108 **Black Tern** △
Chlidonias niger
Recent breeding Ouse Washes (2 years), Ireland, probably Yorkshire. Shallow wetlands with floating vegetation.

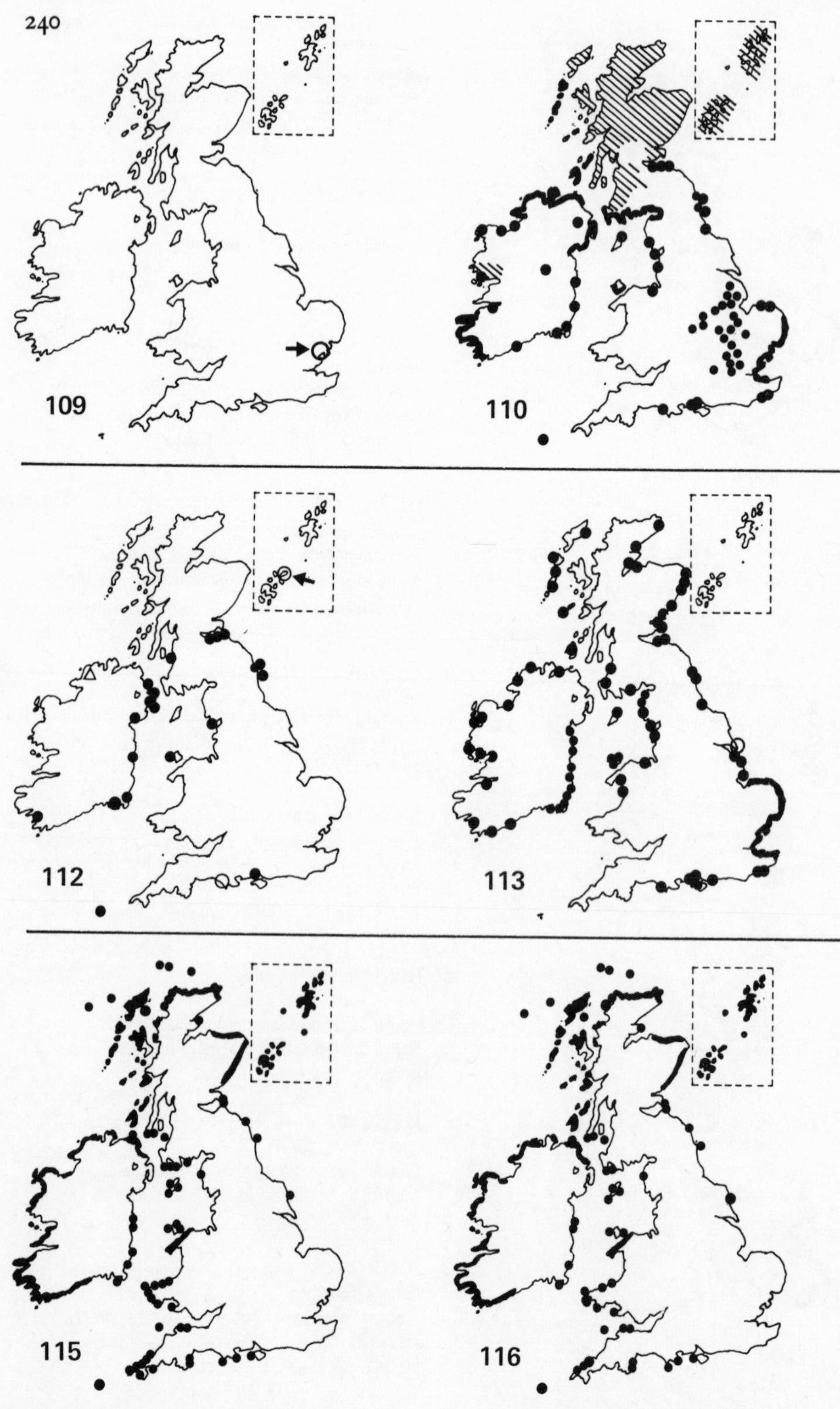
109
110
112
113
115
116

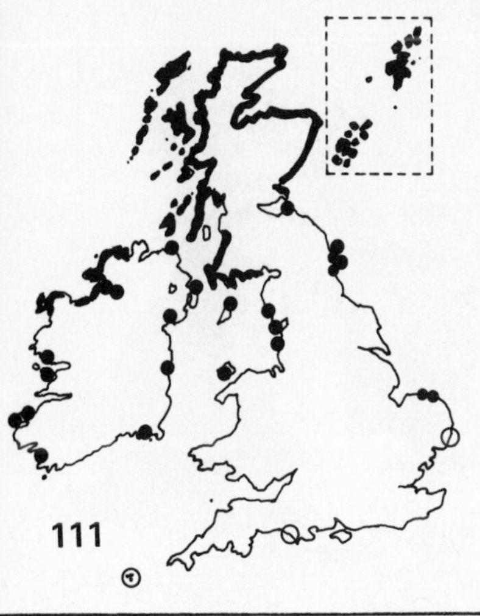

109 **Gull-billed Tern** △
Gelochelidon nilotica
Sporadic; bred Essex 1950.
Only breeding record was on island in reservoir.

110 **Common Tern** ○○○○○
Sterna hirundo
Continued spread inland by small numbers in England. Mainly low-lying coasts; also inland by rivers, lakes.

111 **Arctic Tern** ○○○○○
Sterna paradisaea
No marked recent changes known.
Low-lying coasts and islands.

114

112 **Roseate Tern** ○○○○
Sterna dougallii
About 2000 pairs; small colonies recently found W. Ireland. Chiefly low coastal islands.

113 **Little Tern** ○○○○
Sterna albifrons
About 1600 pairs; further local decreases. Typically in small colonies on sand, shingle or shell beaches.

114 **Sandwich Tern** ○○○○○
Sterna sandvicensis
About 12,000 pairs—a further increase.
Low-lying coasts, also locally on islands in fresh lochs.

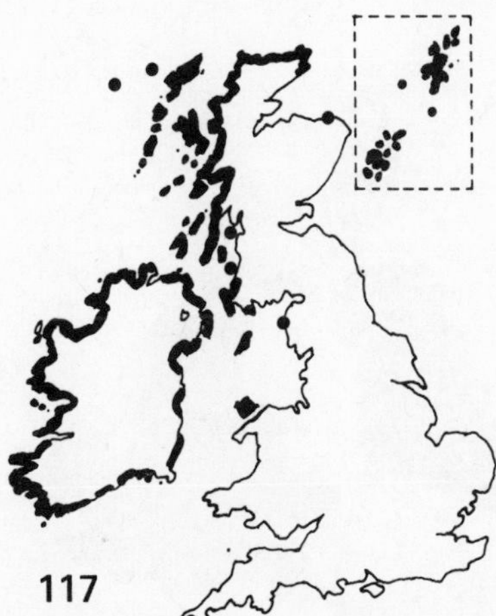

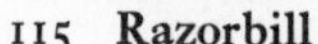

115 **Razorbill** ⊙⊙⊙⊙⊙⊙
Alca torda
Some decrease in Irish Sea, notably in 1970. Rocky seacliffs and islands.

116 **Guillemot** ⊙⊙⊙⊙⊙⊙
Uria aalge
Further decline in Irish Sea, especially in 1970. Rocky seacliffs, stacks and islands.

117 **Black Guillemot** ●●●●
Cepphus grylle
No evidence of recent marked change.
Rocky coasts and islands.

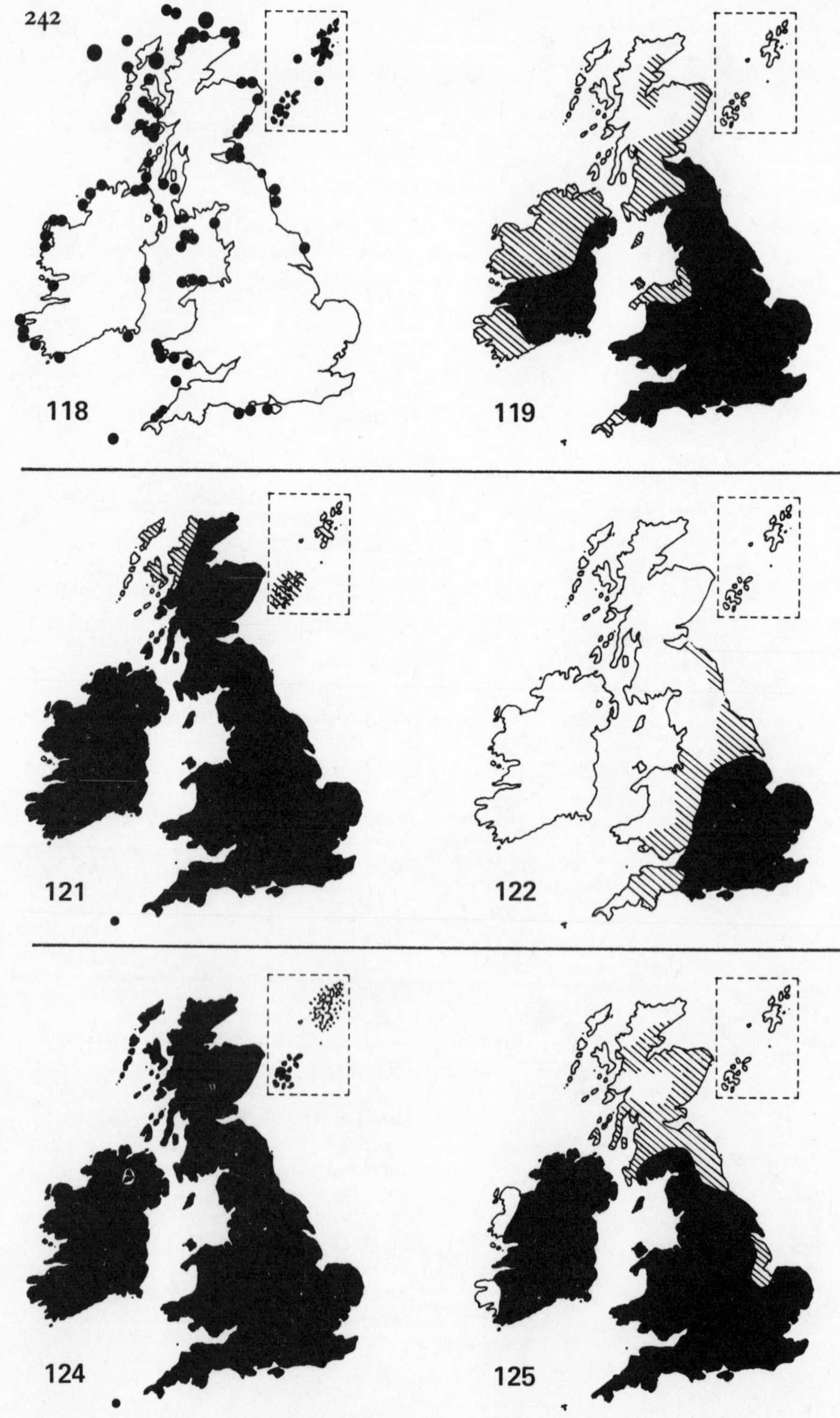
118
119
121
122
124
125

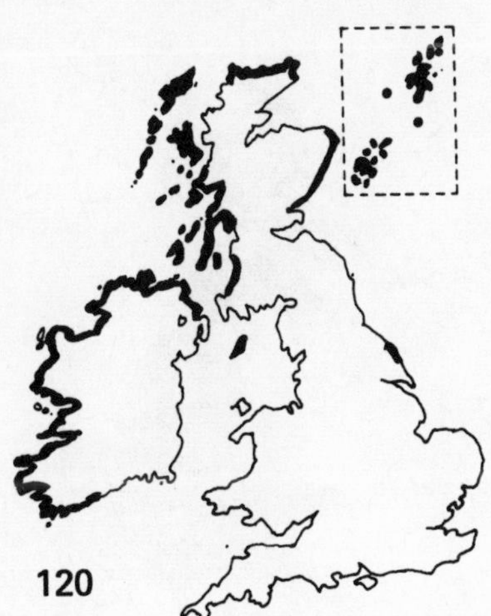

118 **Puffin** ⊙⊙⊙⊙⊙⊙
Fratercula arctica
Heavy recent decrease in N.W. Scotland, Vegetated marine islands; also mainland seacliff slopes.

119 **Stock Dove** ●●●●●
Columba oenas
Some recovery in areas where reduced 1957–64. Farmland, parkland, sea coast.

120 **Rock Dove** ●●●●●
Columba livia
No marked changes known.
Seacliffs. Feral birds (not mapped) mainly in towns.

121 **Woodpigeon** ●●●●●●●
Columba palumbus
Some decrease in last few years.
Farmland and woods of all kinds; also treeless islands.

122 **Turtle Dove** ○○○○○
Streptopelia turtur
No marked recent changes known.
Scrub, tall hedges on farmland, downs, heaths.

123 **Collared Dove** ●●●●●
Streptopelia decaocto
Continued marked increase, but rate now slowing. Typically in large suburban and village gardens with conifers.

126

124 **Cuckoo** ○○○○
Cuculus canorus
No further changes known.
Rural habitats of virtually all kinds.

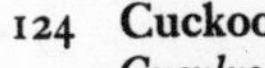

125 **Barn Owl** ●●●●
Tyto alba
Fluctuates, but numbers still generally low.
Lightly wooded country, especially with rough pastures.

126 **Snowy Owl** △
Nyctea scandiaca
Sporadic; one pair Shetland (Fetlar) since 1967. Open moorland with rock outcrops.

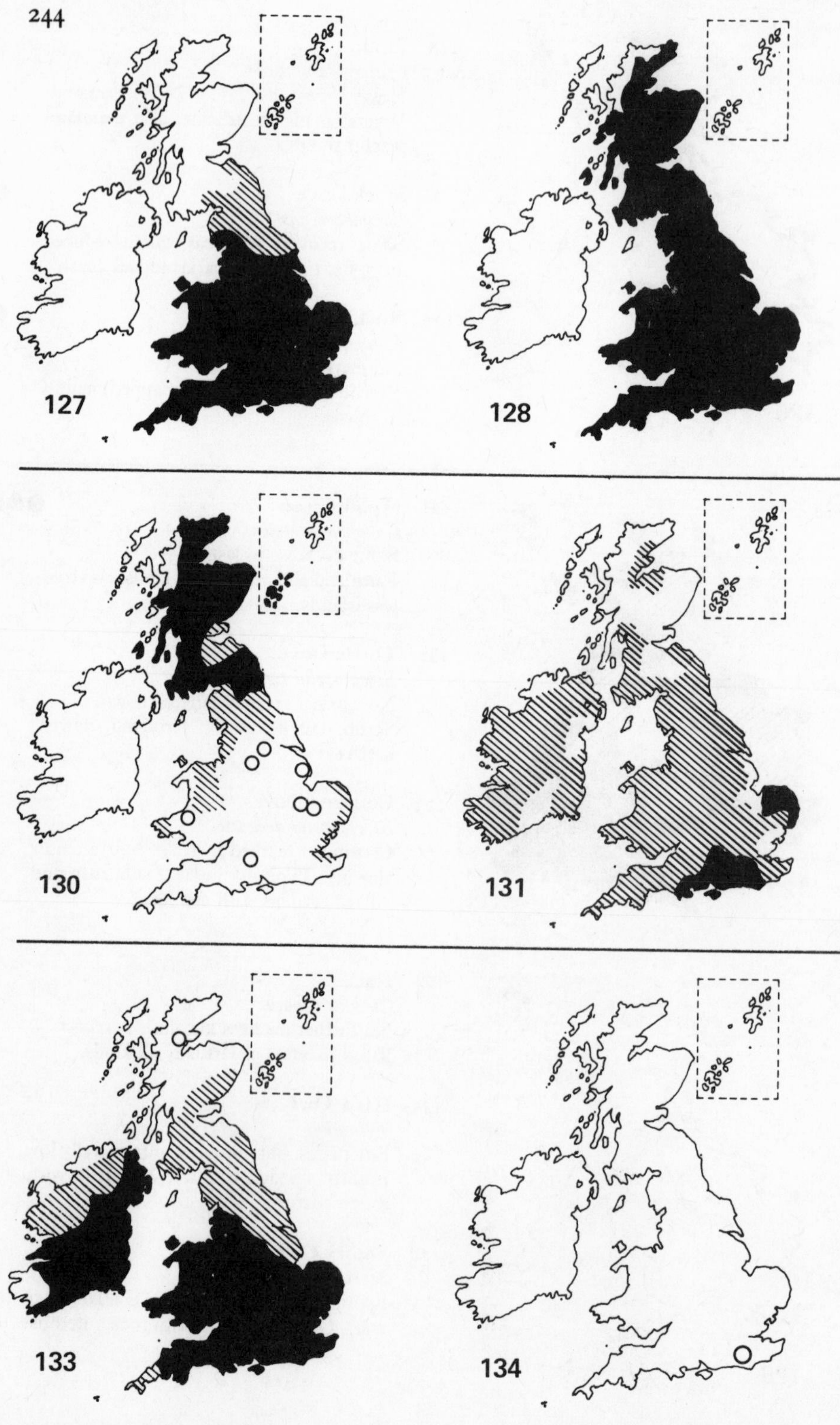
127
128
130
131
133
134

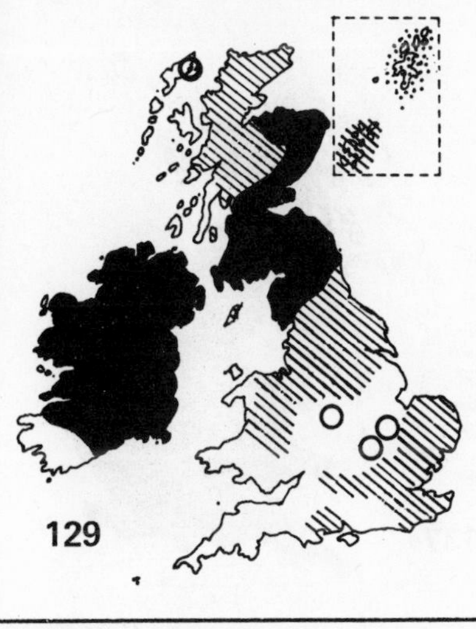

127 **Little Owl** ●●●●
Athene noctua
Still much reduced in lowland England. Chiefly lightly wooded farmland; locally seacliffs.

128 **Tawny Owl** ●●●●●
Strix aluco
No marked recent changes known. Chiefly deciduous woodland; also gardens, town parks.

129 **Long-eared Owl** ●●●●
Asio otus
No marked recent changes known. Chiefly coniferous woods, also isolated spinneys in open country.

130 **Short-eared Owl** ⊙⊙⊙⊙
Asio flammeus
Fluctuates.
Moorland, rough grassland, young conifer plantations.

131 **Nightjar** ○○○○
Caprimulgus europaeus
Perhaps further general decrease.
Open woodlands, heaths, low moors.

132 **Swift** ○○○○○○
Apus apus
No marked recent changes.
Towns and villages, feeding especially over freshwater.

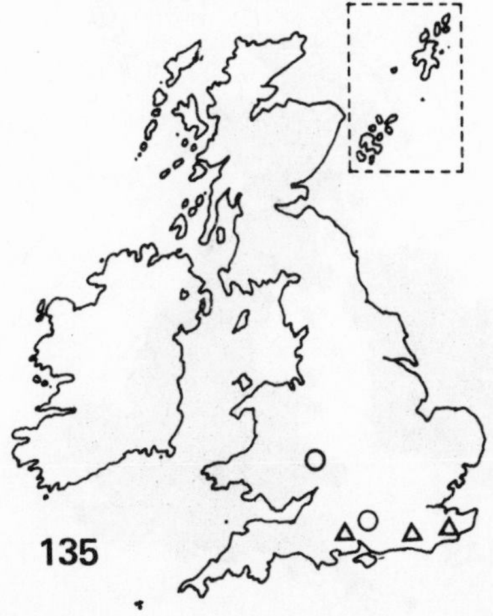

133 **Kingfisher** ●●●●
Alcedo atthis
Recovery from 1963 winter; spreading in Scotland. Slow-moving rivers and streams; lakes.

134 **Bee-eater** △
Merops apiaster
Sporadic; bred Sussex (3 pairs) 1955.
Only breeding record was in sand pit in farmland.

135 **Hoopoe** △
Upupa epops
Occasional breeding records in S. England.
Parkland, large gardens, open wooded country.

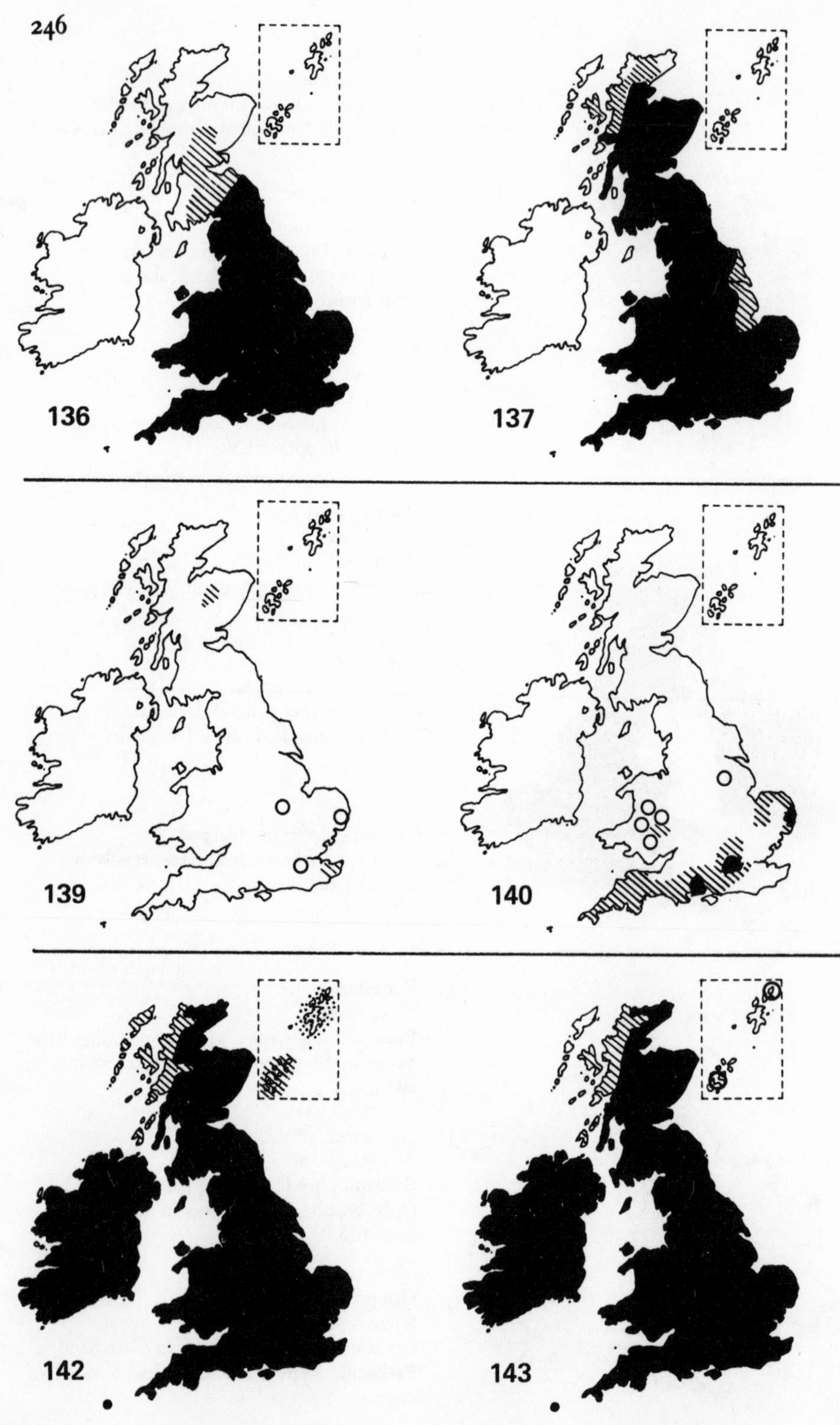
136
137
139
140
142
143

136 **Green Woodpecker** ●●●●
Picus viridis
Gradual recovery from 1963 winter. Wooded country with grasslands.

137 **Great Spotted Woodpecker** ●●●●●
Dendrocopos major
No marked recent changes known. Deciduous and coniferous woodlands.

138 **Lesser Spotted Woodpecker** ●●●●
Dendrocopos minor
No marked recent changes known. Woodlands, old orchards.

139 **Wryneck** ○
Jynx torquilla
Further decline Kent (no longer proved annually); colonisation Inverness (up to 3 pairs since 1969). Gardens, orchards in south; pine and birch woods in north.

140 **Woodlark** ●●●
Lullula arborea
Further decrease; now perhaps fewer than 100 pairs. Heaths and other open ground with scattered trees.

141 **Skylark** ●●●●●●●
Alauda arvensis
Apparent recent increase on farmland. All kinds of open country.

142 **Swallow** ○○○○○○
Hirundo rustica
Fluctuates, but no general increase or decrease. Farmland and other open country, nesting in buildings.

143 **House Martin** ○○○○○○
Delichon urbica
Local fluctuations, but no recent wider changes. Various open rural habitats, also towns.

144 **Sand Martin** ○○○○○○
Riparia riparia
No marked changes known. Usually near water, nesting in sand and gravel pits, river banks, etc.

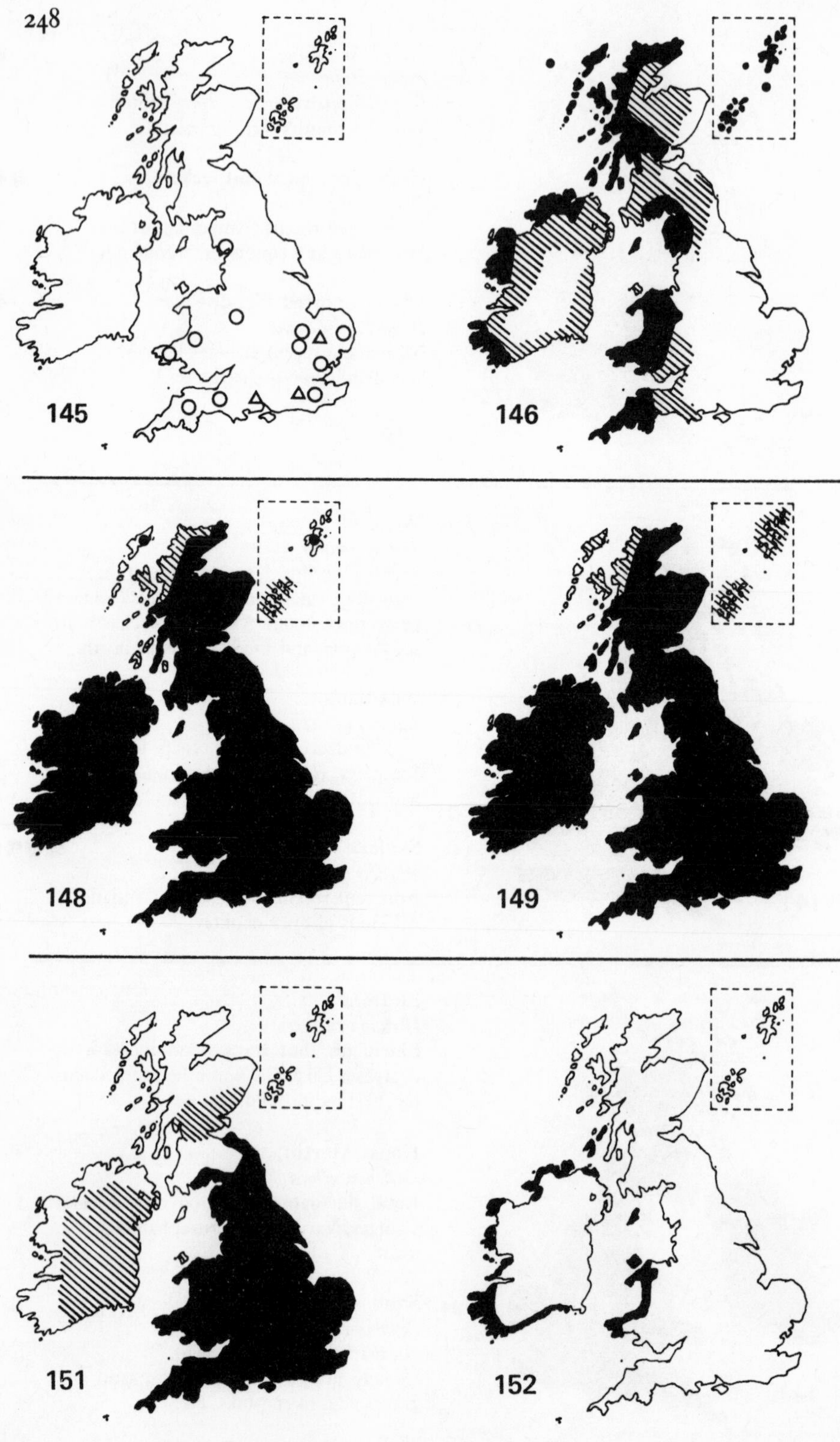
145
146
148
149
151
152

145 **Golden Oriole** △
Oriolus oriolus
Sporadic; several recent summer records but few of nests. Deciduous woodland.

146 **Raven** ●●●●
Corvus corax
No recent marked changes.
Coastal and inland cliffs, locally in trees.

147 **Carrion/Hooded Crow** ●●●●●●
Corvus corone
Further increase in Carrion Crow numbers. Habitats very varied. Cross-hatch shows hybrid zone.

148 **Rook** ●●●●●●●
Corvus frugilegus
Further local decreases recorded.
Farmland with small woods and spinneys.

149 **Jackdaw** ●●●●●●
Corvus monedula
No recent marked changes known.
Parkland, woods, seacliffs, quarries, etc.

150 **Magpie** ●●●●●
Pica pica
No recent marked changes known.
Pastures and other farmland with tall hedges; woodland edge.

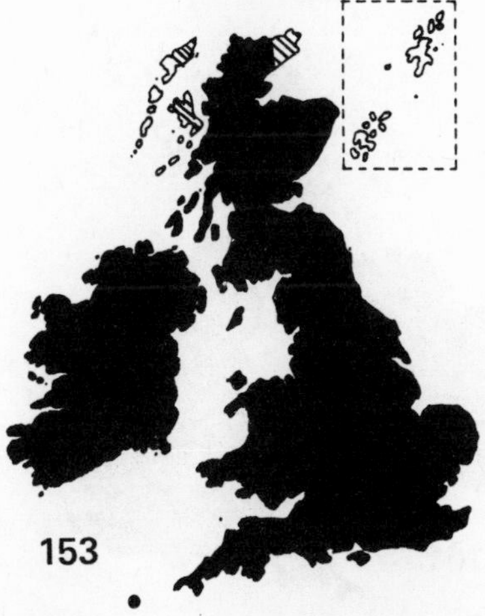

151 **Jay** ●●●●●
Garrulus glandarius
No recent marked changes.
Deciduous woodland, especially oak.

152 **Chough** ●●●
Pyrrhocorax pyrrhocorax
Gradual increase since 1963; now probaby over 700 pairs. Seacliffs, also slate quarries inland.

153 **Great Tit** ●●●●●●
Parus major
No recent marked changes.
Woodland of all kinds; most numerous in oak woods.

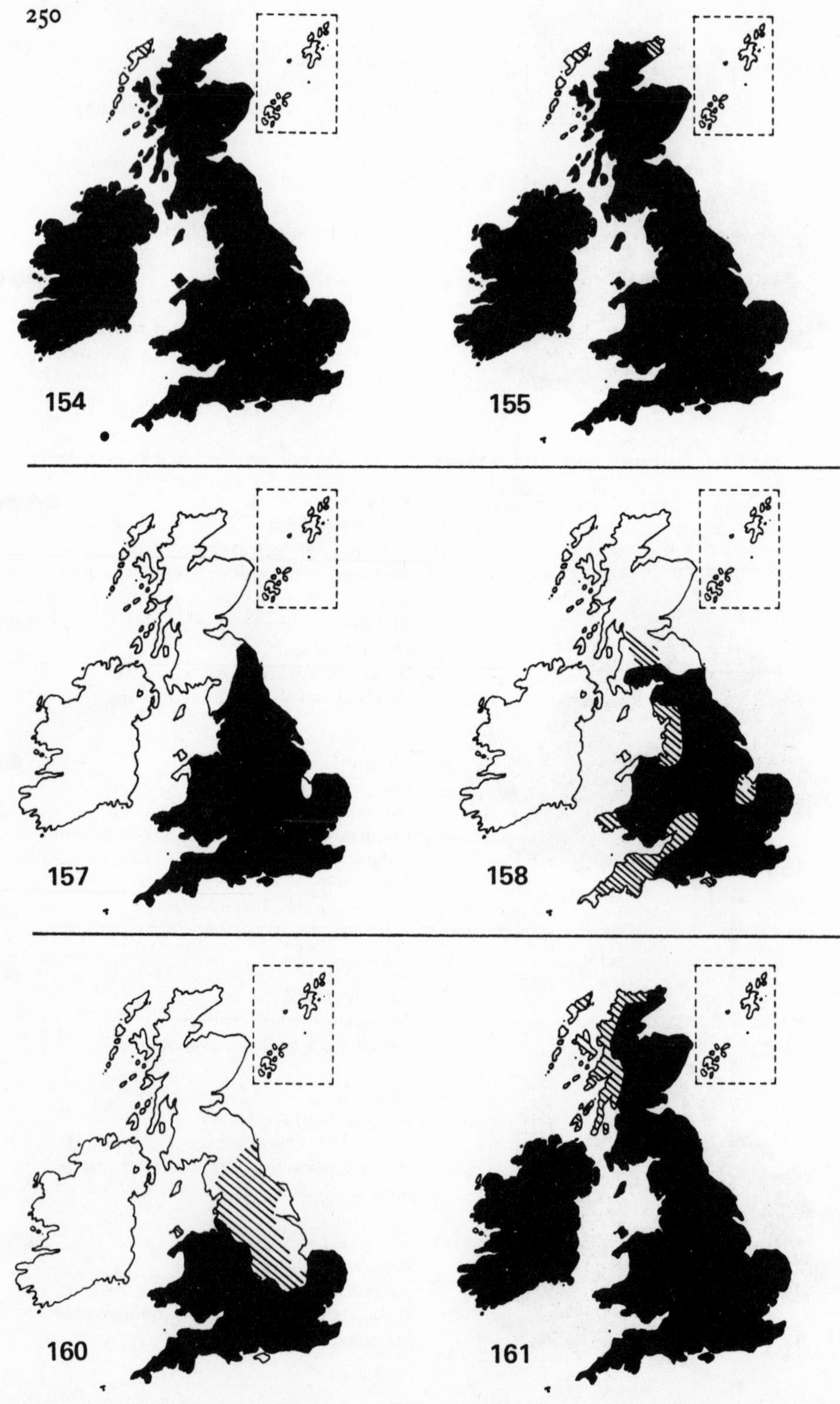
154
155
157
158
160
161

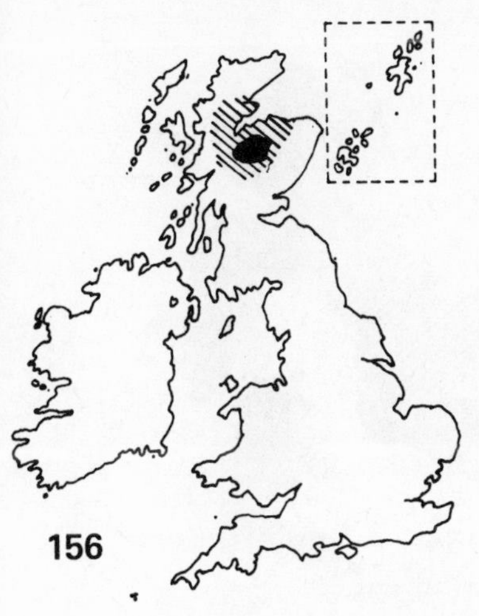

154 **Blue Tit**
Parus caeruleus
No marked changes known.
Woodlands of all kinds, most abundant in oak woods.

155 **Coal Tit**
Parus ater
No marked recent changes.
Chiefly conifer forests, also other woodlands.

156 **Crested Tit**
Parus cristatus
No marked changes known.
Chiefly mature Scots Pine forest.

159

157 **Marsh Tit**
Parus palustris
No marked recent changes.
Various kinds of deciduous woodlands, large gardens, etc.

158 **Willow Tit**
Parus montanus
No marked recent changes.
Chiefly damp woodlands with birch or alder.

159 **Long-tailed Tit**
Aegithalos caudatus
Complete recovery from 1963 hard winter.
Woodlands and scrub of various kinds.

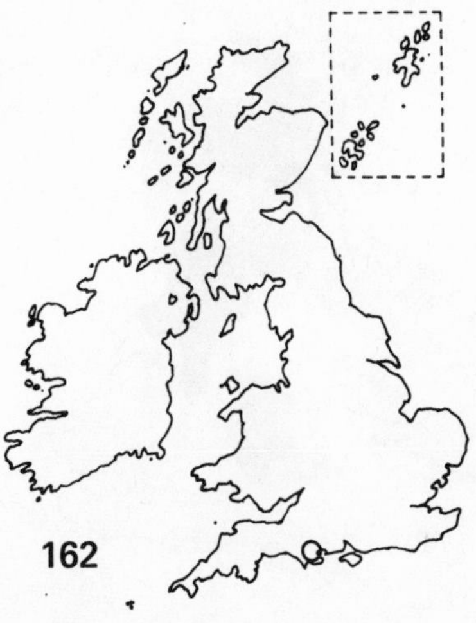

160 **Nuthatch**
Sitta europaea
Increased in north-west of range.
Parklands, deciduous woods, large gardens.

161 **Treecreeper**
Certhia familiaris
No marked recent changes.
Chiefly deciduous and mixed woodland.

162 **Short-toed Treecreeper** △
Certhia brachydactyla
Sporadic; bred E. Dorset 1971; perhaps now elsewhere in S. England. Woodlands.

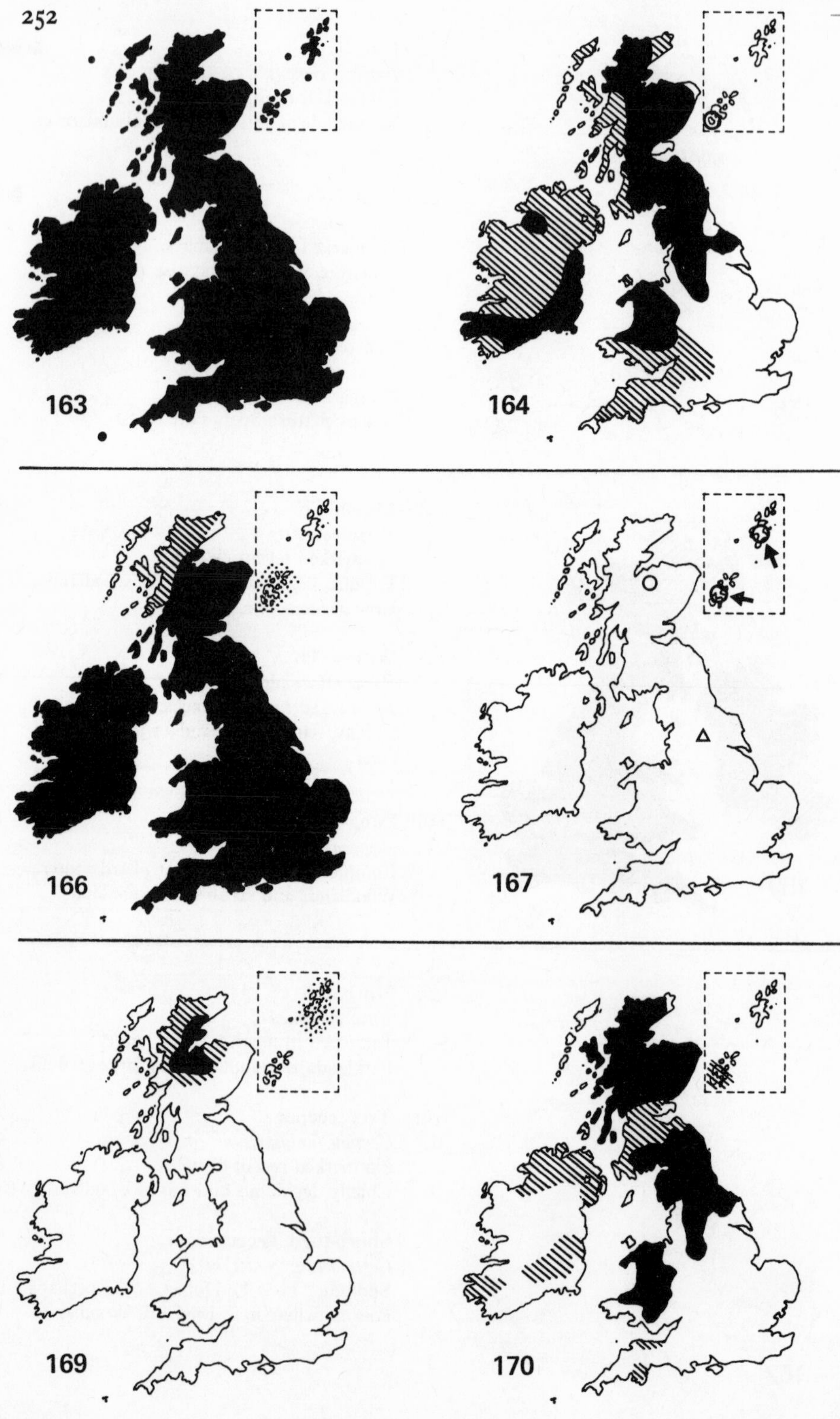
163
164
166
167
169
170

163 **Wren** ●●●●●●●
Troglodytes troglodytes
Steady increase since 1963 hard winter. Habitats very varied—forests to remote maritime islands.

164 **Dipper** ●●●●
Cinclus cinclus
Continued decrease Outer Hebrides; bred Orkney 1970. Fast-running streams, usually in hill country.

165 **Bearded Tit** ●●●
Panurus biarmicus
Marked recent increase and spread.
Phragmites beds.

168

166 **Mistle Thrush** ●●●●●●
Turdus viscivorus
No marked recent changes.
Wooded country of all kinds, including large gardens.

167 **Fieldfare** △
Turdus pilaris
Sporadic, but several recent records in N. Isles, Inverness and once in England. Woodland.

168 **Song Thrush** ●●●●●●●
Turdus philomelos
No marked recent changes.
All kinds of wooded country.

169 **Redwing** ●●
Turdus iliacus
Steady increase; 40–50 occupied territories in 1971. Mixed woodland, alder and birch scrub.

170 **Ring Ouzel** ○○○○
Turdus torquatus
No recent marked changes.
Lower sides of mountains, steep moorland slopes and valleys.

171 **Blackbird** ●●●●●●●
Turdus merula
No marked recent changes.
Wide variety of habitats, including treeless islands.

172

173

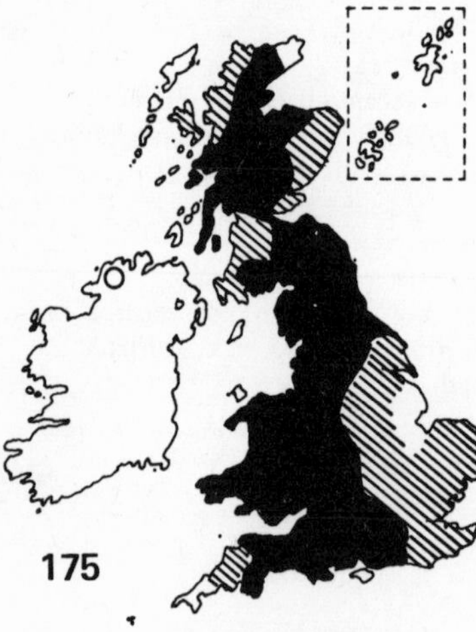

175

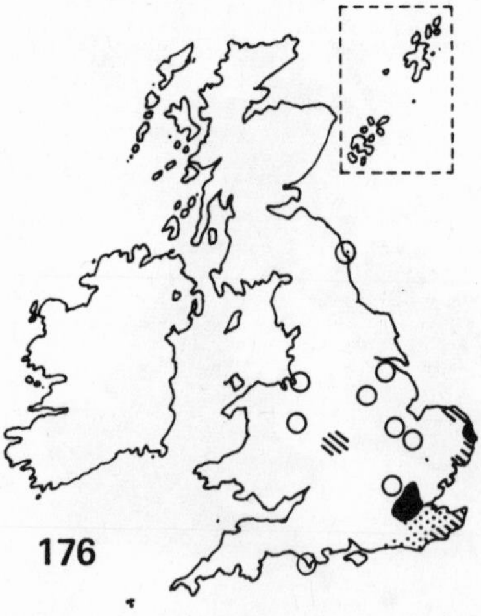

176

178

179

174

172 **Wheatear** ○○○○○
Oenanthe oenanthe
No further marked changes.
Rocky moorlands, coastal turf, heaths, commons, downs.

173 **Stonechat** ⊙⊙⊙⊙
Saxicola torquata
General increase since 1963; now more frequent inland in E. England. Heaths, low moors, usually with gorse and often near coasts.

174 **Whinchat** ○○○○○
Saxicola rubetra
No marked recent changes.
Rough grassland, young conifer plantations, etc.

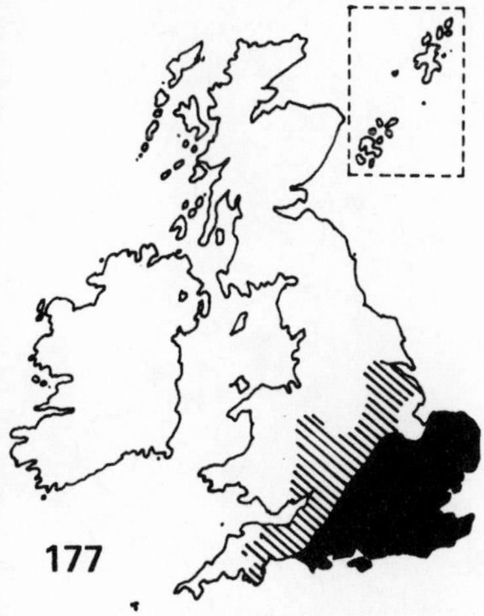

177

175 **Redstart** ○○○○○
Phoenicurus phoenicurus
Fluctuates but no widespread recent changes. Wooded country, often with old or pollarded trees.

176 **Black Redstart** ○○
Phoenicurus ochruros
About 50 pairs, but numbers fluctuate.
Once mainly bombed sites, now mostly at power stations, etc.

177 **Nightingale** ○○○○
Luscinia megarhynchos
Perhaps further decreased but uncertain.
Deciduous woods with shrub understorey; thick hedges, etc.

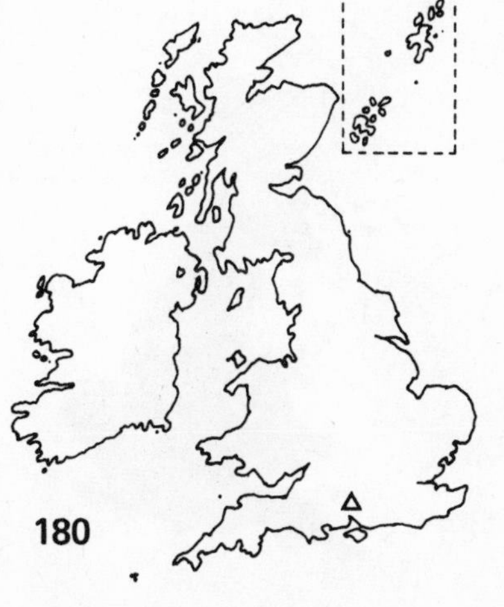

178 **Bluethroat** △
Luscinia svecica
First and only breeding record, Inverness 1968. Only record was in marshy area with *Phragmites*.

179 **Robin** ●●●●●●●
Erithacus rubecula
No evidence of recent marked change.
All kinds of wooded country, including gardens.

180 **Cetti's Warbler** △
Cettia cetti
Sporadic; first breeding record 'S. England', 1972. Lowland marshes with *Phragmites*.

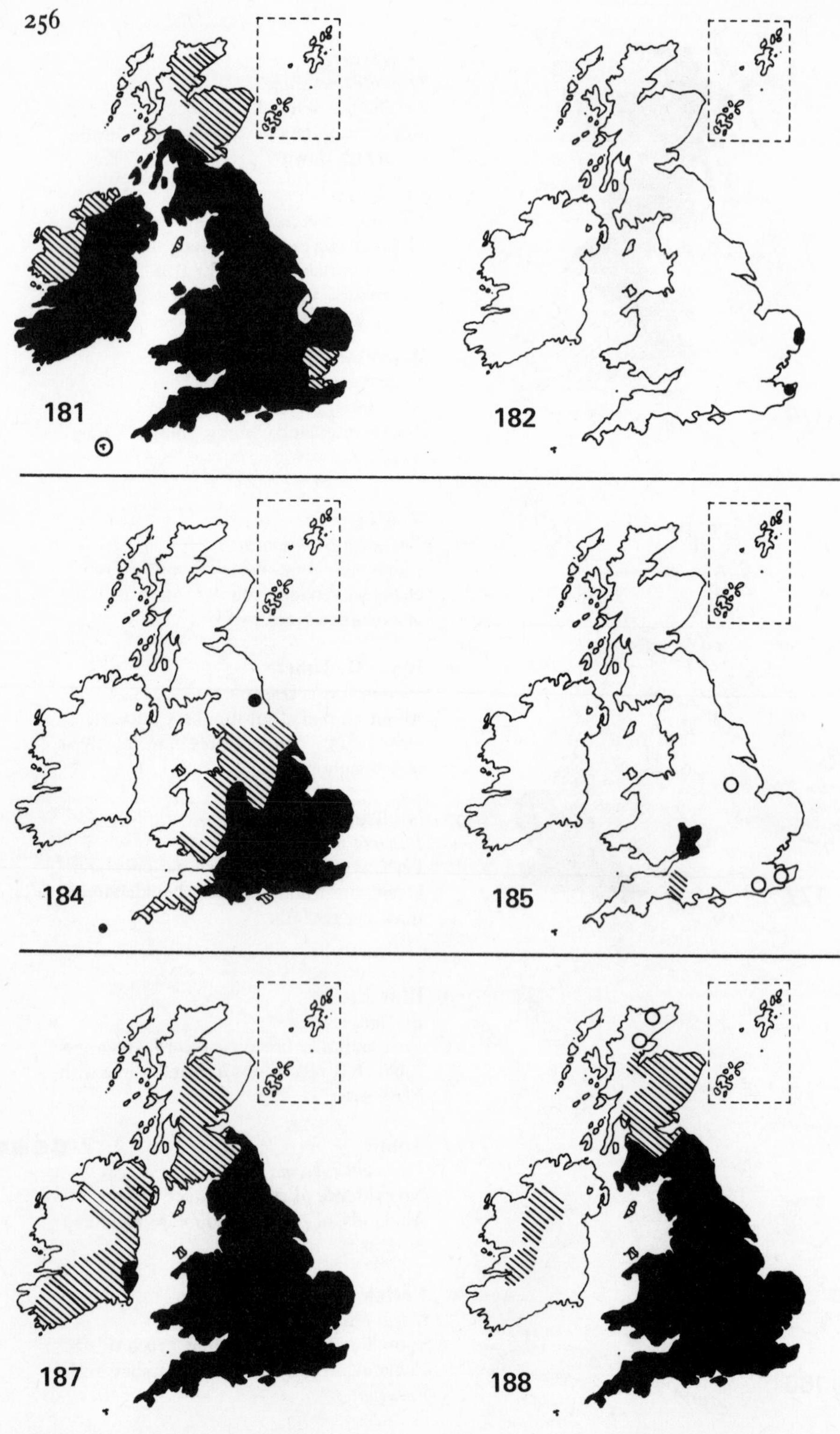
181
182
184
185
187
188

183

181 **Grasshopper Warbler** ○○○○
Locustella naevia
Marked increase E. England; further spread in west and north. Young plantations, commons, etc. with thick, low vegetation.

182 **Savi's Warbler** ○
Locustella luscinioides
Recolonised Kent (1960), Suffolk (1970); increased summer records elsewhere. Extensive *Phragmites* beds.

183 **Moustached Warbler** △
Acrocephalus melanopogon
Sporadic; bred Cambridge 1946.
Only breeding record was in scrub at edge of reed bed.

186

184 **Reed Warbler** 
Acrocephalus scirpaceus
Recent westward spread to Scilly, Carmarthen and Anglesey. Typically in *Phragmites*, in ditches as well as larger waters.

185 **Marsh Warbler** ○○
Acrocephalus palustris
No marked change; about 60–80 pairs. Chiefly in osier beds near rivers.

186 **Sedge Warbler** ○○○○○○
Acrocephalus schoenobaenus
Fluctuates; no recent widespread changes. Coarse vegetation usually near water; also in drier areas.

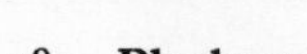

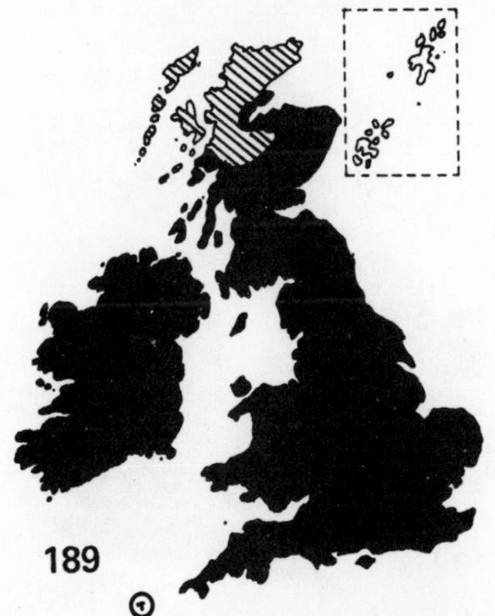

187 **Blackcap** ○○○○○○
Sylvia atricapilla
Fluctuates. Occasional breeding extreme N. Scotland. Mainly deciduous woods with shrub understorey.

188 **Garden Warbler** ○○○○○○
Sylvia borin
Fluctuates. Occasional breeding extreme N. Scotland. Chiefly deciduous woods with shrub understorey.

189 **Whitethroat** ○○○○○○○
Sylvia communis
Sudden, heavy population crash 1969; little recovery since. Low scrub of all kinds, notably hedges, felled and young woods.

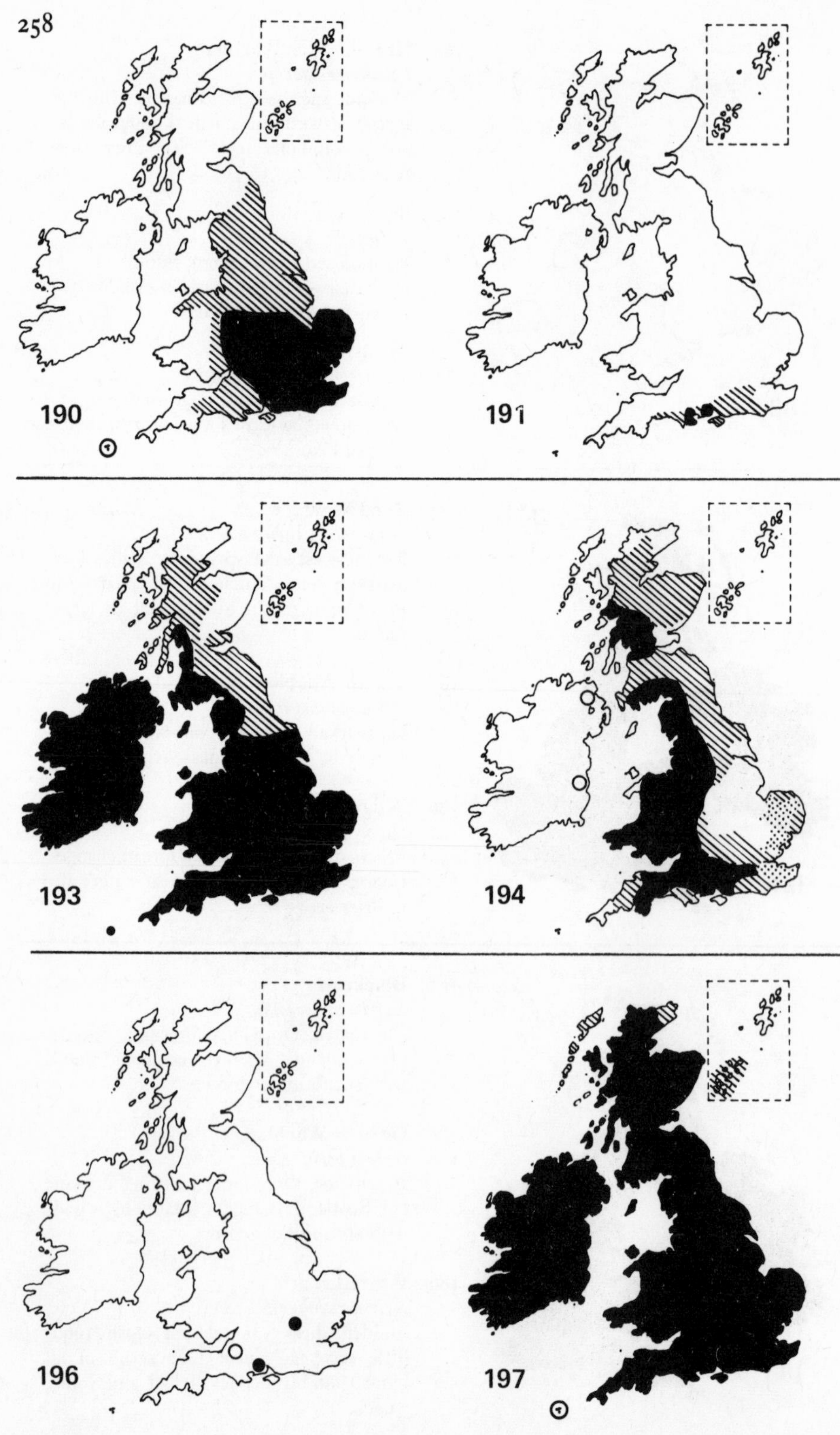
190
191
193
194
196
197

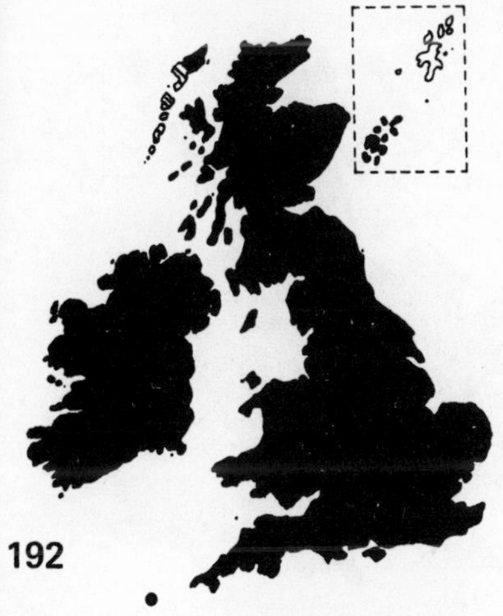
192

190 **Lesser Whitethroat** ○○○○○
Sylvia curruca
Fluctuates; no recent marked changes. Thick scrub, notably overgrown hedges.

191 **Dartford Warbler** ●●●
Sylvia undata
Increase and spread since 1963—about 140 pairs by 1971. Heathlands with gorse and long heather.

192 **Willow Warbler** ○○○○○○○
Phylloscopus trochilus
No marked recent changes.
Wide variety of habitats with trees or tall scrub present.

195

193 **Chiffchaff** ○○○○○○
Phylloscopus collybita
Some indication of spread in N. Scotland. Woodlands, in north usually with rhododendrons.

194 **Wood Warbler** ○○○○○
Phylloscopus sibilatrix
Small numbers recently discovered in Ireland. Chiefly closed woodlands with little or no ground cover.

195 **Goldcrest** ●●●●●●
Regulus regulus
Increasing with spread of conifer plantations. Typically in conifer woods; locally in deciduous woods.

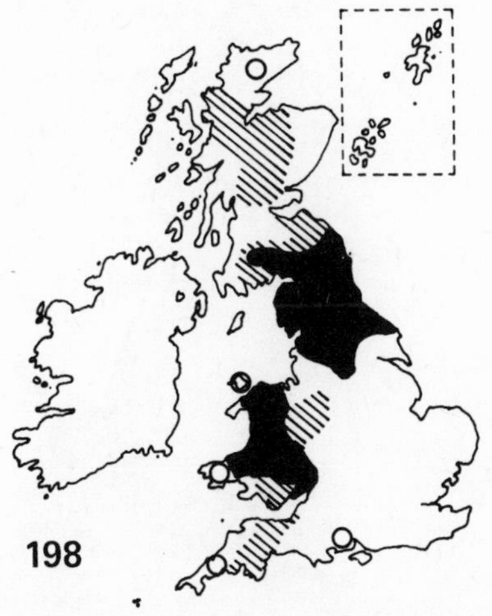
198

196 **Firecrest** ⊙⊙
Regulus ignicapillus
Marked increase and spread; notable concentration Buckingham. Mixed woods usually with spruce or larch.

197 **Spotted Flycatcher** ○○○○○
Muscicapa striata
No marked recent changes known.
Woodland edge, parks, orchards, large gardens.

198 **Pied Flycatcher** ○○○○
Ficedula hypoleuca
Increase in S.W. England; northwards spread in Scotland. Open woods especially of mature oaks.

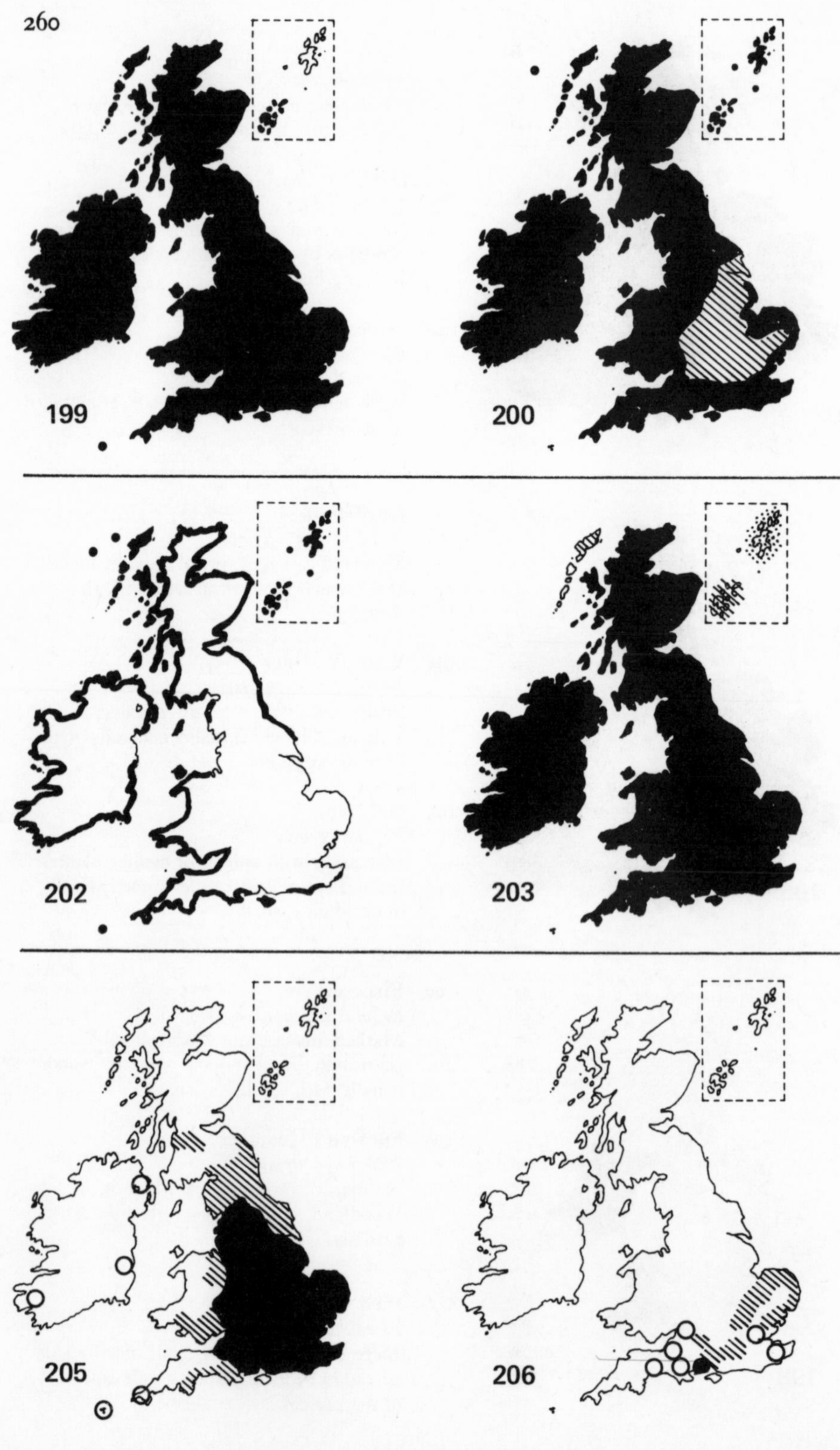
199
200
202
203
205
206

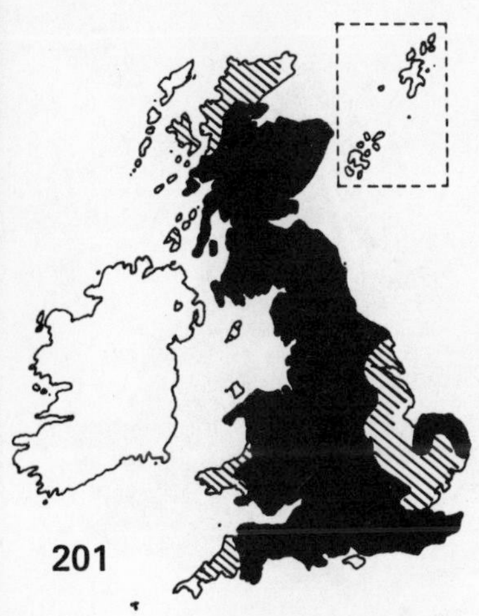

199 **Dunnock** ●●●●●●●
Prunella modularis
No recent marked changes known.
Scrub and other low cover of all kinds.

200 **Meadow Pipit** ⊙⊙⊙⊙⊙⊙⊙
Anthus pratensis
No recent marked changes.
Open moorland, heaths, rough grassland.

201 **Tree Pipit** ○○○○○○
Anthus trivialis
No recent marked changes known.
Woodland edges and clearings, heaths, commons with trees.

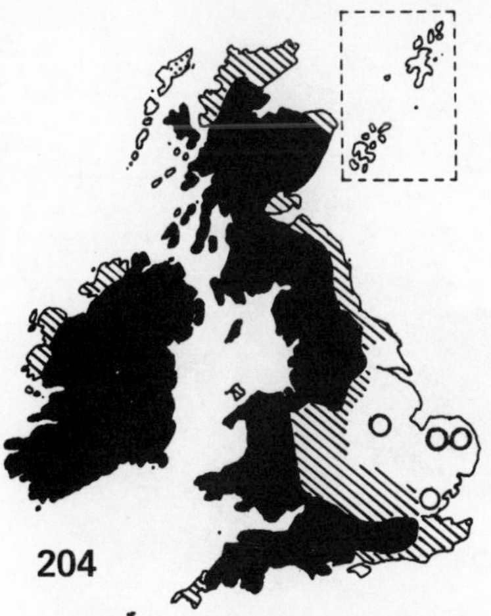

202 **Rock Pipit** ●●●●●
Anthus spinoletta
No recent marked changes.
Typically along rocky coastlines.

203 **Pied/White Wagtail** ⊙⊙⊙⊙⊙⊙
Motacilla alba
No recent marked changes known.
Varied habitats, usually near water or farm buildings.

204 **Grey Wagtail** ●●●●

Motacilla cinerea
Increase since 1963; now more frequent again E. England. Chiefly beside fast streams in hill country; also by weirs.

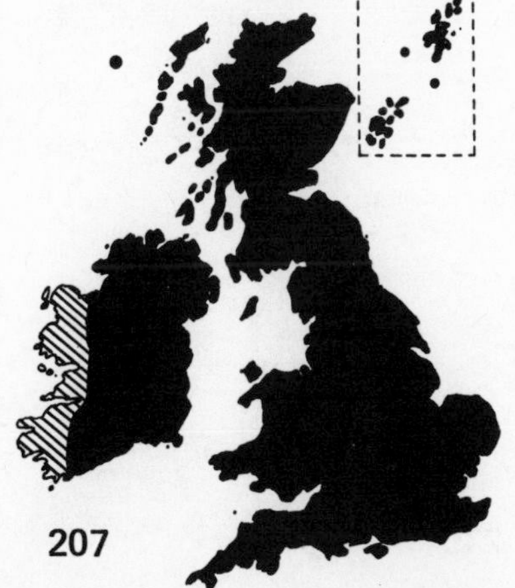

205 **Yellow Wagtail** ○○○○○
Motacilla flava
No marked recent changes.
Typically in damp pastures; also other open habitats near water.

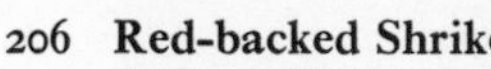

206 **Red-backed Shrike** ○○
Lanius collurio
Further decrease and now only about 80 pairs. Chiefly heathland with hawthorn and other scrub.

207 **Starling** ●●●●●●●
Sturnus vulgaris
No recent marked changes.
Varied habitats including towns, farmland, open woods.

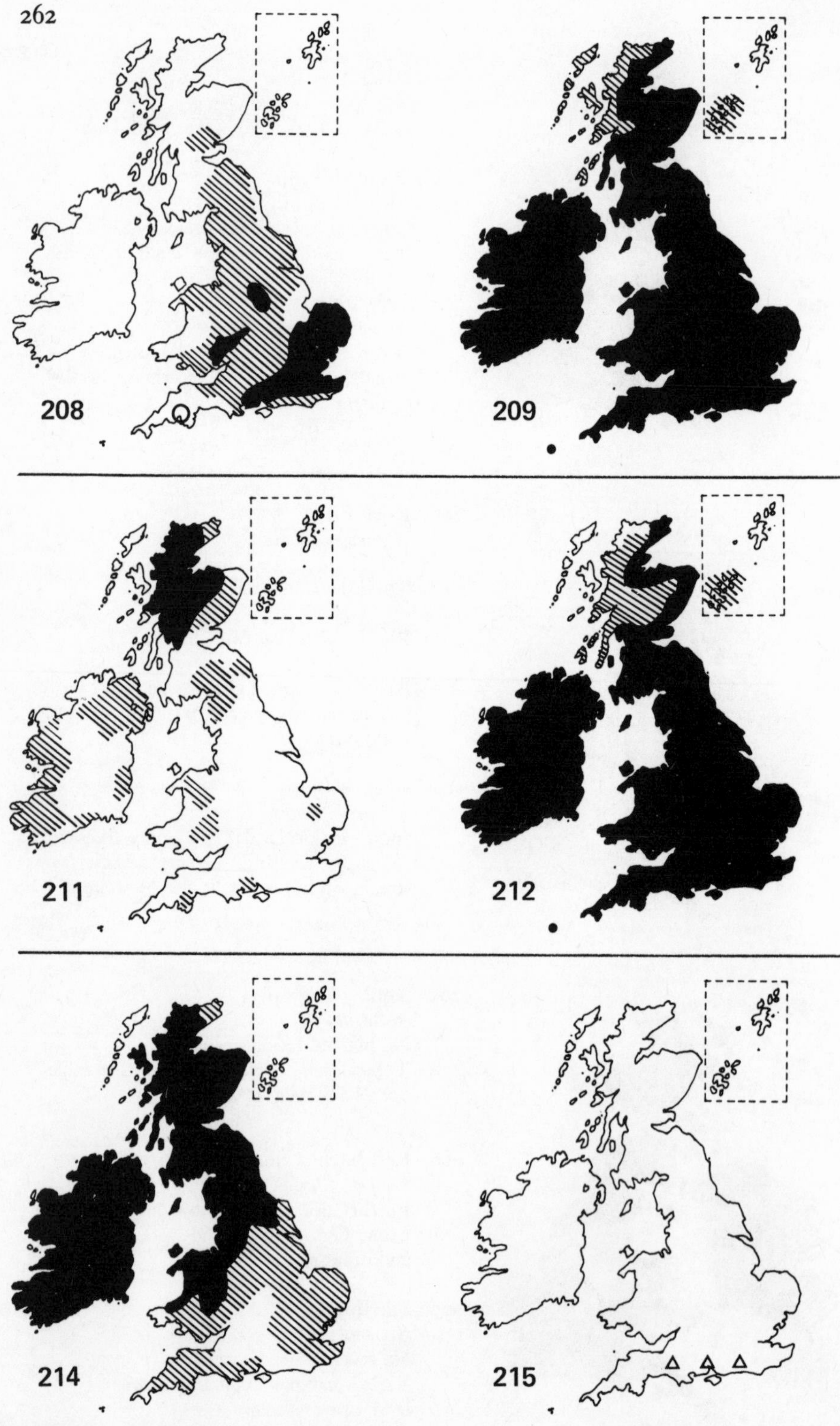
208
209
211
212
214
215

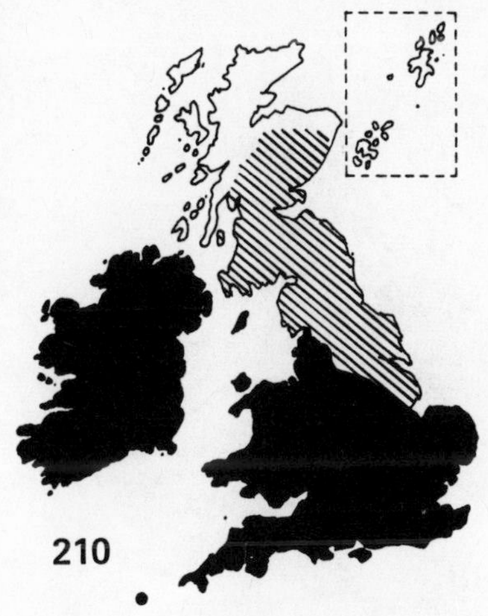

208 **Hawfinch** ●●●●
Coccothraustes coccothraustes
Locally decreased.
Mature, lowland deciduous woods, including orchards.

209 **Greenfinch** ●●●●●●
Carduelis chloris
No recent marked changes known.
Woodland edge, scrub, gardens, thick hedgerows.

210 **Goldfinch** ⊙⊙⊙⊙⊙
Carduelis carduelis
No recent marked changes known.
Open woodland, parks, orchards, large gardens.

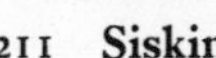
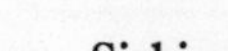

213

211 **Siskin** ●●●●
Carduelis spinus
Continued spread, especially Wales, including Carmarthen and Brecon for first time in 1971. Open coniferous woodland, especially spruce.

212 **Linnet** ⊙⊙⊙⊙⊙⊙
Acanthis cannabina
No recent marked changes known.
Gorse-clad heaths, felled and young woodland, hedges, etc.

213 **Twite** ●●●●
Acanthis flavirostris
Recent increase in Southern Pennines.
Open or rocky moorland; in extreme N.W. in villages, pastures.

216

214 **Redpoll** ⊙⊙⊙⊙⊙
Acanthis flammea
Recent marked expansion, especially in lowland England. In north, chiefly birch scrub; in south, tall hedges, young plantations.

215 **Serin** △
Serinus serinus
Sporadic; has bred S. England on several occasions since 1967. Woodland edge, large gardens.

216 **Bullfinch** ●●●●●●
Pyrrhula pyrrhula
Previous marked expansion may now have ceased. Thick scrub at woodland edge, overgrown hedges, etc.

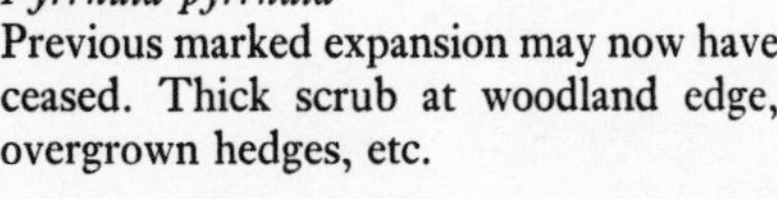

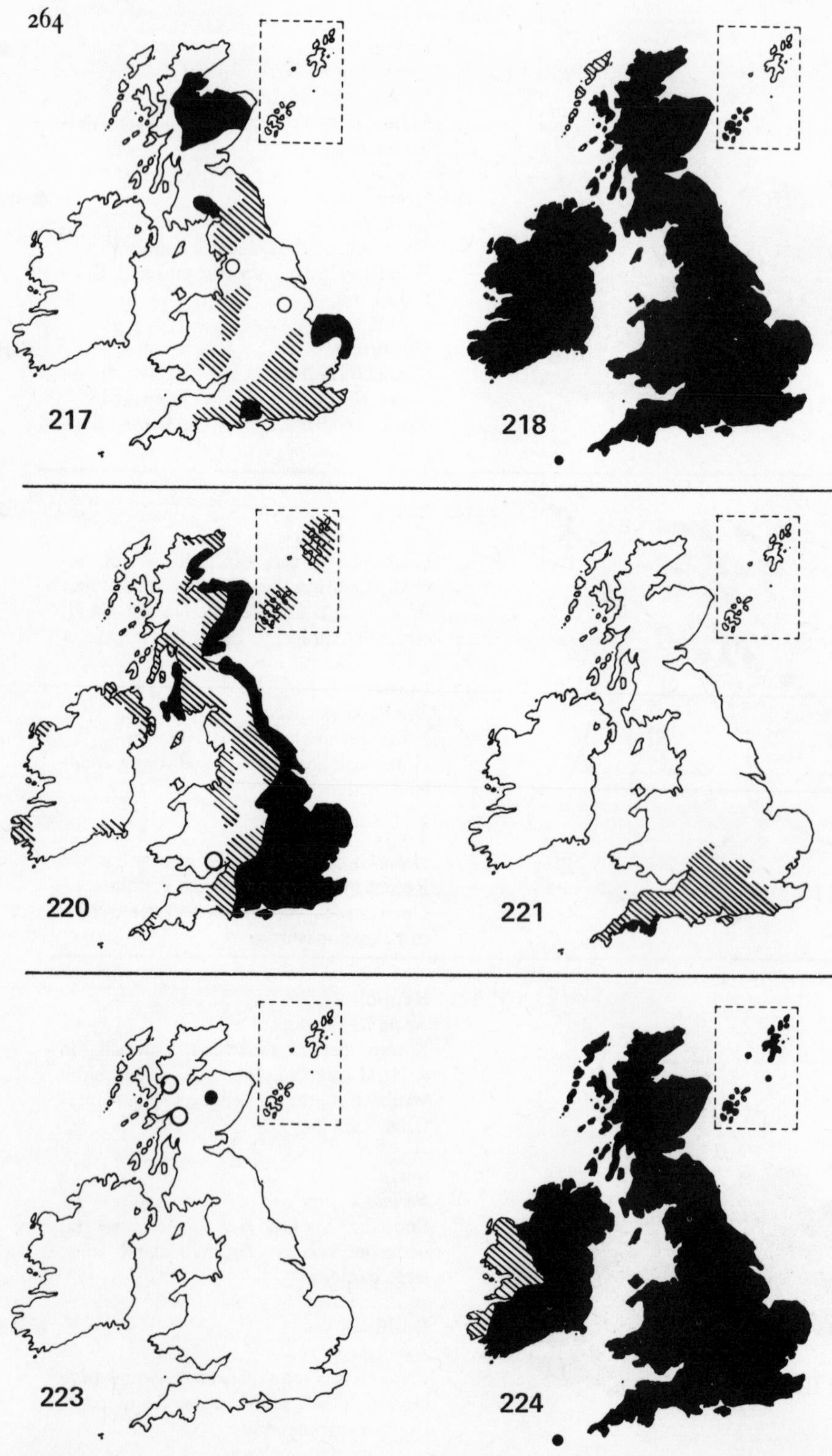
217
218
220
221
223
224

217 **Crossbill**
Loxia curvirostra
Fluctuates—invasion in 1972. (Parrot Crossbill *L. pytyopsittacus* suspected breeding Surrey 1963.) Coniferous woods and shelter belts.

218 **Chaffinch**
Fringilla coelebs
Still much reduced in lowland Britain. Woods, heaths, hedges, parks, gardens, etc.

219 **Yellowhammer**
Emberiza citrinella
No recent marked changes known.
Woodland clearings, young plantations, hedges, scrub.

220 **Corn Bunting**
Emberiza calandra
Recent increase in W. Midlands; bred Monmouth 1970. Dry open farmland; rough ground near sea.

221 **Cirl Bunting**
Emberiza cirlus
Perhaps further decreased.
Hedges and other scrub, mainly in sheltered, sunny valleys.

222 **Reed Bunting**
Emberiza schoeniclus
No recent marked changes.
Typically fens, freshwater margins, but also drier habitats.

223 **Snow Bunting**
Plectrophenax nivalis
Fluctuates, but usually fewer than 3 known pairs. Rock faces near mountain tops.

224 **House Sparrow**
Passer domesticus
No recent marked changes.
Human settlements of all kinds.

225 **Tree Sparrow**
Passer montanus
Former increase and spread now slowing. Open woodlands, old hedgerow trees, quarries, old buildings.

INDEX